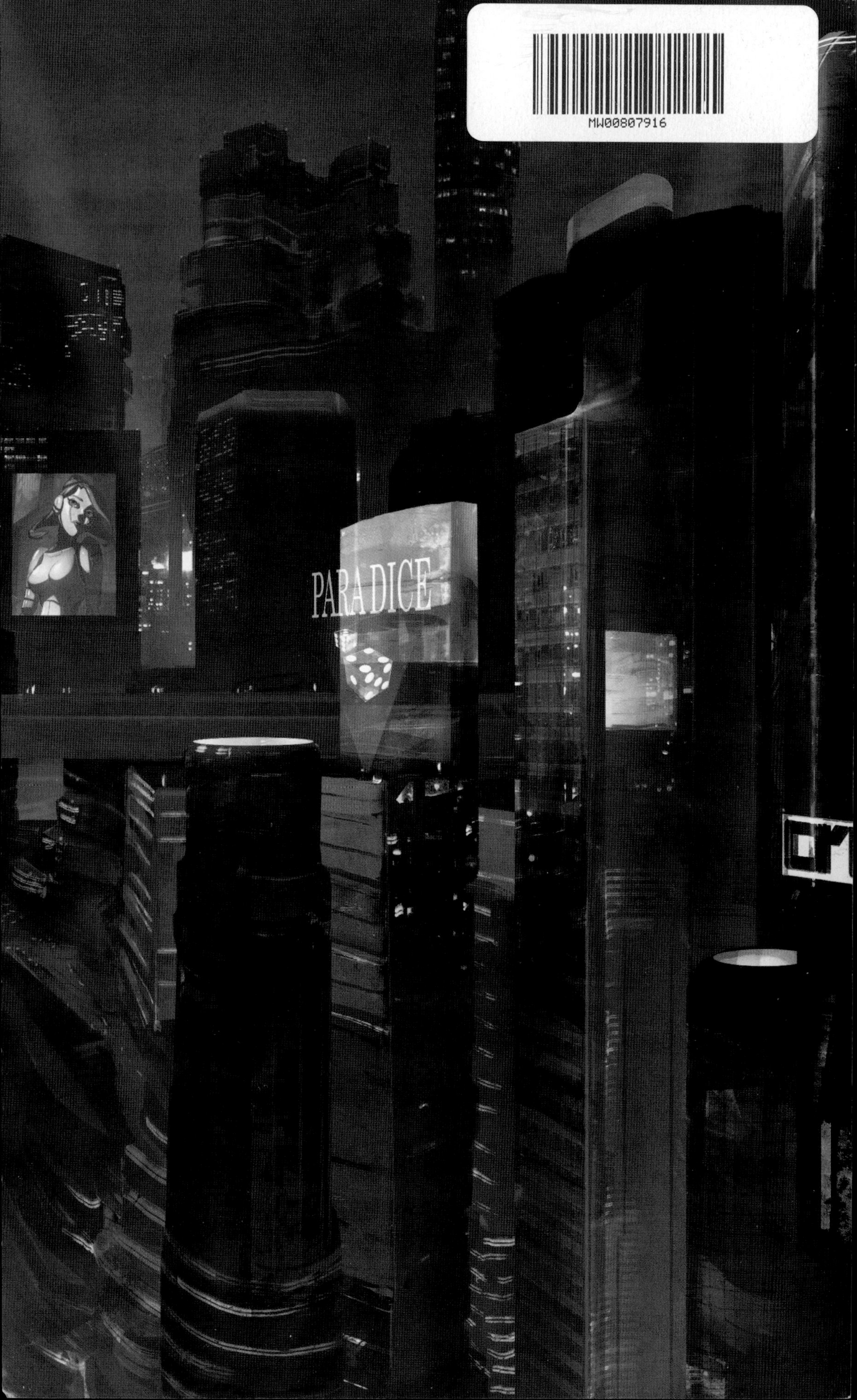
PARA DICE

Created by
FALL OUT BOY, DARREN ROMANELLI and NATHAN CABRERA

TIFFANY BLUES

Script
BRETT LEWIS

Layouts and line art
SAMI BASRI and **HENDRY PRASETYO**

Colorists
SUNNY GHO and **JESSICA KHOLINNE** of **IMAGINARY FRIENDS STUDIOS**

Lettering
RIRI

Production
TEUKU MUHARRAM

Cover
STANLEY "ARTGERM" LAU

Logo
NATHAN CABRERA

End pages
KAI LIM

Editor
DAVE ELLIOTT

Art Directors
DAVE ELLIOTT and **SUNNY GHO**

Design
DREW GILL

A JED/i production

IMAGE COMICS, INC.
Robert Kirkman - chief operating officer
Erik Larsen - chief financial officer
Todd McFarlane - president
Marc Silvestri - chief executive officer
Jim Valentino - vice-president

Eric Stephenson - publisher
Todd Martinez - sales & licensing coordinator
Betsy Gomez - pr & marketing coordinator
Branwyn Bigglestone - accounts manager
Sarah deLaine - administrative assistant
Tyler Shainline - production manager
Drew Gill - art director
Jonathan Chan - production artist
Monica Howard - production artist
Vincent Kukua - production artist
Kevin Yuen - production artist
www.imagecomics.com

Cover art
Issue 1 - Sami Basri and Sunny Gho
Issue 2 - Sami Basri and Sunny Gho
Issue 3 - Stanley 'Artgerm' Lau
Issue 4 - Sami Basri and Admira Wijaya
Issue 5 - Stanley 'Artgerm' Lau

Sketchbook art
Nathan Cabrera, Hendry Prasetyo, and Sami Basri

FALL OUT TOY WORKS, VOL. 1: TIFFANY BLUES
First printing / January 2011
ISBN: 978-1-60706-359-9

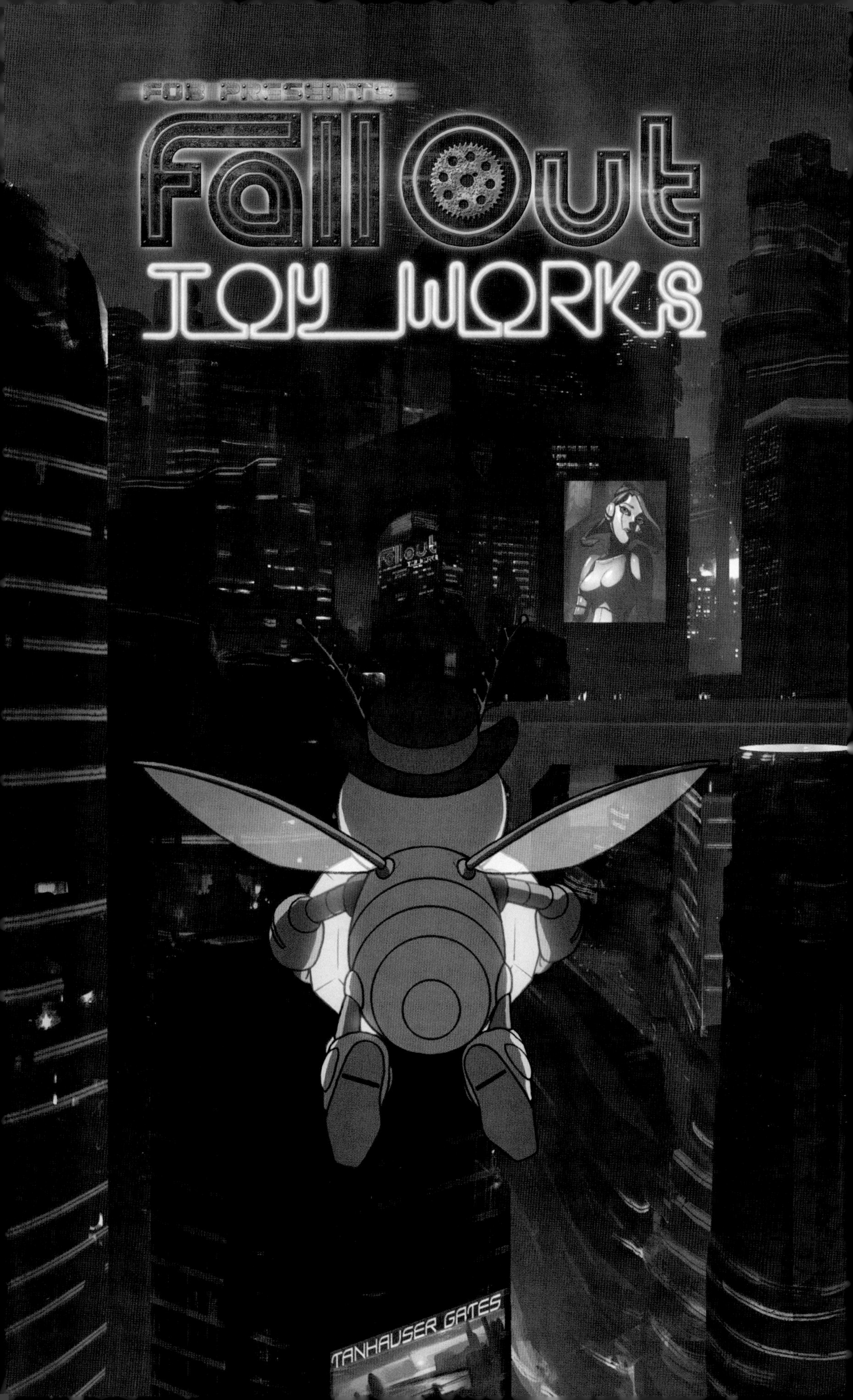
FOB PRESENTS
Fall Out
TOY WORKS
TANHAUSER GATES

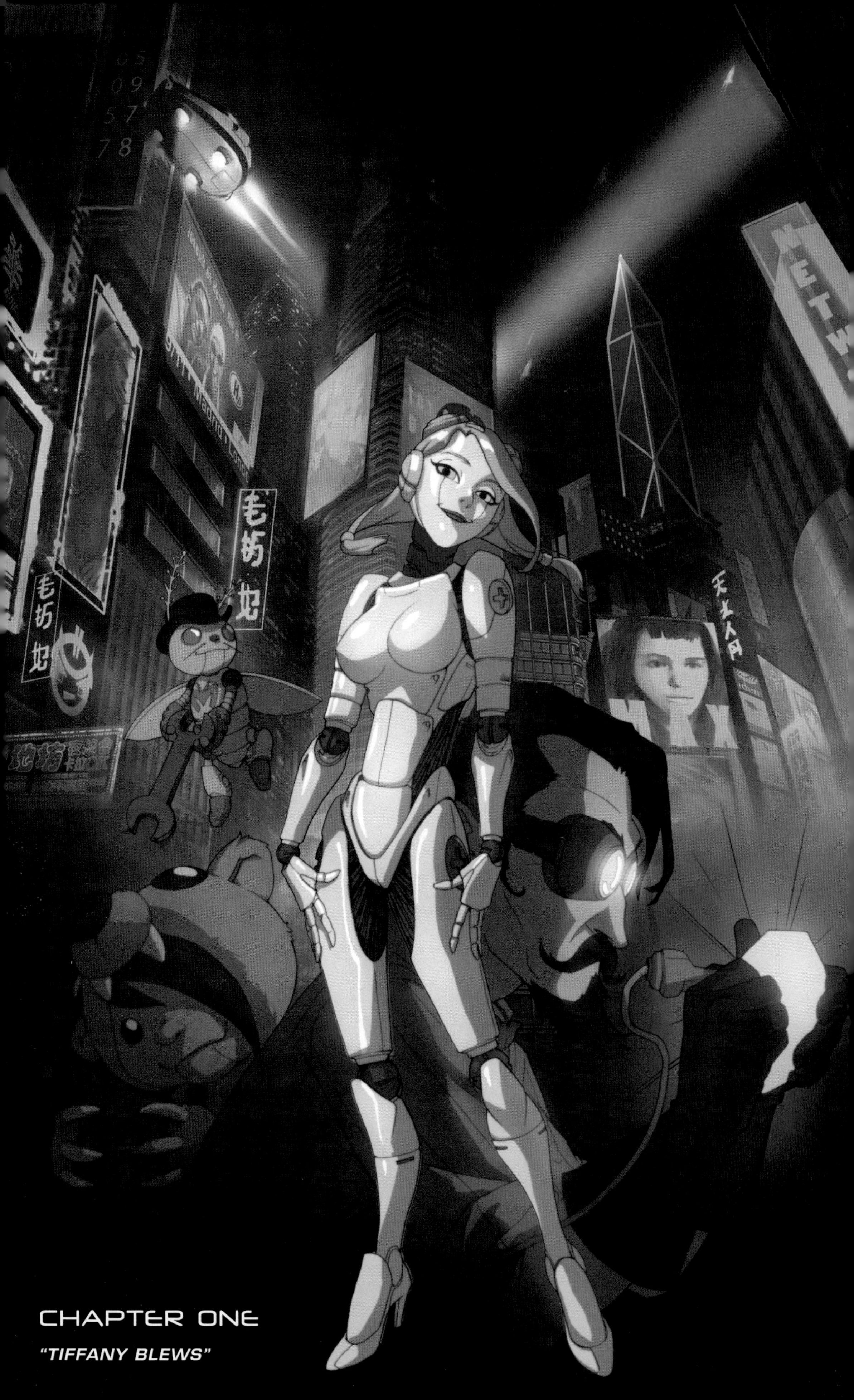

CHAPTER ONE

"TIFFANY BLEWS"

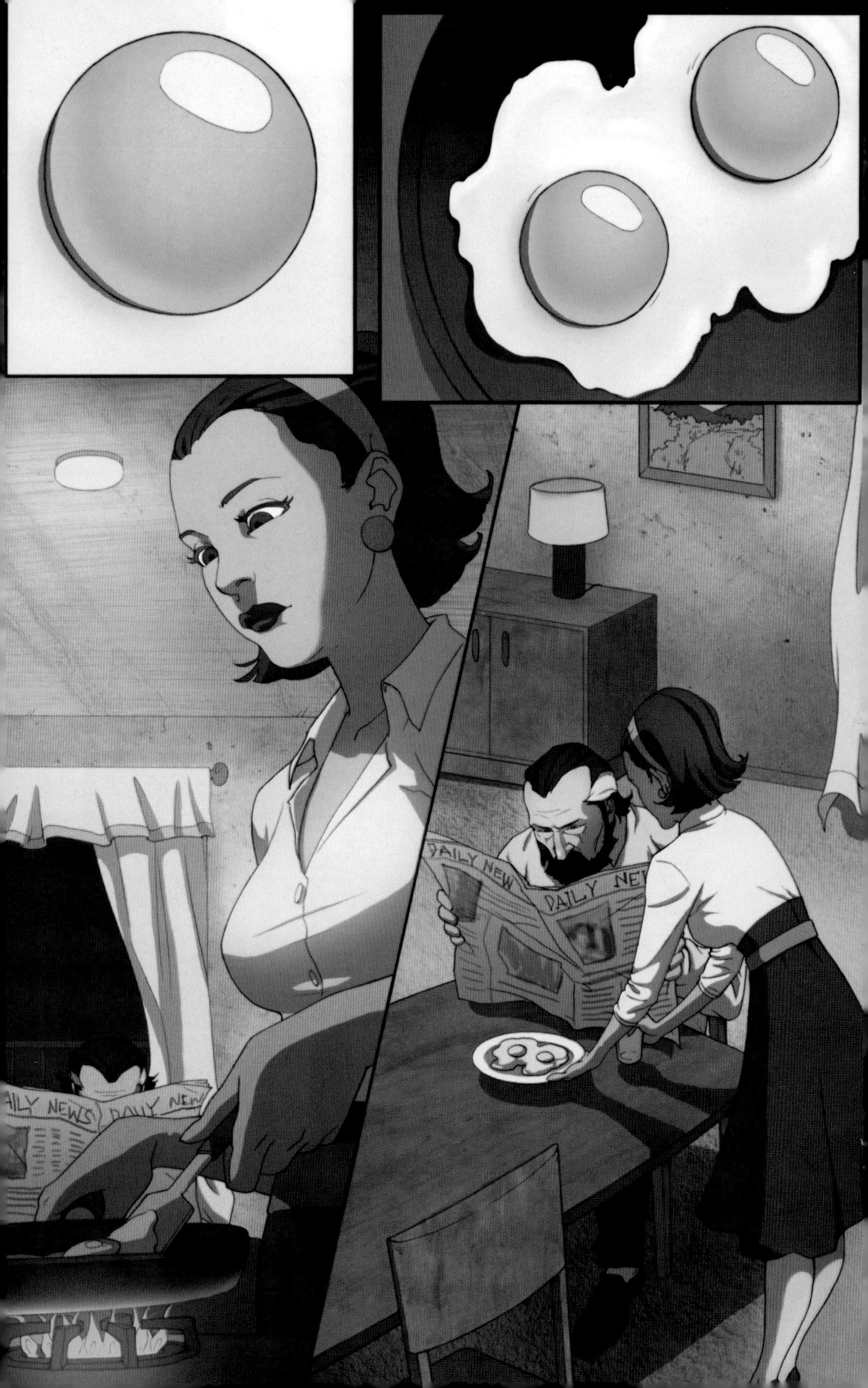

DAILY NEW
DAILY
AILY NEWS

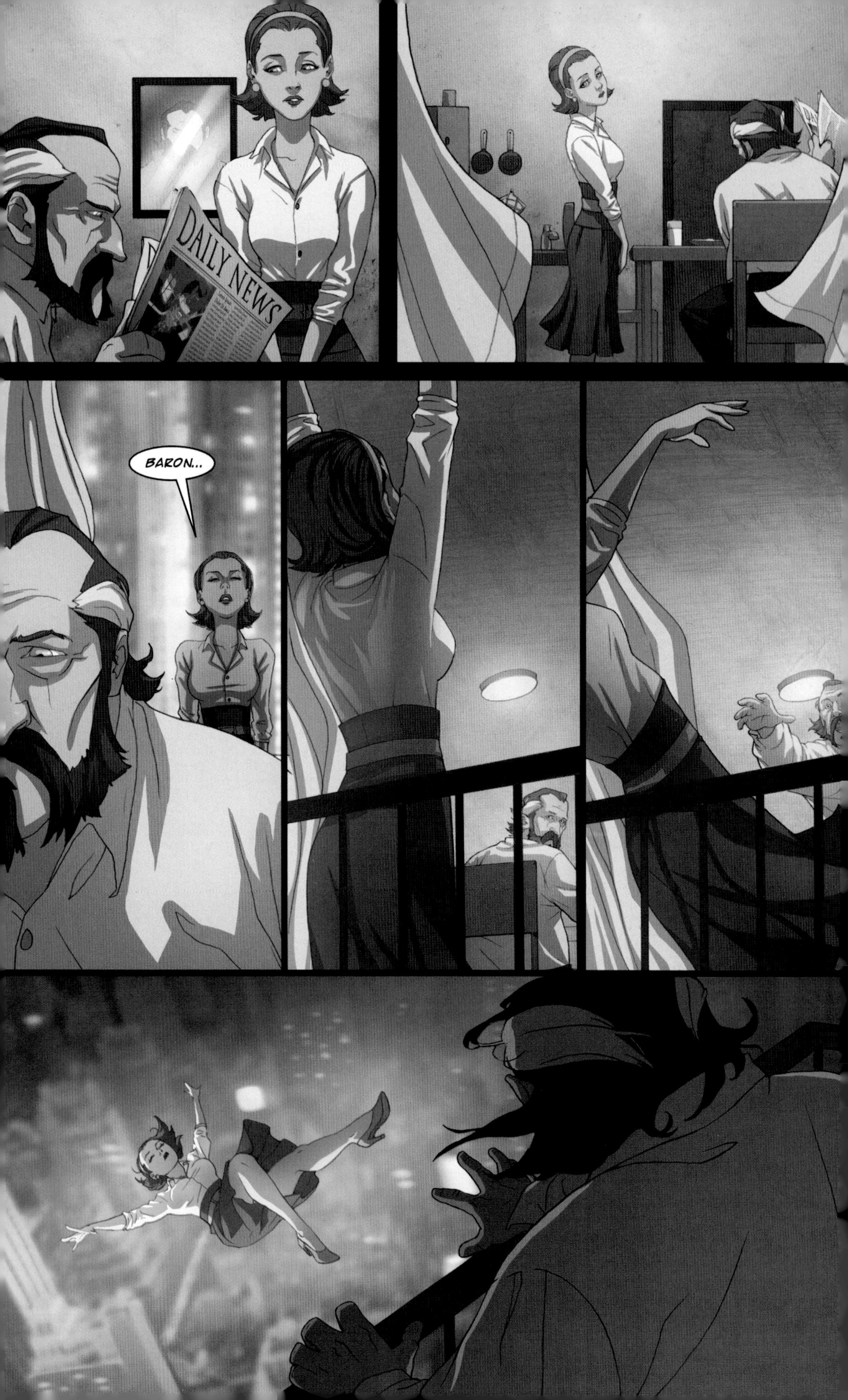
DAILY NEWS
BARON...

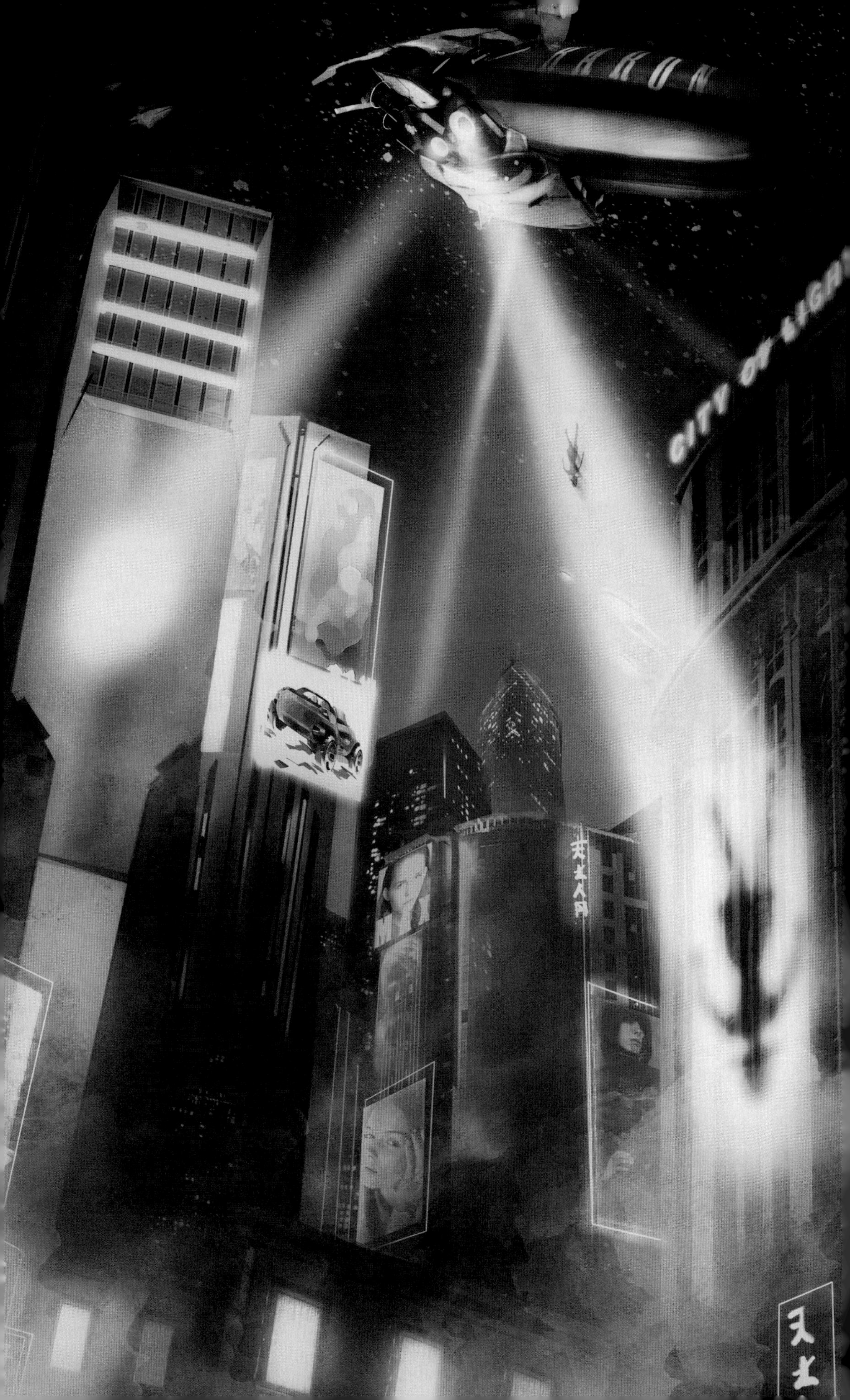
CITY OF LIGH

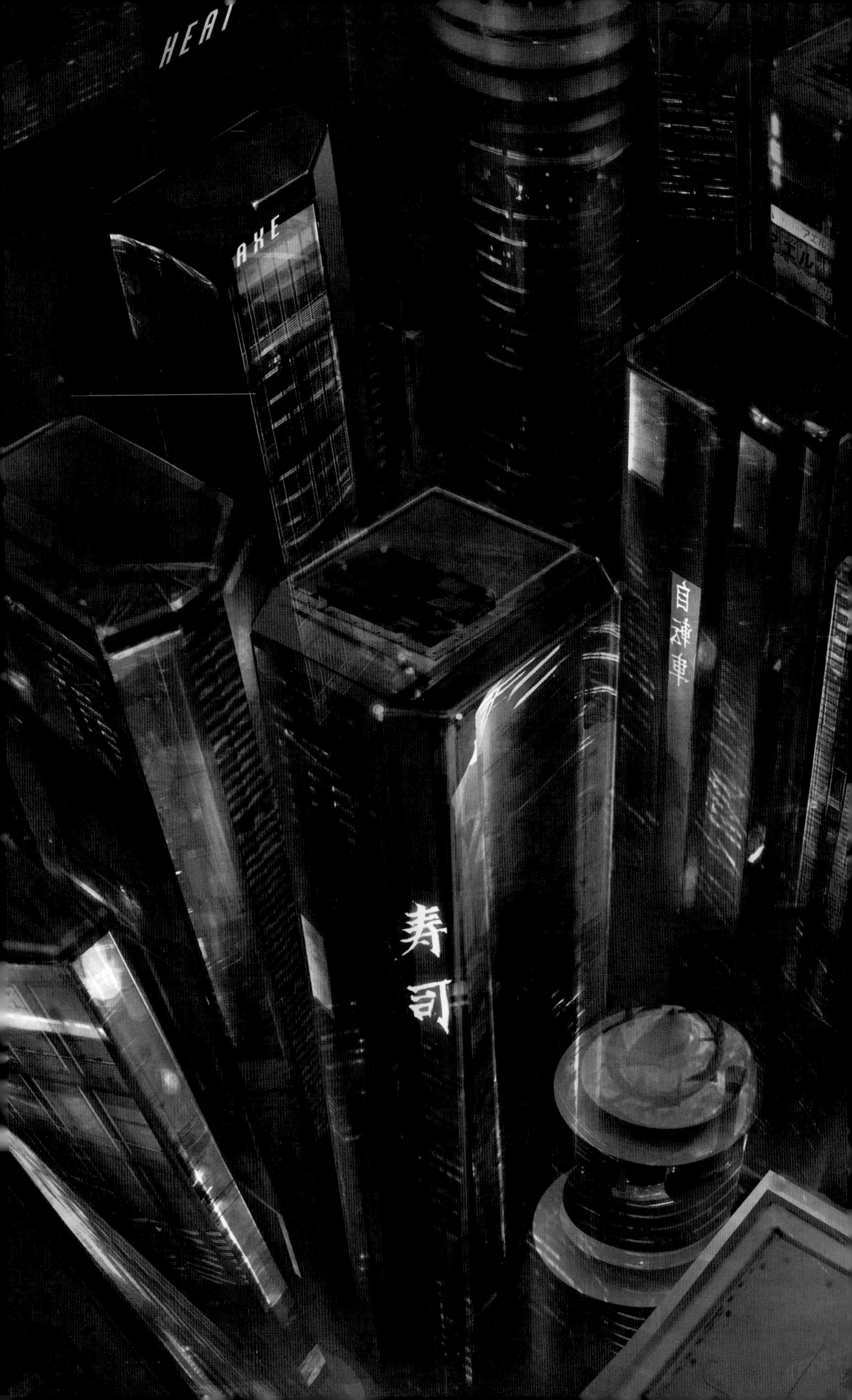
AXE
寿司

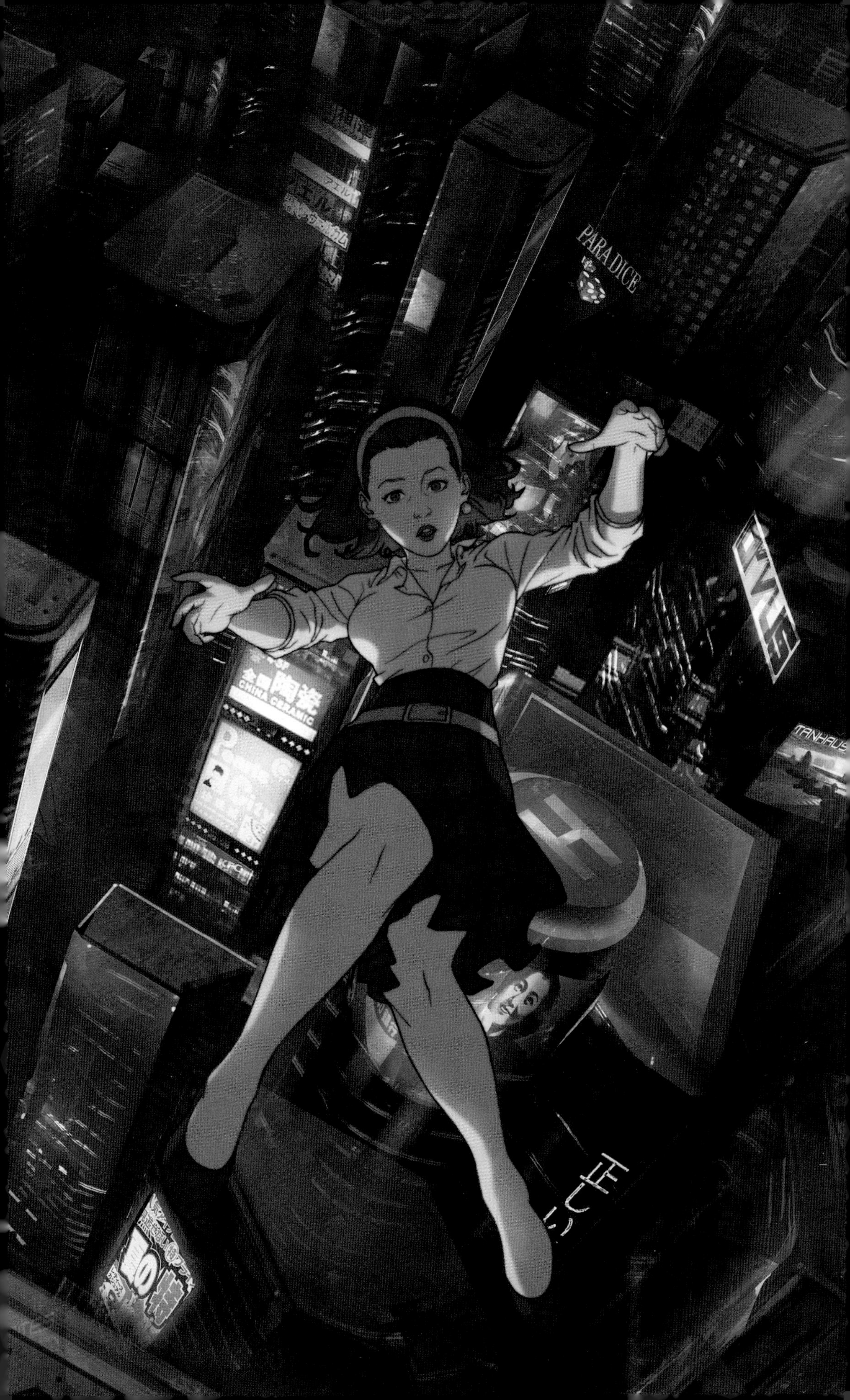
PARADICE
CHINA CERAMIC

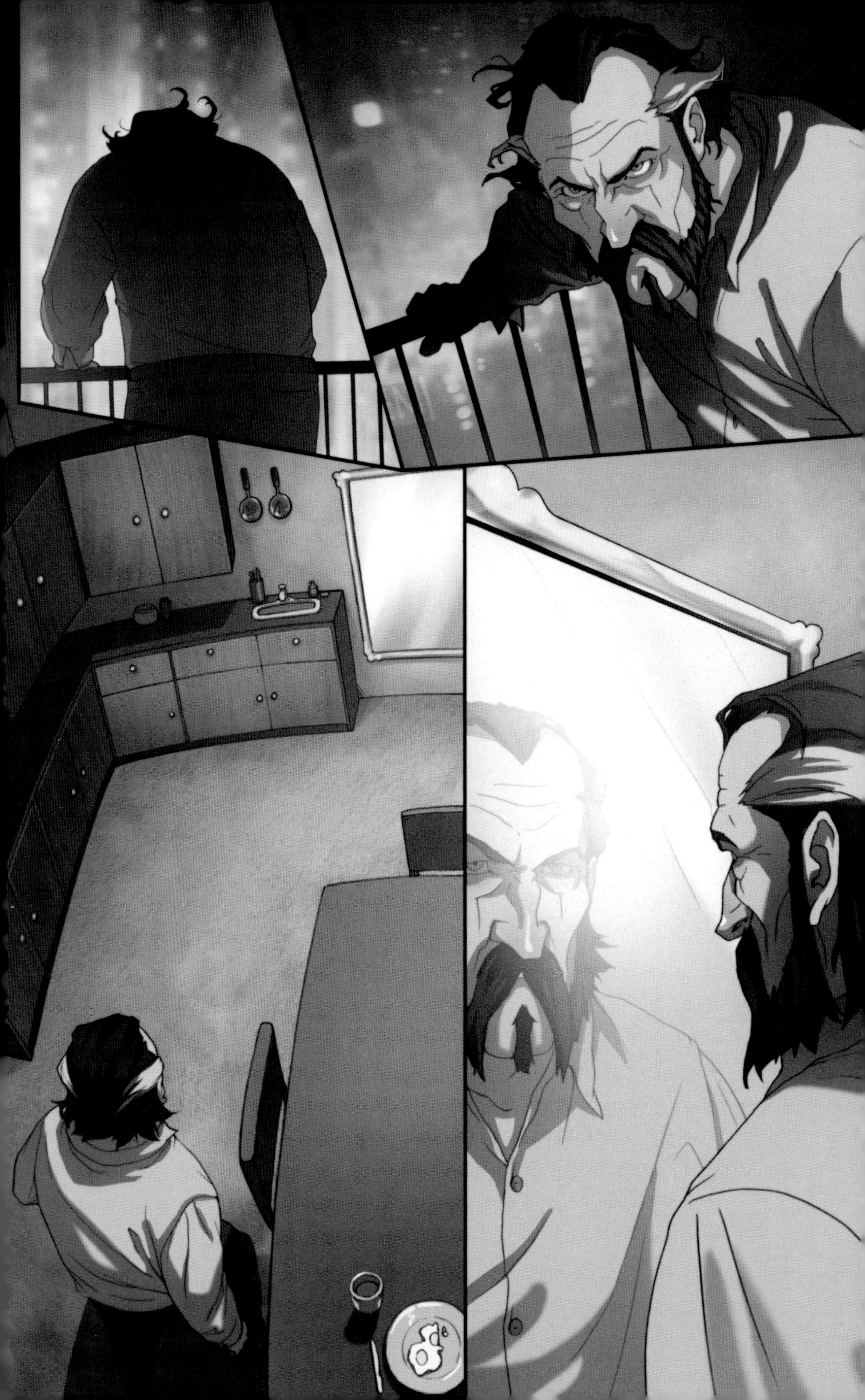

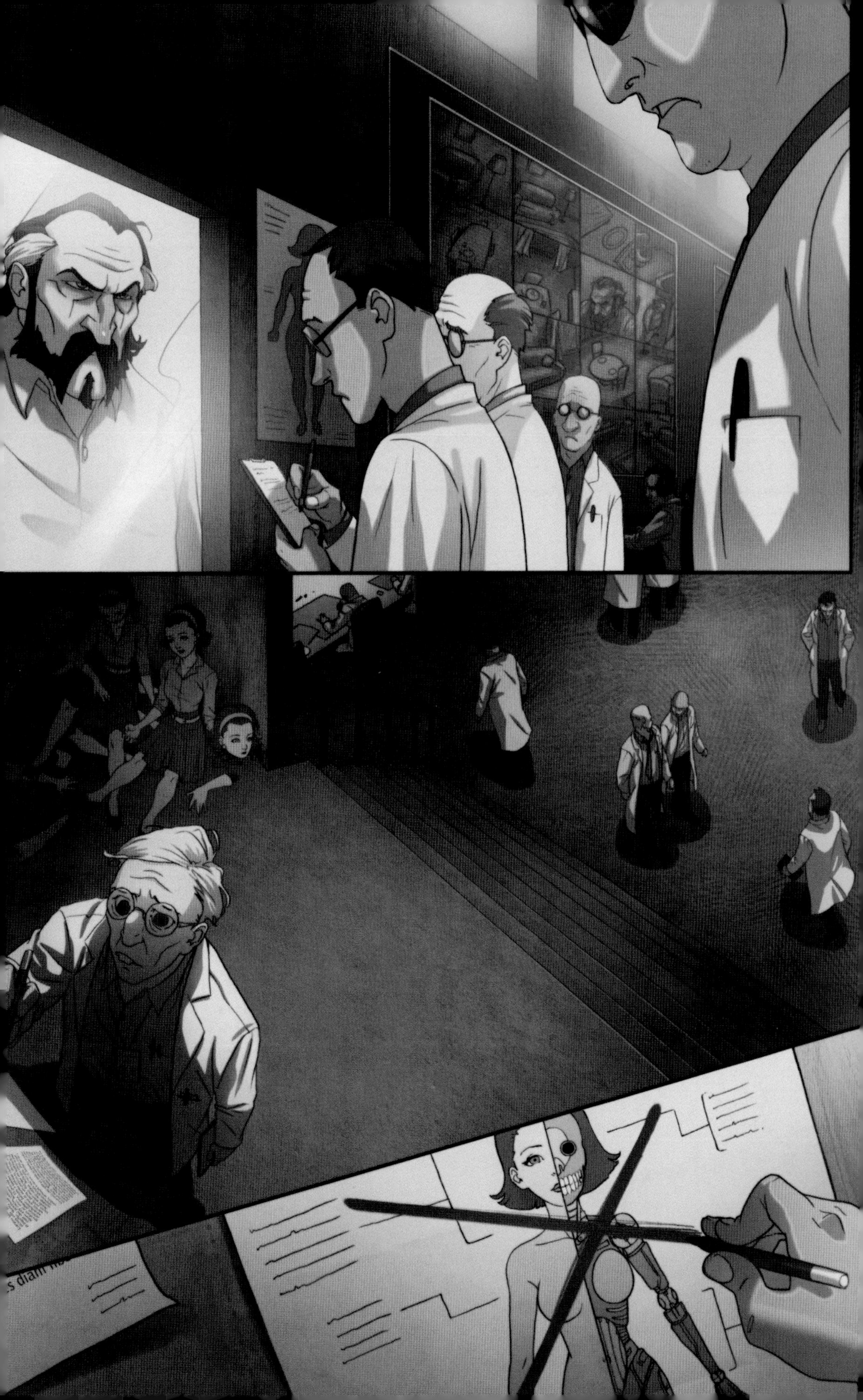

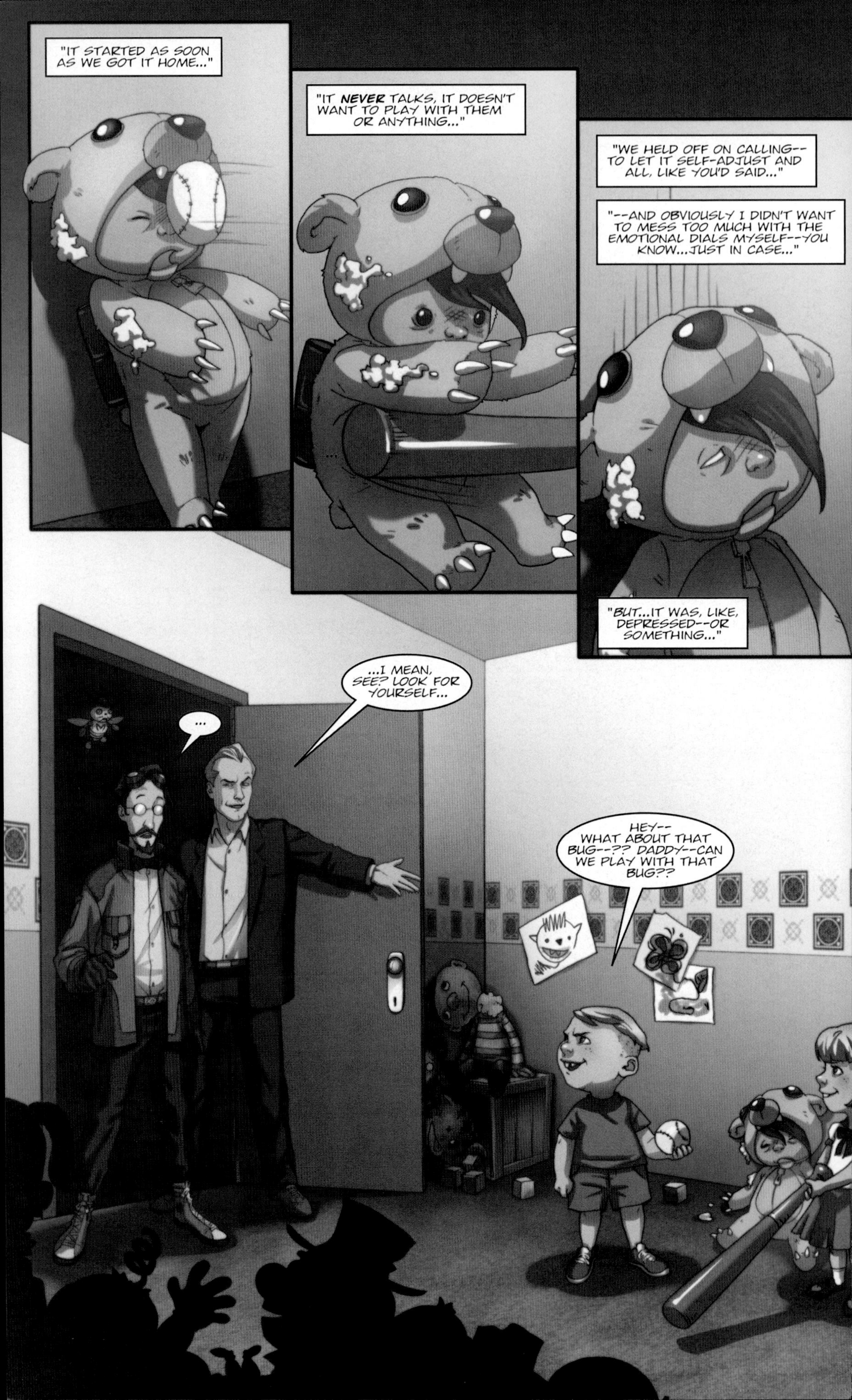
"IT STARTED AS SOON AS WE GOT IT HOME..."
"IT NEVER TALKS, IT DOESN'T WANT TO PLAY WITH THEM OR ANYTHING..."
"WE HELD OFF ON CALLING--TO LET IT SELF-ADJUST AND ALL, LIKE YOU'D SAID..."
"--AND OBVIOUSLY I DIDN'T WANT TO MESS TOO MUCH WITH THE EMOTIONAL DIALS MYSELF--YOU KNOW...JUST IN CASE..."
"BUT...IT WAS, LIKE, DEPRESSED--OR SOMETHING..."
...I MEAN, SEE? LOOK FOR YOURSELF...
...
HEY--WHAT ABOUT THAT BUG--?? DADDY--CAN WE PLAY WITH THAT BUG??

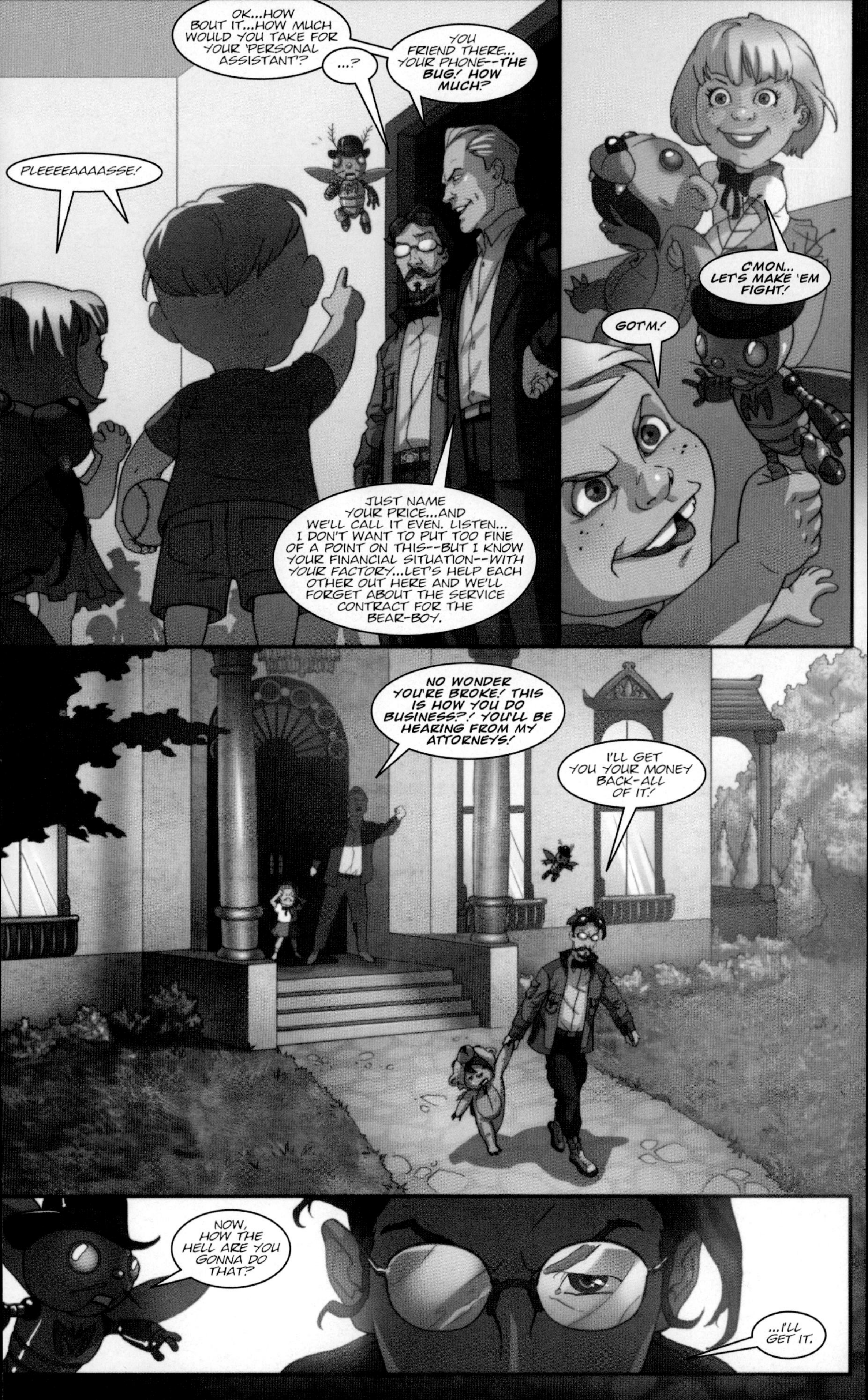

OK...HOW BOUT IT...HOW MUCH WOULD YOU TAKE FOR YOUR 'PERSONAL ASSISTANT'?
...?
YOU FRIEND THERE... YOUR PHONE--THE BUG! HOW MUCH?
PLEEEEAAAAASSE!
JUST NAME YOUR PRICE...AND WE'LL CALL IT EVEN. LISTEN... I DON'T WANT TO PUT TOO FINE OF A POINT ON THIS--BUT I KNOW YOUR FINANCIAL SITUATION--WITH YOUR FACTORY...LET'S HELP EACH OTHER OUT HERE AND WE'LL FORGET ABOUT THE SERVICE CONTRACT FOR THE BEAR-BOY.
C'MON... LET'S MAKE 'EM FIGHT!
GOT'M!
NO WONDER YOU'RE BROKE! THIS IS HOW YOU DO BUSINESS?! YOU'LL BE HEARING FROM MY ATTORNEYS!
I'LL GET YOU YOUR MONEY BACK-ALL OF IT!
NOW, HOW THE HELL ARE YOU GONNA DO THAT?
...I'LL GET IT.

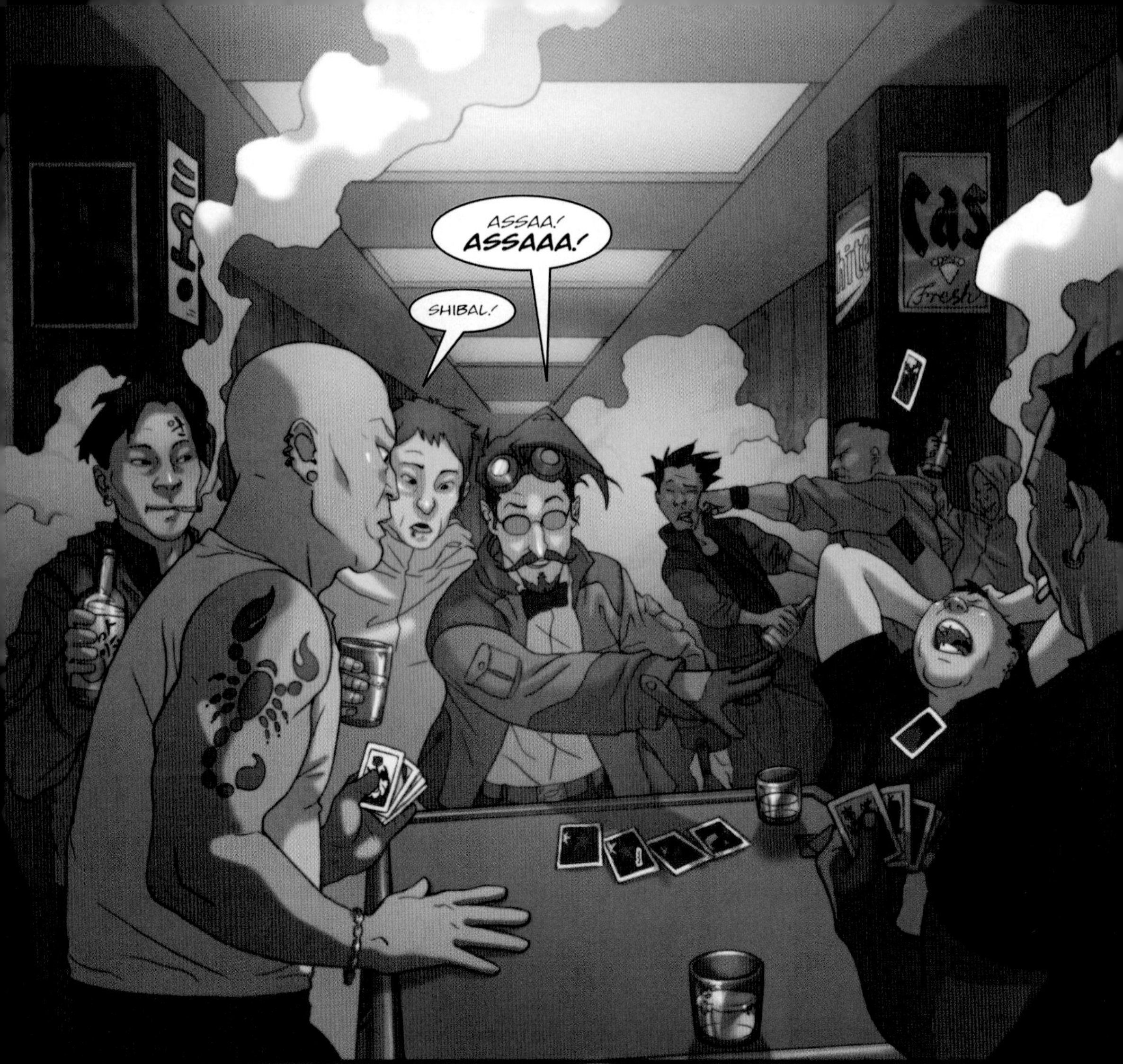
ASSAA! ASSAAA!
SHIBAL!
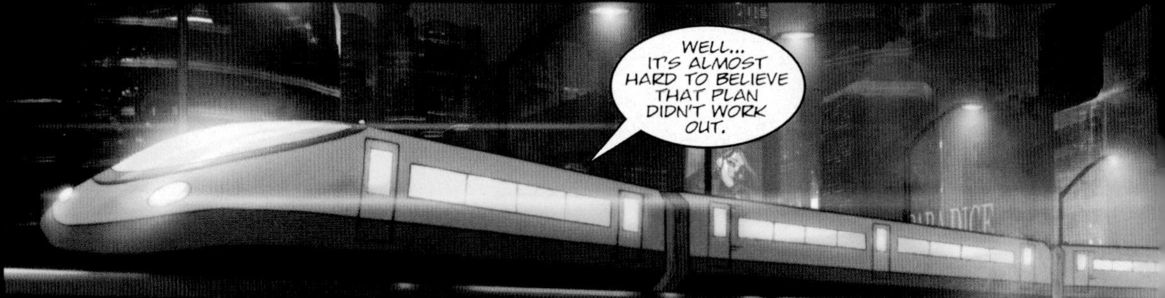
WELL... IT'S ALMOST HARD TO BELIEVE THAT PLAN DIDN'T WORK OUT.
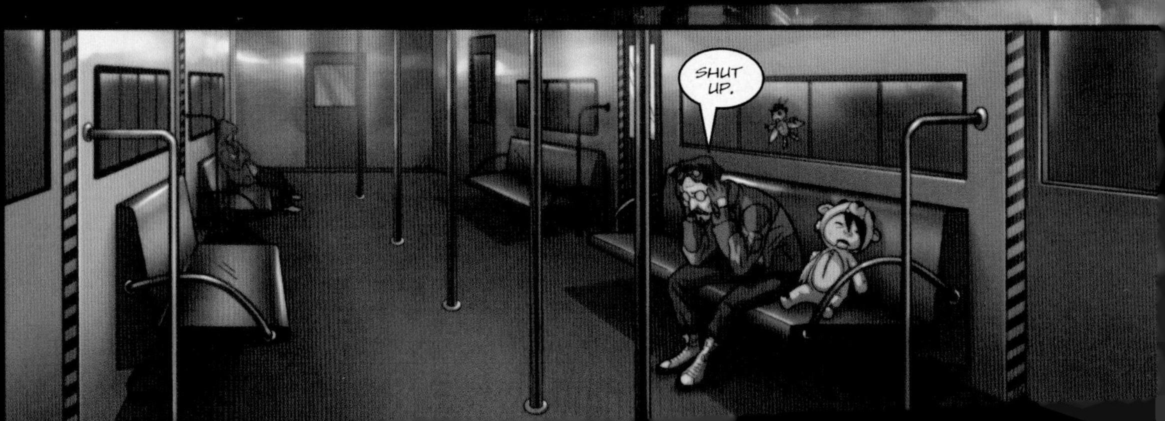
SHUT UP.

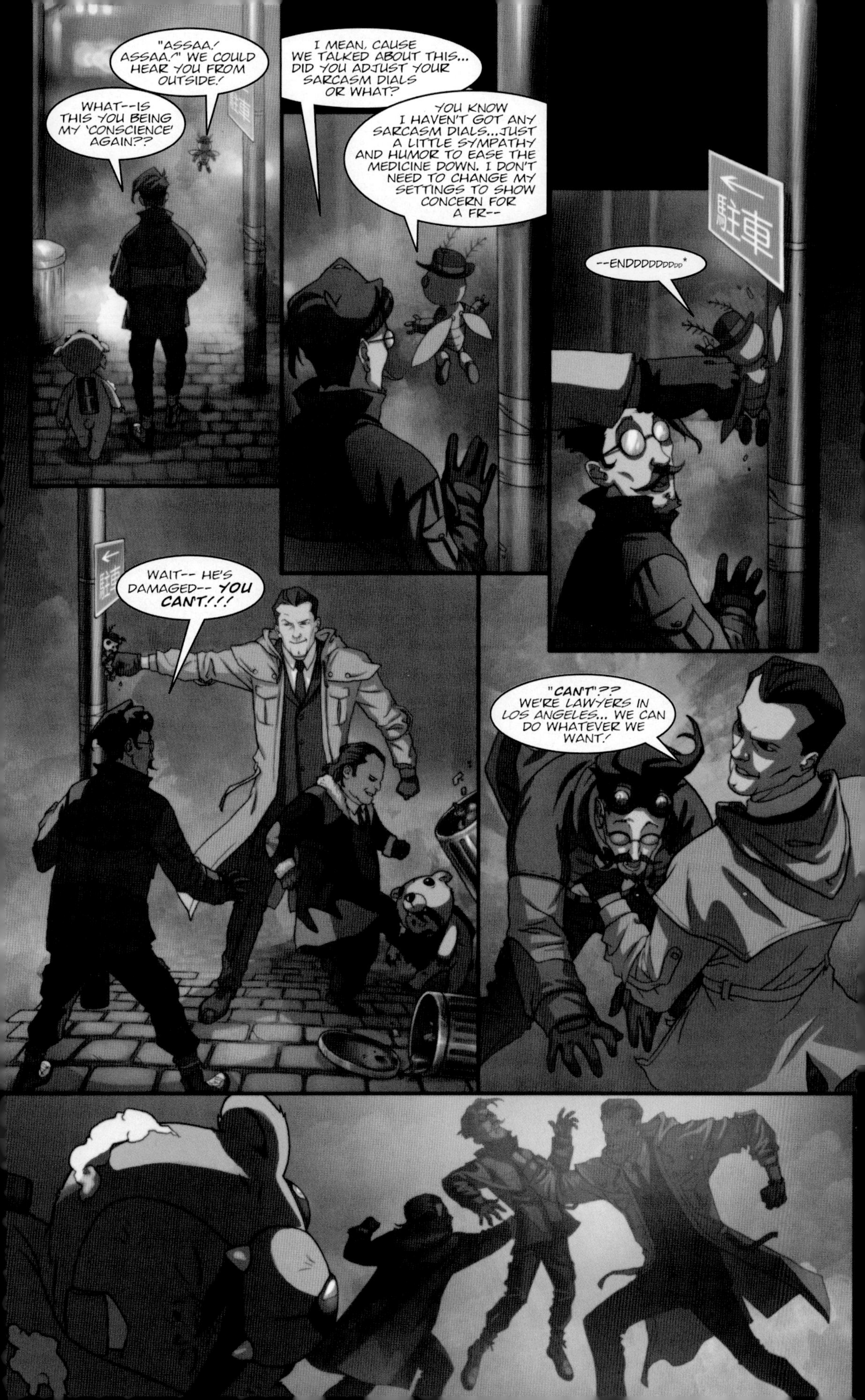

"ASSAA! ASSAA!" WE COULD HEAR YOU FROM OUTSIDE!
WHAT--IS THIS YOU BEING MY 'CONSCIENCE' AGAIN??
駐車
I MEAN, CAUSE WE TALKED ABOUT THIS... DID YOU ADJUST YOUR SARCASM DIALS OR WHAT?
YOU KNOW I HAVEN'T GOT ANY SARCASM DIALS...JUST A LITTLE SYMPATHY AND HUMOR TO EASE THE MEDICINE DOWN. I DON'T NEED TO CHANGE MY SETTINGS TO SHOW CONCERN FOR A FR--
←
駐車
--ENDDDDDDDDD*
WAIT-- HE'S DAMAGED-- YOU CAN'T!!!
"CAN'T"?? WE'RE LAWYERS IN LOS ANGELES... WE CAN DO WHATEVER WE WANT!

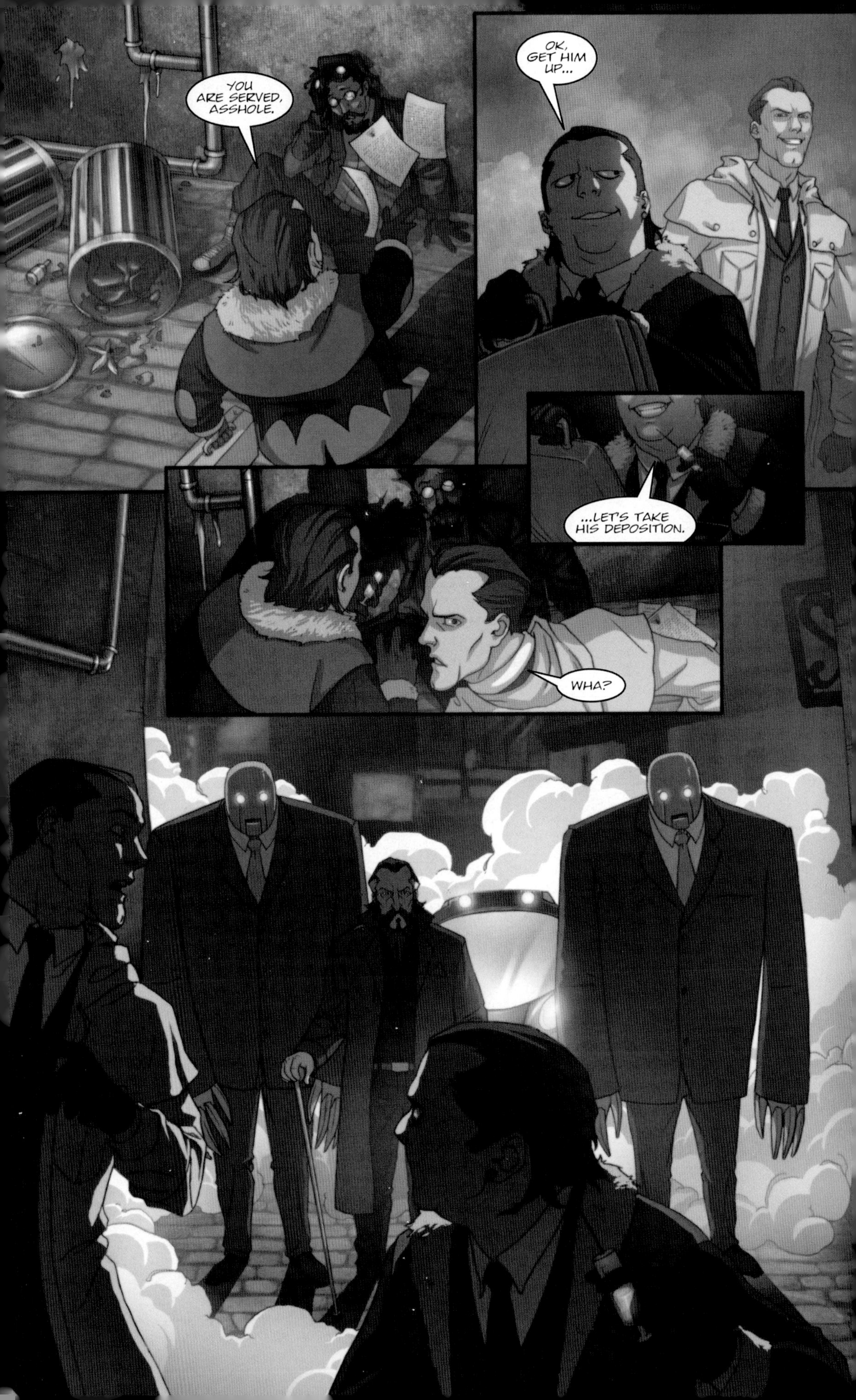
YOU ARE SERVED, ASSHOLE.
OK, GET HIM UP...
...LET'S TAKE HIS DEPOSITION.
WHA?

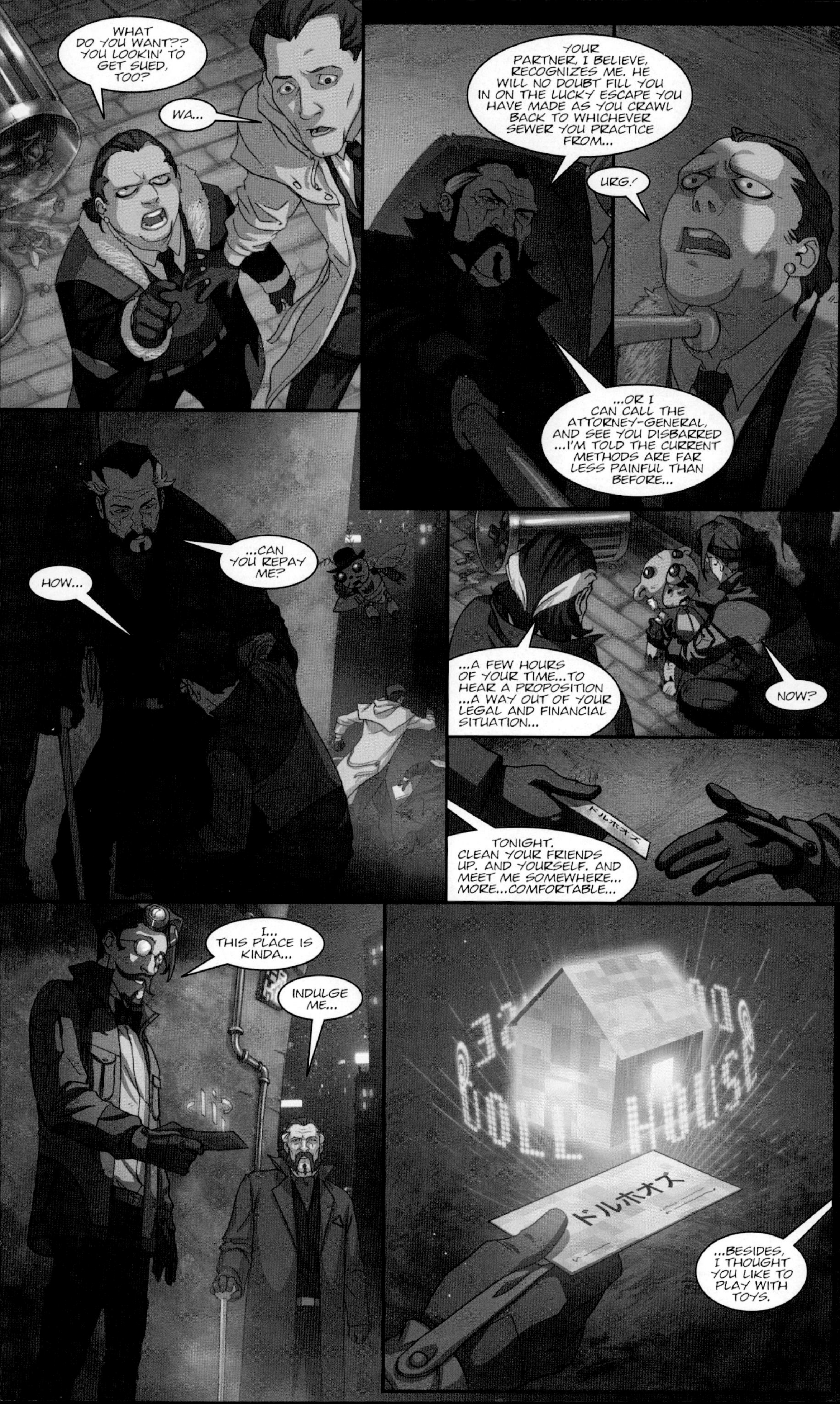
WHAT DO YOU WANT?? YOU LOOKIN' TO GET SUED, TOO?
WA...
YOUR PARTNER, I BELIEVE, RECOGNIZES ME. HE WILL NO DOUBT FILL YOU IN ON THE LUCKY ESCAPE YOU HAVE MADE AS YOU CRAWL BACK TO WHICHEVER SEWER YOU PRACTICE FROM...
URG!
...OR I CAN CALL THE ATTORNEY-GENERAL, AND SEE YOU DISBARRED ...I'M TOLD THE CURRENT METHODS ARE FAR LESS PAINFUL THAN BEFORE...
HOW...
...CAN YOU REPAY ME?
...A FEW HOURS OF YOUR TIME...TO HEAR A PROPOSITION ...A WAY OUT OF YOUR LEGAL AND FINANCIAL SITUATION...
NOW?
ドルホオズ
TONIGHT. CLEAN YOUR FRIENDS UP. AND YOURSELF. AND MEET ME SOMEWHERE... MORE...COMFORTABLE...
I... THIS PLACE IS KINDA...
INDULGE ME...
DOLL HOUSE
ドルホオズ
...BESIDES, I THOUGHT YOU LIKE TO PLAY WITH TOYS.

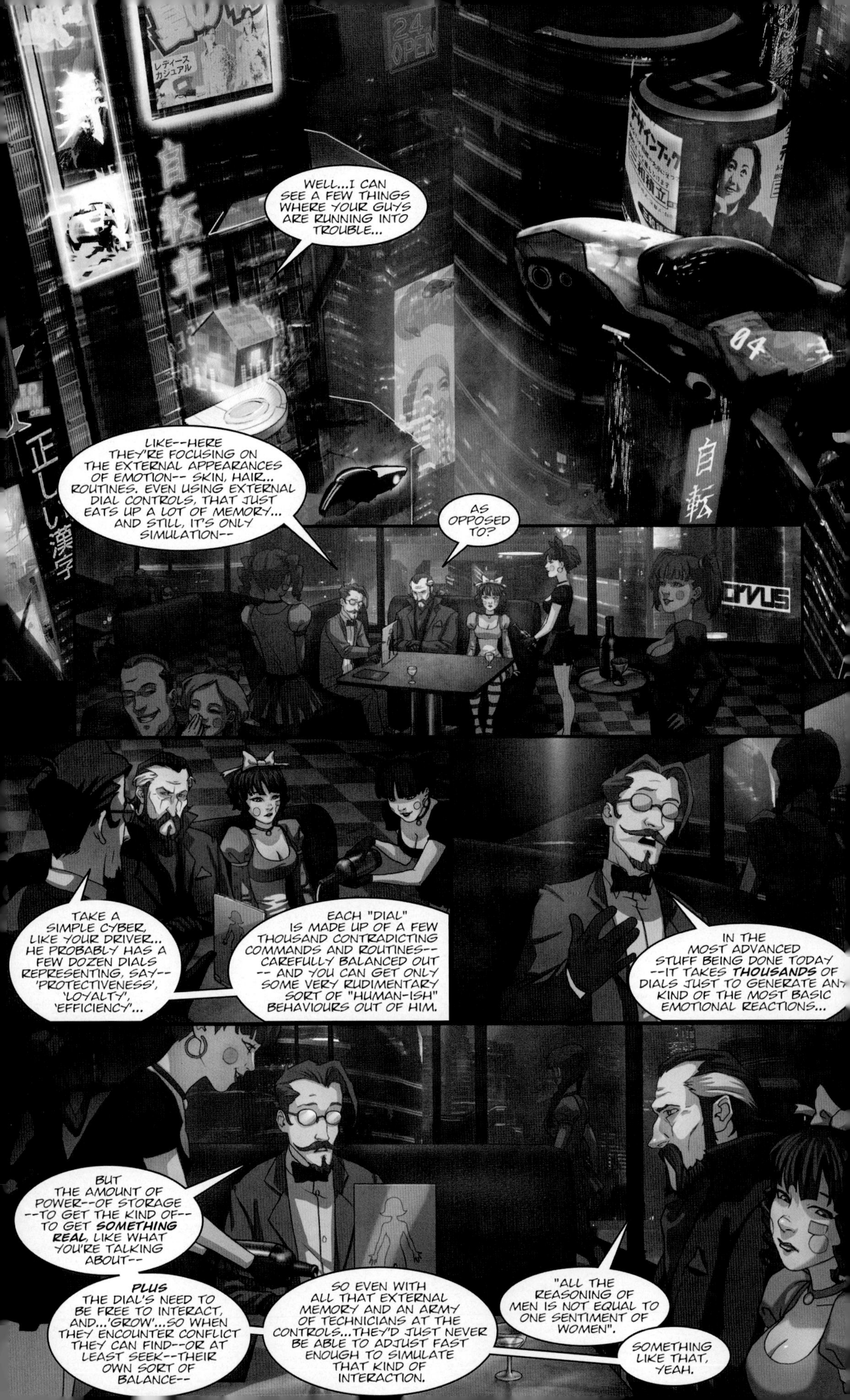
レディースカジュアル
24 OPEN
自転車
WELL...I CAN SEE A FEW THINGS WHERE YOUR GUYS ARE RUNNING INTO TROUBLE...
04
正しい漢字
自転
LIKE--HERE THEY'RE FOCUSING ON THE EXTERNAL APPEARANCES OF EMOTION-- SKIN, HAIR... ROUTINES. EVEN USING EXTERNAL DIAL CONTROLS, THAT JUST EATS UP A LOT OF MEMORY... AND STILL, IT'S ONLY SIMULATION--
AS OPPOSED TO?
TAKE A SIMPLE CYBER, LIKE YOUR DRIVER... HE PROBABLY HAS A FEW DOZEN DIALS REPRESENTING, SAY-- 'PROTECTIVENESS', 'LOYALTY', 'EFFICIENCY'...
EACH "DIAL" IS MADE UP OF A FEW THOUSAND CONTRADICTING COMMANDS AND ROUTINES-- CAREFULLY BALANCED OUT --AND YOU CAN GET ONLY SOME VERY RUDIMENTARY SORT OF "HUMAN-ISH" BEHAVIOURS OUT OF HIM.
IN THE MOST ADVANCED STUFF BEING DONE TODAY --IT TAKES **THOUSANDS** OF DIALS JUST TO GENERATE ANY KIND OF THE MOST BASIC EMOTIONAL REACTIONS...
BUT THE AMOUNT OF POWER--OF STORAGE --TO GET THE KIND OF-- TO GET **SOMETHING REAL**, LIKE WHAT YOU'RE TALKING ABOUT--
PLUS THE DIAL'S NEED TO BE FREE TO INTERACT, AND...'GROW'...SO WHEN THEY ENCOUNTER CONFLICT THEY CAN FIND--OR AT LEAST SEEK--THEIR OWN SORT OF BALANCE--
SO EVEN WITH ALL THAT EXTERNAL MEMORY AND AN ARMY OF TECHNICIANS AT THE CONTROLS...THEY'D JUST NEVER BE ABLE TO ADJUST FAST ENOUGH TO SIMULATE THAT KIND OF INTERACTION.
"ALL THE REASONING OF MEN IS NOT EQUAL TO ONE SENTIMENT OF WOMEN".
SOMETHING LIKE THAT, YEAH.

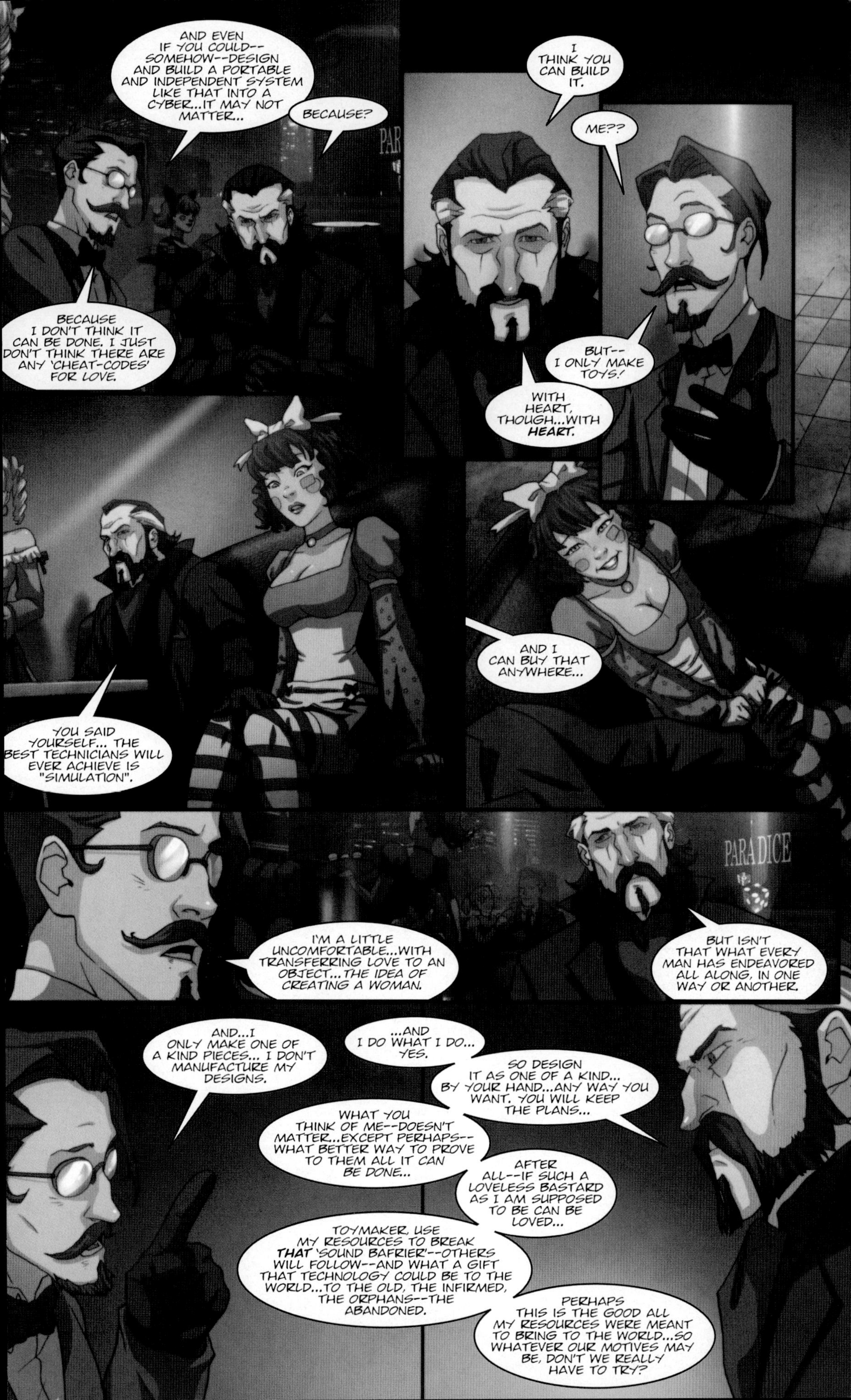
AND EVEN IF YOU COULD-- SOMEHOW--DESIGN AND BUILD A PORTABLE AND INDEPENDENT SYSTEM LIKE THAT INTO A CYBER...IT MAY NOT MATTER...
BECAUSE?
BECAUSE I DON'T THINK IT CAN BE DONE. I JUST DON'T THINK THERE ARE ANY 'CHEAT-CODES' FOR LOVE.
PAR
I THINK YOU CAN BUILD IT.
ME??
BUT-- I ONLY MAKE TOYS!
WITH HEART, THOUGH...WITH **HEART.**
YOU SAID YOURSELF... THE BEST TECHNICIANS WILL EVER ACHIEVE IS "SIMULATION".
AND I CAN BUY THAT ANYWHERE...
I'M A LITTLE UNCOMFORTABLE...WITH TRANSFERRING LOVE TO AN OBJECT...THE IDEA OF CREATING A WOMAN.
PARA DICE
BUT ISN'T THAT WHAT EVERY MAN HAS ENDEAVORED ALL ALONG, IN ONE WAY OR ANOTHER.
AND...I ONLY MAKE ONE OF A KIND PIECES... I DON'T MANUFACTURE MY DESIGNS.
...AND I DO WHAT I DO... YES.
SO DESIGN IT AS ONE OF A KIND... BY YOUR HAND...ANY WAY YOU WANT. YOU WILL KEEP THE PLANS...
WHAT YOU THINK OF ME--DOESN'T MATTER...EXCEPT PERHAPS-- WHAT BETTER WAY TO PROVE TO THEM ALL IT CAN BE DONE...
AFTER ALL--IF SUCH A LOVELESS BASTARD AS I AM SUPPOSED TO BE CAN BE LOVED...
TOYMAKER, USE MY RESOURCES TO BREAK **THAT** 'SOUND BAFRIER'--OTHERS WILL FOLLOW--AND WHAT A GIFT THAT TECHNOLOGY COULD BE TO THE WORLD...TO THE OLD, THE INFIRMED, THE ORPHANS--THE ABANDONED.
PERHAPS THIS IS THE GOOD ALL MY RESOURCES WERE MEANT TO BRING TO THE WORLD...SO WHATEVER OUR MOTIVES MAY BE, DON'T WE REALLY HAVE TO TRY?

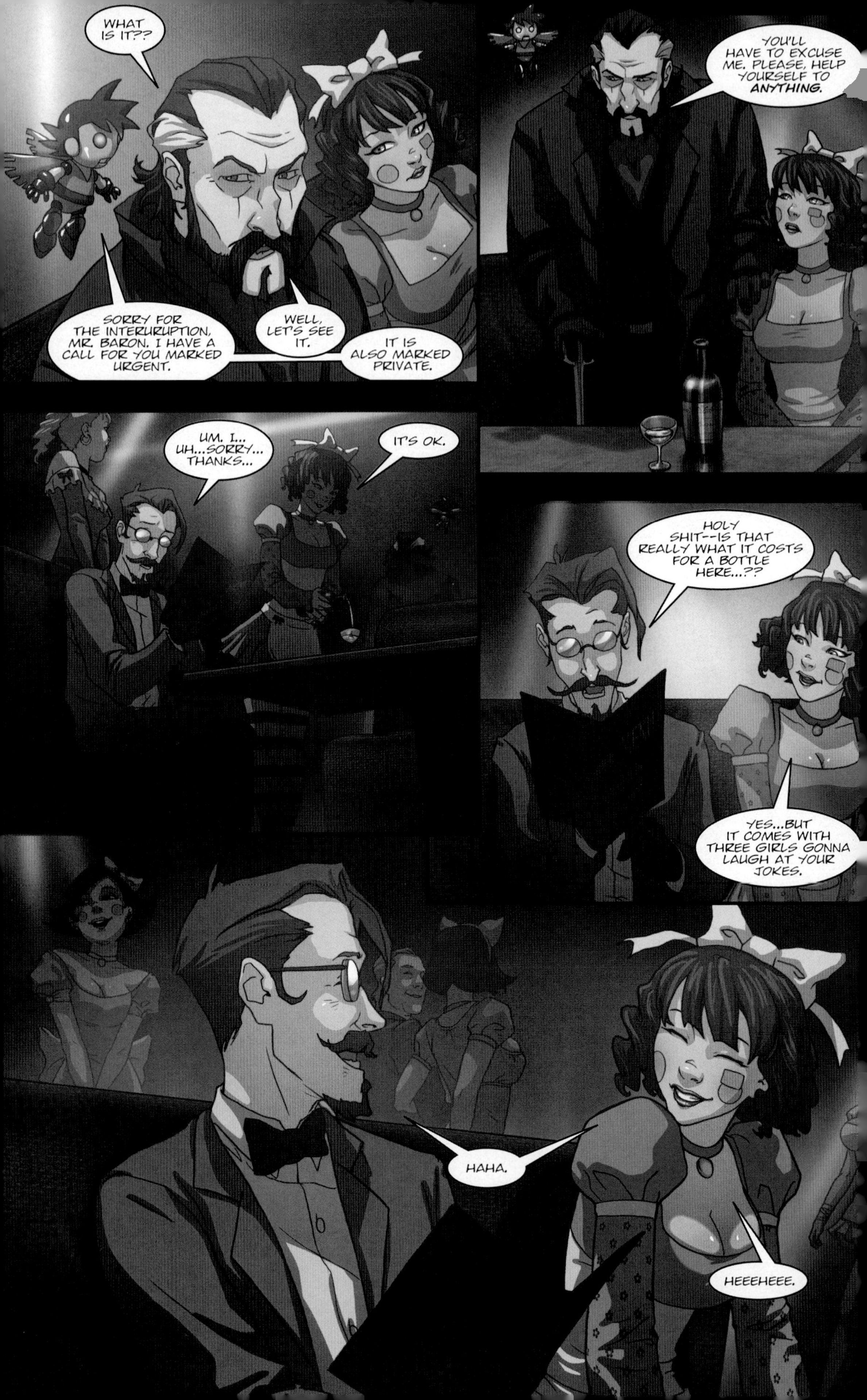
WHAT IS IT??
SORRY FOR THE INTERURUPTION, MR. BARON. I HAVE A CALL FOR YOU MARKED URGENT.
WELL, LET'S SEE IT.
IT IS ALSO MARKED PRIVATE.
YOU'LL HAVE TO EXCUSE ME. PLEASE, HELP YOURSELF TO ANYTHING.
UM. I... UH...SORRY... THANKS...
IT'S OK.
HOLY SHIT--IS THAT REALLY WHAT IT COSTS FOR A BOTTLE HERE...??
YES...BUT IT COMES WITH THREE GIRLS GONNA LAUGH AT YOUR JOKES.
HAHA.
HEEEHEEE.

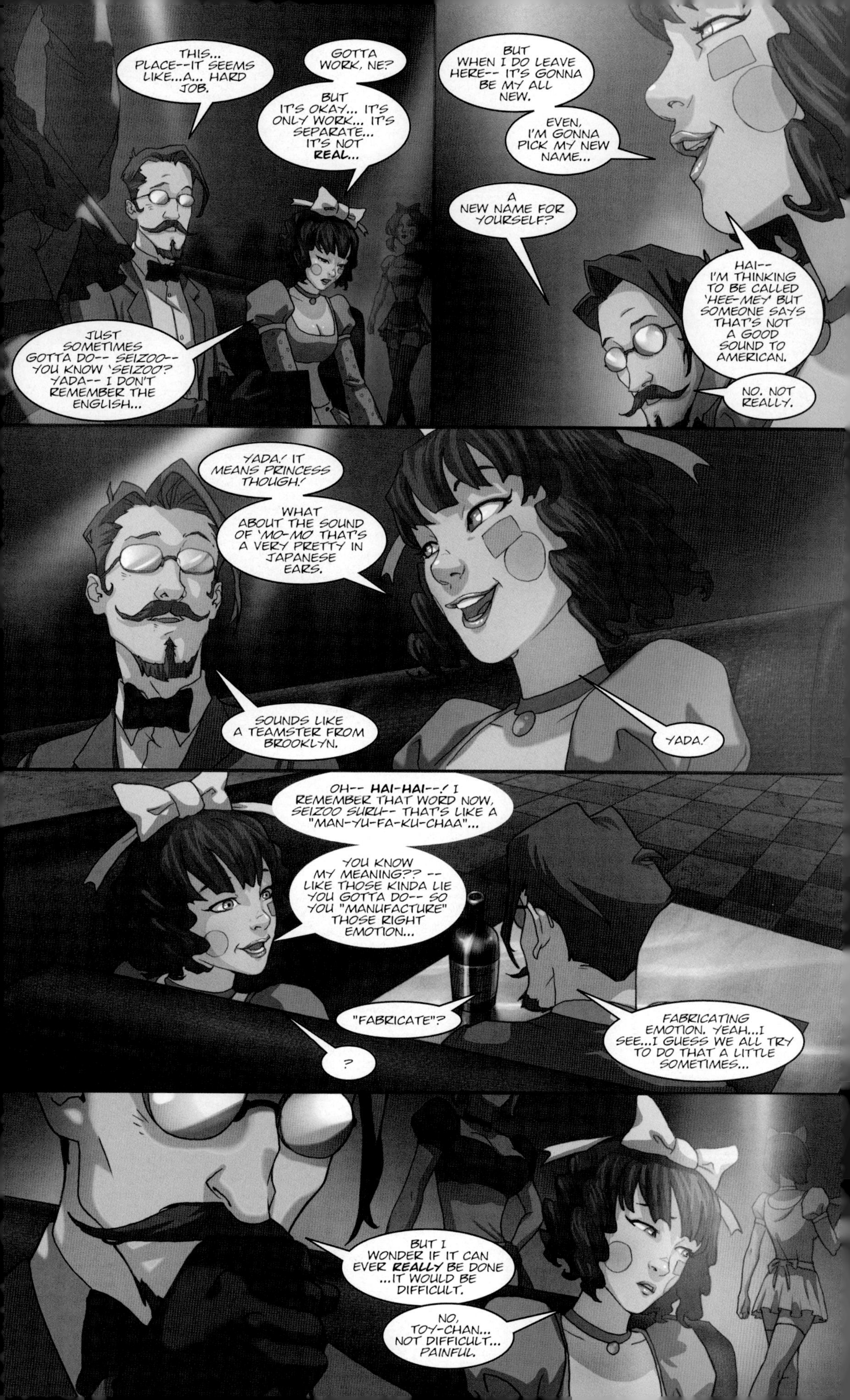
THIS... PLACE--IT SEEMS LIKE...A... HARD JOB.
GOTTA WORK, NE?
BUT IT'S OKAY... IT'S ONLY WORK... IT'S SEPARATE... IT'S NOT **REAL**...
JUST SOMETIMES GOTTA DO-- SEIZOO-- YOU KNOW 'SEIZOO'? YADA-- I DON'T REMEMBER THE ENGLISH...
BUT WHEN I DO LEAVE HERE-- IT'S GONNA BE MY ALL NEW.
EVEN, I'M GONNA PICK MY NEW NAME...
A NEW NAME FOR YOURSELF?
HAI-- I'M THINKING TO BE CALLED 'HEE-MEY' BUT SOMEONE SAYS THAT'S NOT A GOOD SOUND TO AMERICAN.
NO. NOT REALLY.
YADA! IT MEANS PRINCESS THOUGH!
WHAT ABOUT THE SOUND OF 'MO-MO' THAT'S A VERY PRETTY IN JAPANESE EARS.
SOUNDS LIKE A TEAMSTER FROM BROOKLYN.
YADA!
OH-- **HAI-HAI--!** I REMEMBER THAT WORD NOW, SEIZOO SURU-- THAT'S LIKE A "MAN-YU-FA-KU-CHAA"...
YOU KNOW MY MEANING?? --LIKE THOSE KINDA LIE YOU GOTTA DO-- SO YOU "MANUFACTURE" THOSE RIGHT EMOTION...
"FABRICATE"?
?
FABRICATING EMOTION. YEAH...I SEE...I GUESS WE ALL TRY TO DO THAT A LITTLE SOMETIMES...
BUT I WONDER IF IT CAN EVER **REALLY** BE DONE ...IT WOULD BE DIFFICULT.
NO, TOY-CHAN... NOT DIFFICULT... PAINFUL.

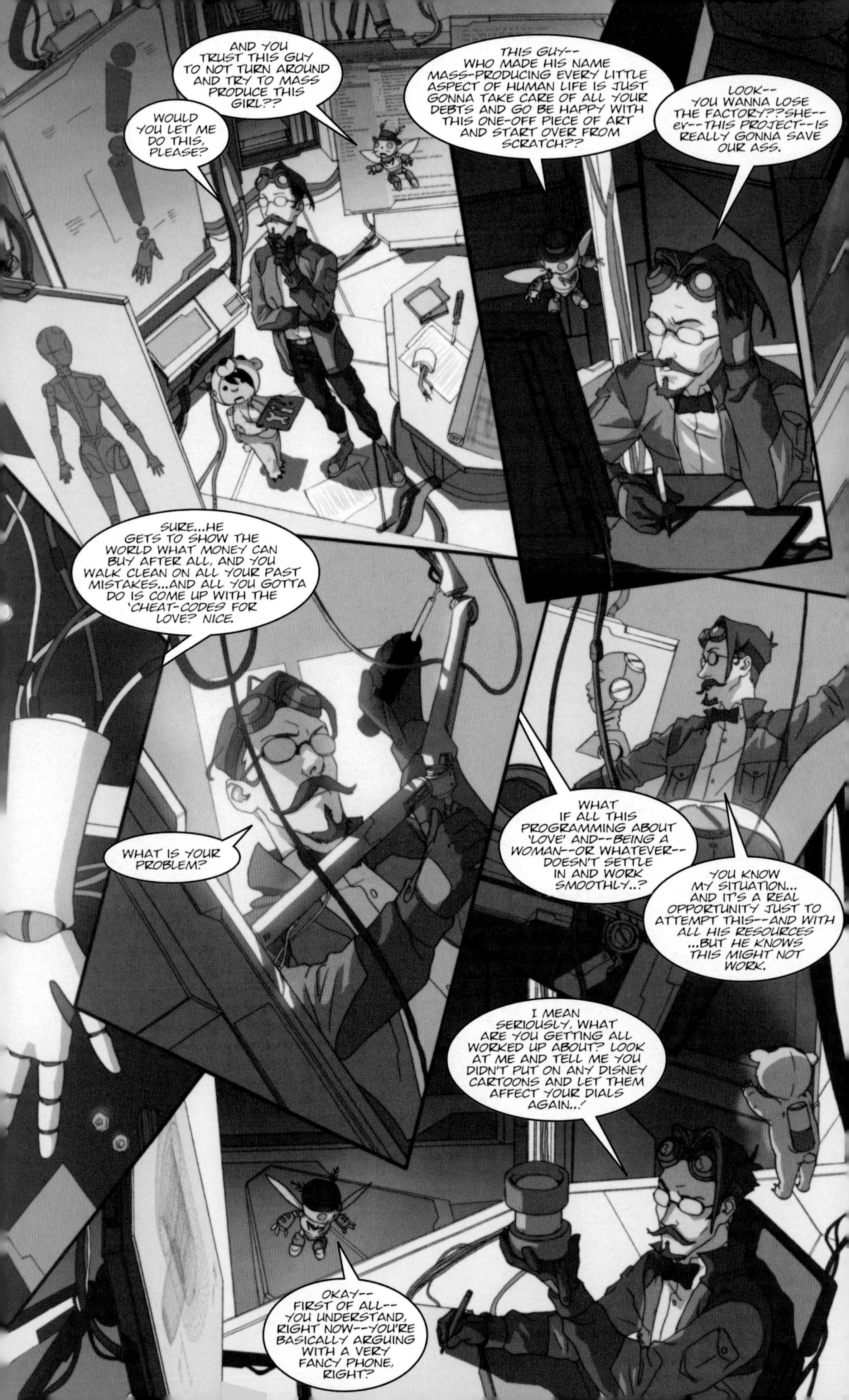
AND YOU TRUST THIS GUY TO NOT TURN AROUND AND TRY TO MASS PRODUCE THIS GIRL??
WOULD YOU LET ME DO THIS, PLEASE?
THIS GUY-- WHO MADE HIS NAME MASS-PRODUCING EVERY LITTLE ASPECT OF HUMAN LIFE IS JUST GONNA TAKE CARE OF ALL YOUR DEBTS AND GO BE HAPPY WITH THIS ONE-OFF PIECE OF ART AND START OVER FROM SCRATCH??
LOOK-- YOU WANNA LOSE THE FACTORY??SHE-- ev--THIS PROJECT--IS REALLY GONNA SAVE OUR ASS.
SURE...HE GETS TO SHOW THE WORLD WHAT MONEY CAN BUY AFTER ALL, AND YOU WALK CLEAN ON ALL YOUR PAST MISTAKES...AND ALL YOU GOTTA DO IS COME UP WITH THE 'CHEAT-CODES' FOR LOVE? NICE.
WHAT IS YOUR PROBLEM?
WHAT IF ALL THIS PROGRAMMING ABOUT 'LOVE' AND--BEING A WOMAN--OR WHATEVER-- DOESN'T SETTLE IN AND WORK SMOOTHLY..?
YOU KNOW MY SITUATION... AND IT'S A REAL OPPORTUNITY JUST TO ATTEMPT THIS--AND WITH ALL HIS RESOURCES ...BUT HE KNOWS THIS MIGHT NOT WORK.
I MEAN SERIOUSLY, WHAT ARE YOU GETTING ALL WORKED UP ABOUT? LOOK AT ME AND TELL ME YOU DIDN'T PUT ON ANY DISNEY CARTOONS AND LET THEM AFFECT YOUR DIALS AGAIN...'
OKAY-- FIRST OF ALL-- YOU UNDERSTAND, RIGHT NOW--YOU'RE BASICALLY ARGUING WITH A VERY FANCY PHONE, RIGHT?

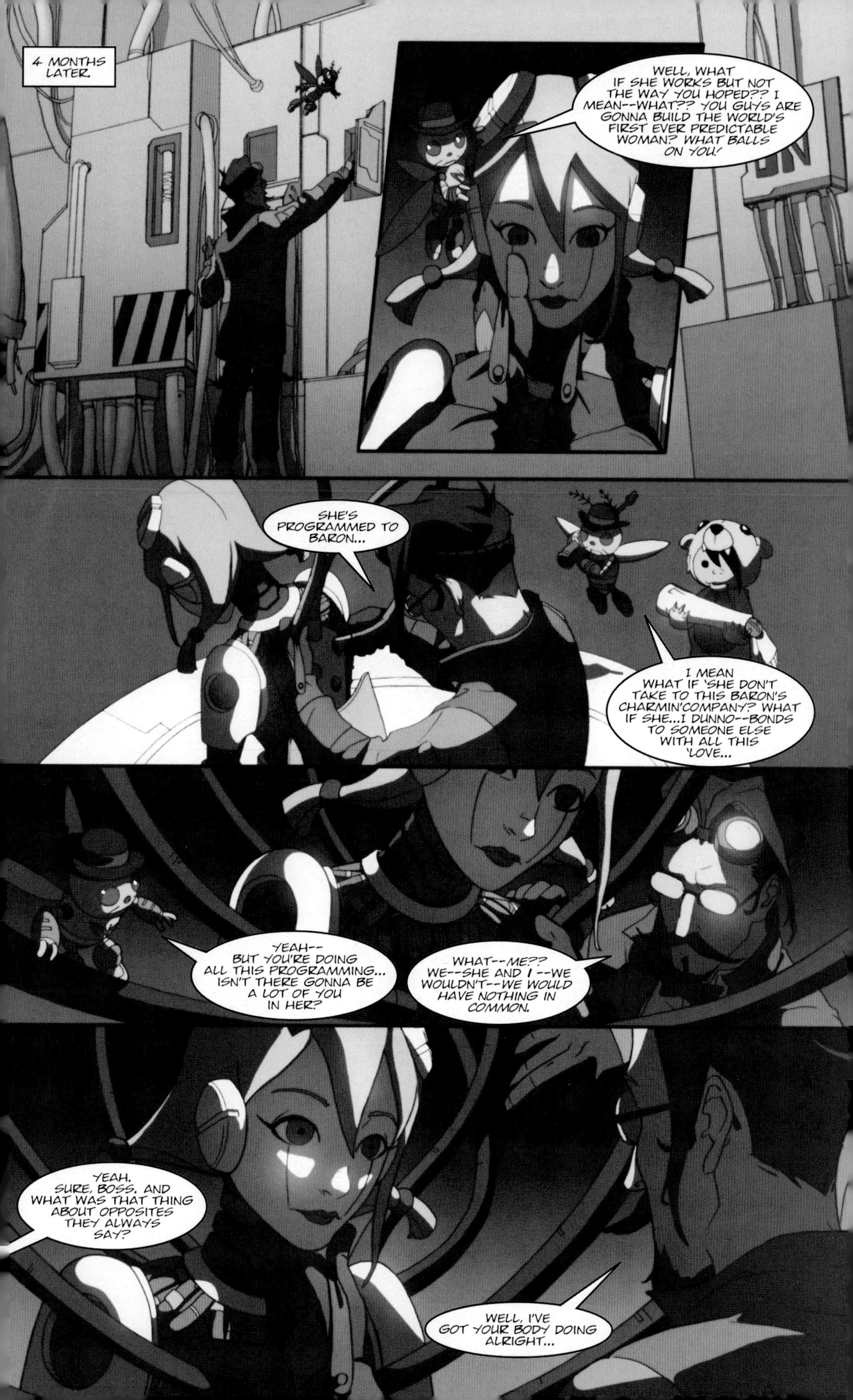
4 MONTHS LATER.
WELL, WHAT IF SHE WORKS BUT NOT THE WAY YOU HOPED?? I MEAN--WHAT?? YOU GUYS ARE GONNA BUILD THE WORLD'S FIRST EVER PREDICTABLE WOMAN? WHAT BALLS ON YOU!
SHE'S PROGRAMMED TO BARON...
I MEAN WHAT IF 'SHE DON'T TAKE TO THIS BARON'S CHARMIN'COMPANY? WHAT IF SHE...I DUNNO--BONDS TO SOMEONE ELSE WITH ALL THIS 'LOVE...
YEAH-- BUT YOU'RE DOING ALL THIS PROGRAMMING... ISN'T THERE GONNA BE A LOT OF YOU IN HER?
WHAT--ME?? WE--SHE AND I --WE WOULDN'T--WE WOULD HAVE NOTHING IN COMMON.
YEAH. SURE, BOSS. AND WHAT WAS THAT THING ABOUT OPPOSITES THEY ALWAYS SAY?
WELL, I'VE GOT YOUR BODY DOING ALRIGHT...

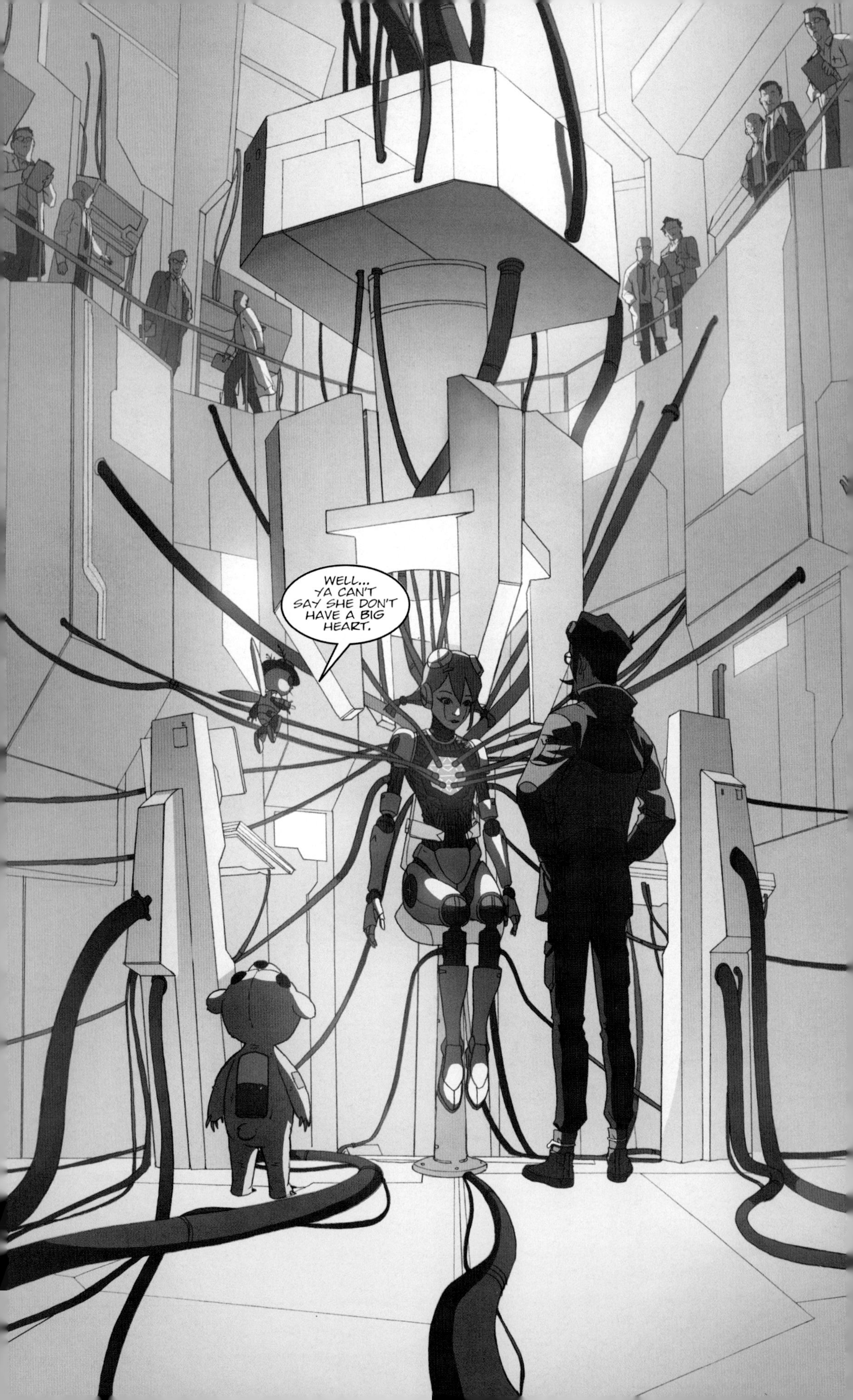
WELL... YA CAN'T SAY SHE DON'T HAVE A BIG HEART.

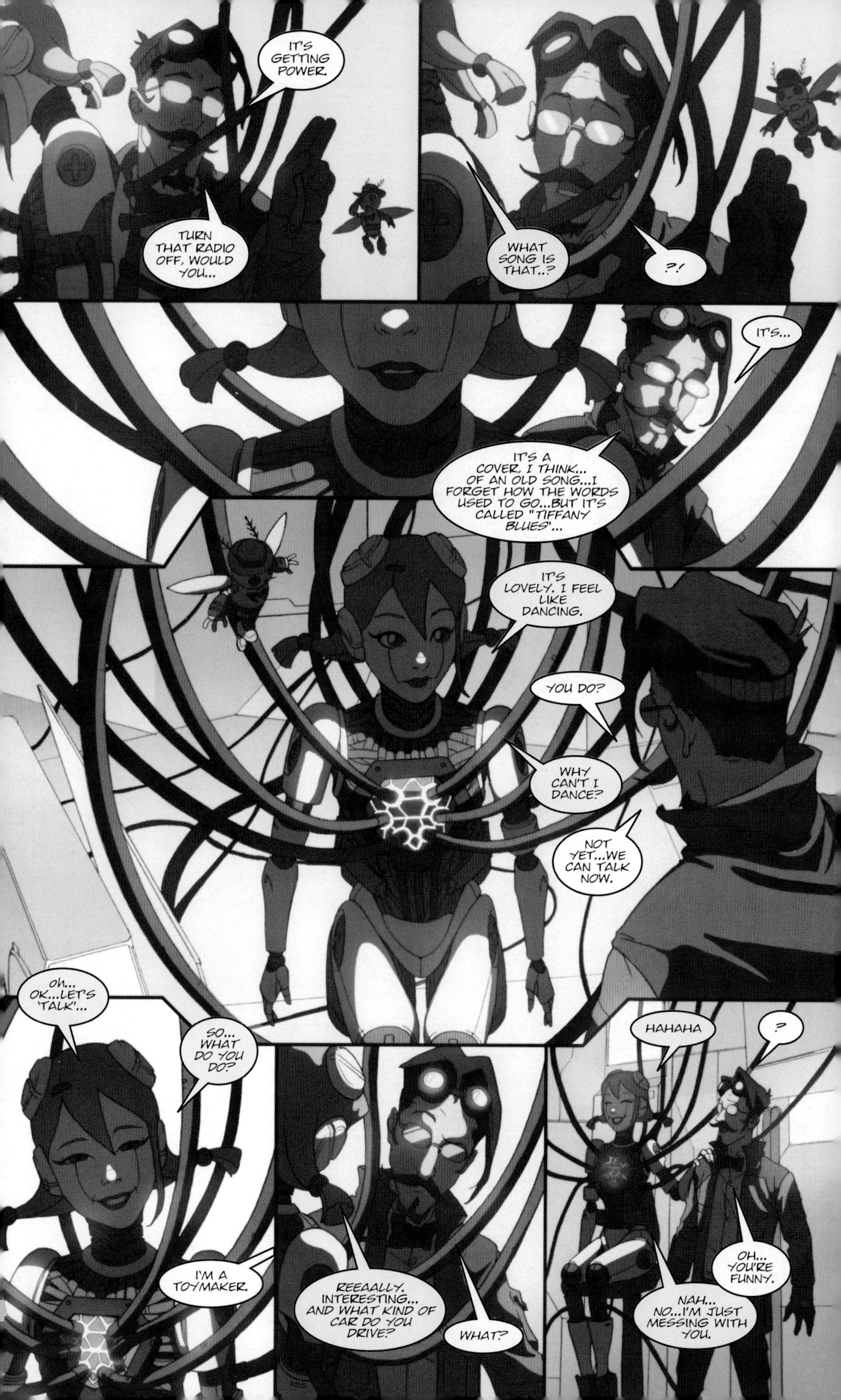
IT'S GETTING POWER.
TURN THAT RADIO OFF, WOULD YOU...
WHAT SONG IS THAT..?
?!
IT'S...
IT'S A COVER, I THINK... OF AN OLD SONG...I FORGET HOW THE WORDS USED TO GO...BUT IT'S CALLED "TIFFANY BLUES"...
IT'S LOVELY. I FEEL LIKE DANCING.
YOU DO?
WHY CAN'T I DANCE?
NOT YET...WE CAN TALK NOW.
oh... OK...LET'S 'TALK'...
SO... WHAT DO YOU DO?
I'M A TOYMAKER.
REEAALLY. INTERESTING... AND WHAT KIND OF CAR DO YOU DRIVE?
WHAT?
HAHAHA
?
OH... YOU'RE FUNNY.
NAH... NO...I'M JUST MESSING WITH YOU.

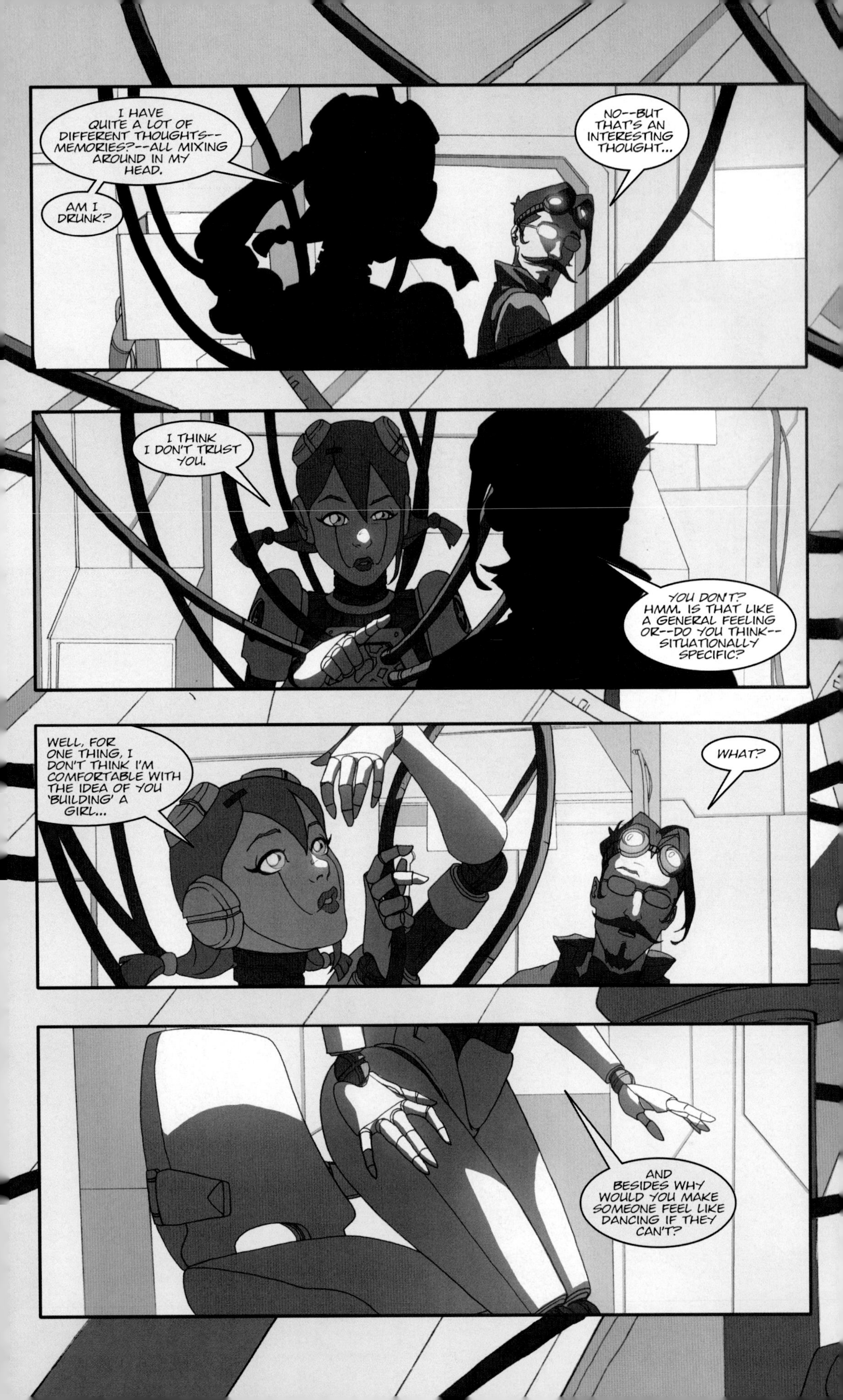
I HAVE QUITE A LOT OF DIFFERENT THOUGHTS--MEMORIES?--ALL MIXING AROUND IN MY HEAD.
AM I DRUNK?
NO--BUT THAT'S AN INTERESTING THOUGHT...
I THINK I DON'T TRUST YOU.
YOU DON'T? HMM. IS THAT LIKE A GENERAL FEELING OR--DO YOU THINK--SITUATIONALLY SPECIFIC?
WELL, FOR ONE THING, I DON'T THINK I'M COMFORTABLE WITH THE IDEA OF YOU 'BUILDING' A GIRL...
WHAT?
AND BESIDES WHY WOULD YOU MAKE SOMEONE FEEL LIKE DANCING IF THEY CAN'T?

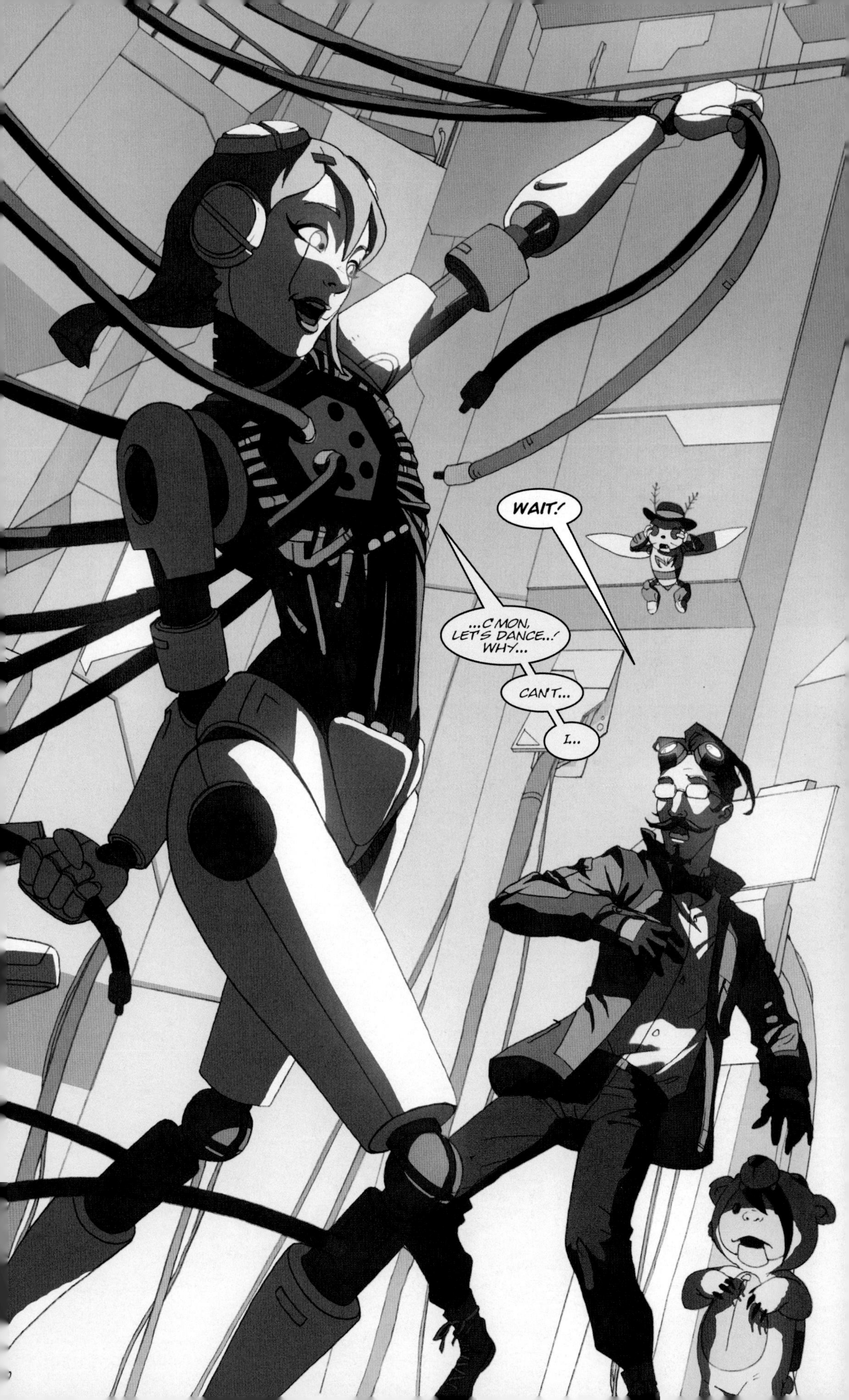
WAIT!
...C'MON, LET'S DANCE..! WHY...
CAN'T...
I...

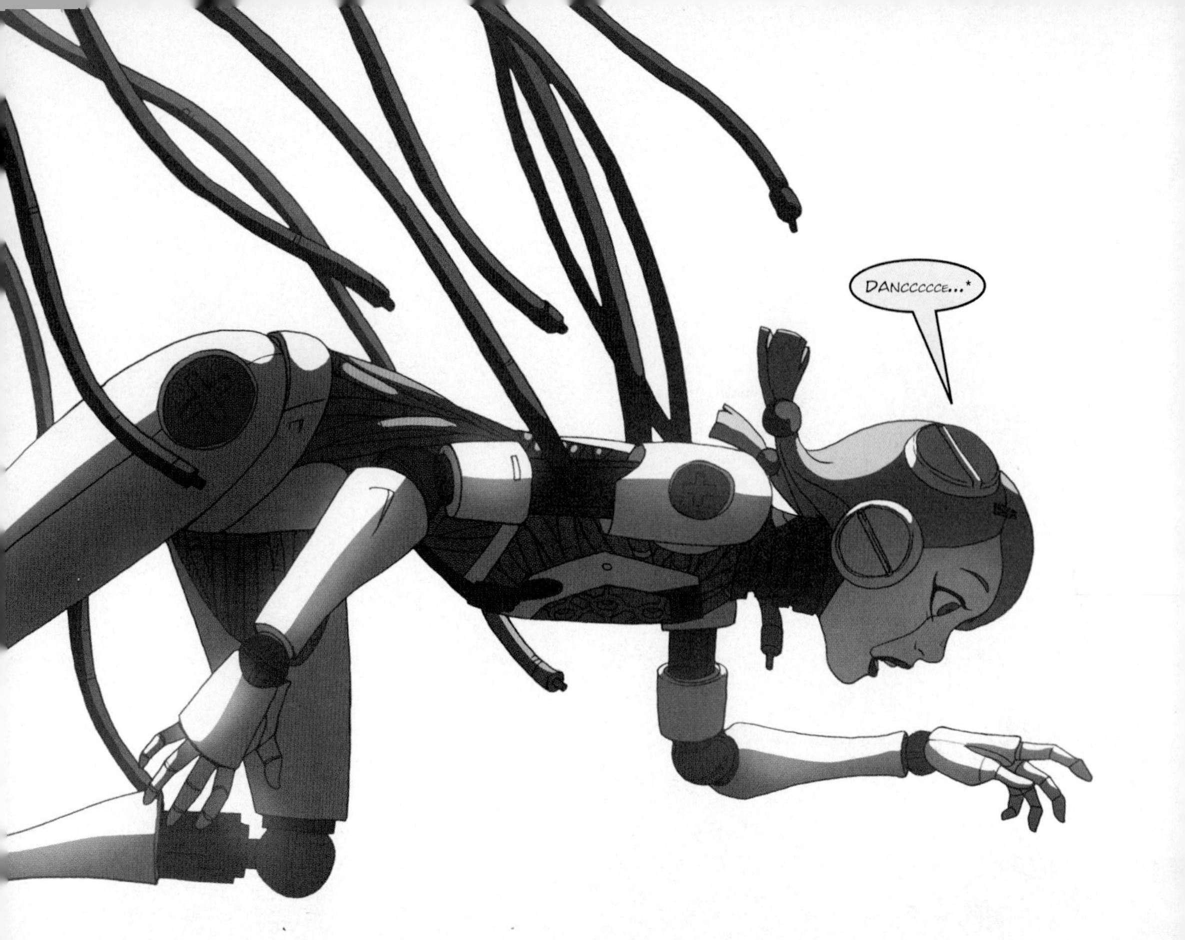
DANCCCCCE...*

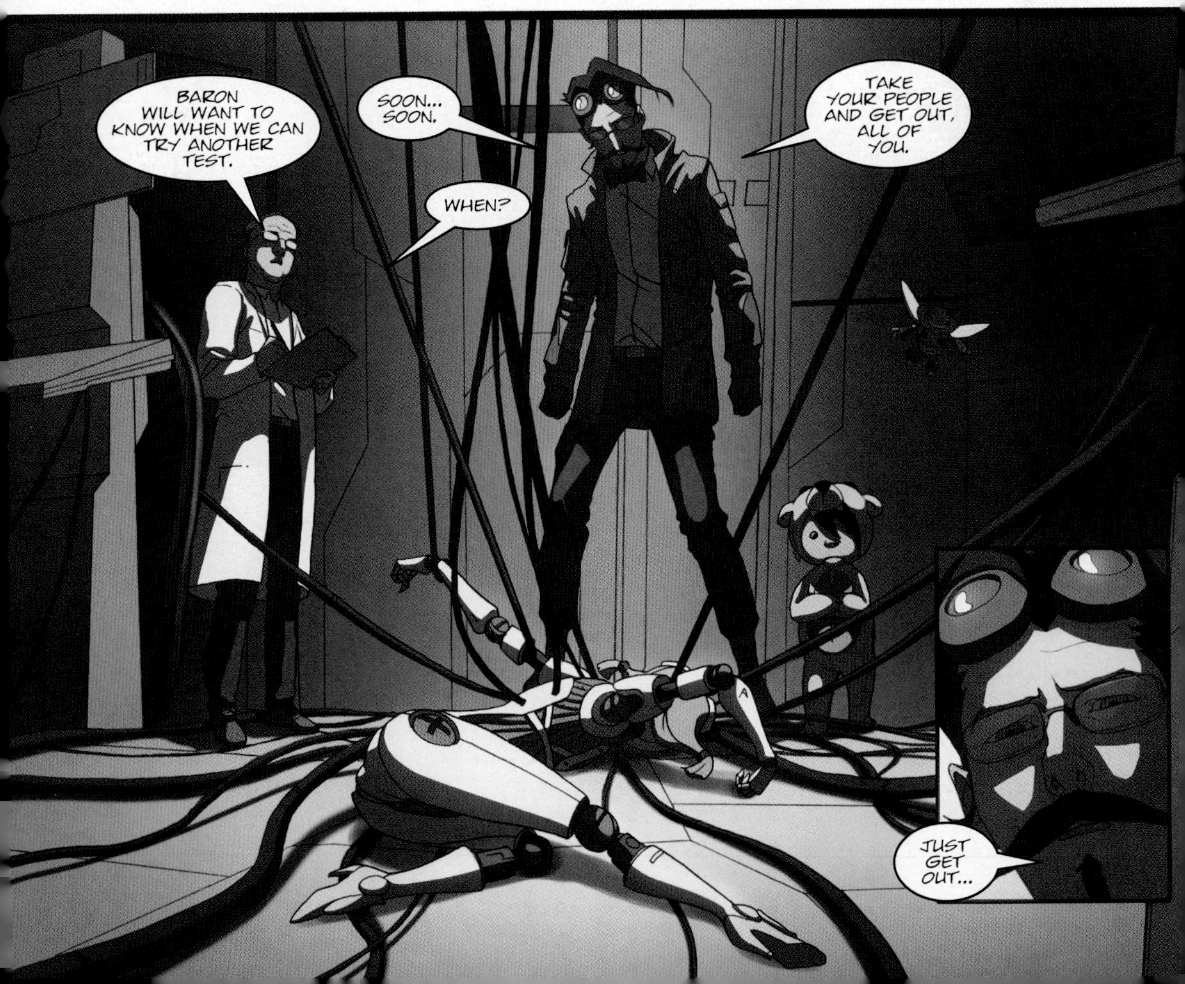
BARON WILL WANT TO KNOW WHEN WE CAN TRY ANOTHER TEST.
SOON... SOON.
WHEN?
TAKE YOUR PEOPLE AND GET OUT, ALL OF YOU.
JUST GET OUT...

CHAPTER TWO

"MY EVENING OUT WITH YOUR GIRLFRIEND"

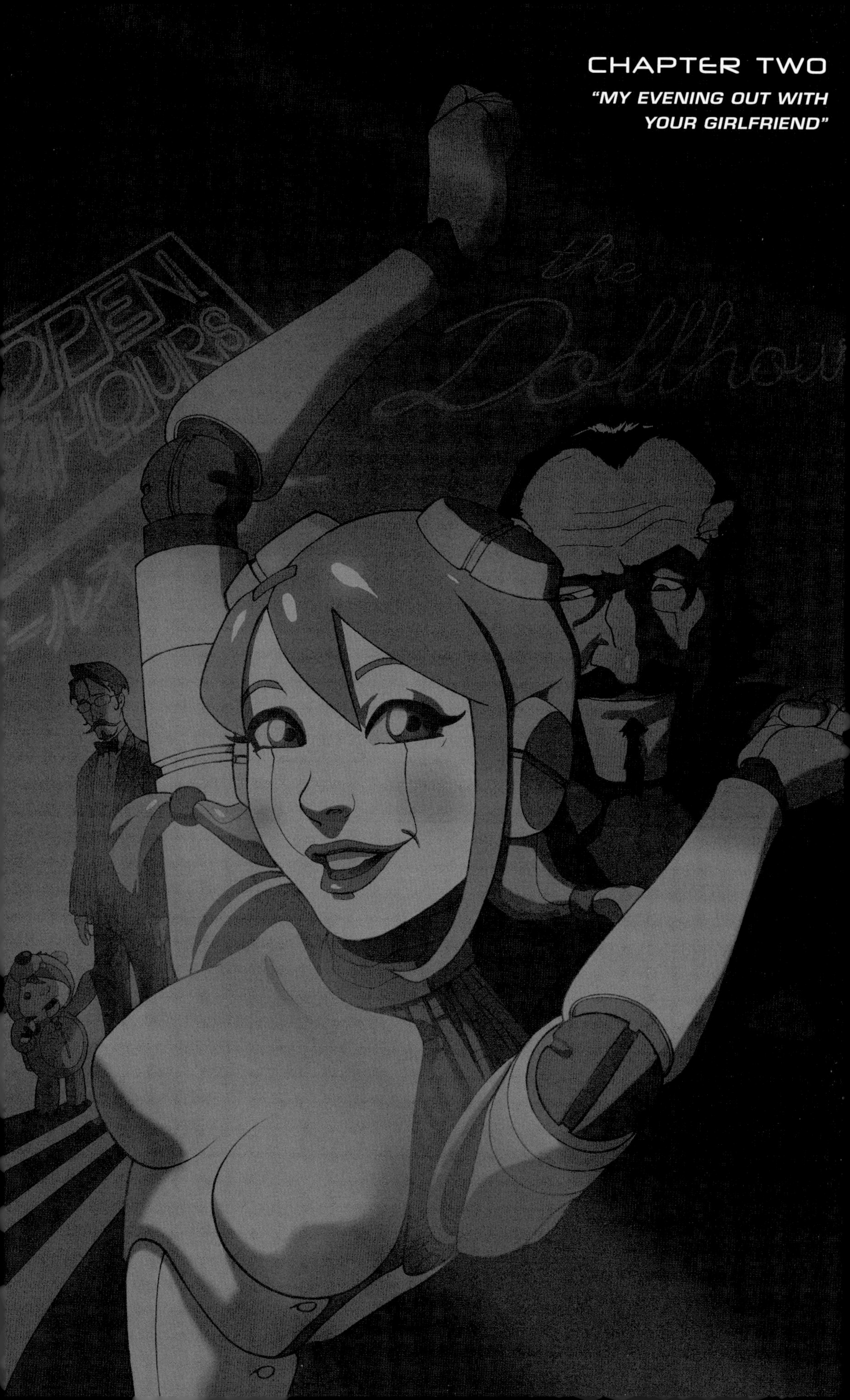
OPEN
HOURS

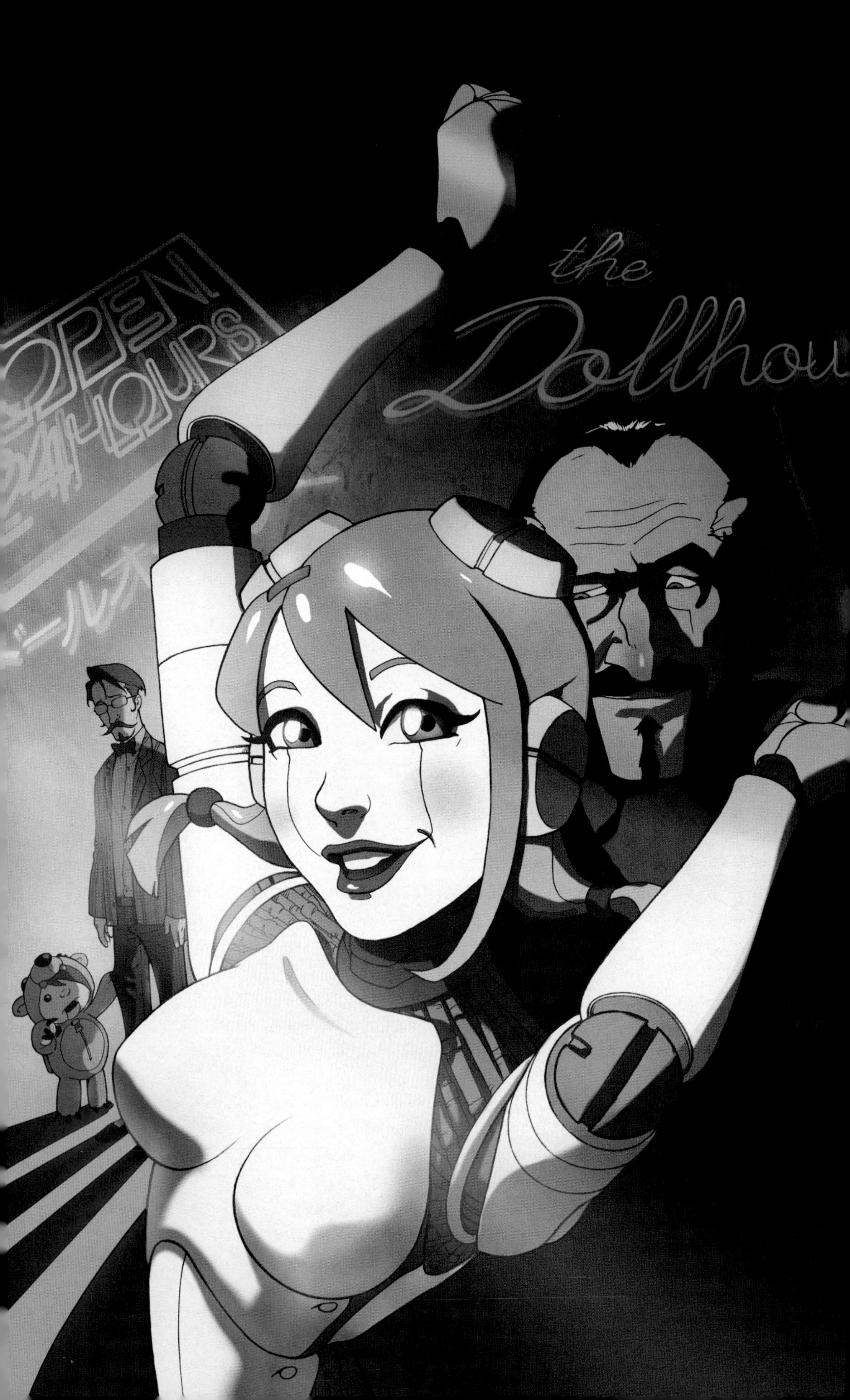
OPEN
24 HOURS
the Dollhou

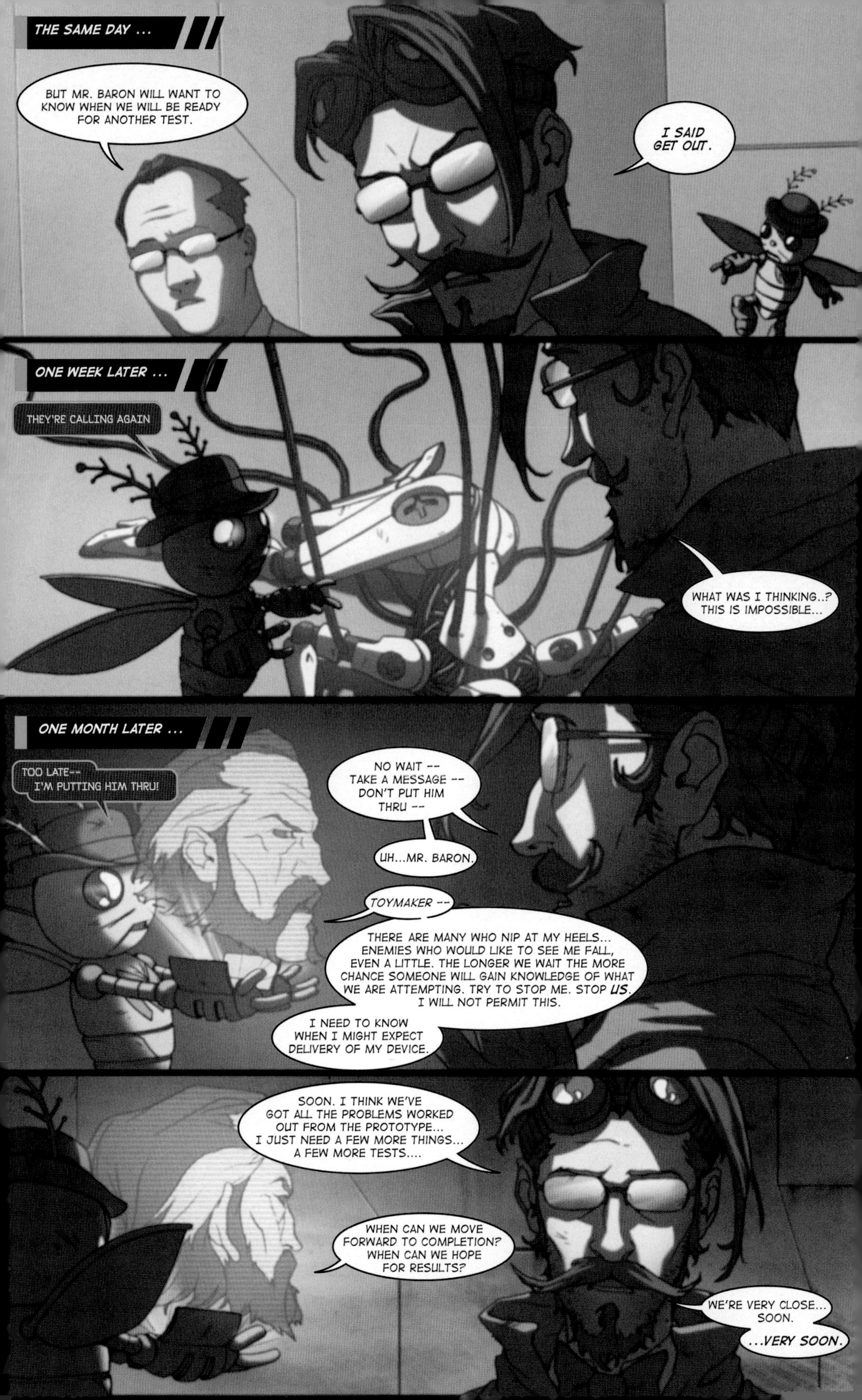
THE SAME DAY ...
BUT MR. BARON WILL WANT TO KNOW WHEN WE WILL BE READY FOR ANOTHER TEST.
I SAID GET OUT.
ONE WEEK LATER ...
THEY'RE CALLING AGAIN
WHAT WAS I THINKING..? THIS IS IMPOSSIBLE...
ONE MONTH LATER ...
TOO LATE-- I'M PUTTING HIM THRU!
NO WAIT -- TAKE A MESSAGE -- DON'T PUT HIM THRU --
UH...MR. BARON.
TOYMAKER --
THERE ARE MANY WHO NIP AT MY HEELS... ENEMIES WHO WOULD LIKE TO SEE ME FALL, EVEN A LITTLE. THE LONGER WE WAIT THE MORE CHANCE SOMEONE WILL GAIN KNOWLEDGE OF WHAT WE ARE ATTEMPTING. TRY TO STOP ME. STOP *US*. I WILL NOT PERMIT THIS.
I NEED TO KNOW WHEN I MIGHT EXPECT DELIVERY OF MY DEVICE.
SOON. I THINK WE'VE GOT ALL THE PROBLEMS WORKED OUT FROM THE PROTOTYPE... I JUST NEED A FEW MORE THINGS... A FEW MORE TESTS....
WHEN CAN WE MOVE FORWARD TO COMPLETION? WHEN CAN WE HOPE FOR RESULTS?
WE'RE VERY CLOSE... SOON.
...*VERY SOON*.

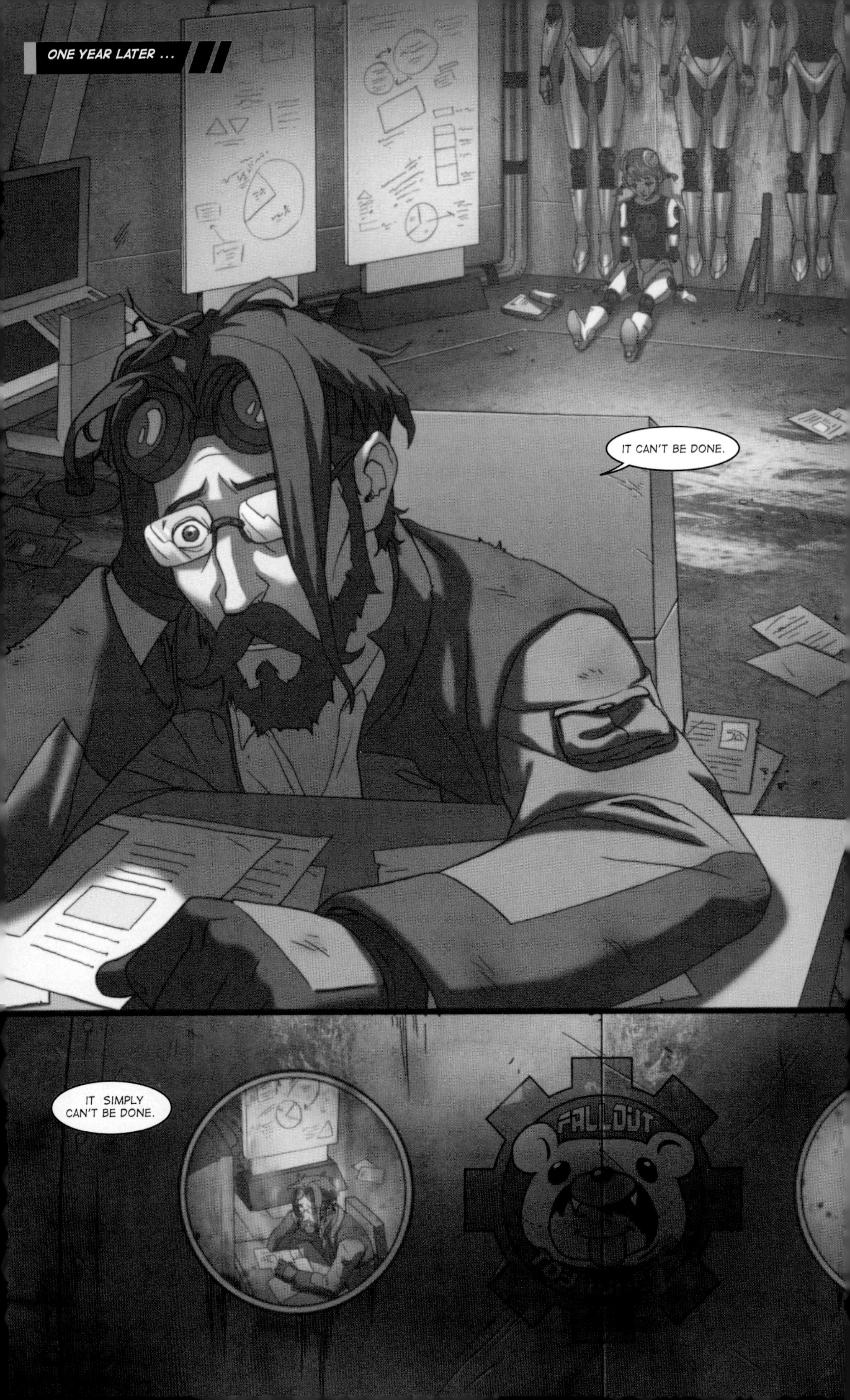
ONE YEAR LATER ...
IT CAN'T BE DONE.
IT SIMPLY CAN'T BE DONE.
FALLOUT

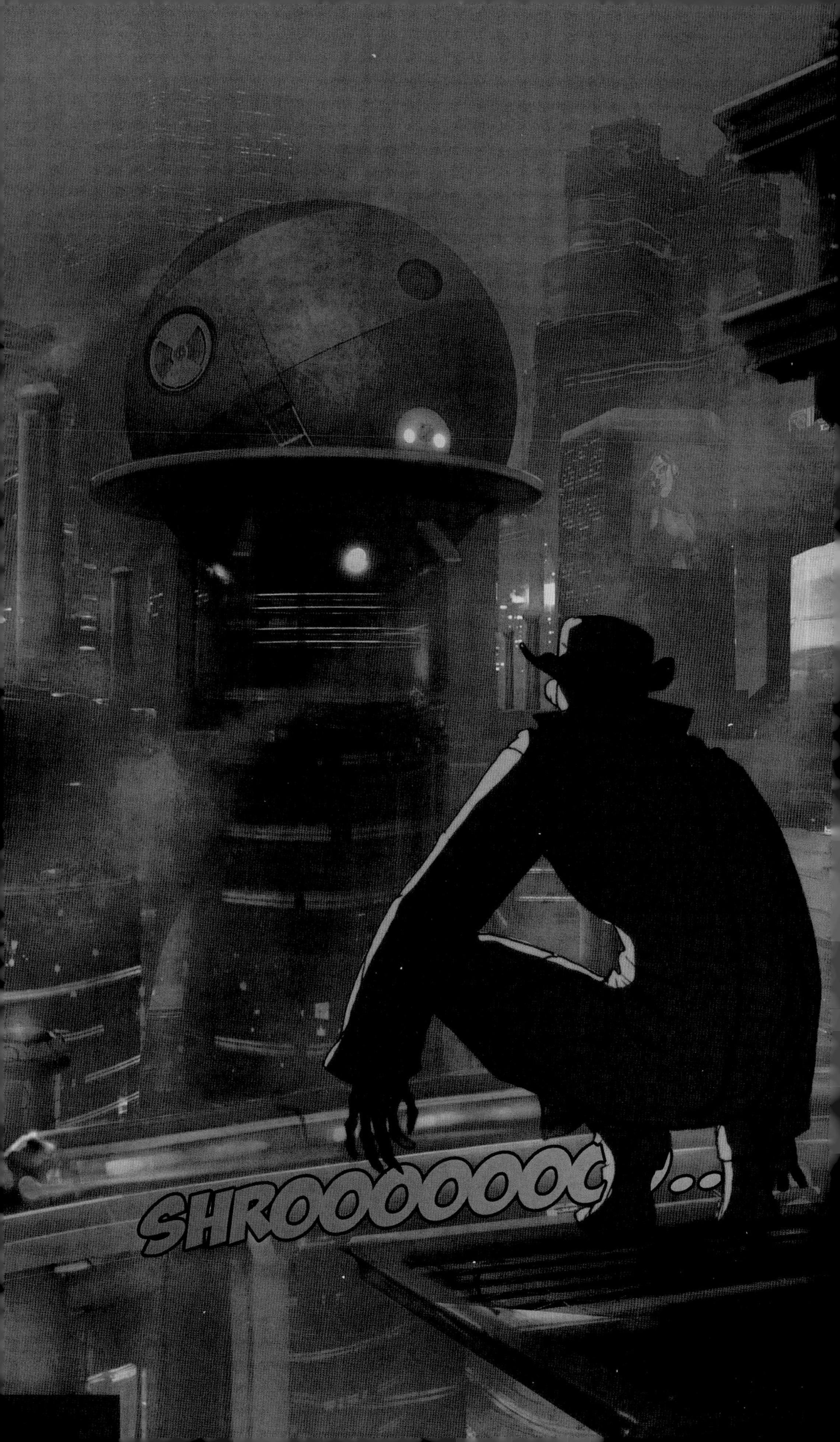
SHROOOOOOOO..

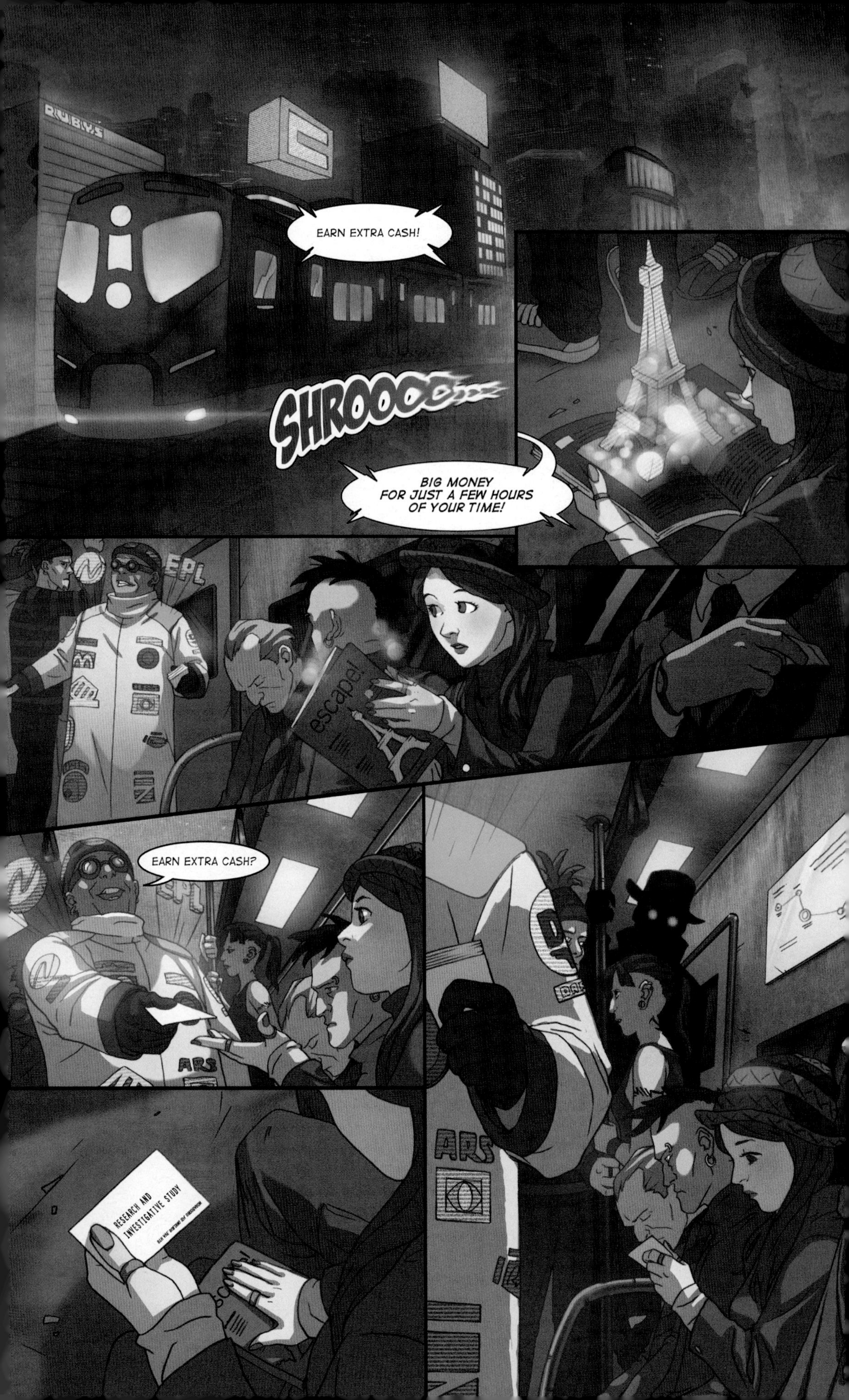
RUBYS
EARN EXTRA CASH!
SHROOOO
BIG MONEY FOR JUST A FEW HOURS OF YOUR TIME!
EPL
escape!
EARN EXTRA CASH?
ARS
RESEARCH AND INVESTIGATIVE STUDY

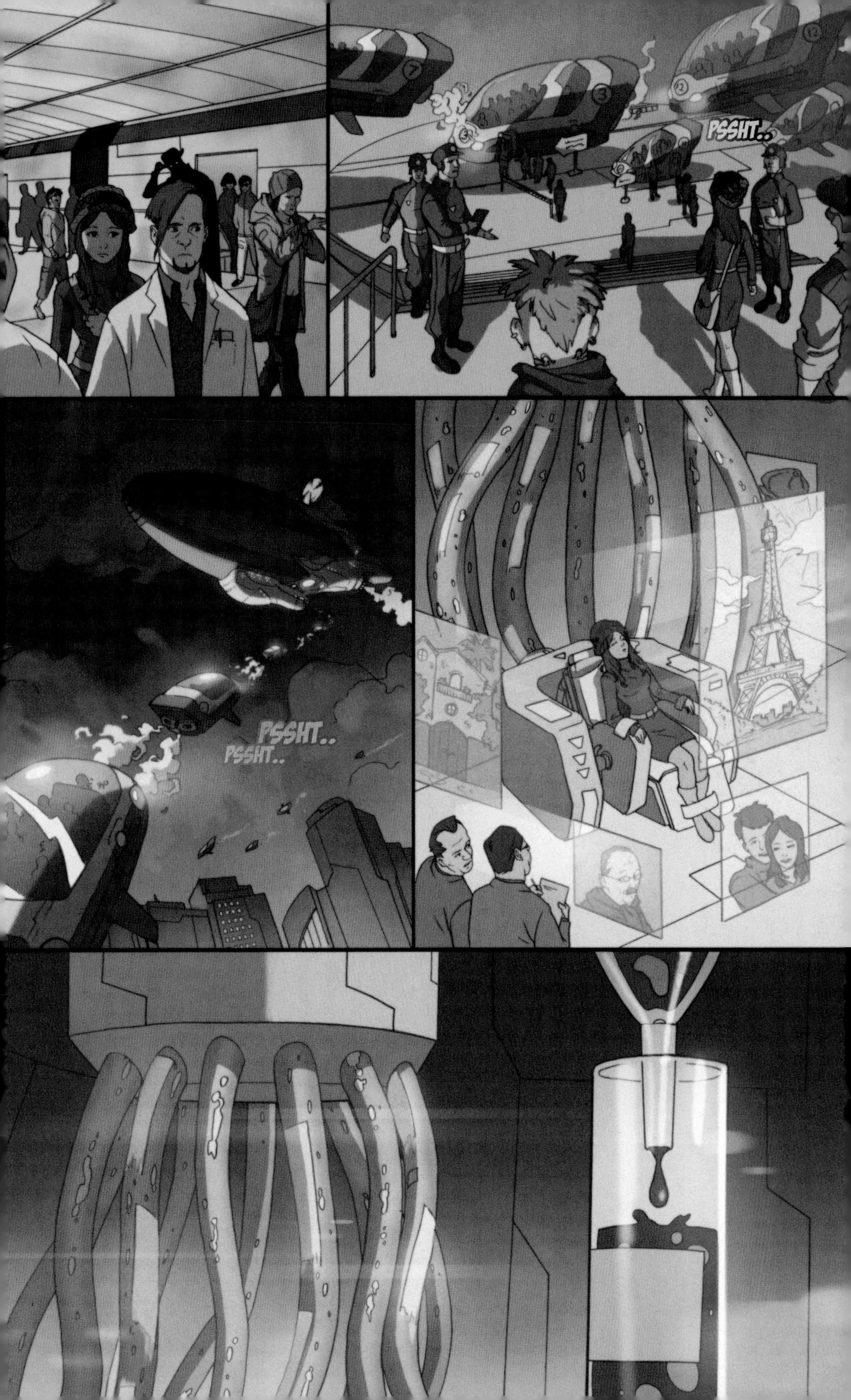
PSSHT..
PSSHT..
PSSHT..

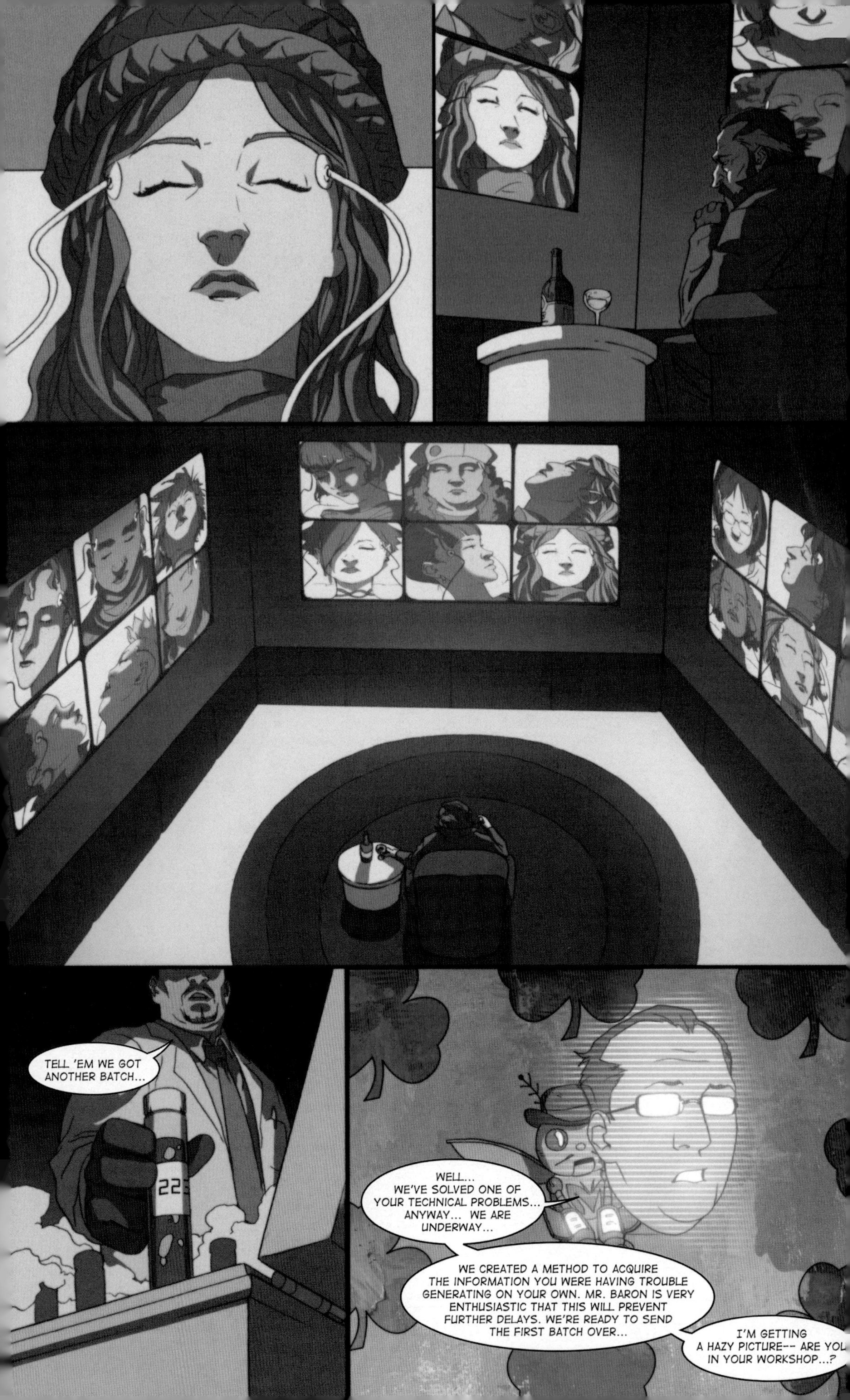
TELL 'EM WE GOT ANOTHER BATCH...
223
WELL... WE'VE SOLVED ONE OF YOUR TECHNICAL PROBLEMS... ANYWAY... WE ARE UNDERWAY...
WE CREATED A METHOD TO ACQUIRE THE INFORMATION YOU WERE HAVING TROUBLE GENERATING ON YOUR OWN. MR. BARON IS VERY ENTHUSIASTIC THAT THIS WILL PREVENT FURTHER DELAYS. WE'RE READY TO SEND THE FIRST BATCH OVER...
I'M GETTING A HAZY PICTURE-- ARE YOU IN YOUR WORKSHOP...?

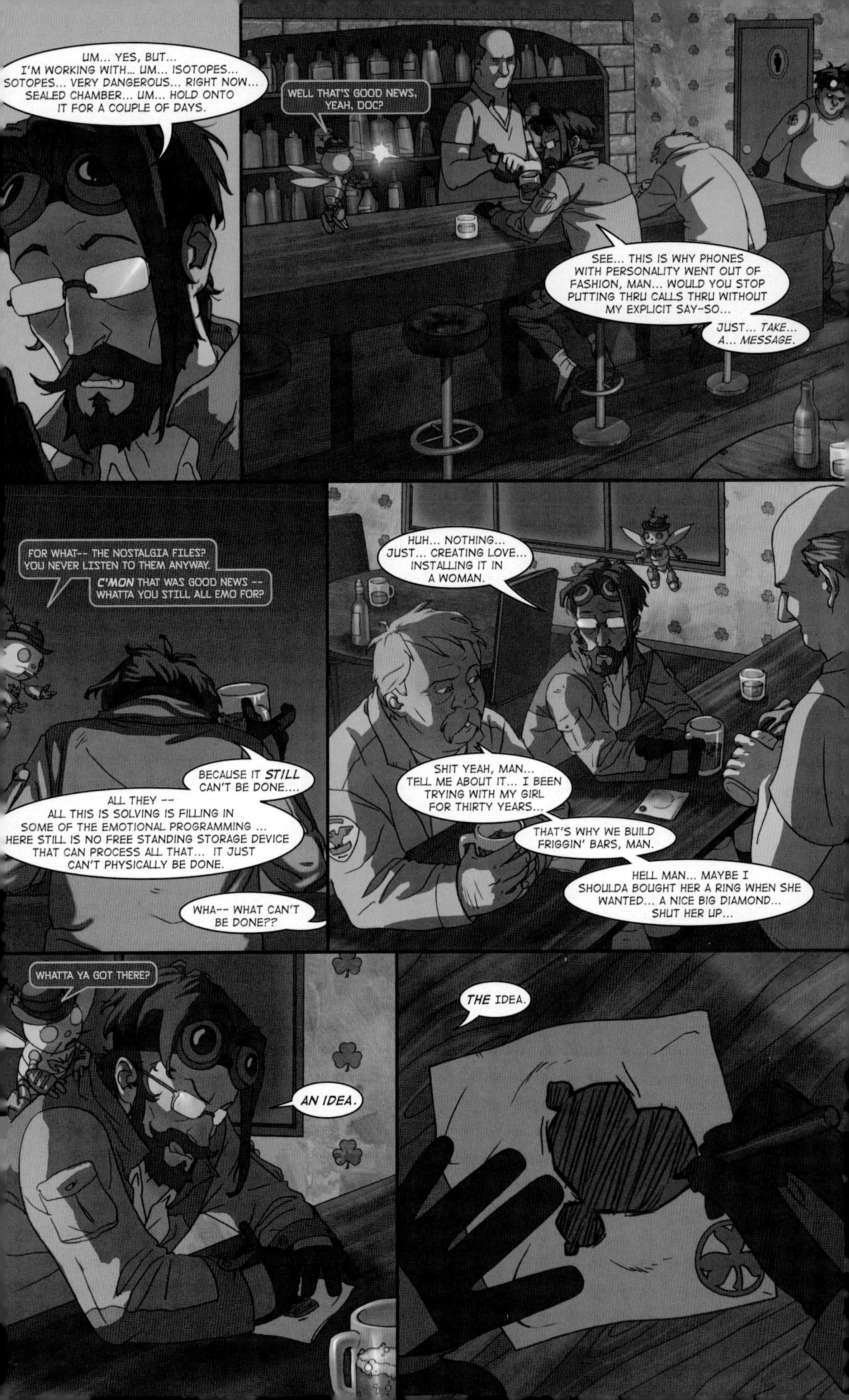
UM... YES, BUT... I'M WORKING WITH... UM... ISOTOPES... SOTOPES... VERY DANGEROUS... RIGHT NOW... SEALED CHAMBER... UM... HOLD ONTO IT FOR A COUPLE OF DAYS.
WELL THAT'S GOOD NEWS, YEAH, DOC?
SEE... THIS IS WHY PHONES WITH PERSONALITY WENT OUT OF FASHION, MAN... WOULD YOU STOP PUTTING THRU CALLS THRU WITHOUT MY EXPLICIT SAY-SO...
JUST... *TAKE*... A... *MESSAGE*.
FOR WHAT-- THE NOSTALGIA FILES? YOU NEVER LISTEN TO THEM ANYWAY.
C'MON THAT WAS GOOD NEWS -- WHATTA YOU STILL ALL EMO FOR?
BECAUSE IT ***STILL*** CAN'T BE DONE....
ALL THEY -- ALL THIS IS SOLVING IS FILLING IN SOME OF THE EMOTIONAL PROGRAMMING ... HERE STILL IS NO FREE STANDING STORAGE DEVICE THAT CAN PROCESS ALL THAT... IT JUST CAN'T PHYSICALLY BE DONE.
WHA-- WHAT CAN'T BE DONE??
HUH... NOTHING... JUST... CREATING LOVE... INSTALLING IT IN A WOMAN.
SHIT YEAH, MAN... TELL ME ABOUT IT... I BEEN TRYING WITH MY GIRL FOR THIRTY YEARS...
THAT'S WHY WE BUILD FRIGGIN' BARS, MAN.
HELL MAN... MAYBE I SHOULDA BOUGHT HER A RING WHEN SHE WANTED... A NICE BIG DIAMOND... SHUT HER UP...
WHATTA YA GOT THERE?
AN IDEA.
THE IDEA.

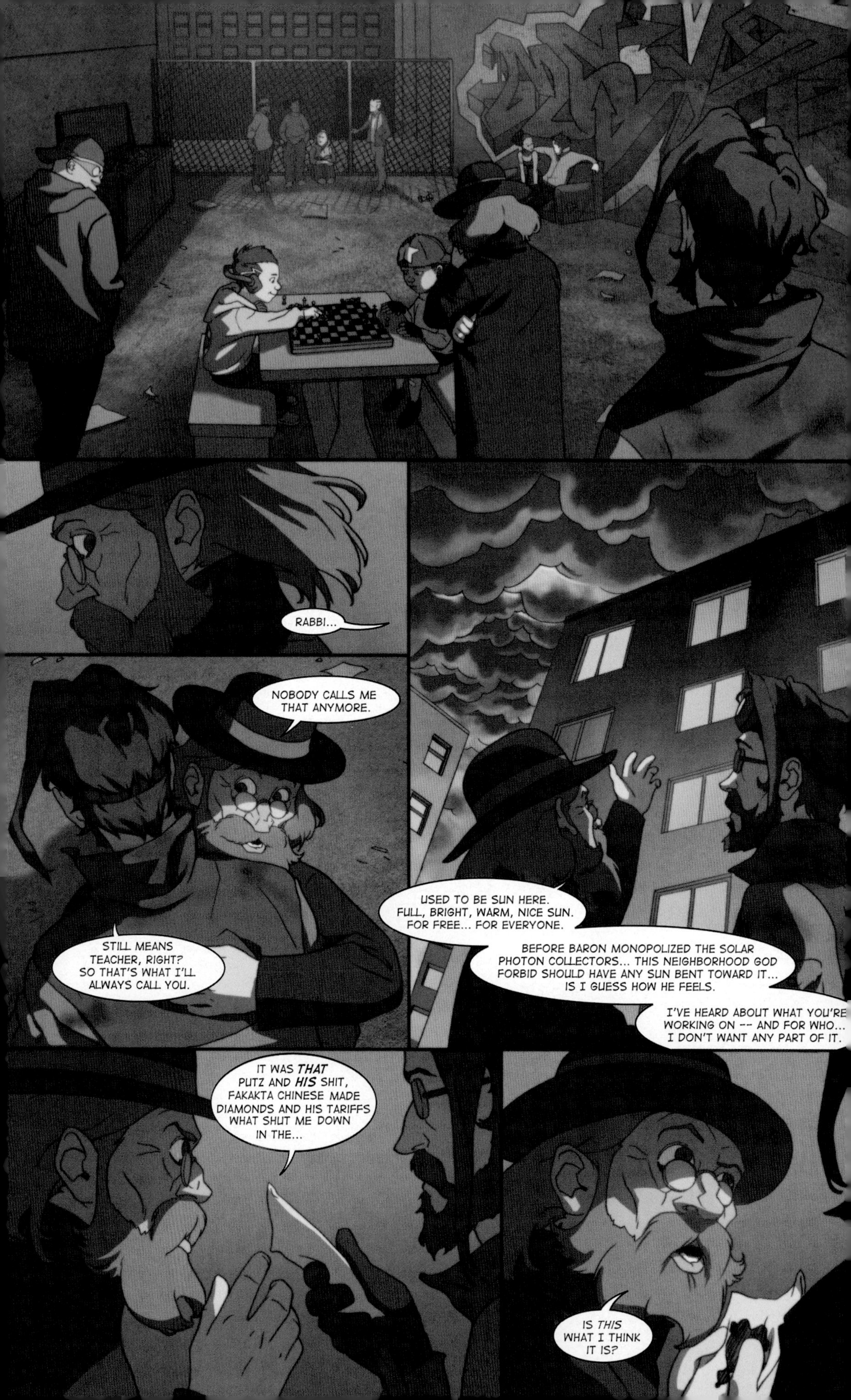
RABBI...
NOBODY CALLS ME THAT ANYMORE.
STILL MEANS TEACHER, RIGHT? SO THAT'S WHAT I'LL ALWAYS CALL YOU.
USED TO BE SUN HERE. FULL, BRIGHT, WARM, NICE SUN. FOR FREE... FOR EVERYONE.
BEFORE BARON MONOPOLIZED THE SOLAR PHOTON COLLECTORS... THIS NEIGHBORHOOD GOD FORBID SHOULD HAVE ANY SUN BENT TOWARD IT... IS I GUESS HOW HE FEELS.
I'VE HEARD ABOUT WHAT YOU'RE WORKING ON -- AND FOR WHO... I DON'T WANT ANY PART OF IT.
IT WAS *THAT* PUTZ AND *HIS* SHIT, FAKAKTA CHINESE MADE DIAMONDS AND HIS TARIFFS WHAT SHUT ME DOWN IN THE...
IS *THIS* WHAT I THINK IT IS?

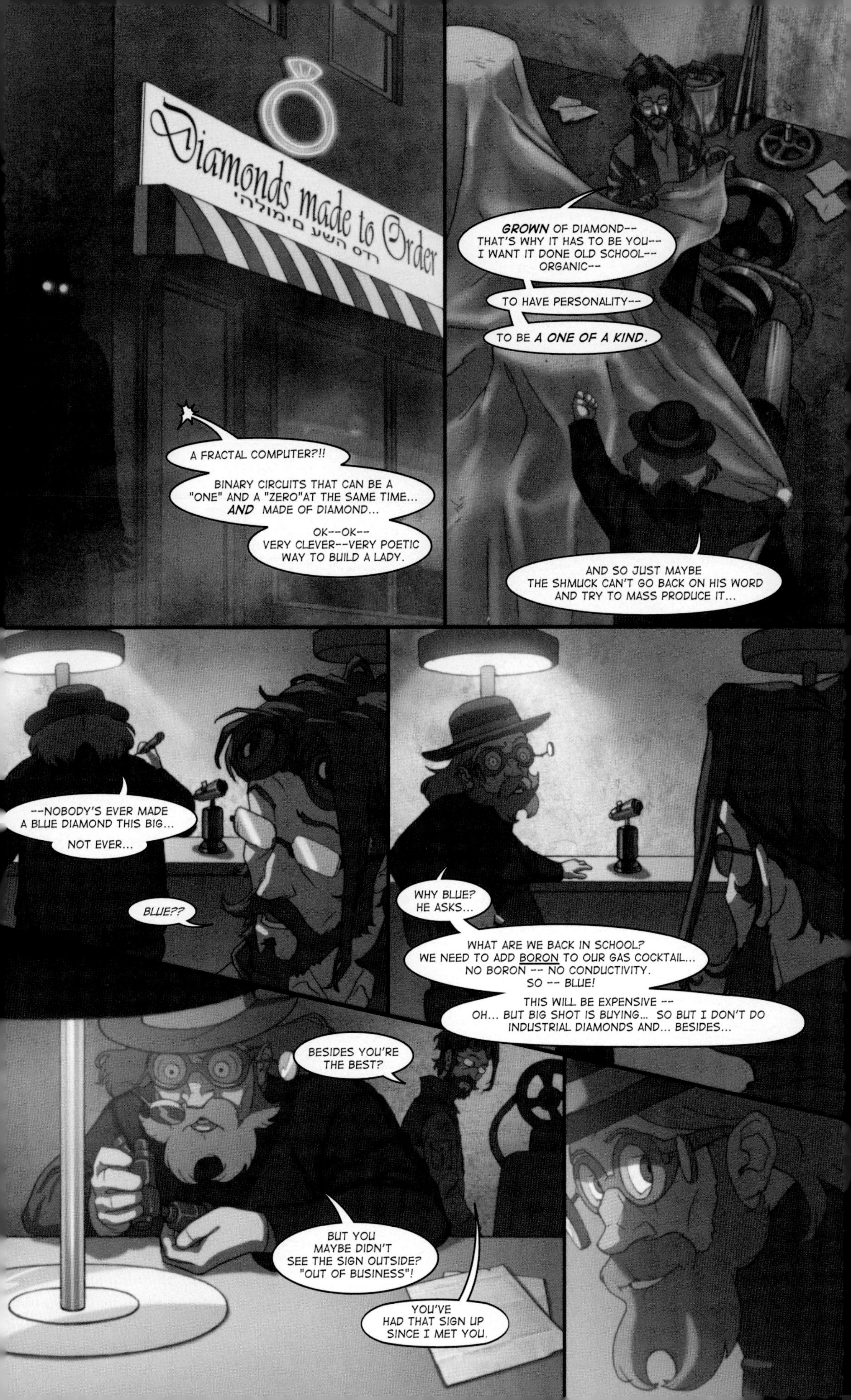
Diamonds made to Order
רדס השע סימולהי!
A FRACTAL COMPUTER?!!
BINARY CIRCUITS THAT CAN BE A "ONE" AND A "ZERO"AT THE SAME TIME... AND MADE OF DIAMOND...
OK--OK-- VERY CLEVER--VERY POETIC WAY TO BUILD A LADY.
GROWN OF DIAMOND-- THAT'S WHY IT HAS TO BE YOU-- I WANT IT DONE OLD SCHOOL-- ORGANIC--
TO HAVE PERSONALITY--
TO BE A ONE OF A KIND.
AND SO JUST MAYBE THE SHMUCK CAN'T GO BACK ON HIS WORD AND TRY TO MASS PRODUCE IT...
--NOBODY'S EVER MADE A BLUE DIAMOND THIS BIG...
NOT EVER...
BLUE??
WHY BLUE? HE ASKS...
WHAT ARE WE BACK IN SCHOOL? WE NEED TO ADD BORON TO OUR GAS COCKTAIL... NO BORON -- NO CONDUCTIVITY. SO -- BLUE!
THIS WILL BE EXPENSIVE -- OH... BUT BIG SHOT IS BUYING... SO BUT I DON'T DO INDUSTRIAL DIAMONDS AND... BESIDES...
BESIDES YOU'RE THE BEST?
BUT YOU MAYBE DIDN'T SEE THE SIGN OUTSIDE? "OUT OF BUSINESS"!
YOU'VE HAD THAT SIGN UP SINCE I MET YOU.

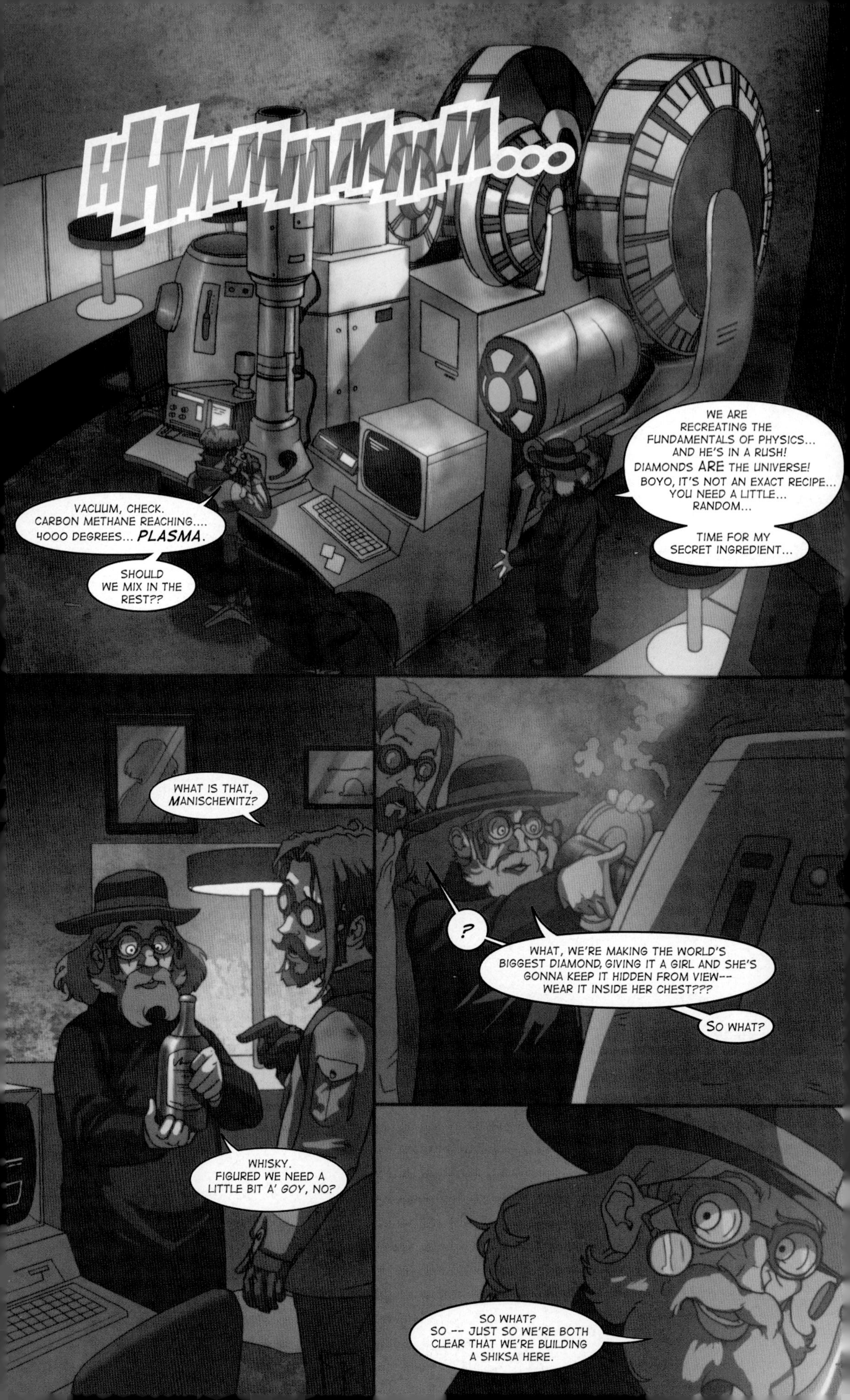
HHMMMMMMMM...
VACUUM, CHECK. CARBON METHANE REACHING.... 4000 DEGREES... PLASMA.
SHOULD WE MIX IN THE REST??
WE ARE RECREATING THE FUNDAMENTALS OF PHYSICS... AND HE'S IN A RUSH! DIAMONDS ARE THE UNIVERSE! BOYO, IT'S NOT AN EXACT RECIPE... YOU NEED A LITTLE... RANDOM...
TIME FOR MY SECRET INGREDIENT...
WHAT IS THAT, MANISCHEWITZ?
WHISKY. FIGURED WE NEED A LITTLE BIT A' GOY, NO?
?
WHAT, WE'RE MAKING THE WORLD'S BIGGEST DIAMOND, GIVING IT A GIRL AND SHE'S GONNA KEEP IT HIDDEN FROM VIEW-- WEAR IT INSIDE HER CHEST???
SO WHAT?
SO WHAT? SO -- JUST SO WE'RE BOTH CLEAR THAT WE'RE BUILDING A SHIKSA HERE.

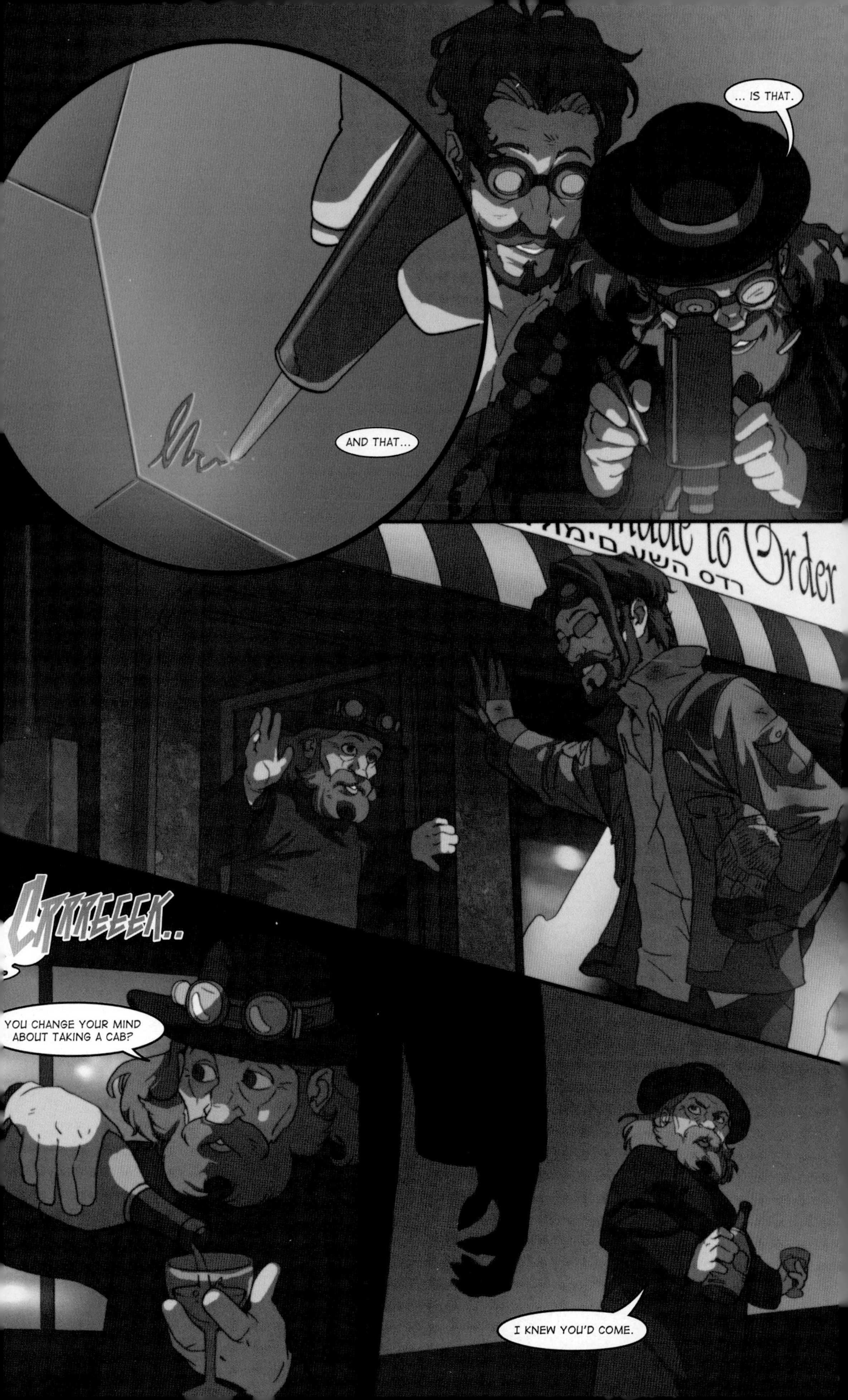
AND THAT...
... IS THAT.
to Order
CRRRREEEK..
YOU CHANGE YOUR MIND ABOUT TAKING A CAB?
I KNEW YOU'D COME.

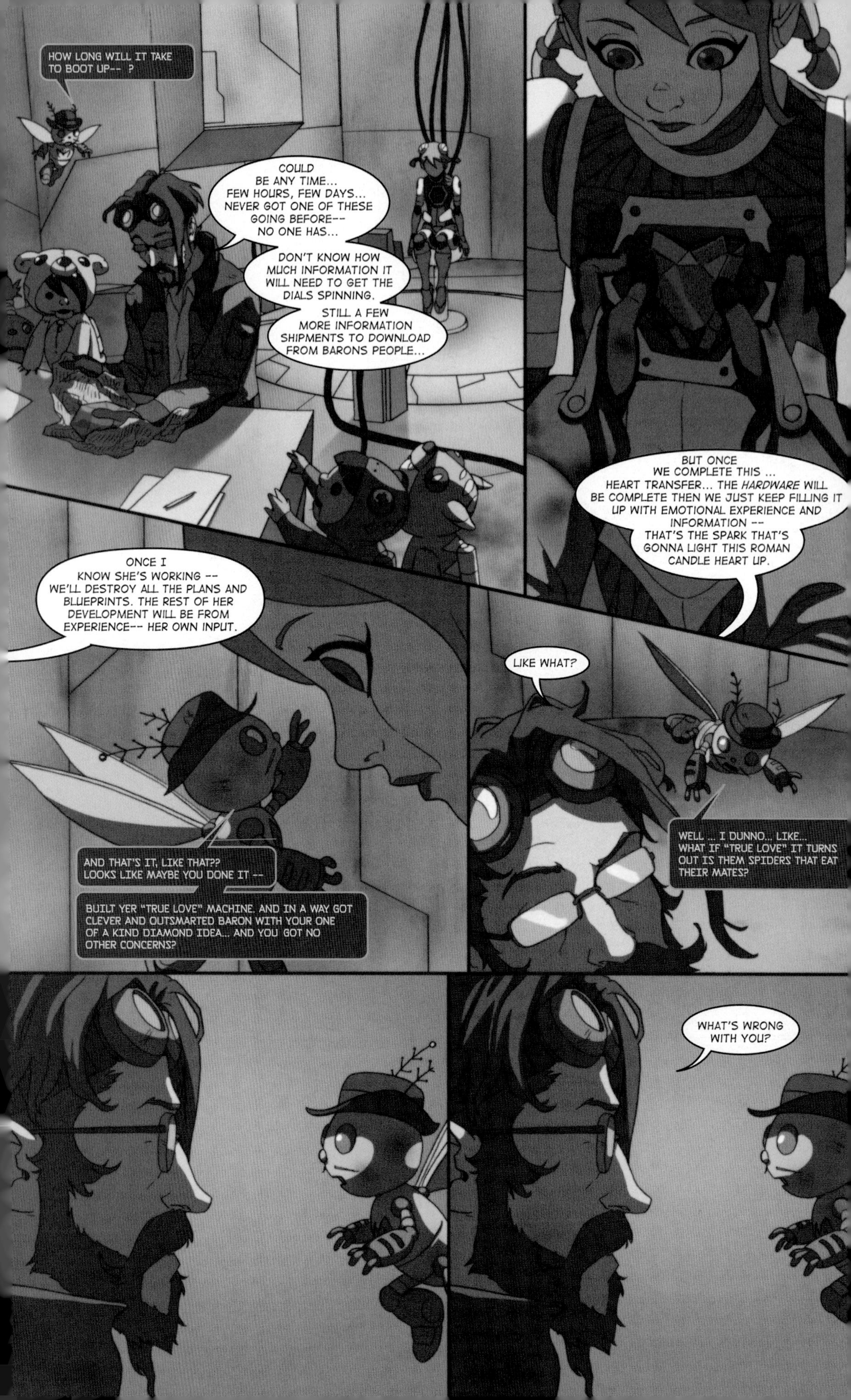
HOW LONG WILL IT TAKE TO BOOT UP-- ?
COULD BE ANY TIME... FEW HOURS, FEW DAYS... NEVER GOT ONE OF THESE GOING BEFORE-- NO ONE HAS...
DON'T KNOW HOW MUCH INFORMATION IT WILL NEED TO GET THE DIALS SPINNING.
STILL A FEW MORE INFORMATION SHIPMENTS TO DOWNLOAD FROM BARONS PEOPLE...
BUT ONCE WE COMPLETE THIS ... HEART TRANSFER... THE *HARDWARE* WILL BE COMPLETE THEN WE JUST KEEP FILLING IT UP WITH EMOTIONAL EXPERIENCE AND INFORMATION -- THAT'S THE SPARK THAT'S GONNA LIGHT THIS ROMAN CANDLE HEART UP.
ONCE I KNOW SHE'S WORKING -- WE'LL DESTROY ALL THE PLANS AND BLUEPRINTS. THE REST OF HER DEVELOPMENT WILL BE FROM EXPERIENCE-- HER OWN INPUT.
AND THAT'S IT, LIKE THAT?? LOOKS LIKE MAYBE YOU DONE IT --
BUILT YER "TRUE LOVE" MACHINE. AND IN A WAY GOT CLEVER AND OUTSMARTED BARON WITH YOUR ONE OF A KIND DIAMOND IDEA... AND YOU GOT NO OTHER CONCERNS?
LIKE WHAT?
WELL ... I DUNNO... LIKE... WHAT IF "TRUE LOVE" IT TURNS OUT IS THEM SPIDERS THAT EAT THEIR MATES?
WHAT'S WRONG WITH YOU?

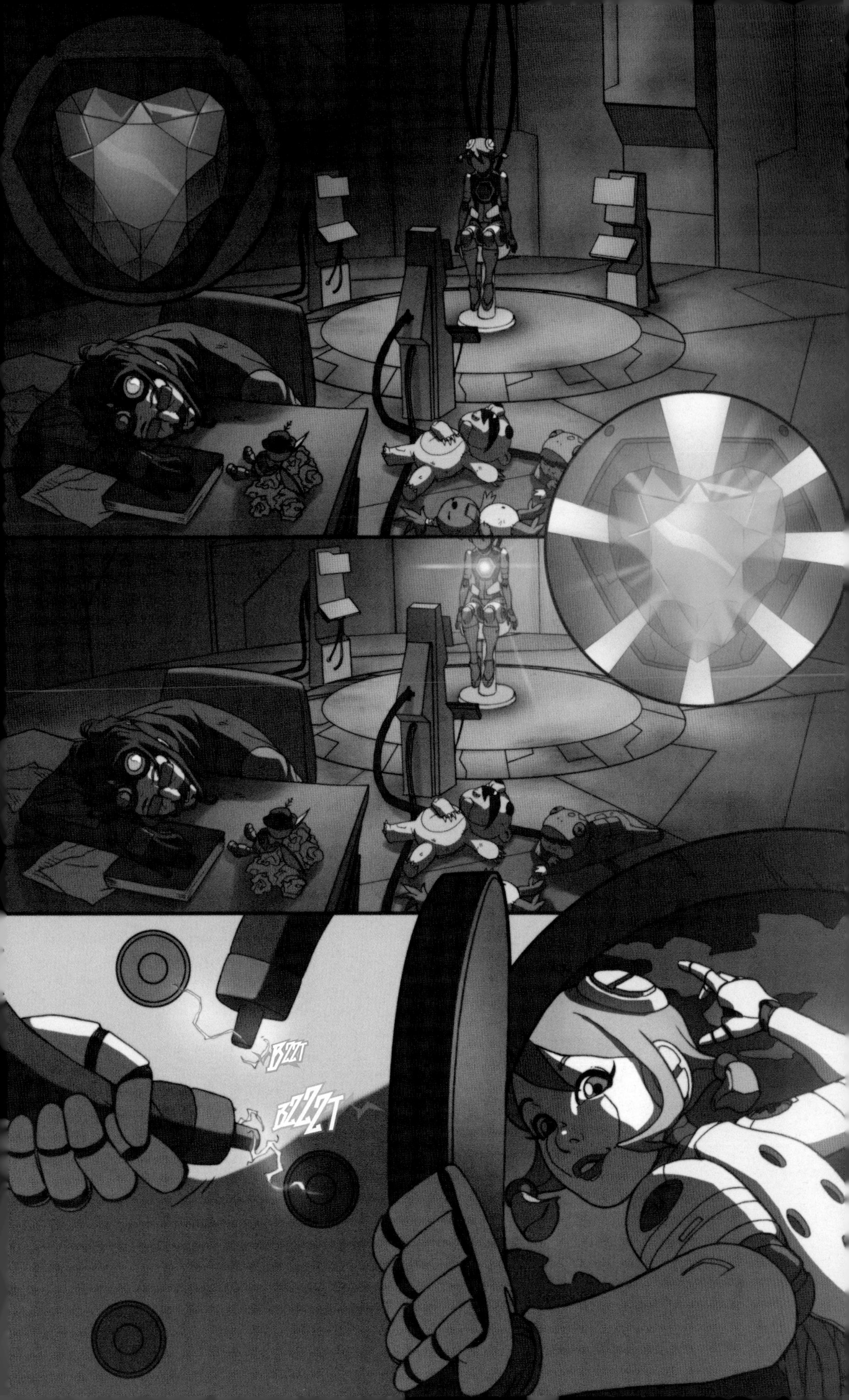
BZZT
BZZZT

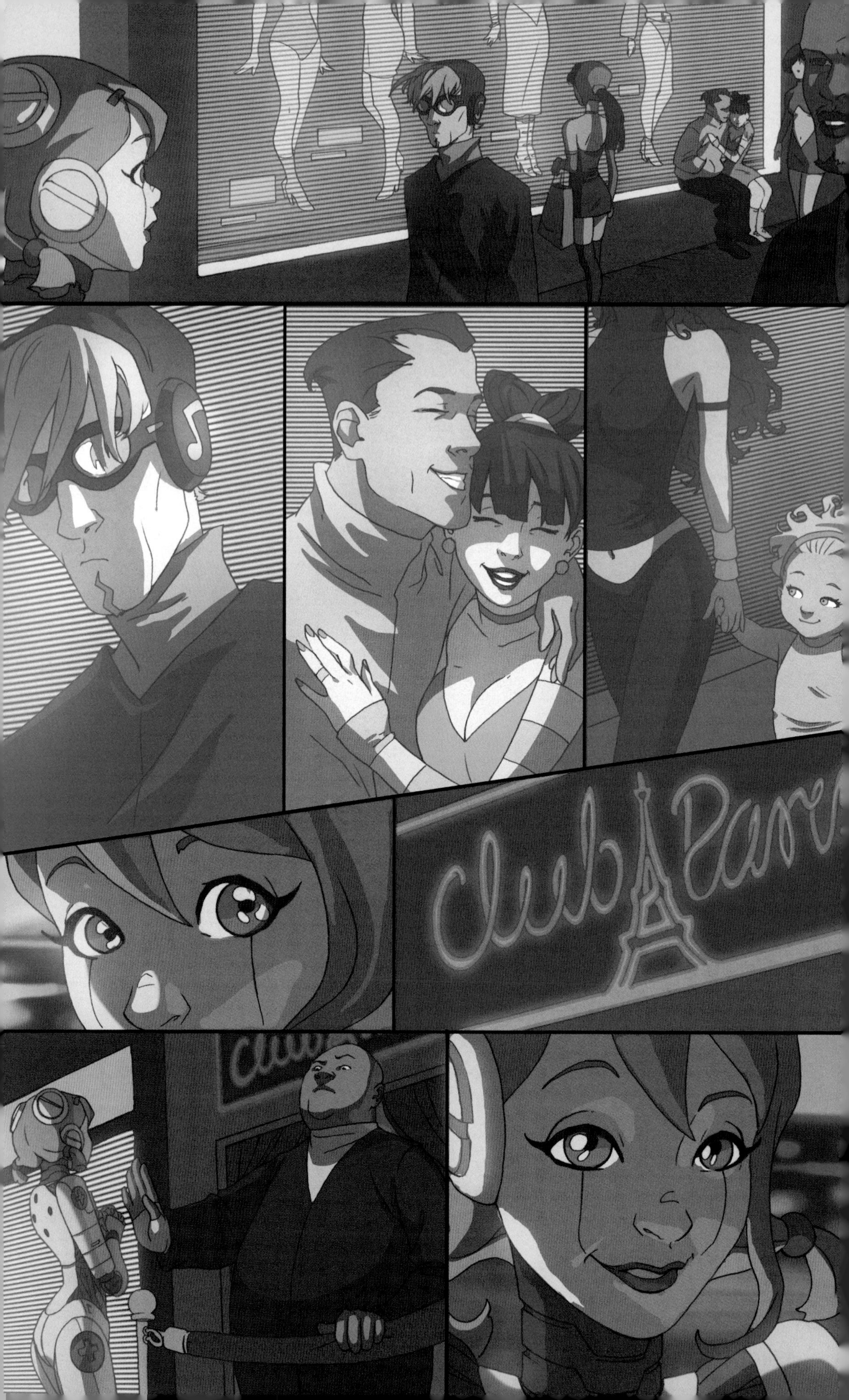
club

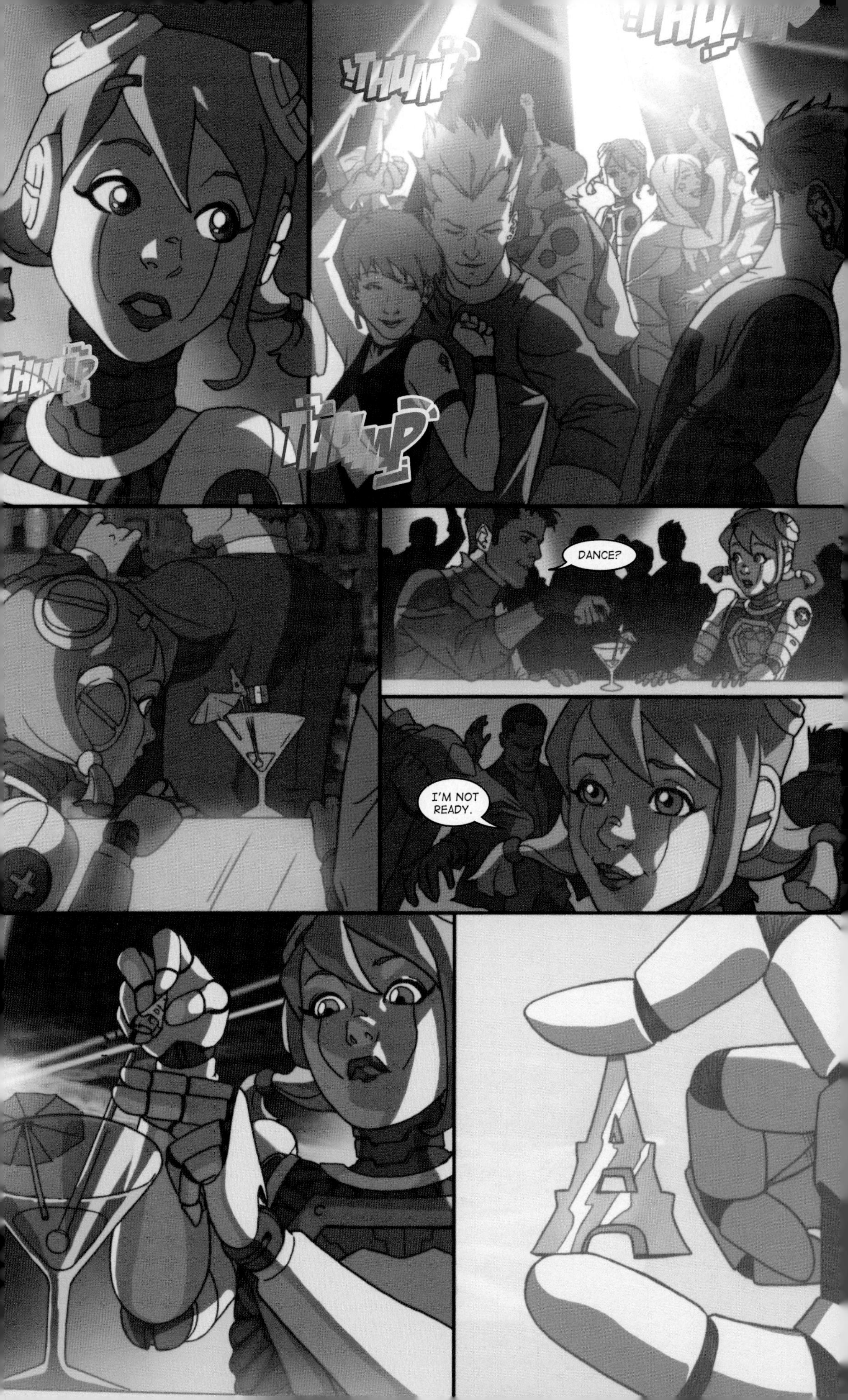
THUMP
THUMP
THUMP
THUMP
DANCE?
I'M NOT READY.

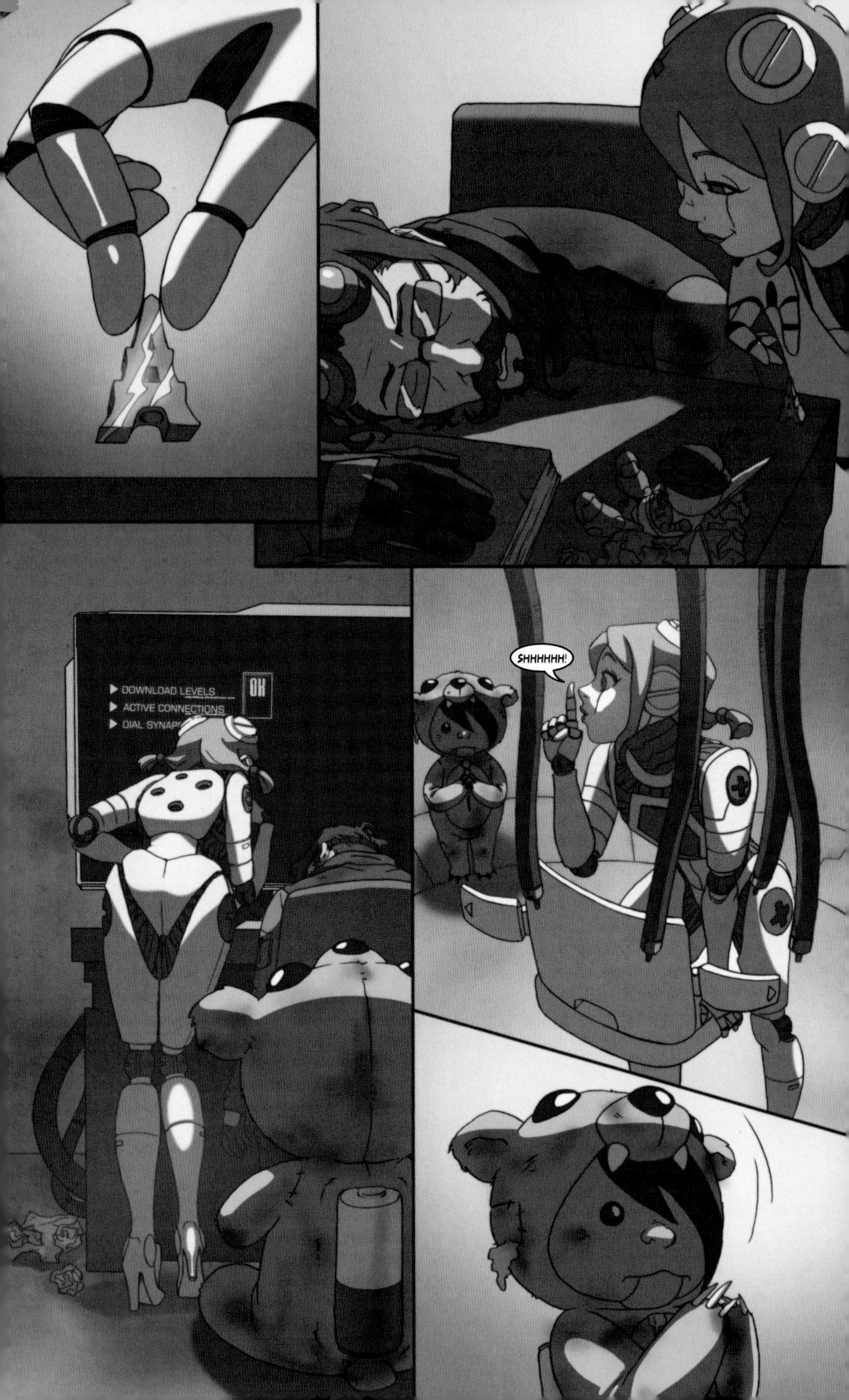
DOWNLOAD LEVELS
ACTIVE CONNECTIONS
OK
SHHHHHH!

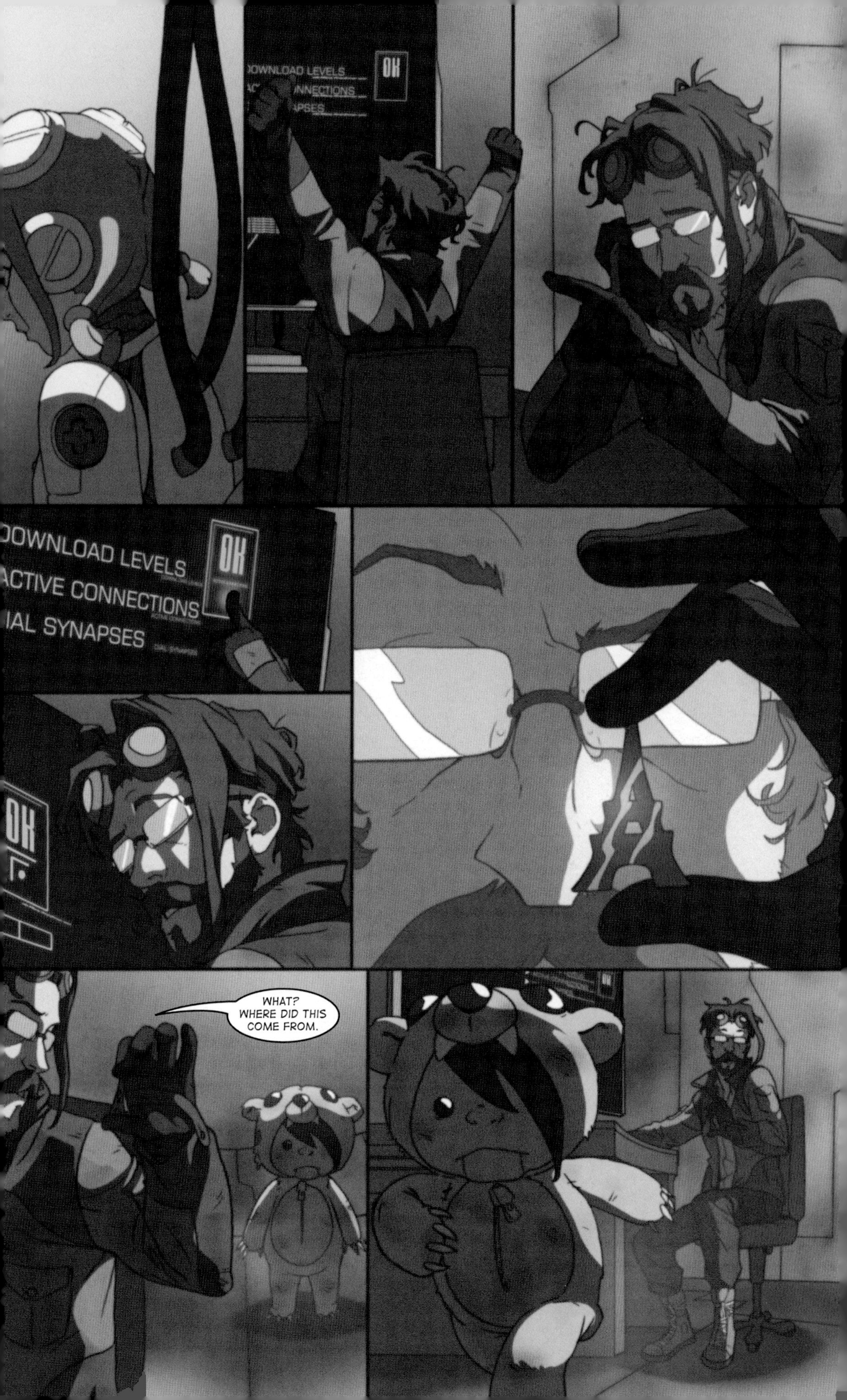
DOWNLOAD LEVELS
OK
DOWNLOAD LEVELS
ACTIVE CONNECTIONS
IAL SYNAPSES
OK
WHAT? WHERE DID THIS COME FROM.

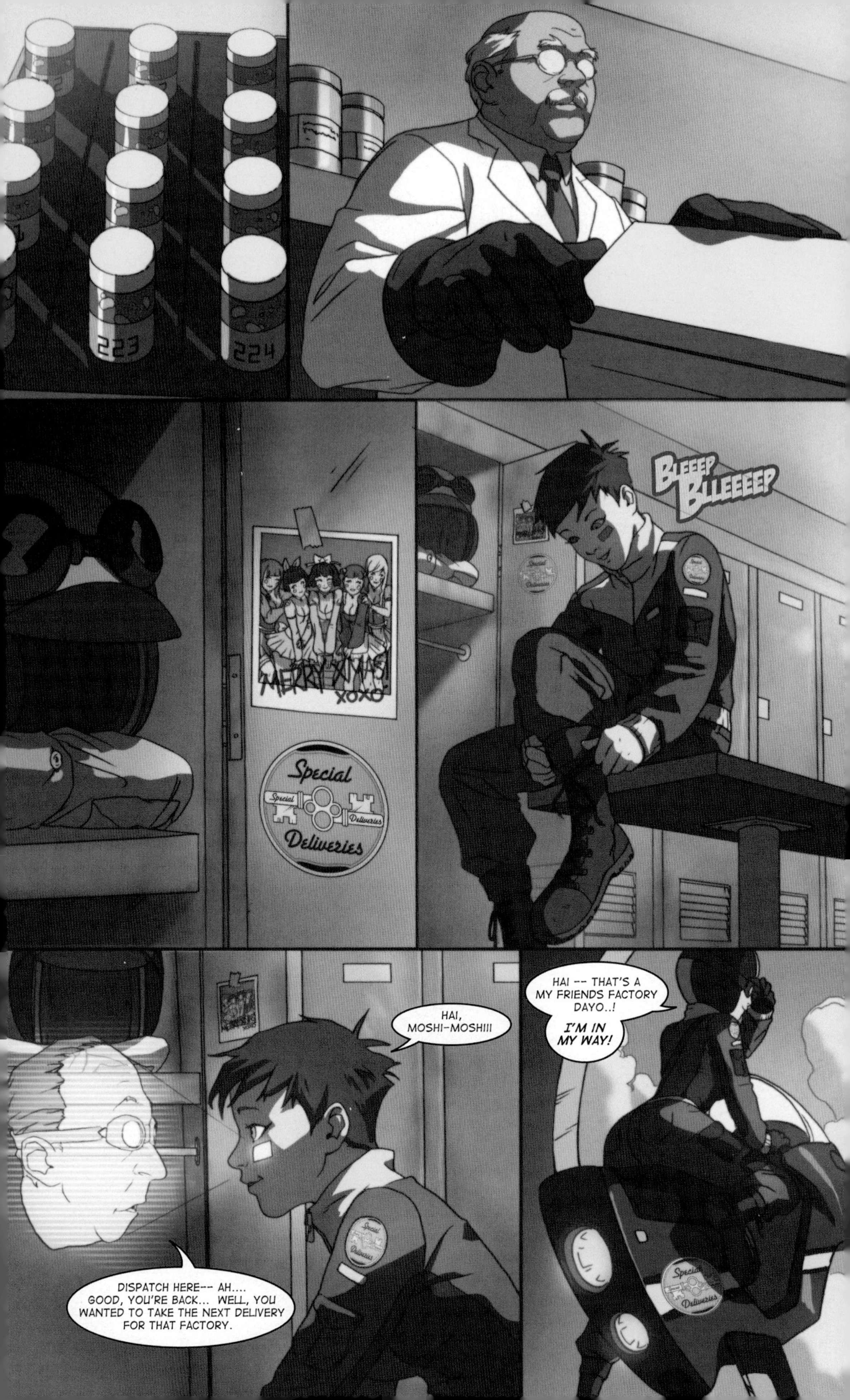
223
224
Special Deliveries
MERRY XMAS!
XOXO
BLEEEP BLLEEEEP
HAI, MOSHI-MOSHI!!!
DISPATCH HERE-- AH.... GOOD, YOU'RE BACK... WELL, YOU WANTED TO TAKE THE NEXT DELIVERY FOR THAT FACTORY.
HAI -- THAT'S A MY FRIENDS FACTORY DAYO..!
I'M IN MY WAY!

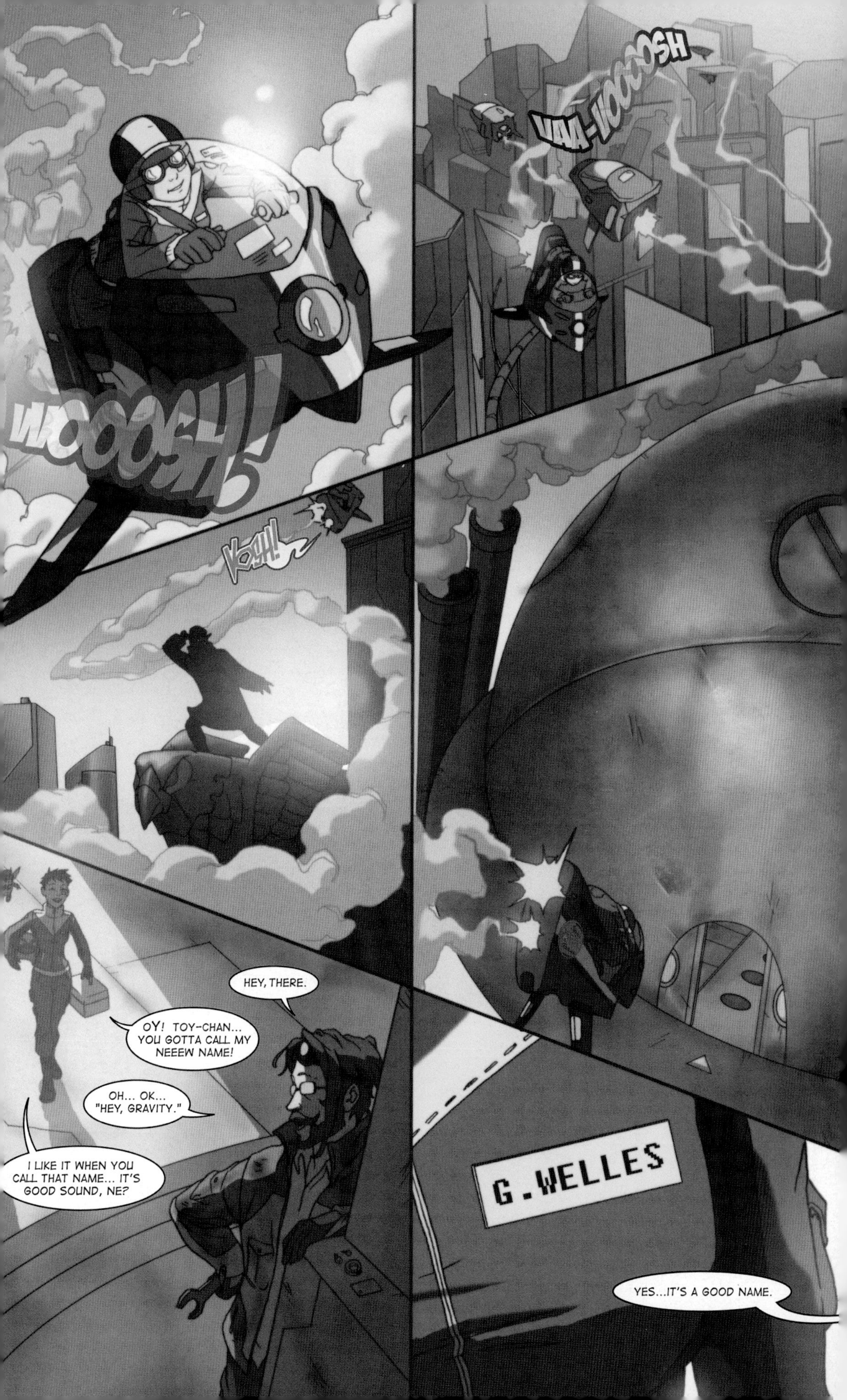
WOOOSH!
VAA-VOOOOSH
KOSH!
HEY, THERE.
OY! TOY-CHAN... YOU GOTTA CALL MY NEEEW NAME!
OH... OK... "HEY, GRAVITY."
I LIKE IT WHEN YOU CALL THAT NAME... IT'S GOOD SOUND, NE?
G.WELLES
YES...IT'S A GOOD NAME.

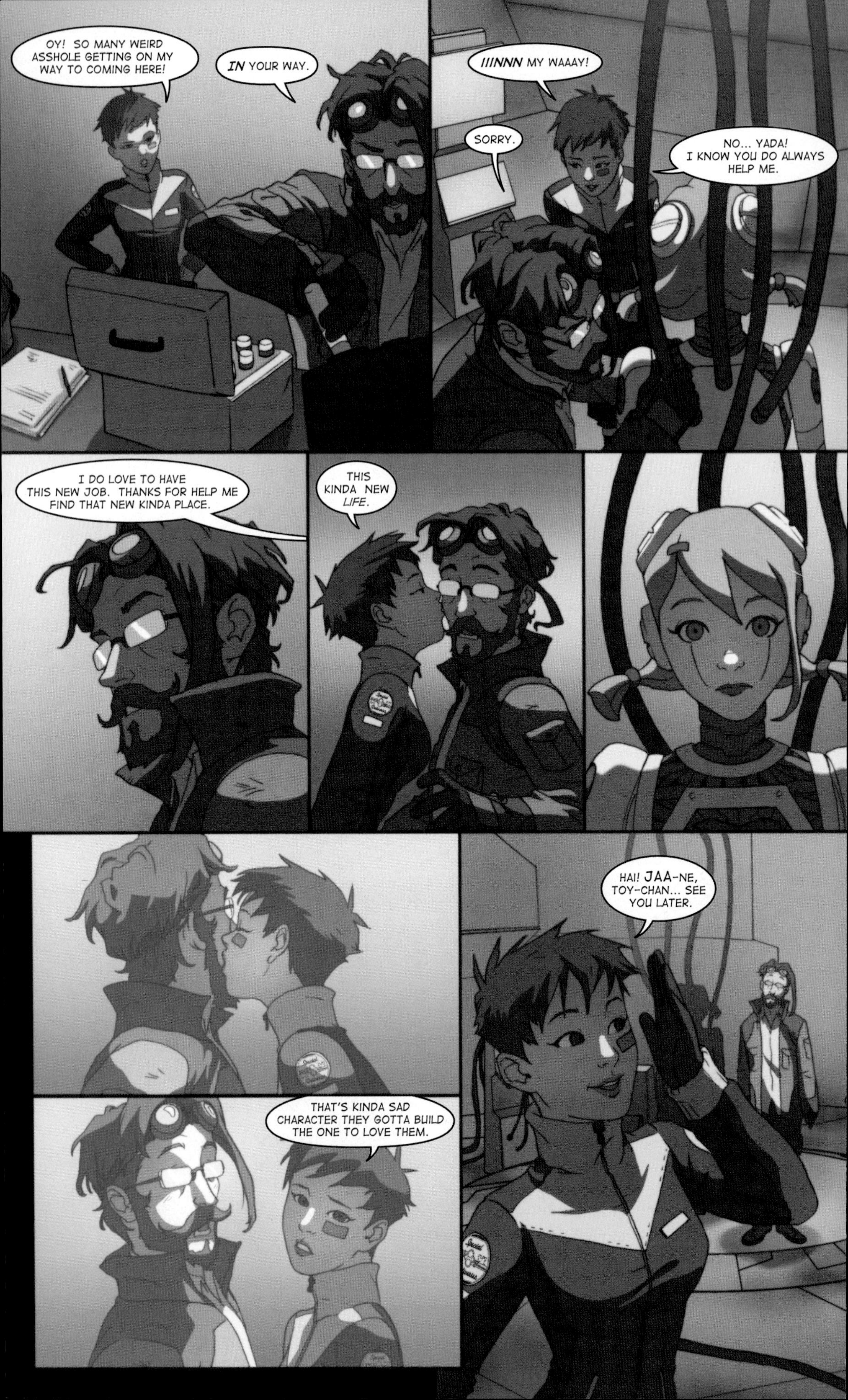
OY! SO MANY WEIRD ASSHOLE GETTING ON MY WAY TO COMING HERE!
IN YOUR WAY.
IIINNN MY WAAAY!
SORRY.
NO... YADA! I KNOW YOU DO ALWAYS HELP ME.
I DO LOVE TO HAVE THIS NEW JOB. THANKS FOR HELP ME FIND THAT NEW KINDA PLACE.
THIS KINDA NEW LIFE.
THAT'S KINDA SAD CHARACTER THEY GOTTA BUILD THE ONE TO LOVE THEM.
HAI! JAA-NE, TOY-CHAN... SEE YOU LATER.

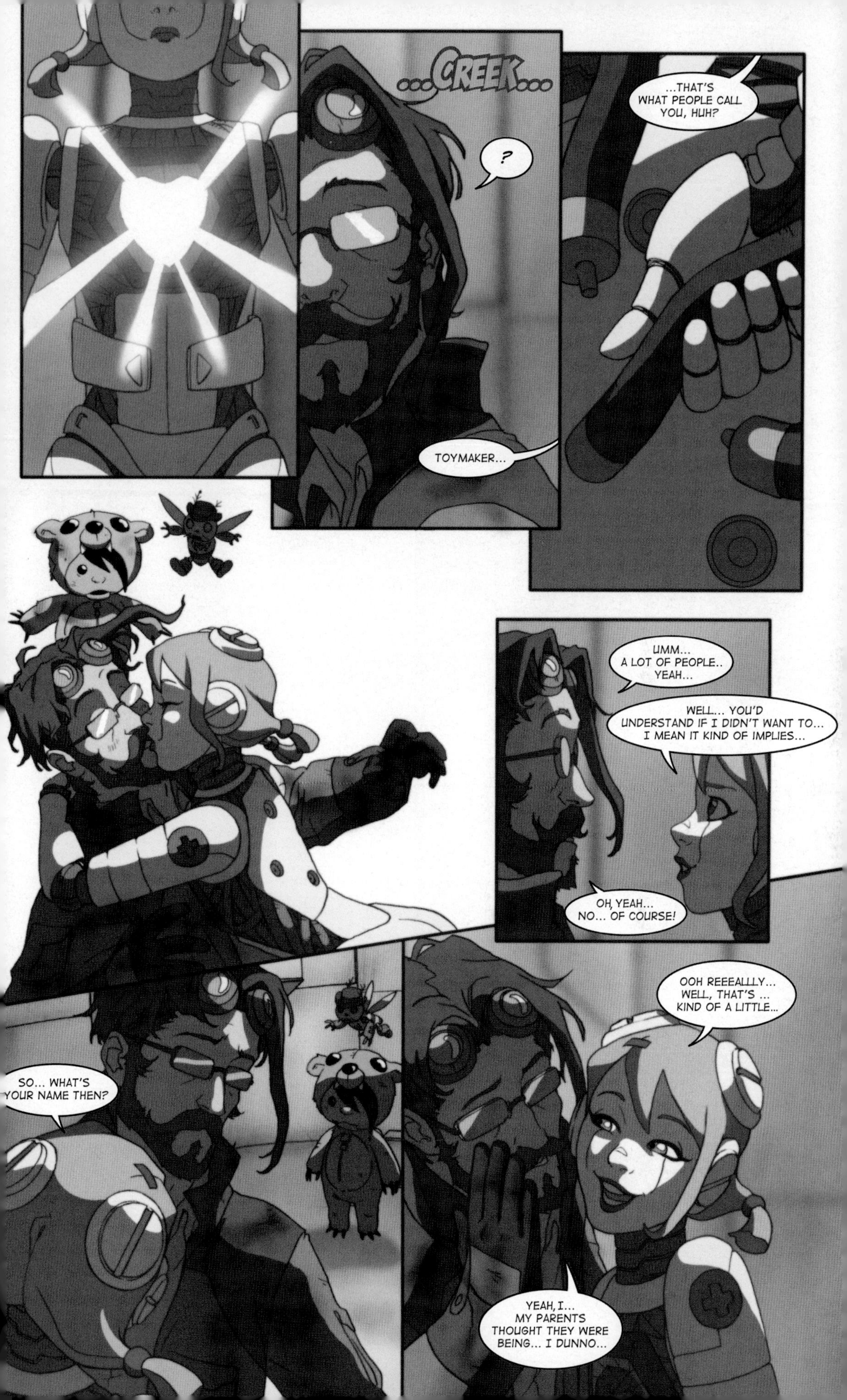
...CREEK...
?
TOYMAKER...
...THAT'S WHAT PEOPLE CALL YOU, HUH?
UMM... A LOT OF PEOPLE.. YEAH...
WELL... YOU'D UNDERSTAND IF I DIDN'T WANT TO... I MEAN IT KIND OF IMPLIES...
OH, YEAH... NO... OF COURSE!
SO... WHAT'S YOUR NAME THEN?
OOH REEEALLLY... WELL, THAT'S ... KIND OF A LITTLE...
YEAH, I... MY PARENTS THOUGHT THEY WERE BEING... I DUNNO...

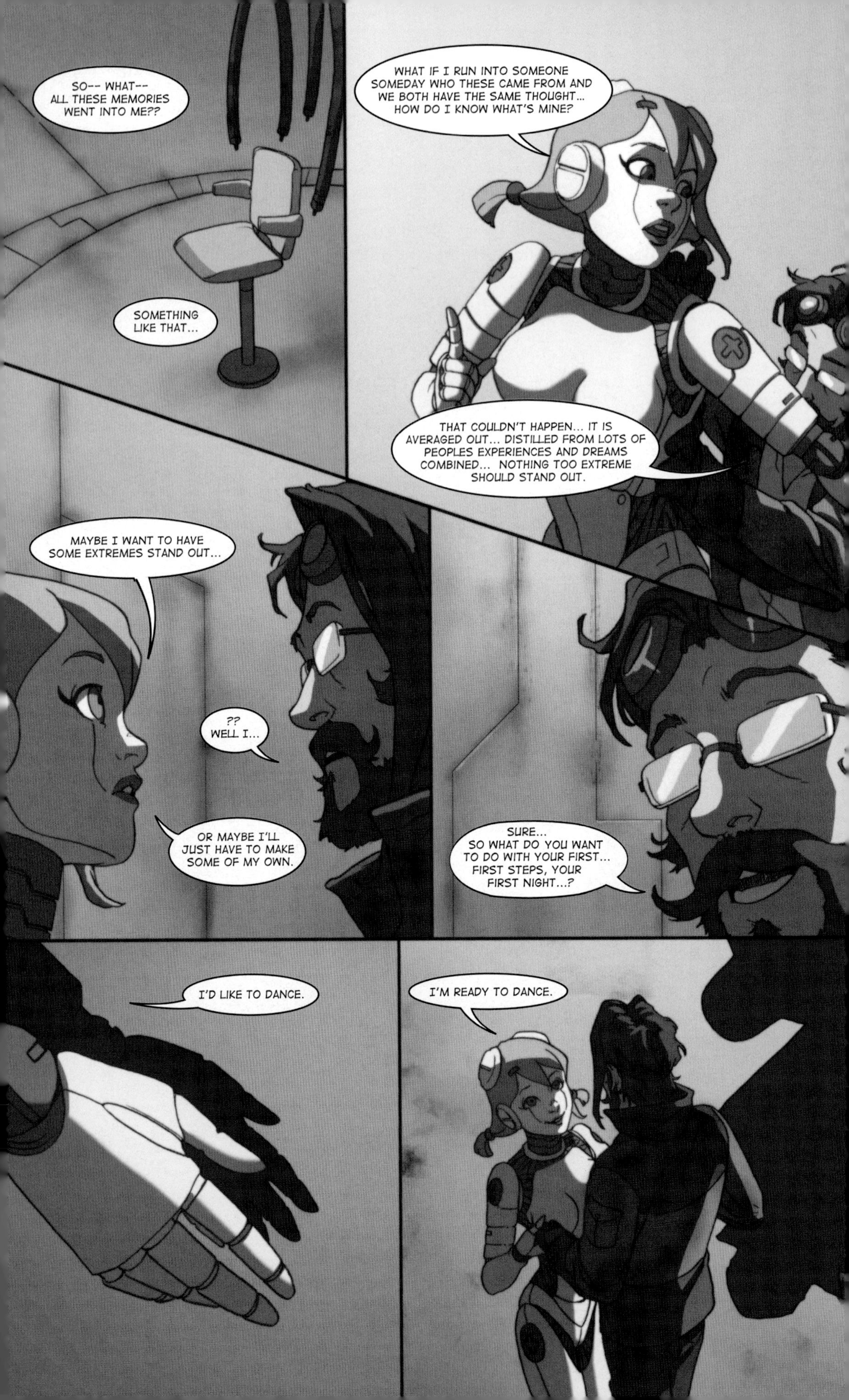
SO-- WHAT--
ALL THESE MEMORIES WENT INTO ME??
SOMETHING LIKE THAT...
WHAT IF I RUN INTO SOMEONE SOMEDAY WHO THESE CAME FROM AND WE BOTH HAVE THE SAME THOUGHT... HOW DO I KNOW WHAT'S MINE?
THAT COULDN'T HAPPEN... IT IS AVERAGED OUT... DISTILLED FROM LOTS OF PEOPLES EXPERIENCES AND DREAMS COMBINED... NOTHING TOO EXTREME SHOULD STAND OUT.
MAYBE I WANT TO HAVE SOME EXTREMES STAND OUT...
?? WELL I...
OR MAYBE I'LL JUST HAVE TO MAKE SOME OF MY OWN.
SURE... SO WHAT DO YOU WANT TO DO WITH YOUR FIRST... FIRST STEPS, YOUR FIRST NIGHT...?
I'D LIKE TO DANCE.
I'M READY TO DANCE.

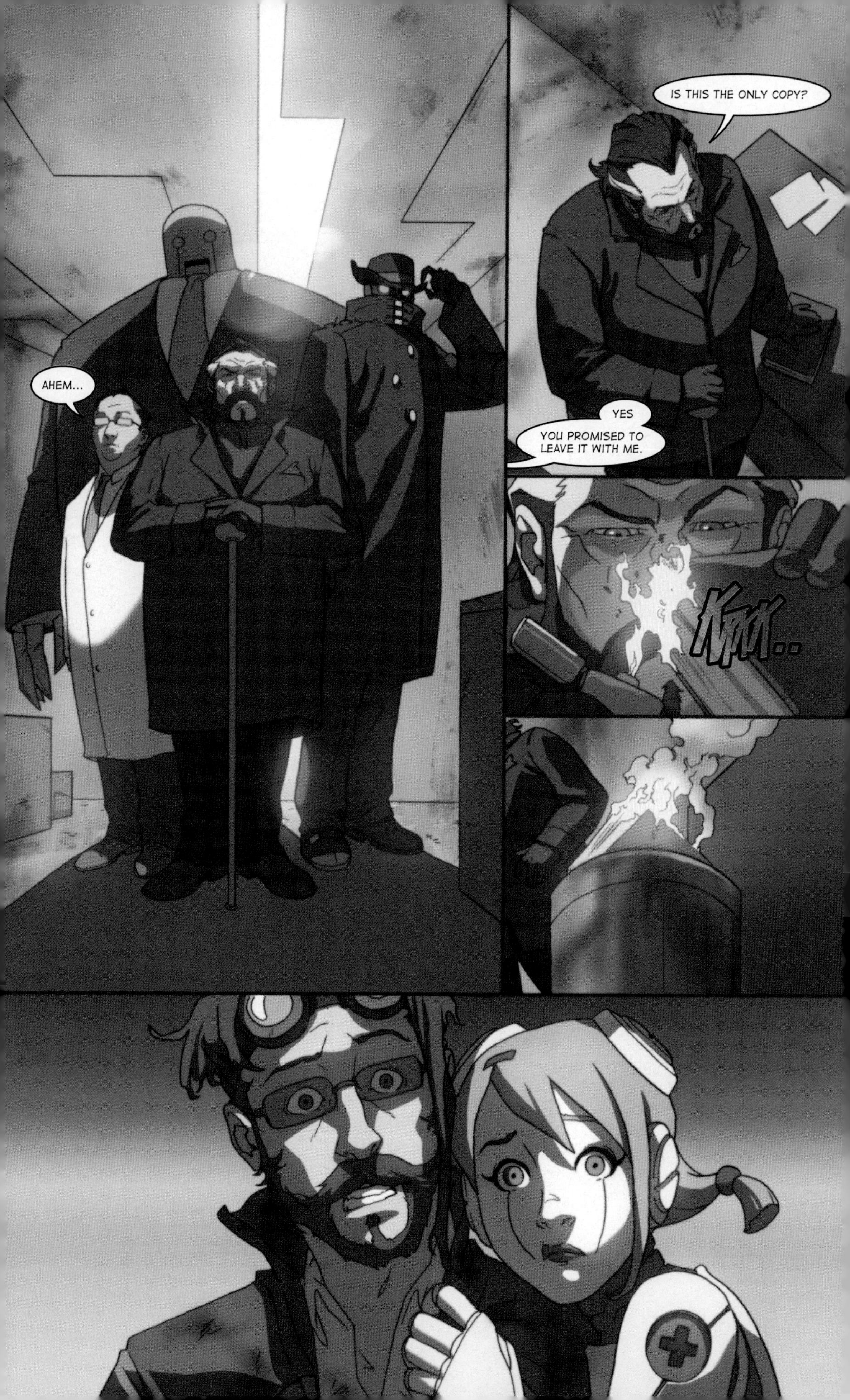
AHEM...
IS THIS THE ONLY COPY?
YES
YOU PROMISED TO LEAVE IT WITH ME.
KRKK..

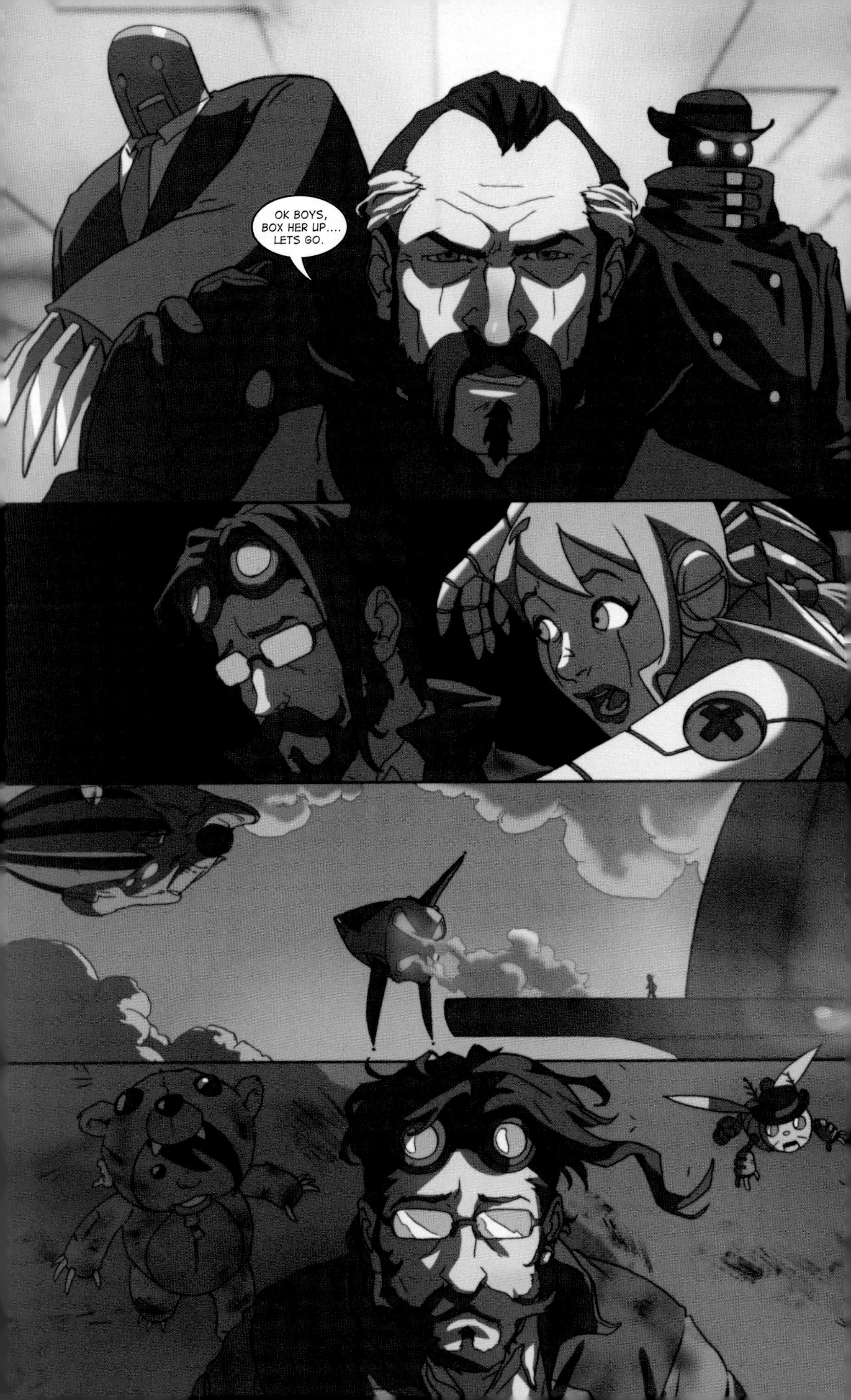
OK BOYS,
BOX HER UP....
LETS GO.

CHAPTER THREE

"BUT AREN'T ALL DREAMS INTERLUDES ANYWAY?"

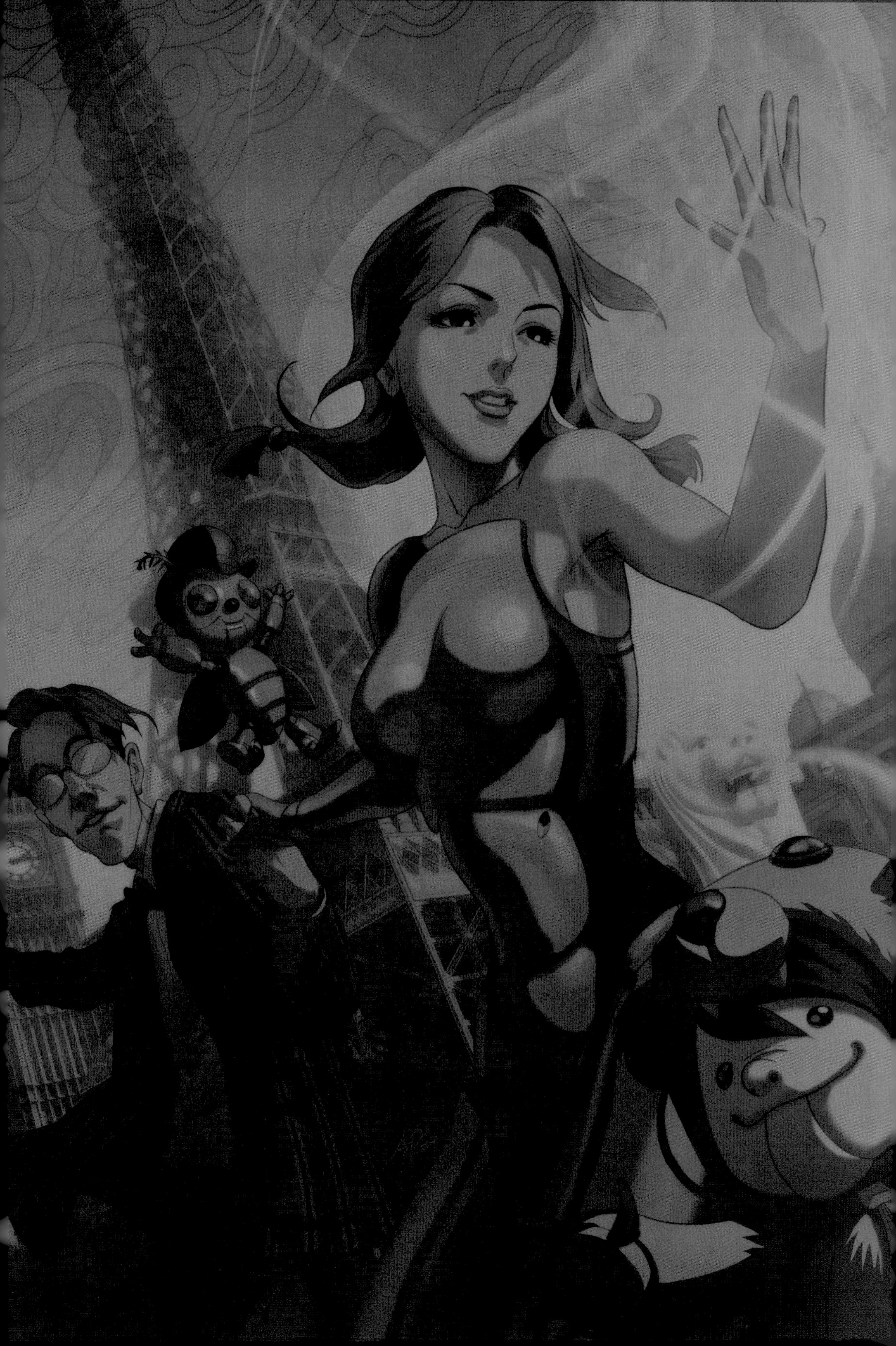

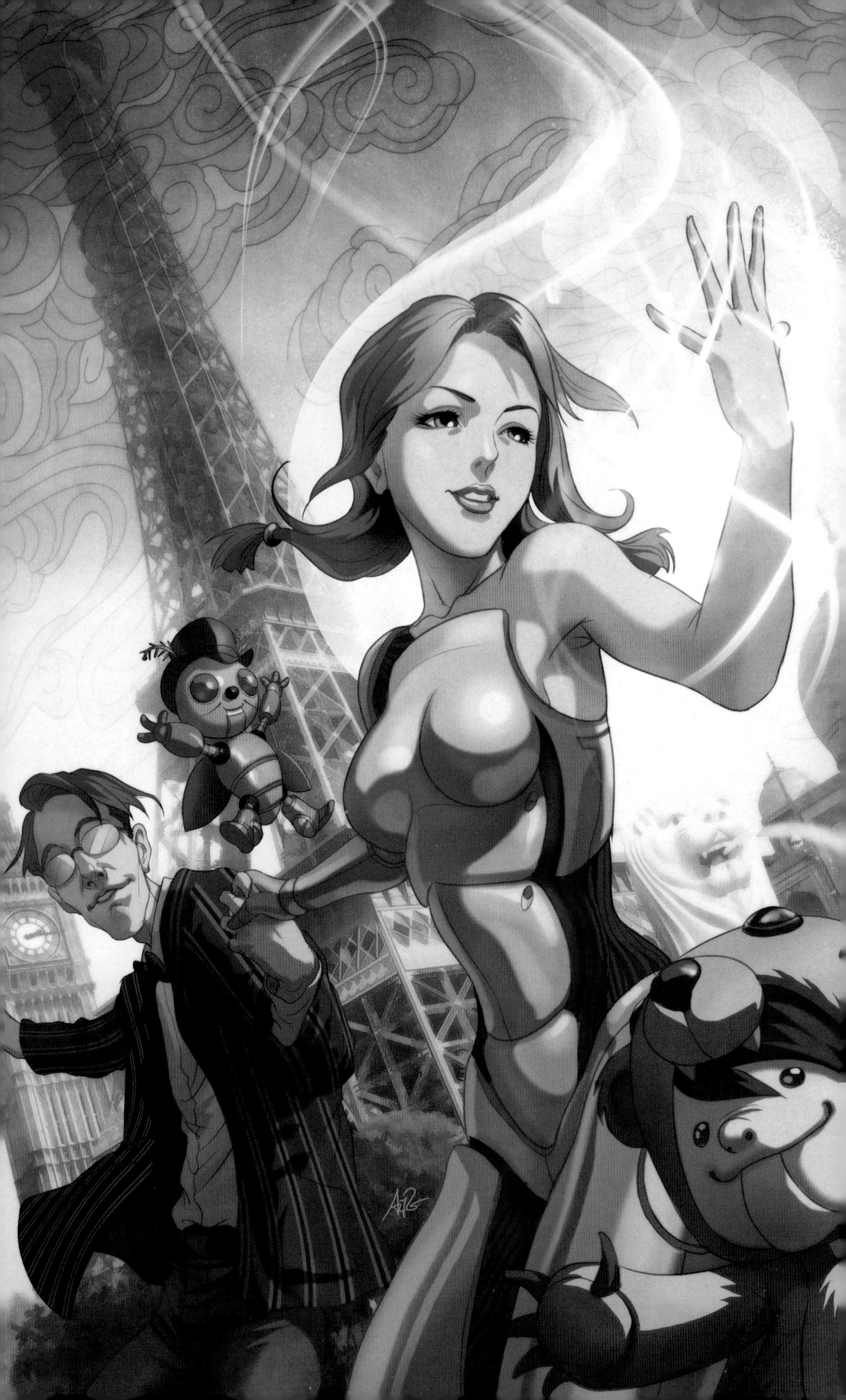

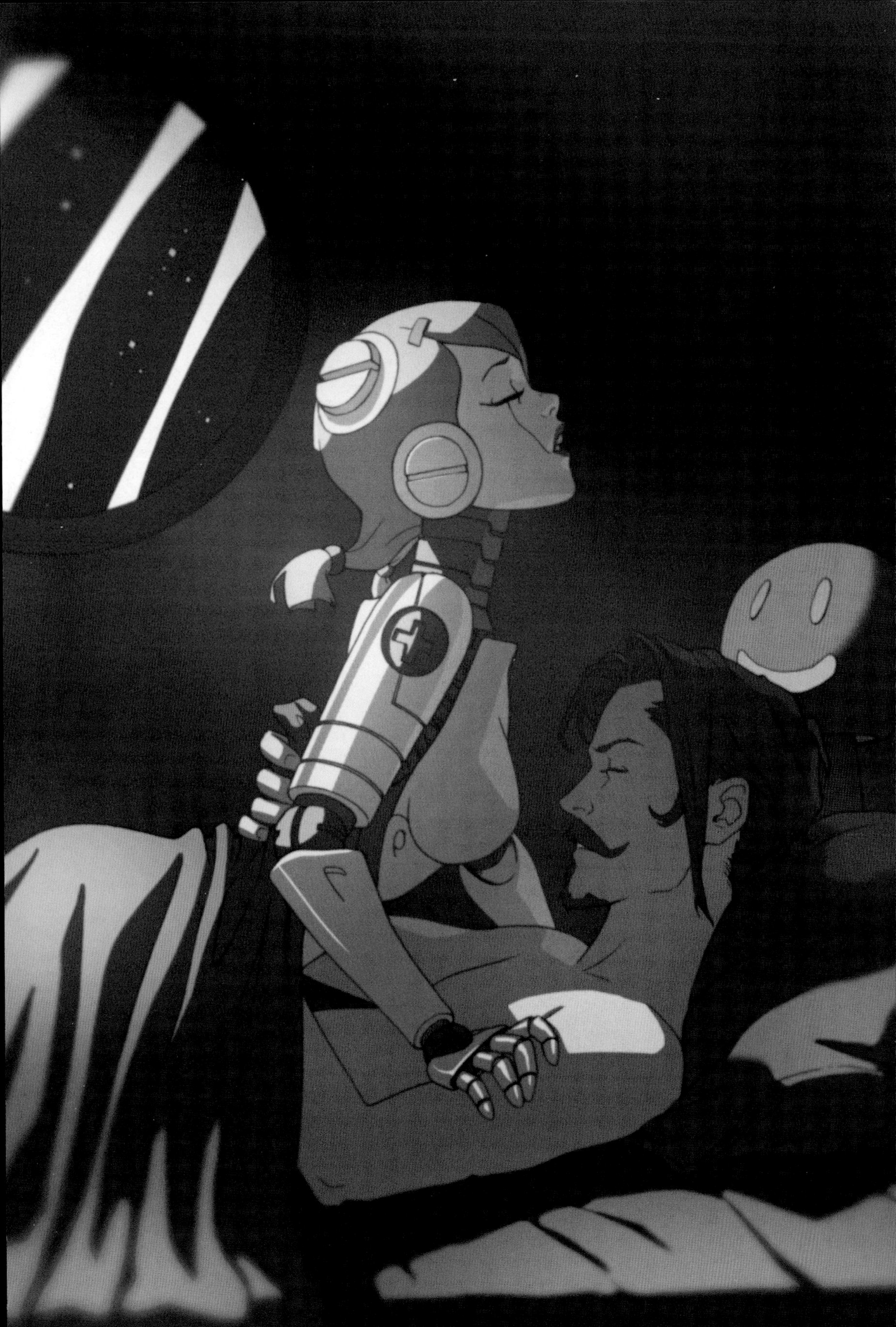

YAAAA.

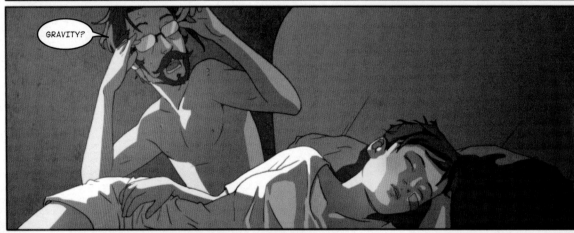

GRAVITY?

OIY! *NANDAYO*-- YOU WAKING ME THAT KINDA WAY!!

I JUST WORRY THAT... I GUESS IT'S THAT FEELING LIKE I LEFT SOMETHING INCOMPLETE...

YOU DID YOUR JOB, *NE*... SHE'S WITH THAT DOUCHE DID TRICK YOU.

WHAT YOU EXPECT!? OF COURSE TWO EMPTY PEOPLE'S GONNA LOVE EACH OTHER.

YOU GOTTA THINK ABOUT *YOUR* OWN SELF!

I...SORRY... I WAS DREAMING.

DREAMIN' BOUT THAT OTHER ONE AGAIN, NE? THAT'S A YOUR PAST BAD BUSINESS, TOY-CHAN... YOU GOTTA DREAM MORE FUTURE KIND OF THING.

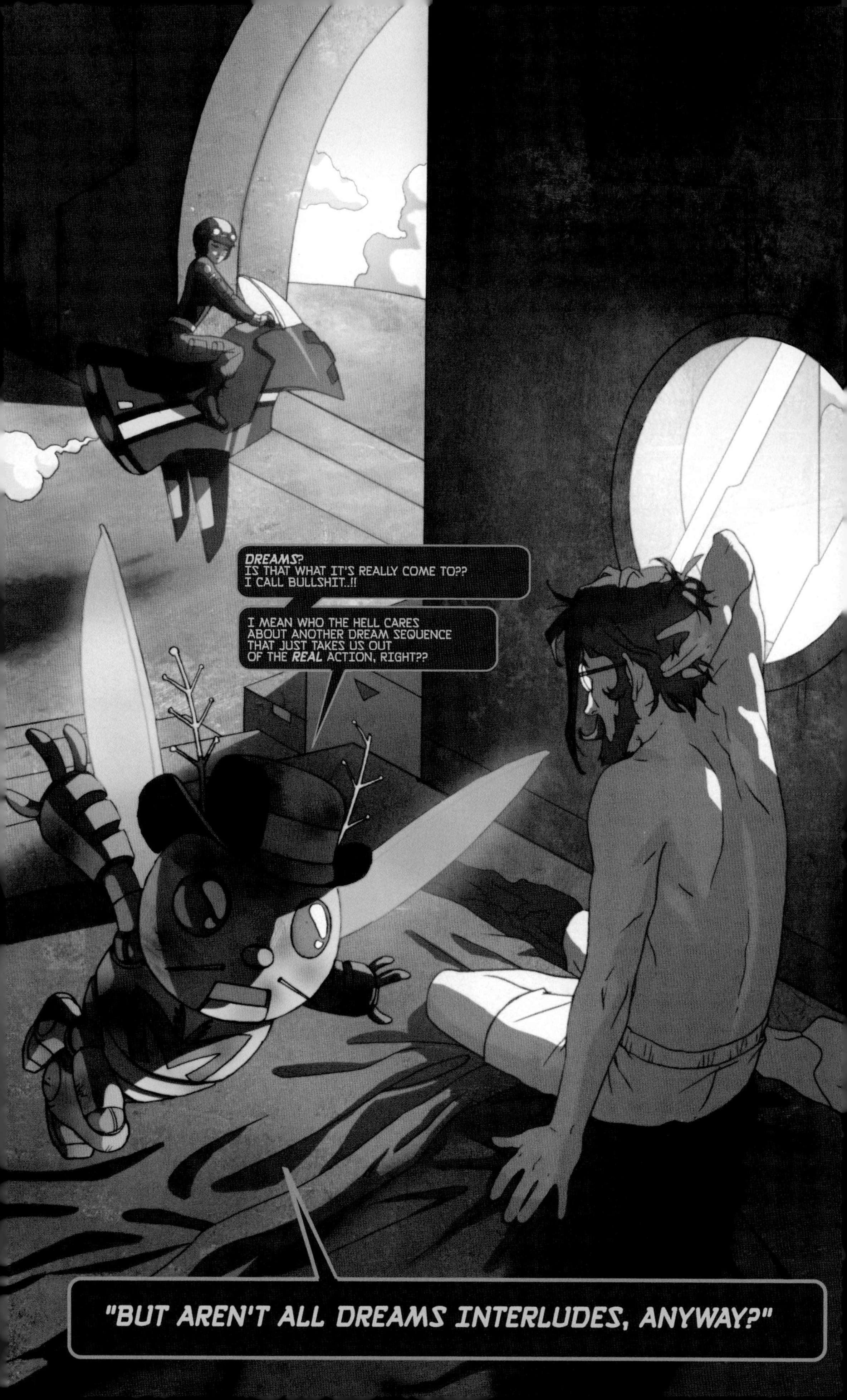
DREAMS?
IS THAT WHAT IT'S REALLY COME TO??
I CALL BULLSHIT..!!
I MEAN WHO THE HELL CARES
ABOUT ANOTHER DREAM SEQUENCE
THAT JUST TAKES US OUT
OF THE REAL ACTION, RIGHT??
"BUT AREN'T ALL DREAMS INTERLUDES, ANYWAY?"

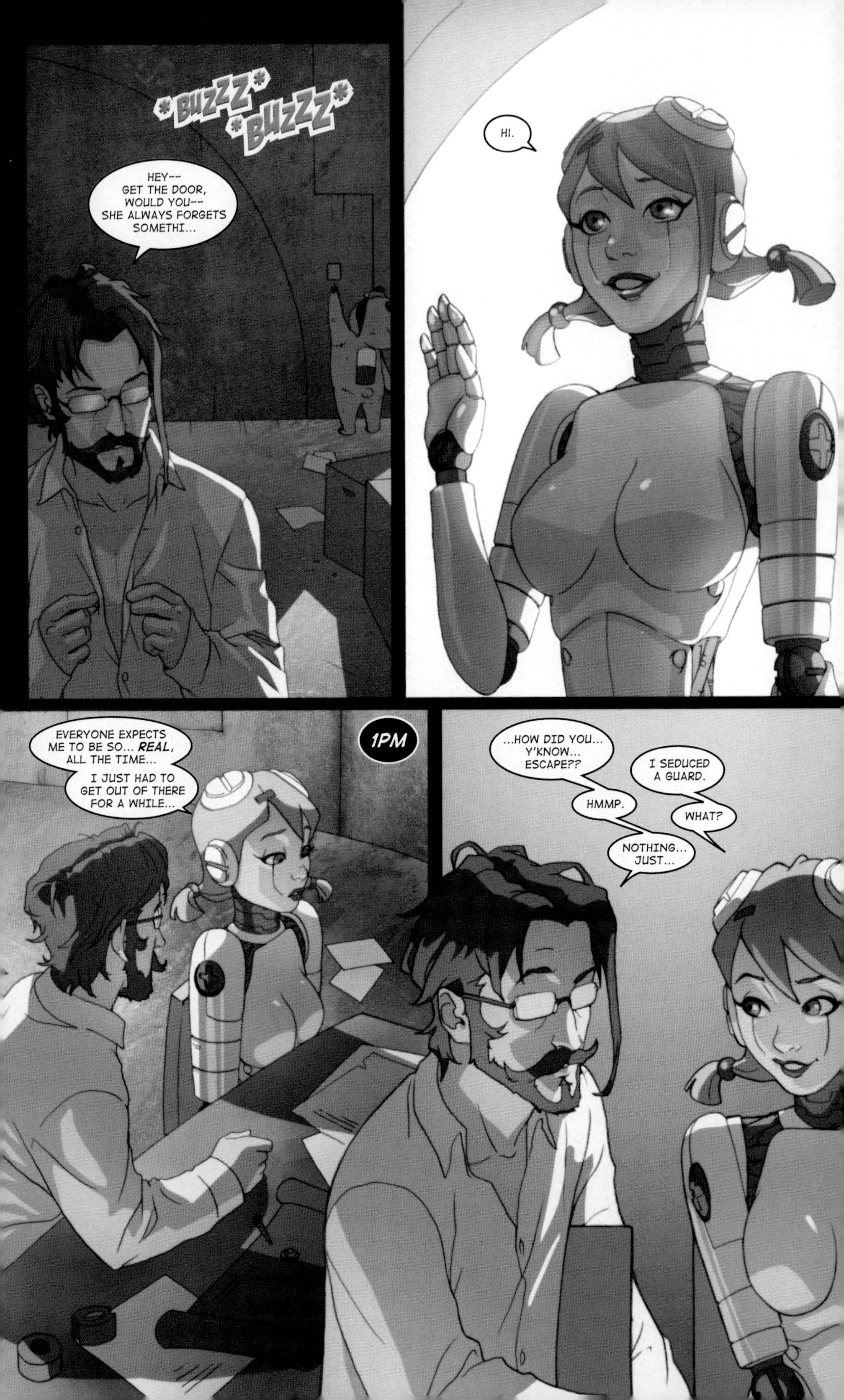
BUZZZ *BUZZZ*
HEY-- GET THE DOOR, WOULD YOU-- SHE ALWAYS FORGETS SOMETHI...
HI.
1PM
EVERYONE EXPECTS ME TO BE SO... REAL, ALL THE TIME...
I JUST HAD TO GET OUT OF THERE FOR A WHILE...
...HOW DID YOU... Y'KNOW... ESCAPE??
I SEDUCED A GUARD.
HMMP.
WHAT?
NOTHING... JUST...

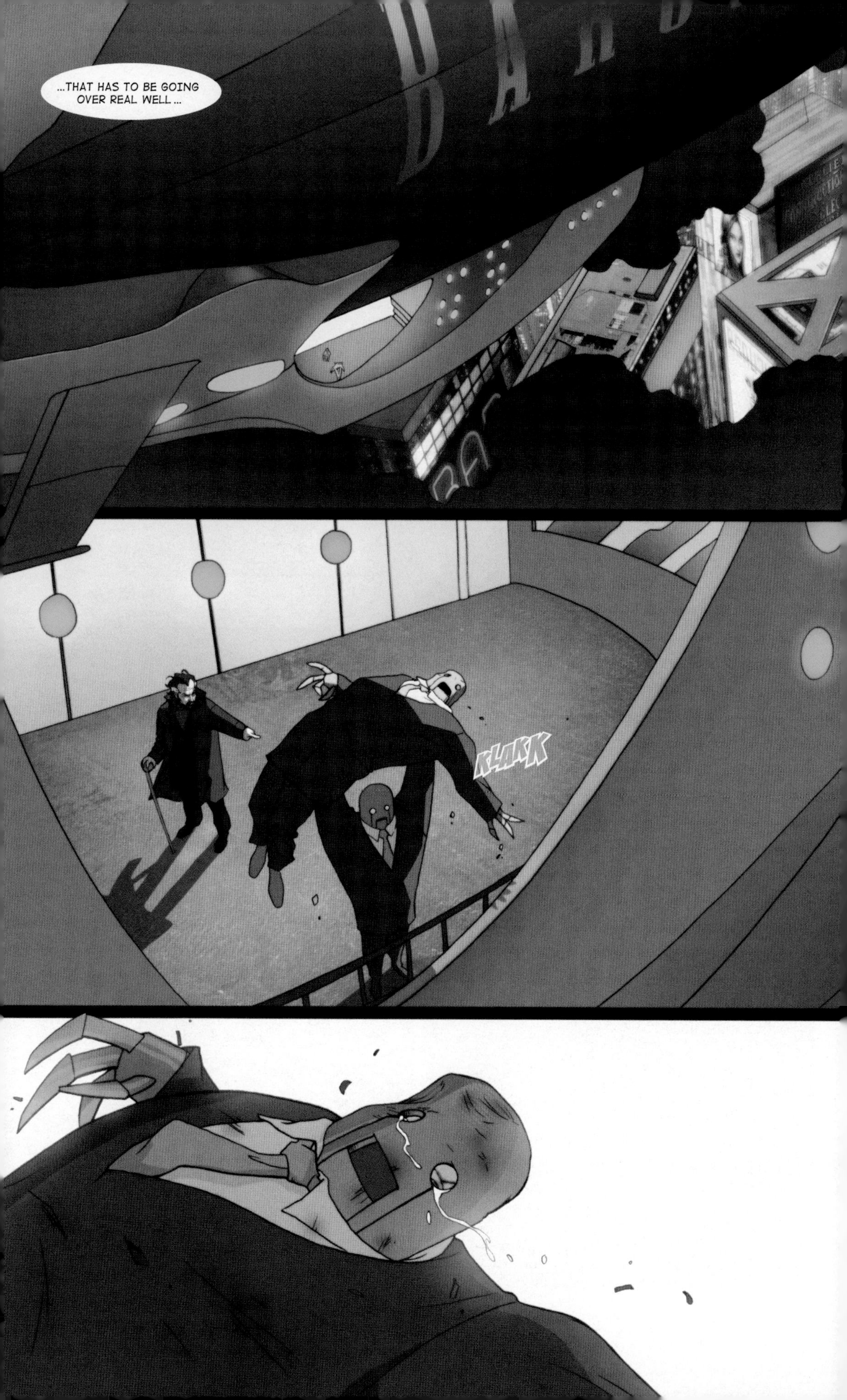
...THAT HAS TO BE GOING OVER REAL WELL ...
KLAKK

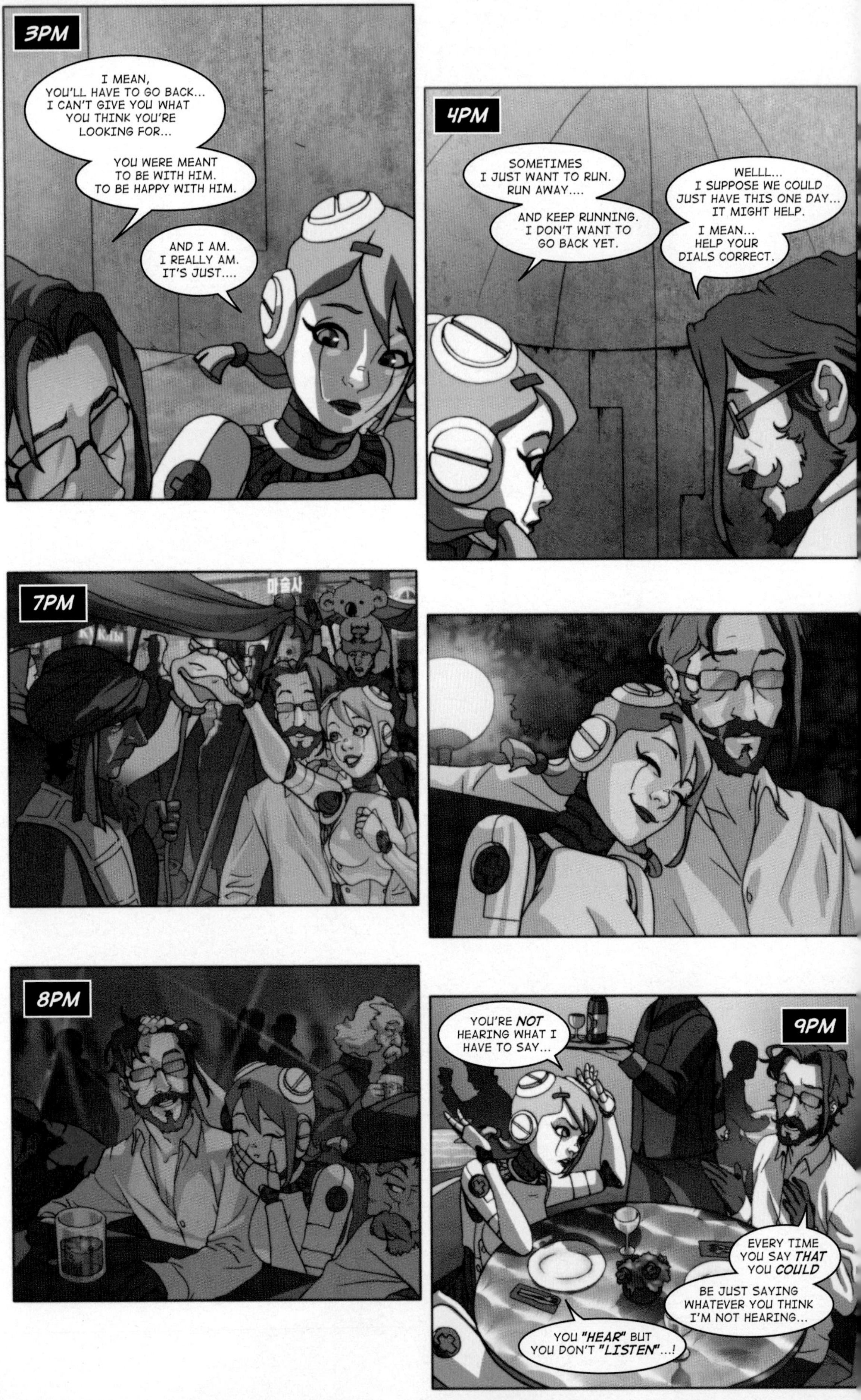
3PM
I MEAN, YOU'LL HAVE TO GO BACK... I CAN'T GIVE YOU WHAT YOU THINK YOU'RE LOOKING FOR...
YOU WERE MEANT TO BE WITH HIM. TO BE HAPPY WITH HIM.
AND I AM. I REALLY AM. IT'S JUST....
4PM
SOMETIMES I JUST WANT TO RUN. RUN AWAY....
AND KEEP RUNNING. I DON'T WANT TO GO BACK YET.
WELLL... I SUPPOSE WE COULD JUST HAVE THIS ONE DAY... IT MIGHT HELP.
I MEAN... HELP YOUR DIALS CORRECT.
7PM
마술사
8PM
9PM
YOU'RE *NOT* HEARING WHAT I HAVE TO SAY...
EVERY TIME YOU SAY *THAT* YOU *COULD*
BE JUST SAYING WHATEVER YOU THINK I'M NOT HEARING...
YOU *"HEAR"* BUT YOU DON'T *"LISTEN"*...!

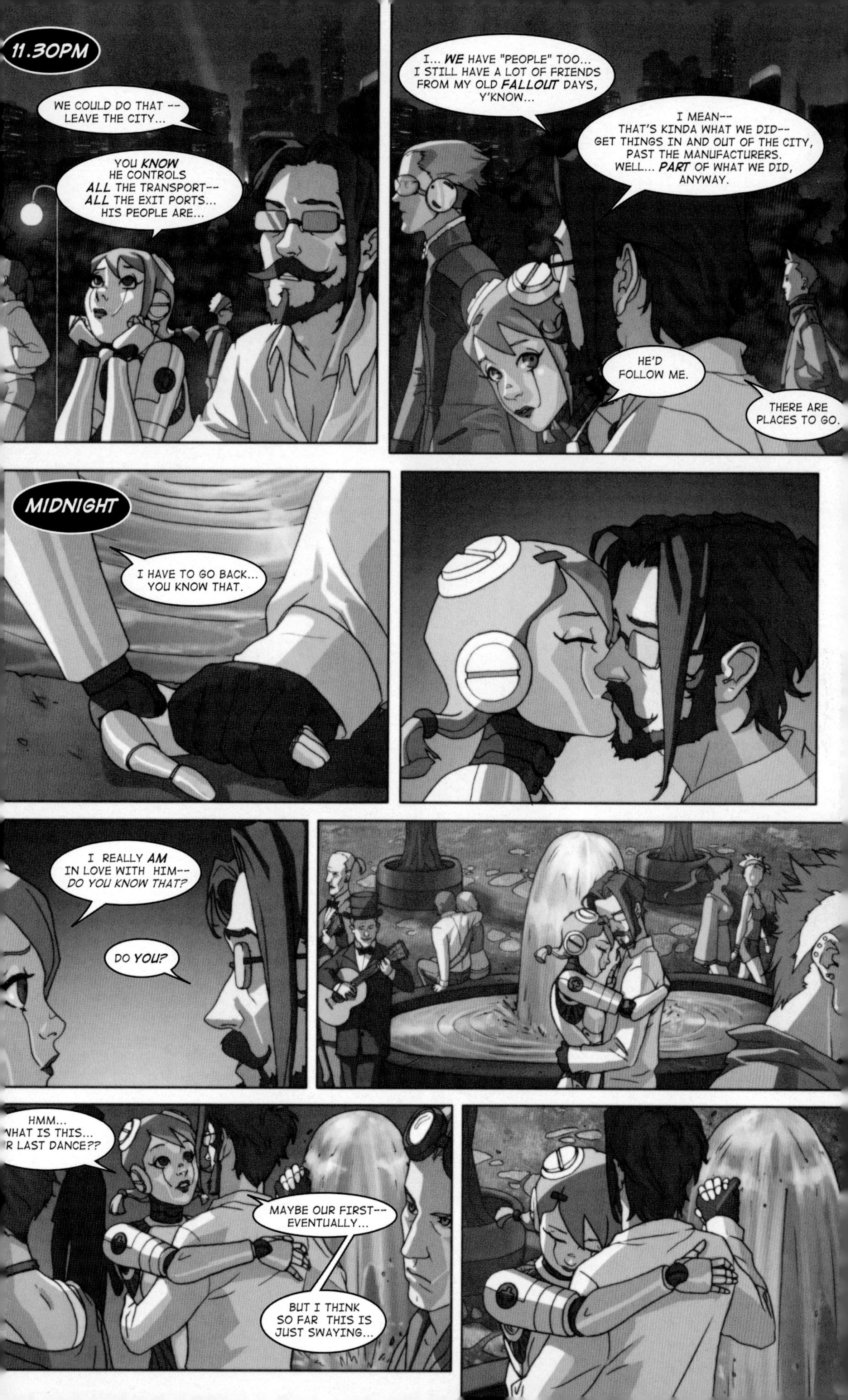

11.30PM
WE COULD DO THAT -- LEAVE THE CITY...
YOU KNOW HE CONTROLS ALL THE TRANSPORT-- ALL THE EXIT PORTS... HIS PEOPLE ARE...
I... WE HAVE "PEOPLE" TOO... I STILL HAVE A LOT OF FRIENDS FROM MY OLD FALLOUT DAYS, Y'KNOW...
I MEAN-- THAT'S KINDA WHAT WE DID-- GET THINGS IN AND OUT OF THE CITY, PAST THE MANUFACTURERS. WELL... PART OF WHAT WE DID, ANYWAY.
HE'D FOLLOW ME.
THERE ARE PLACES TO GO.
MIDNIGHT
I HAVE TO GO BACK... YOU KNOW THAT.
I REALLY AM IN LOVE WITH HIM-- DO YOU KNOW THAT?
DO YOU?
HMM... WHAT IS THIS... R LAST DANCE??
MAYBE OUR FIRST-- EVENTUALLY...
BUT I THINK SO FAR THIS IS JUST SWAYING...

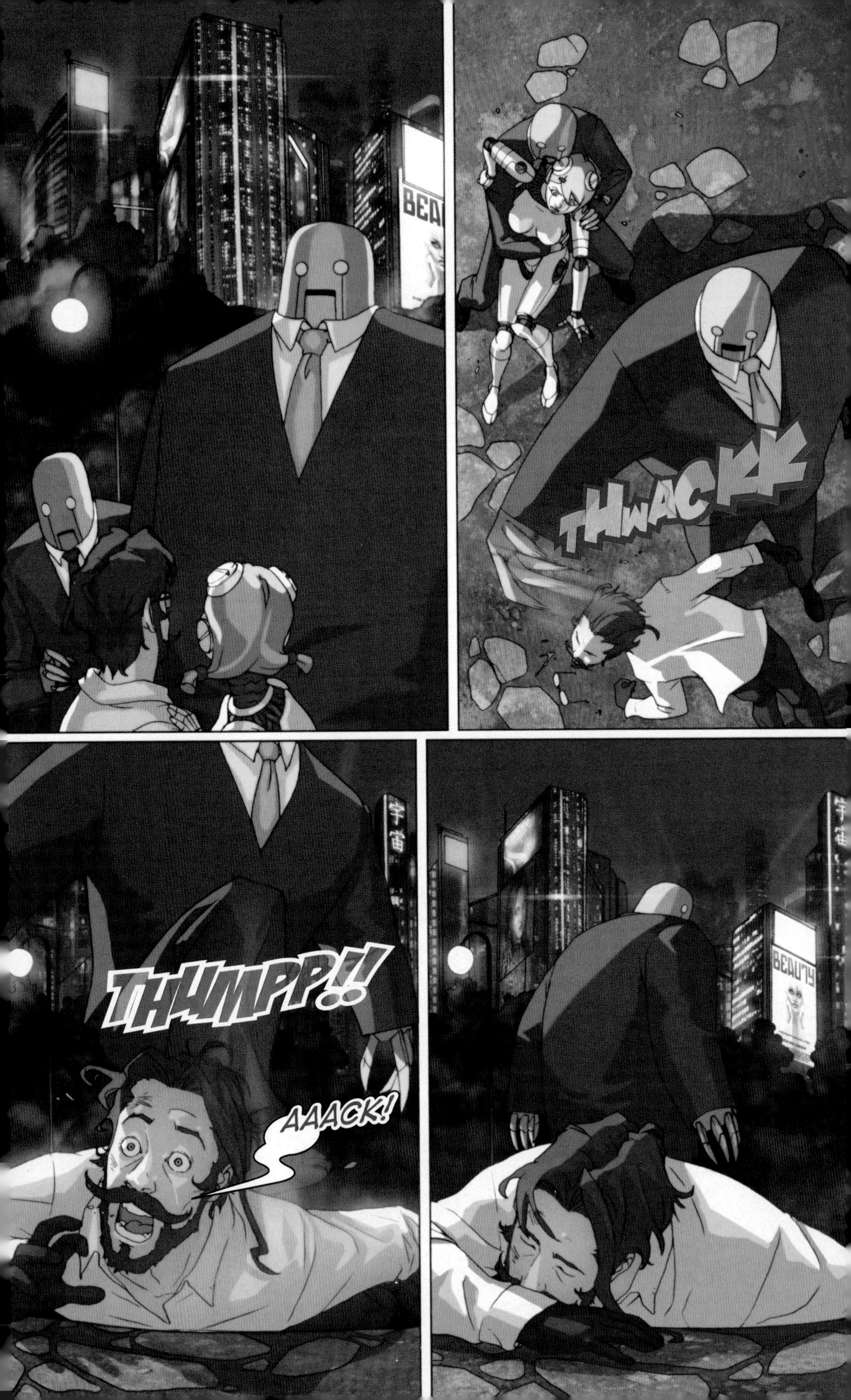
THWACKK
THUMPP!!
AAACK!
BEAUTY

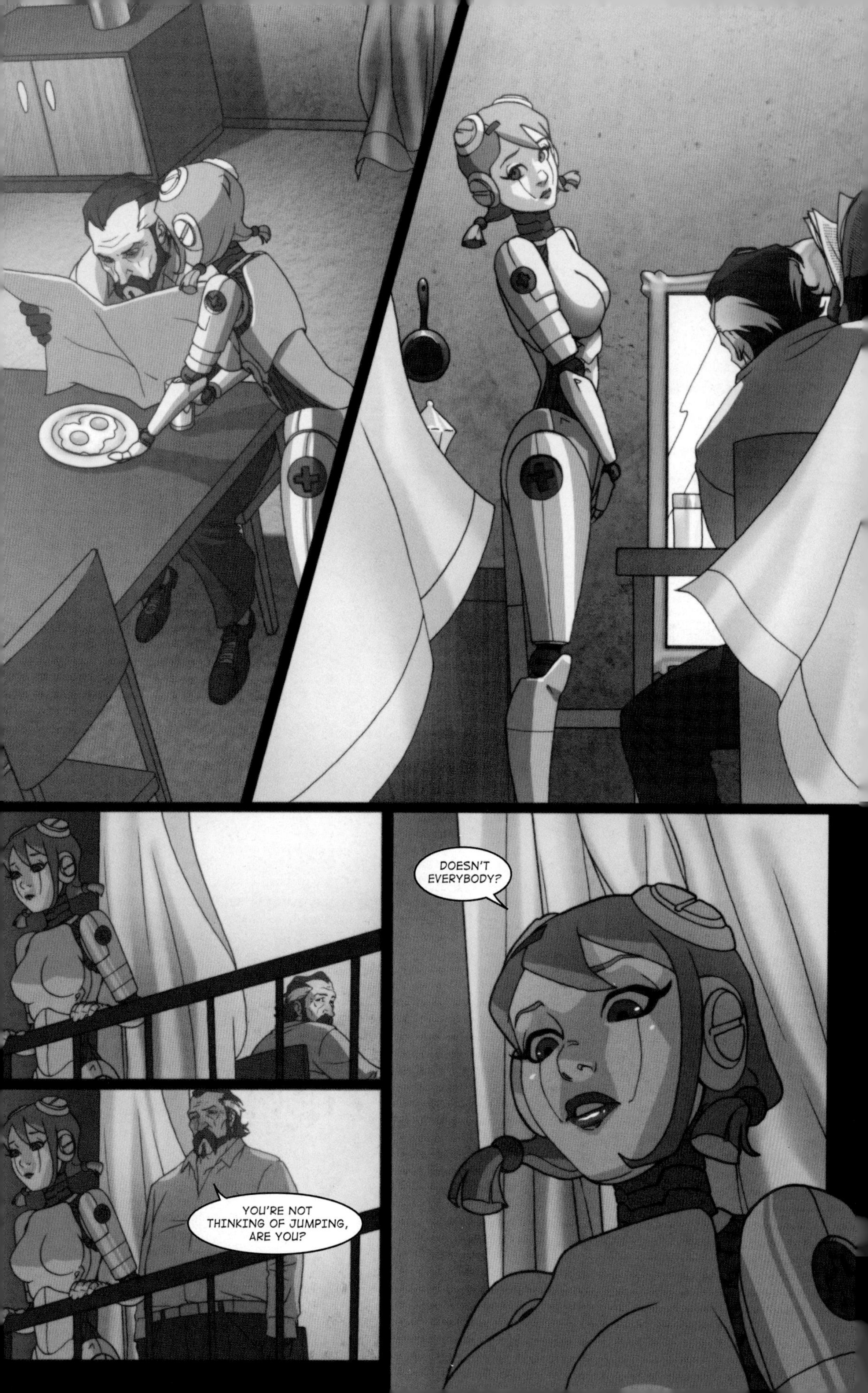
DOESN'T EVERYBODY?
YOU'RE NOT THINKING OF JUMPING, ARE YOU?

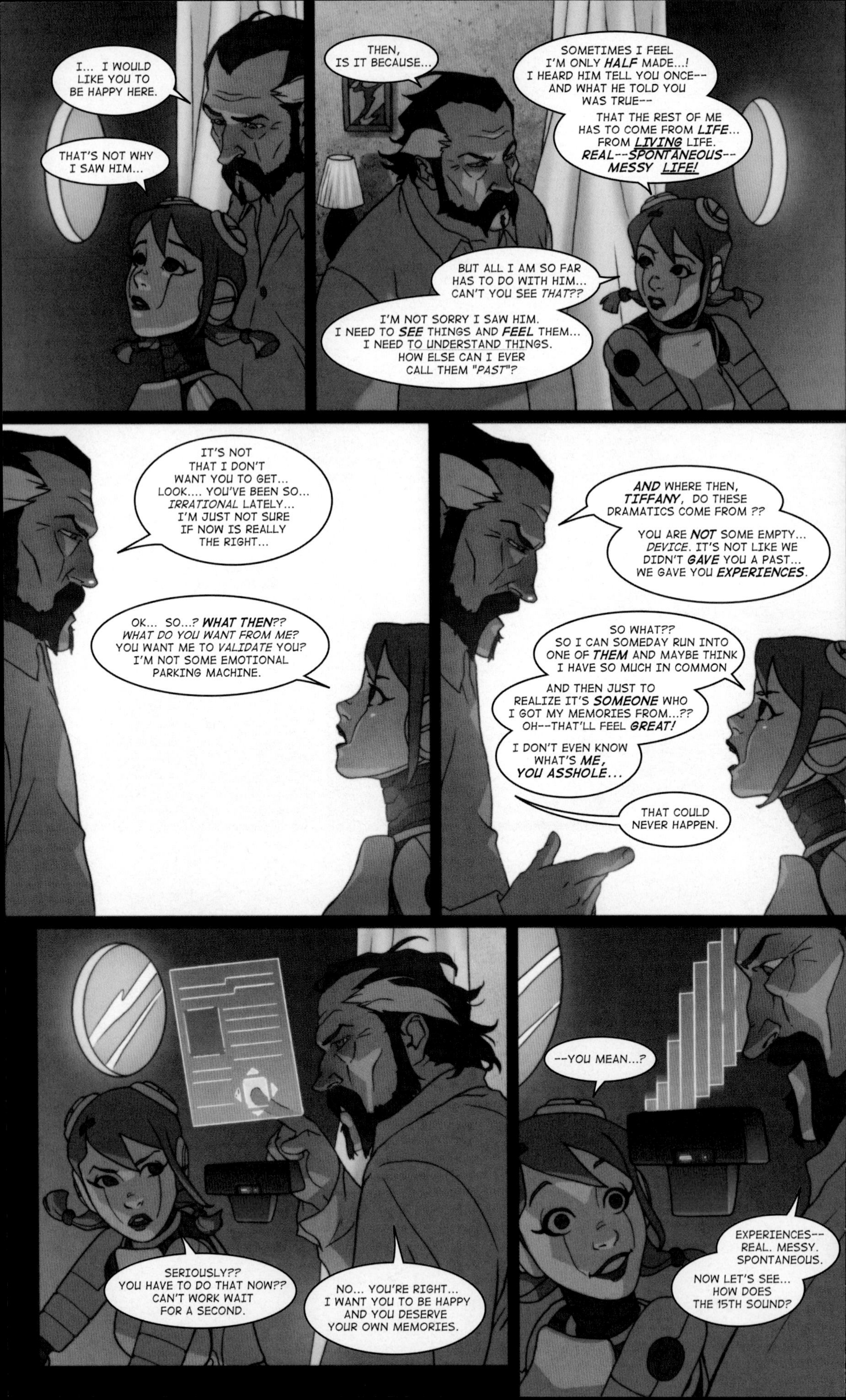
I... I WOULD LIKE YOU TO BE HAPPY HERE.
THAT'S NOT WHY I SAW HIM...
THEN, IS IT BECAUSE...
SOMETIMES I FEEL I'M ONLY HALF MADE...! I HEARD HIM TELL YOU ONCE-- AND WHAT HE TOLD YOU WAS TRUE--
THAT THE REST OF ME HAS TO COME FROM LIFE... FROM LIVING LIFE. REAL--SPONTANEOUS-- MESSY LIFE!
BUT ALL I AM SO FAR HAS TO DO WITH HIM... CAN'T YOU SEE THAT??
I'M NOT SORRY I SAW HIM. I NEED TO SEE THINGS AND FEEL THEM... I NEED TO UNDERSTAND THINGS. HOW ELSE CAN I EVER CALL THEM "PAST"?
IT'S NOT THAT I DON'T WANT YOU TO GET... LOOK.... YOU'VE BEEN SO... IRRATIONAL LATELY... I'M JUST NOT SURE IF NOW IS REALLY THE RIGHT...
OK... SO...? WHAT THEN?? WHAT DO YOU WANT FROM ME? YOU WANT ME TO VALIDATE YOU? I'M NOT SOME EMOTIONAL PARKING MACHINE.
AND WHERE THEN, TIFFANY, DO THESE DRAMATICS COME FROM ??
YOU ARE NOT SOME EMPTY... DEVICE. IT'S NOT LIKE WE DIDN'T GAVE YOU A PAST... WE GAVE YOU EXPERIENCES.
SO WHAT?? SO I CAN SOMEDAY RUN INTO ONE OF THEM AND MAYBE THINK I HAVE SO MUCH IN COMMON
AND THEN JUST TO REALIZE IT'S SOMEONE WHO I GOT MY MEMORIES FROM...?? OH--THAT'LL FEEL GREAT!
I DON'T EVEN KNOW WHAT'S ME, YOU ASSHOLE...
THAT COULD NEVER HAPPEN.
SERIOUSLY?? YOU HAVE TO DO THAT NOW?? CAN'T WORK WAIT FOR A SECOND.
NO... YOU'RE RIGHT... I WANT YOU TO BE HAPPY AND YOU DESERVE YOUR OWN MEMORIES.
--YOU MEAN...?
EXPERIENCES-- REAL. MESSY. SPONTANEOUS.
NOW LET'S SEE... HOW DOES THE 15TH SOUND?

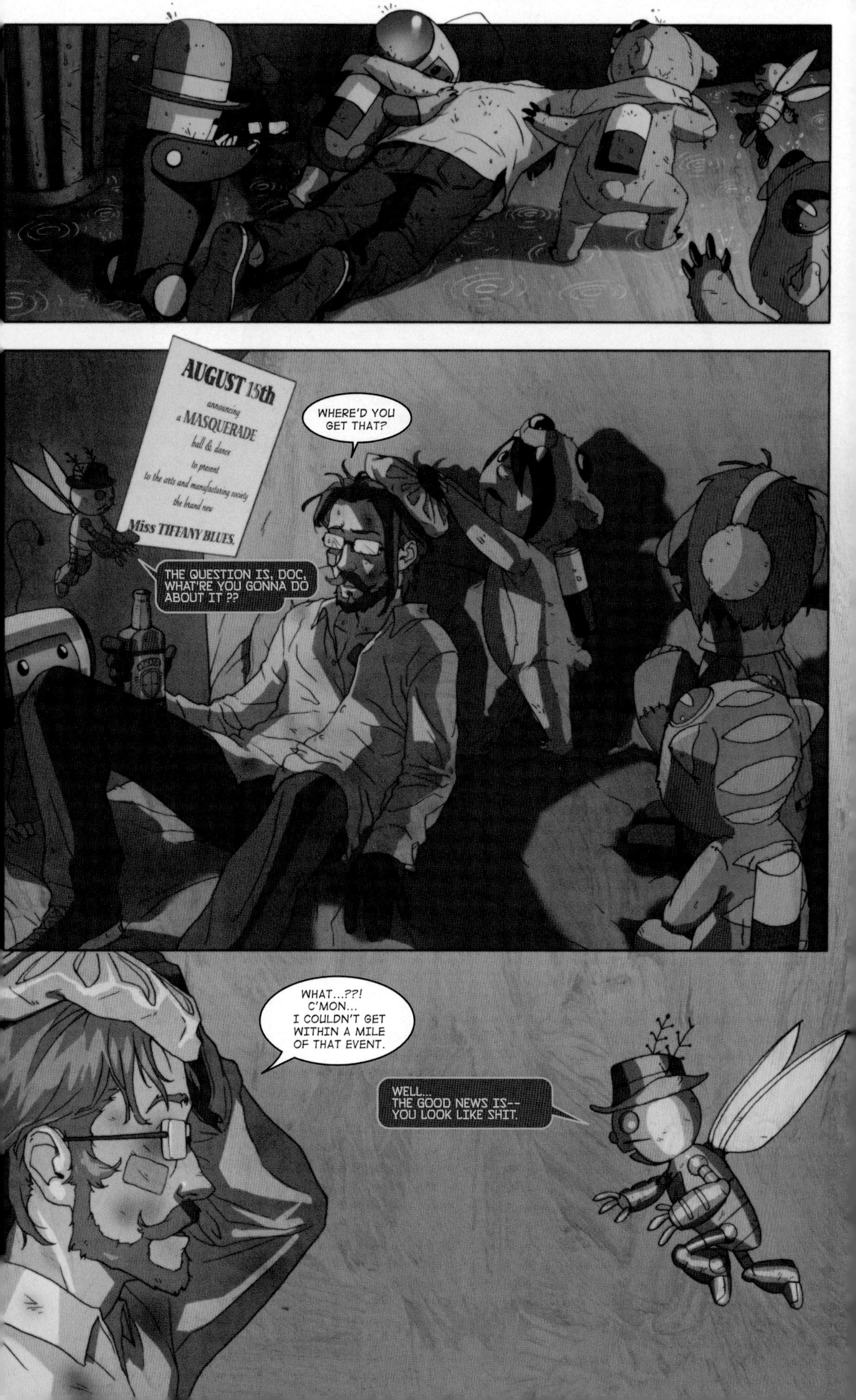
AUGUST 15th
announcing
a MASQUERADE
ball & dance
to present
to the arts and manufacturing society
the brand new
Miss TIFFANY BLUES.
WHERE'D YOU GET THAT?
THE QUESTION IS, DOC, WHAT'RE YOU GONNA DO ABOUT IT ??
WHAT...??! C'MON... I COULDN'T GET WITHIN A MILE OF THAT EVENT.
WELL... THE GOOD NEWS IS-- YOU LOOK LIKE SHIT.

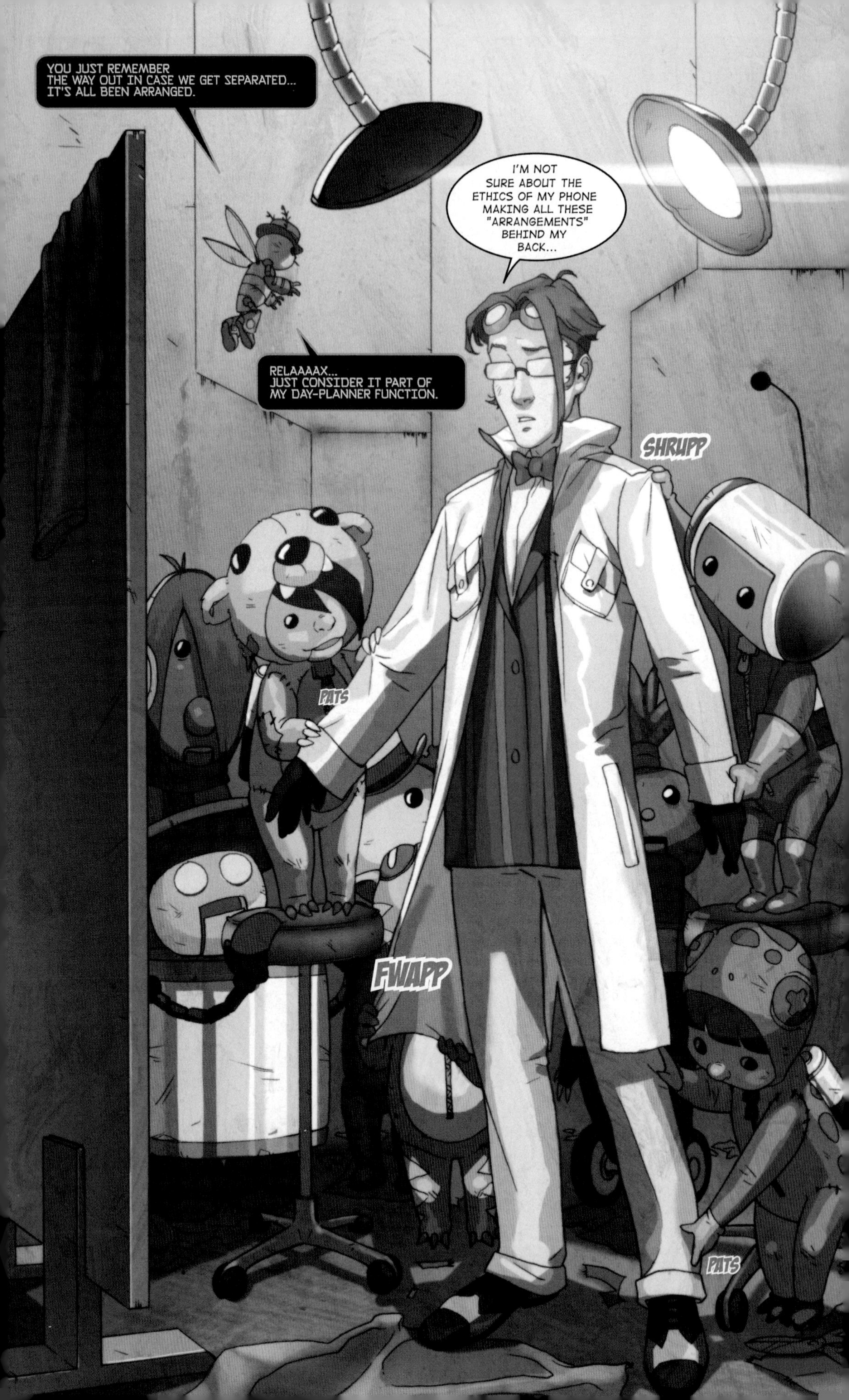
YOU JUST REMEMBER THE WAY OUT IN CASE WE GET SEPARATED... IT'S ALL BEEN ARRANGED.
I'M NOT SURE ABOUT THE ETHICS OF MY PHONE MAKING ALL THESE "ARRANGEMENTS" BEHIND MY BACK...
RELAAAAX... JUST CONSIDER IT PART OF MY DAY-PLANNER FUNCTION.
SHRUPP
PATS
FWAPP
PATS

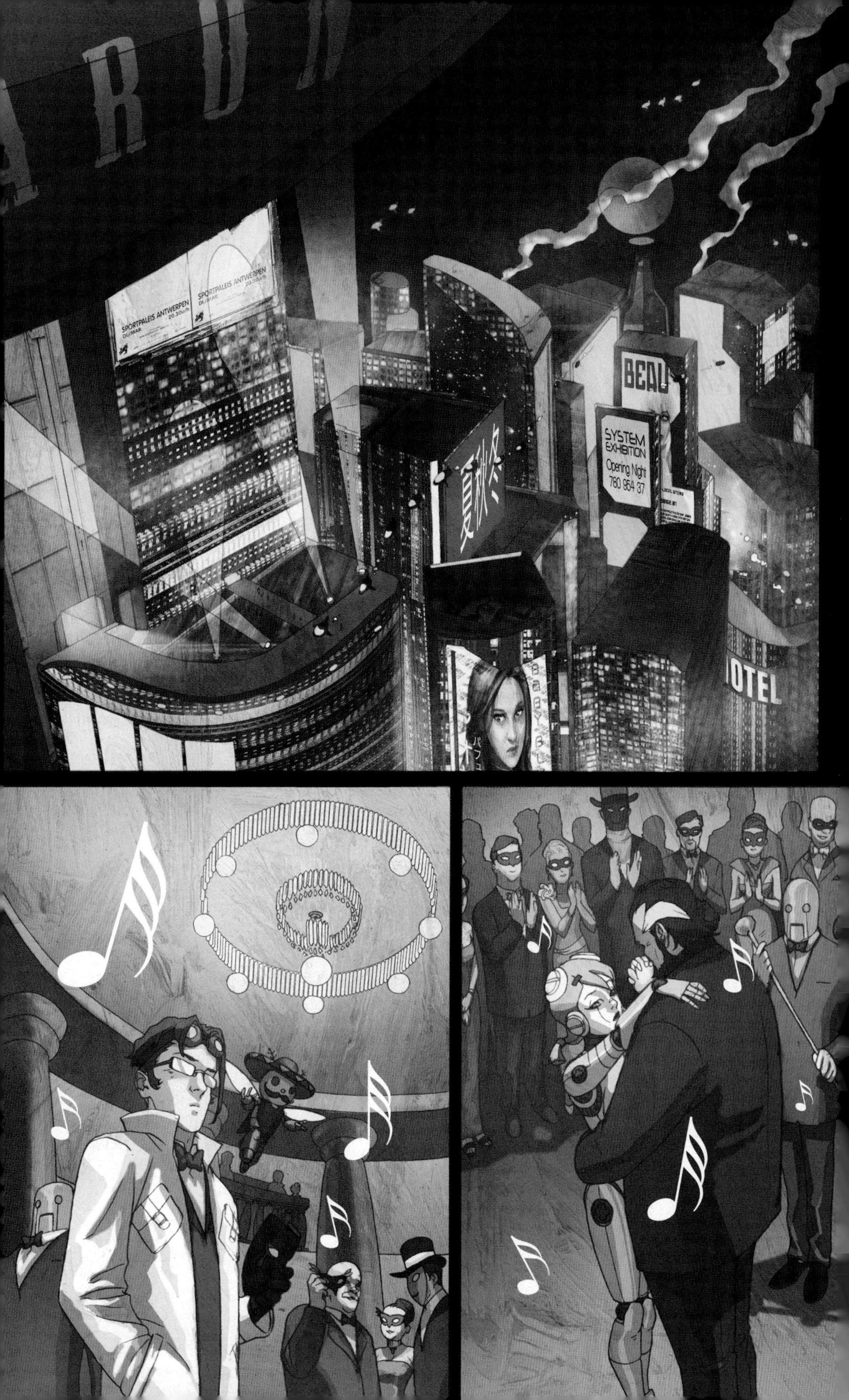
SPORTPALEIS ANTWERPEN
DI/MAR.
20.30u/h
SPORTPALEIS ANTWERPEN
DI/MAR.
20.30u/h
BEAU
SYSTEM
EXHIBITION
Opening Night
780 954 37
夏秋冬
OTEL

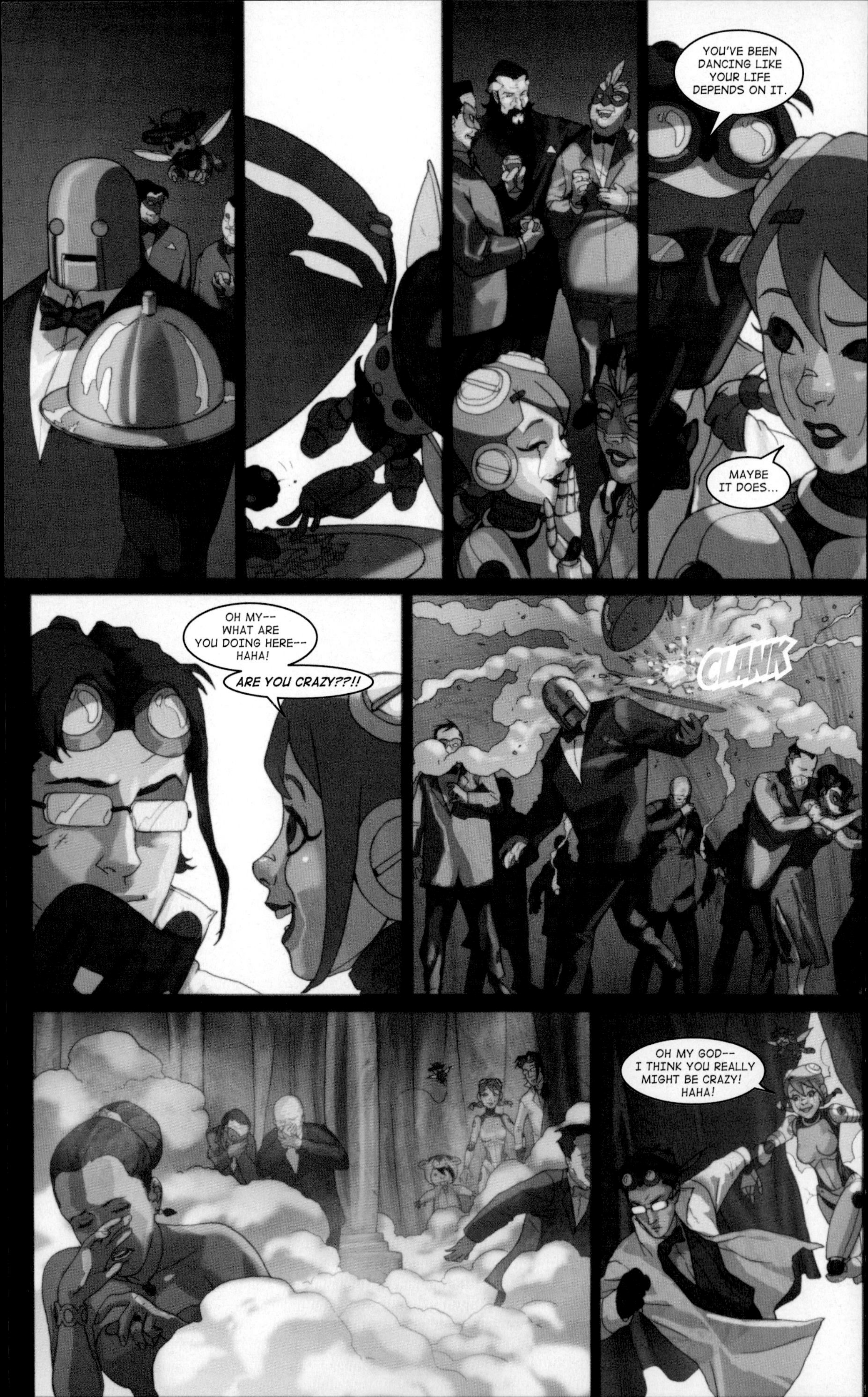
YOU'VE BEEN DANCING LIKE YOUR LIFE DEPENDS ON IT.
MAYBE IT DOES...
OH MY-- WHAT ARE YOU DOING HERE-- HAHA!
ARE YOU CRAZY??!!
CLANK
OH MY GOD-- I THINK YOU REALLY MIGHT BE CRAZY! HAHA!

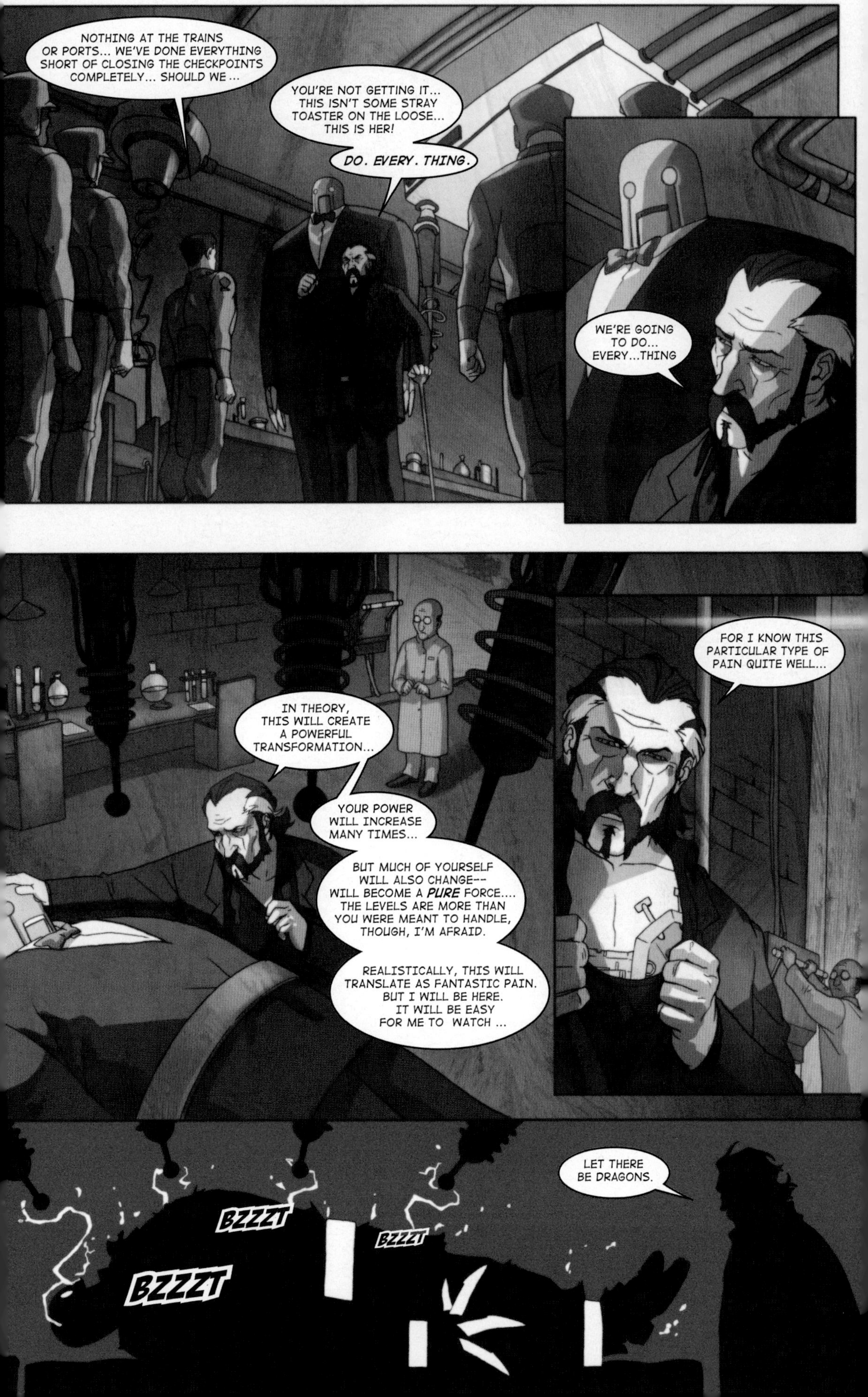

NOTHING AT THE TRAINS OR PORTS... WE'VE DONE EVERYTHING SHORT OF CLOSING THE CHECKPOINTS COMPLETELY... SHOULD WE ...
YOU'RE NOT GETTING IT... THIS ISN'T SOME STRAY TOASTER ON THE LOOSE... THIS IS HER!
DO. EVERY. THING.
WE'RE GOING TO DO... EVERY...THING
IN THEORY, THIS WILL CREATE A POWERFUL TRANSFORMATION...
YOUR POWER WILL INCREASE MANY TIMES...
BUT MUCH OF YOURSELF WILL ALSO CHANGE-- WILL BECOME A PURE FORCE.... THE LEVELS ARE MORE THAN YOU WERE MEANT TO HANDLE, THOUGH, I'M AFRAID.
REALISTICALLY, THIS WILL TRANSLATE AS FANTASTIC PAIN. BUT I WILL BE HERE. IT WILL BE EASY FOR ME TO WATCH ...
FOR I KNOW THIS PARTICULAR TYPE OF PAIN QUITE WELL...
LET THERE BE DRAGONS.
BZZZT
BZZZT
BZZZT

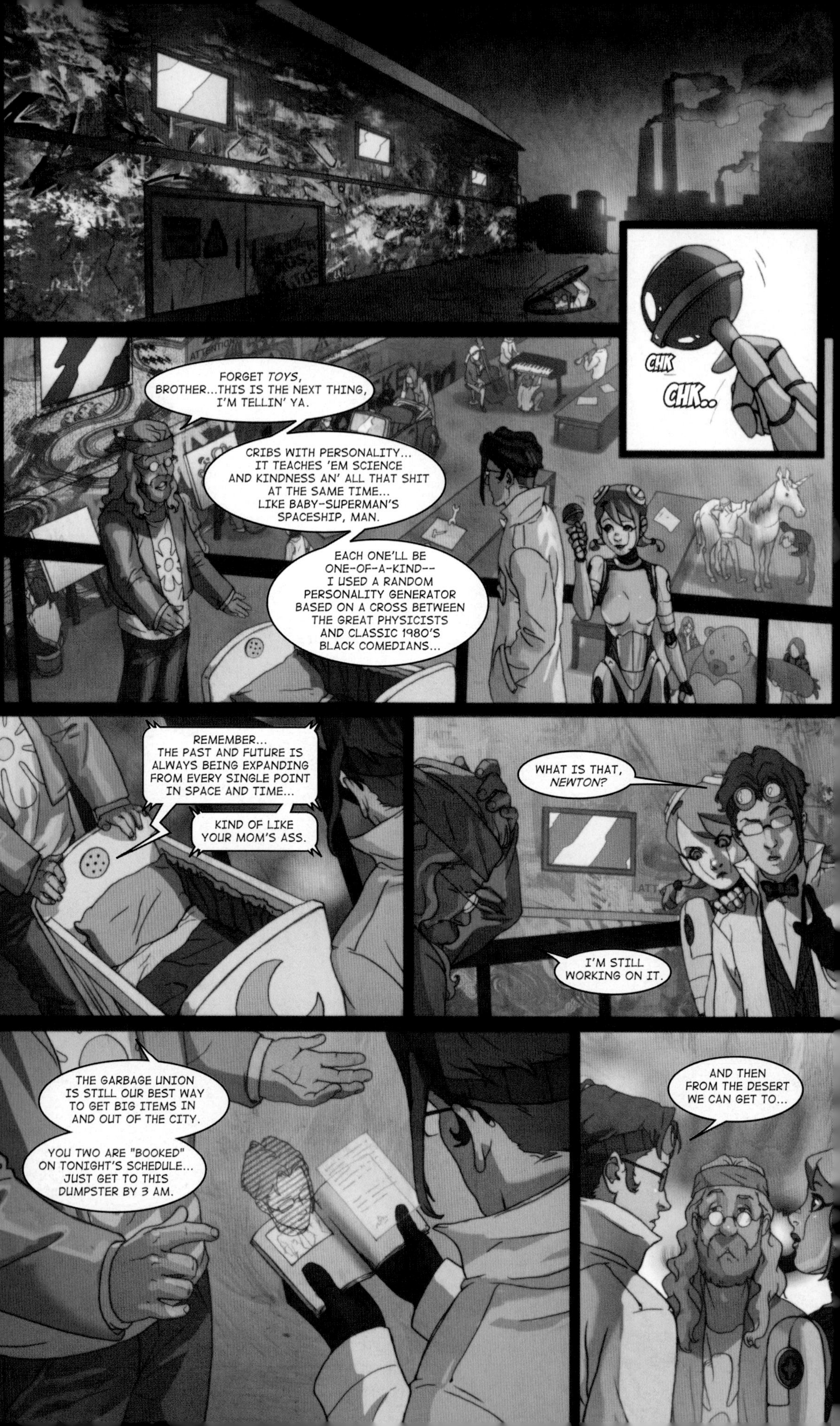
CHK
CHK..
FORGET *TOYS*, BROTHER...THIS IS THE NEXT THING, I'M TELLIN' YA.
CRIBS WITH PERSONALITY... IT TEACHES 'EM SCIENCE AND KINDNESS AN' ALL THAT SHIT AT THE SAME TIME... LIKE BABY-SUPERMAN'S SPACESHIP, MAN.
EACH ONE'LL BE ONE-OF-A-KIND-- I USED A RANDOM PERSONALITY GENERATOR BASED ON A CROSS BETWEEN THE GREAT PHYSICISTS AND CLASSIC 1980'S BLACK COMEDIANS...
REMEMBER... THE PAST AND FUTURE IS ALWAYS BEING EXPANDING FROM EVERY SINGLE POINT IN SPACE AND TIME...
KIND OF LIKE YOUR MOM'S ASS.
WHAT IS THAT, *NEWTON?*
I'M STILL WORKING ON IT.
THE GARBAGE UNION IS STILL OUR BEST WAY TO GET BIG ITEMS IN AND OUT OF THE CITY.
YOU TWO ARE "BOOKED" ON TONIGHT'S SCHEDULE... JUST GET TO THIS DUMPSTER BY 3 AM.
AND THEN FROM THE DESERT WE CAN GET TO...

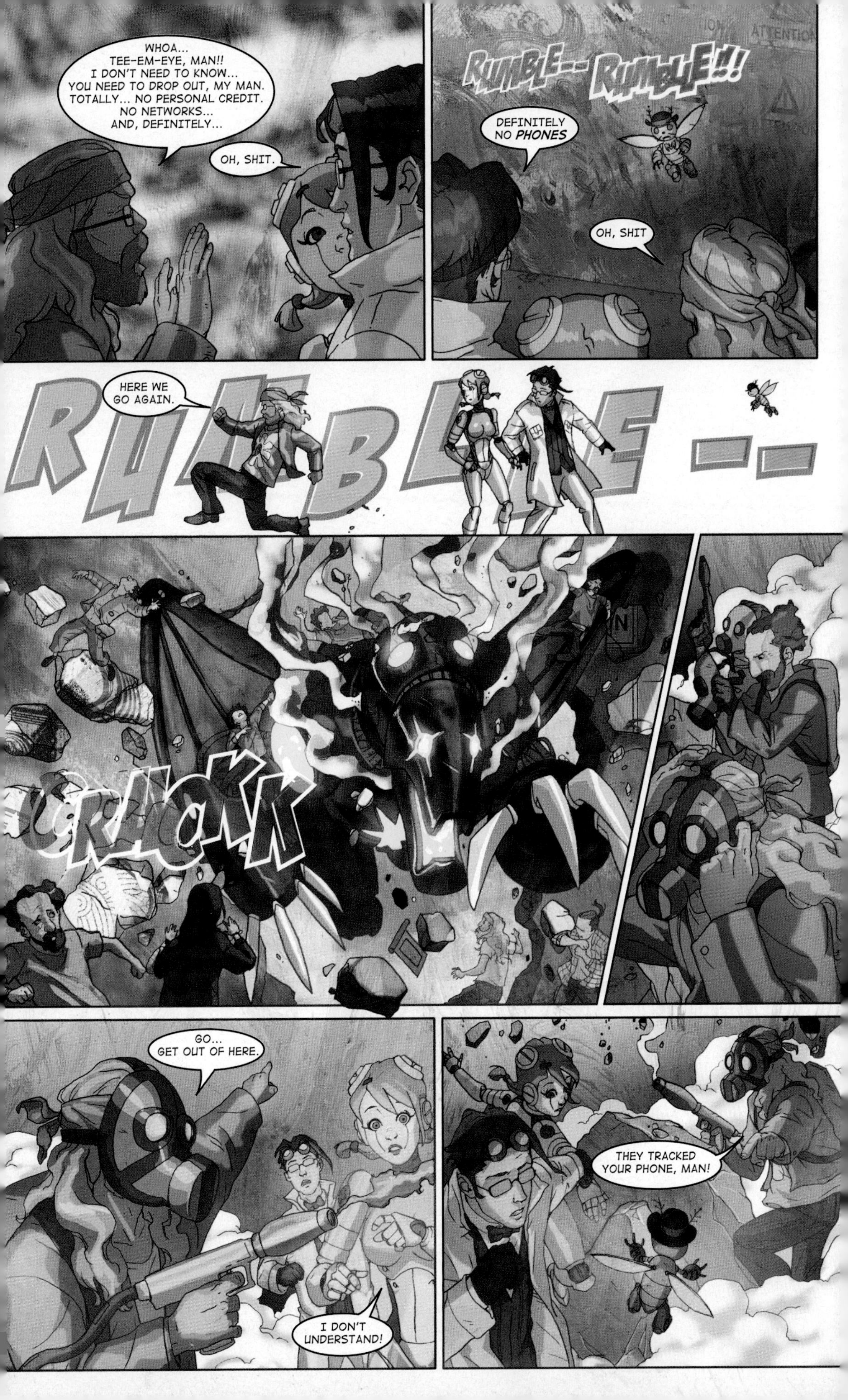
WHOA...
TEE-EM-EYE, MAN!!
I DON'T NEED TO KNOW...
YOU NEED TO DROP OUT, MY MAN.
TOTALLY... NO PERSONAL CREDIT.
NO NETWORKS...
AND, DEFINITELY...
OH, SHIT.
RUMBLE-- RUMBLE!!!
DEFINITELY NO *PHONES*
OH, SHIT
HERE WE GO AGAIN.
RUMBLE --
CRACK
GO...
GET OUT OF HERE.
I DON'T UNDERSTAND!
THEY TRACKED YOUR PHONE, MAN!

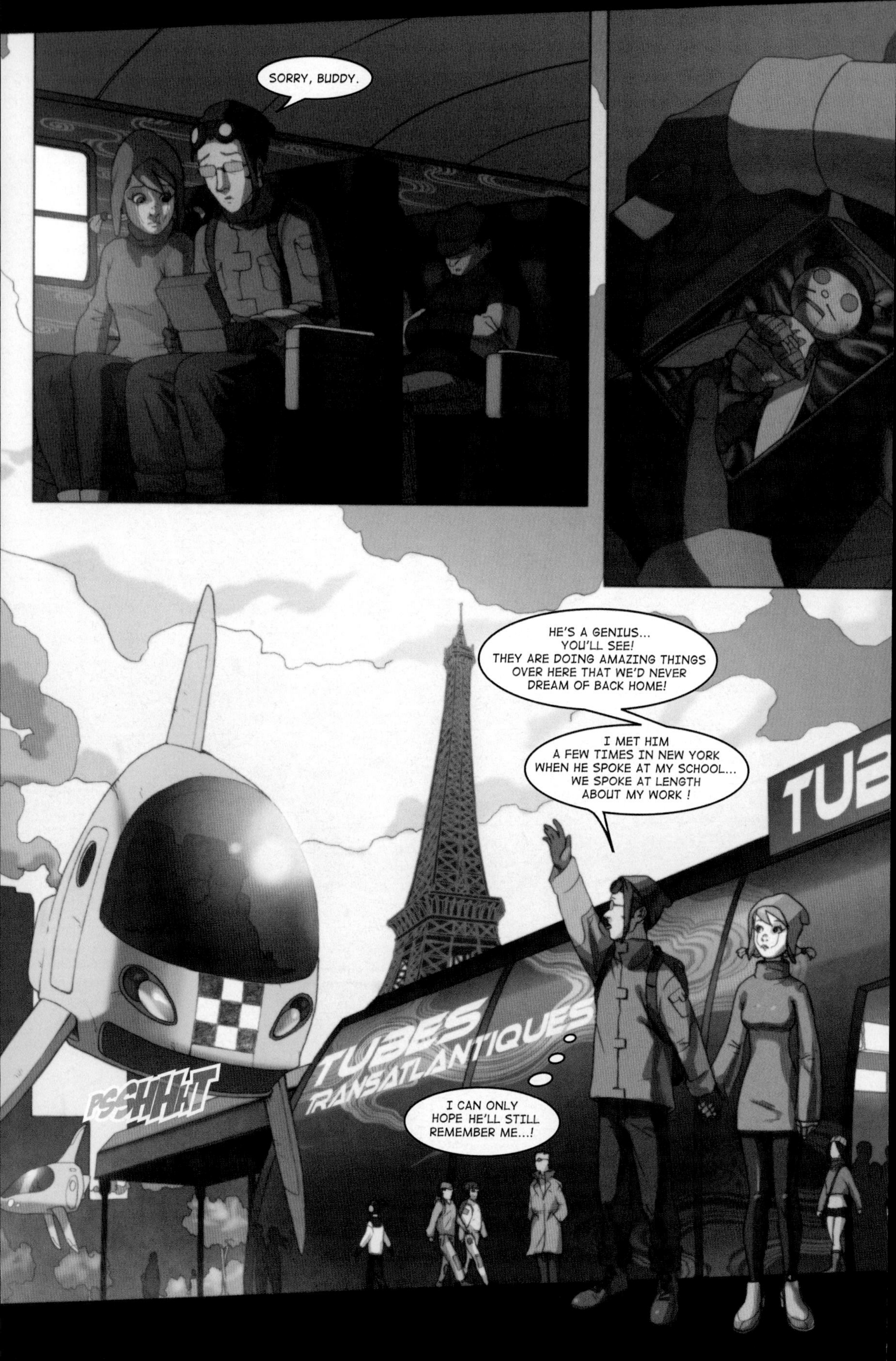
SORRY, BUDDY.
HE'S A GENIUS... YOU'LL SEE! THEY ARE DOING AMAZING THINGS OVER HERE THAT WE'D NEVER DREAM OF BACK HOME!
I MET HIM A FEW TIMES IN NEW YORK WHEN HE SPOKE AT MY SCHOOL... WE SPOKE AT LENGTH ABOUT MY WORK !
TUBES TRANSATLANTIQUES
PSSHHHT
I CAN ONLY HOPE HE'LL STILL REMEMBER ME...!

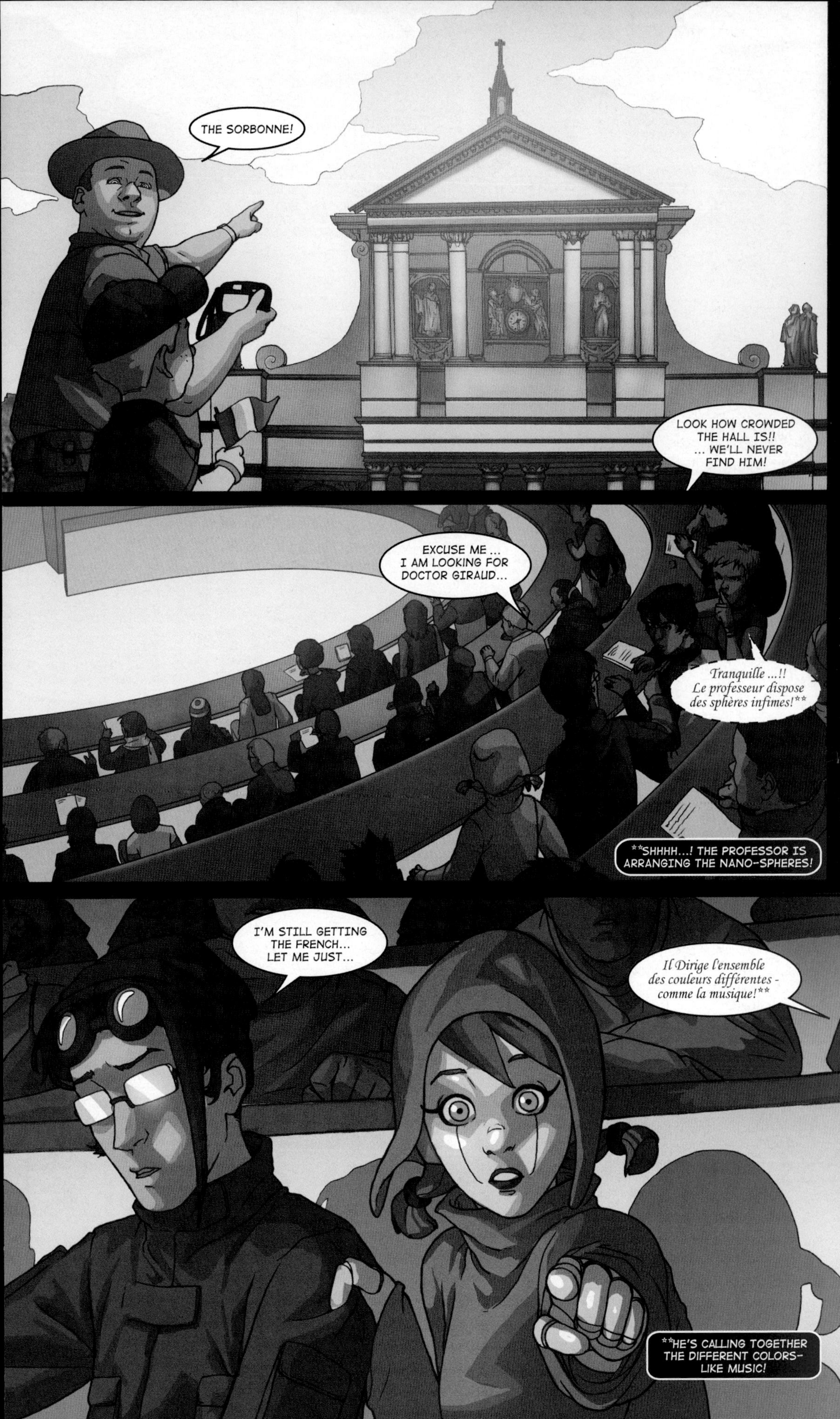
THE SORBONNE!
LOOK HOW CROWDED THE HALL IS!! ... WE'LL NEVER FIND HIM!
EXCUSE ME ... I AM LOOKING FOR DOCTOR GIRAUD...
Tranquille ...!! Le professeur dispose des sphères infimes!**
**SHHHH...! THE PROFESSOR IS ARRANGING THE NANO-SPHERES!
I'M STILL GETTING THE FRENCH... LET ME JUST...
Il Dirige l'ensemble des couleurs différentes - comme la musique!**
**HE'S CALLING TOGETHER THE DIFFERENT COLORS- LIKE MUSIC!

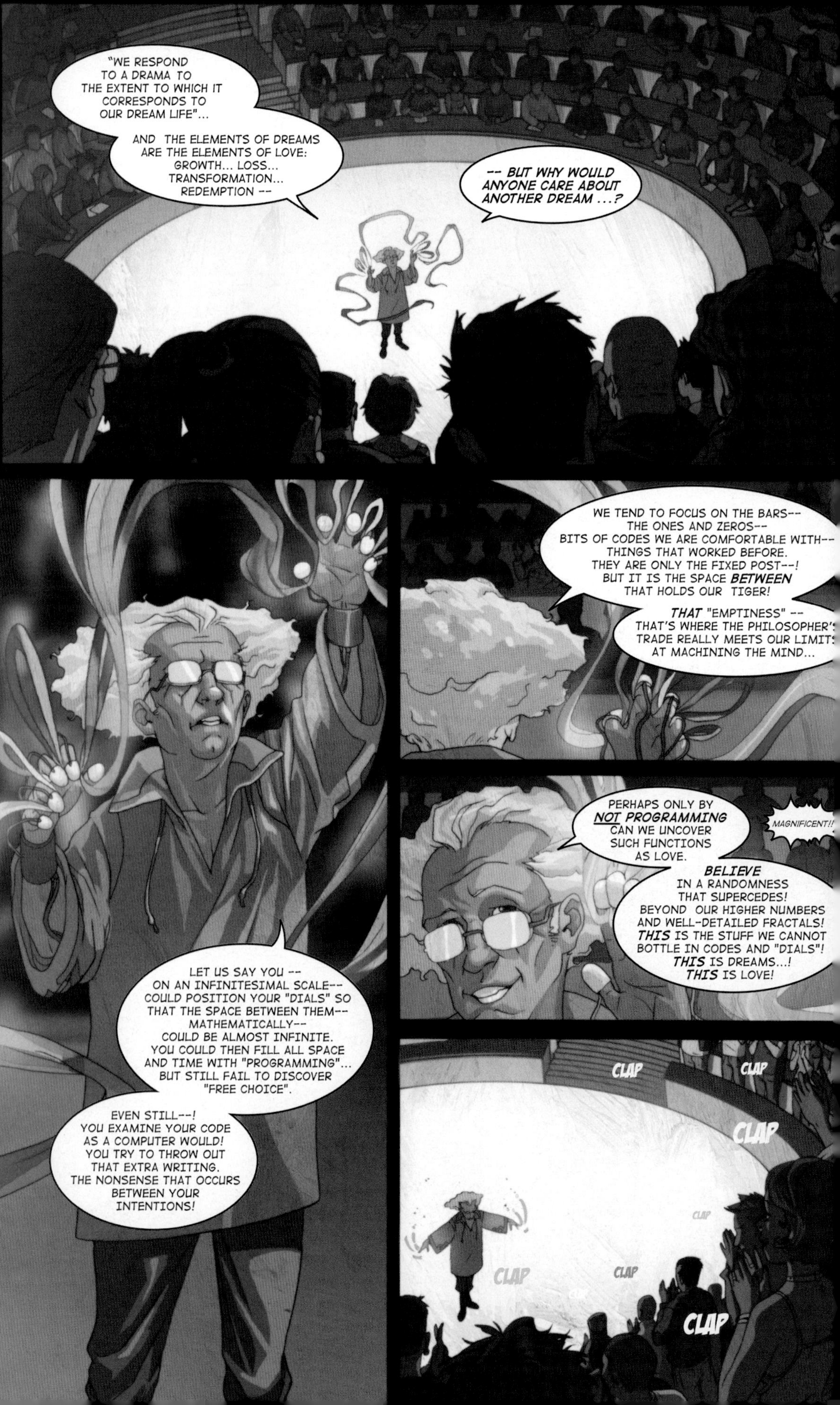
"WE RESPOND TO A DRAMA TO THE EXTENT TO WHICH IT CORRESPONDS TO OUR DREAM LIFE"...
AND THE ELEMENTS OF DREAMS ARE THE ELEMENTS OF LOVE: GROWTH... LOSS... TRANSFORMATION... REDEMPTION --
-- BUT WHY WOULD ANYONE CARE ABOUT ANOTHER DREAM ...?
WE TEND TO FOCUS ON THE BARS-- THE ONES AND ZEROS-- BITS OF CODES WE ARE COMFORTABLE WITH-- THINGS THAT WORKED BEFORE. THEY ARE ONLY THE FIXED POST--! BUT IT IS THE SPACE BETWEEN THAT HOLDS OUR TIGER!
THAT "EMPTINESS" -- THAT'S WHERE THE PHILOSOPHER'S TRADE REALLY MEETS OUR LIMITS AT MACHINING THE MIND...
LET US SAY YOU -- ON AN INFINITESIMAL SCALE-- COULD POSITION YOUR "DIALS" SO THAT THE SPACE BETWEEN THEM-- MATHEMATICALLY-- COULD BE ALMOST INFINITE. YOU COULD THEN FILL ALL SPACE AND TIME WITH "PROGRAMMING"... BUT STILL FAIL TO DISCOVER "FREE CHOICE".
EVEN STILL--! YOU EXAMINE YOUR CODE AS A COMPUTER WOULD! YOU TRY TO THROW OUT THAT EXTRA WRITING. THE NONSENSE THAT OCCURS BETWEEN YOUR INTENTIONS!
PERHAPS ONLY BY NOT PROGRAMMING CAN WE UNCOVER SUCH FUNCTIONS AS LOVE.
MAGNIFICENT!!
BELIEVE IN A RANDOMNESS THAT SUPERCEDES! BEYOND OUR HIGHER NUMBERS AND WELL-DETAILED FRACTALS! THIS IS THE STUFF WE CANNOT BOTTLE IN CODES AND "DIALS"! THIS IS DREAMS...! THIS IS LOVE!
CLAP
CLAP
CLAP
CLAP
CLAP
CLAP
CLAP

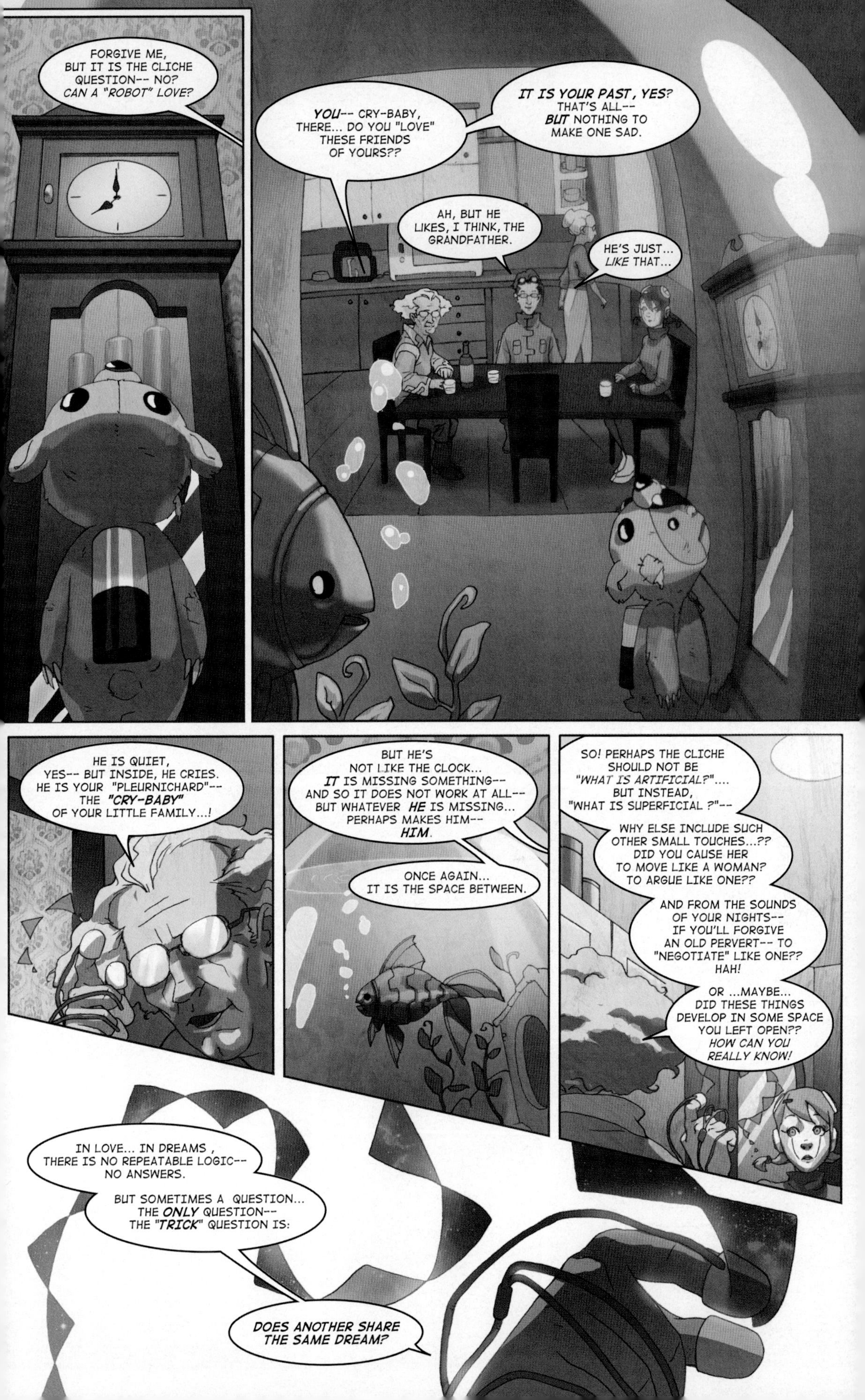
FORGIVE ME, BUT IT IS THE CLICHE QUESTION-- NO? CAN A "ROBOT" LOVE?
YOU-- CRY-BABY, THERE... DO YOU "LOVE" THESE FRIENDS OF YOURS??
IT IS YOUR PAST, YES? THAT'S ALL-- BUT NOTHING TO MAKE ONE SAD.
AH, BUT HE LIKES, I THINK, THE GRANDFATHER.
HE'S JUST... LIKE THAT...
HE IS QUIET, YES-- BUT INSIDE, HE CRIES. HE IS YOUR "PLEURNICHARD"-- THE "CRY-BABY" OF YOUR LITTLE FAMILY...!
BUT HE'S NOT LIKE THE CLOCK... IT IS MISSING SOMETHING-- AND SO IT DOES NOT WORK AT ALL-- BUT WHATEVER HE IS MISSING... PERHAPS MAKES HIM-- HIM.
ONCE AGAIN... IT IS THE SPACE BETWEEN.
SO! PERHAPS THE CLICHE SHOULD NOT BE "WHAT IS ARTIFICIAL?".... BUT INSTEAD, "WHAT IS SUPERFICIAL ?"--
WHY ELSE INCLUDE SUCH OTHER SMALL TOUCHES...?? DID YOU CAUSE HER TO MOVE LIKE A WOMAN? TO ARGUE LIKE ONE??
AND FROM THE SOUNDS OF YOUR NIGHTS-- IF YOU'LL FORGIVE AN OLD PERVERT-- TO "NEGOTIATE" LIKE ONE?? HAH!
OR ...MAYBE... DID THESE THINGS DEVELOP IN SOME SPACE YOU LEFT OPEN?? HOW CAN YOU REALLY KNOW!
IN LOVE... IN DREAMS , THERE IS NO REPEATABLE LOGIC-- NO ANSWERS.
BUT SOMETIMES A QUESTION... THE ONLY QUESTION-- THE "TRICK" QUESTION IS:
DOES ANOTHER SHARE THE SAME DREAM?

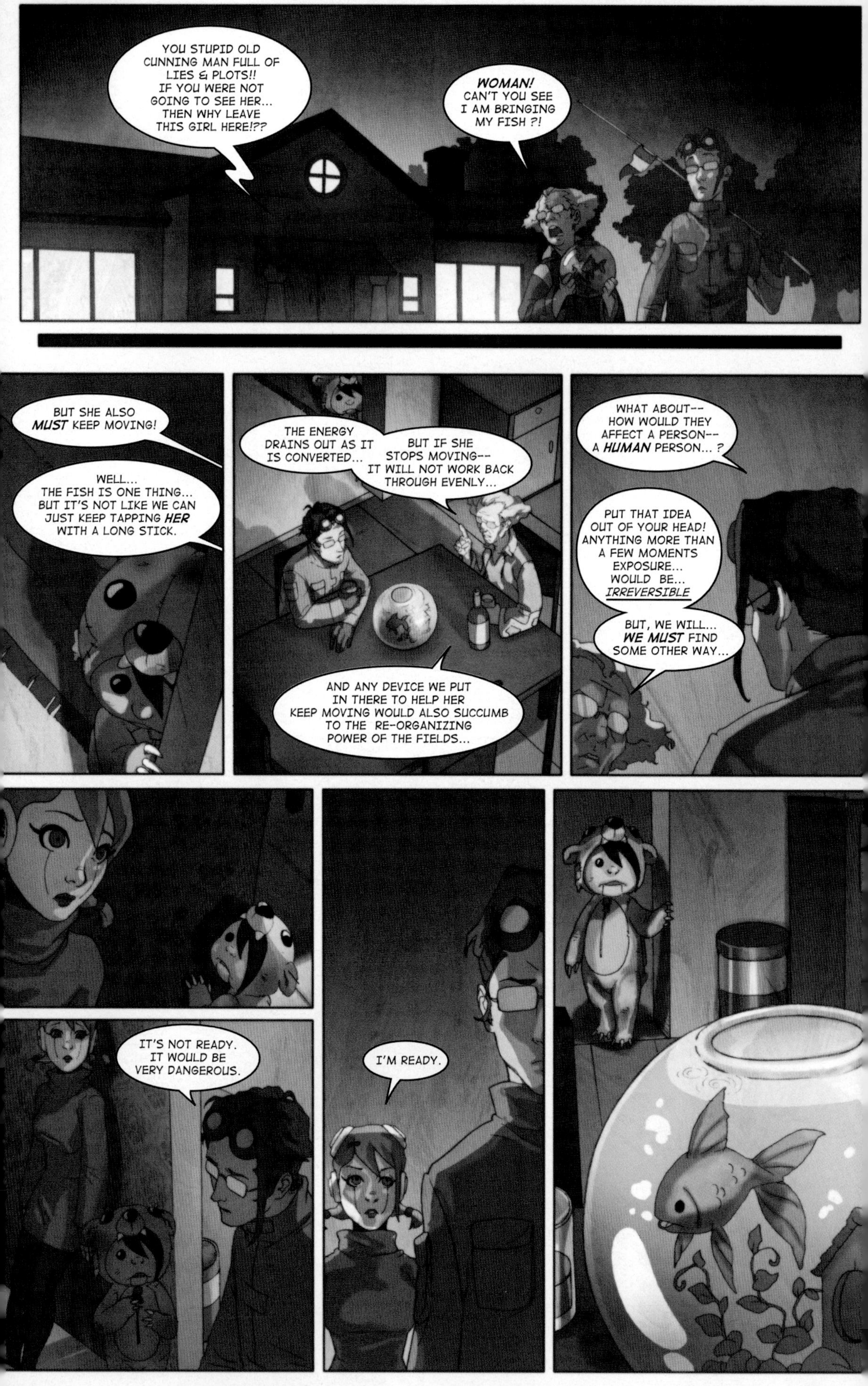
YOU STUPID OLD CUNNING MAN FULL OF LIES & PLOTS!! IF YOU WERE NOT GOING TO SEE HER... THEN WHY LEAVE THIS GIRL HERE!??
WOMAN! CAN'T YOU SEE I AM BRINGING MY FISH ?!
BUT SHE ALSO MUST KEEP MOVING!
WELL... THE FISH IS ONE THING... BUT IT'S NOT LIKE WE CAN JUST KEEP TAPPING HER WITH A LONG STICK.
THE ENERGY DRAINS OUT AS IT IS CONVERTED...
BUT IF SHE STOPS MOVING-- IT WILL NOT WORK BACK THROUGH EVENLY...
AND ANY DEVICE WE PUT IN THERE TO HELP HER KEEP MOVING WOULD ALSO SUCCUMB TO THE RE-ORGANIZING POWER OF THE FIELDS...
WHAT ABOUT-- HOW WOULD THEY AFFECT A PERSON-- A HUMAN PERSON... ?
PUT THAT IDEA OUT OF YOUR HEAD! ANYTHING MORE THAN A FEW MOMENTS EXPOSURE... WOULD BE... IRREVERSIBLE
BUT, WE WILL... WE MUST FIND SOME OTHER WAY...
IT'S NOT READY. IT WOULD BE VERY DANGEROUS.
I'M READY.

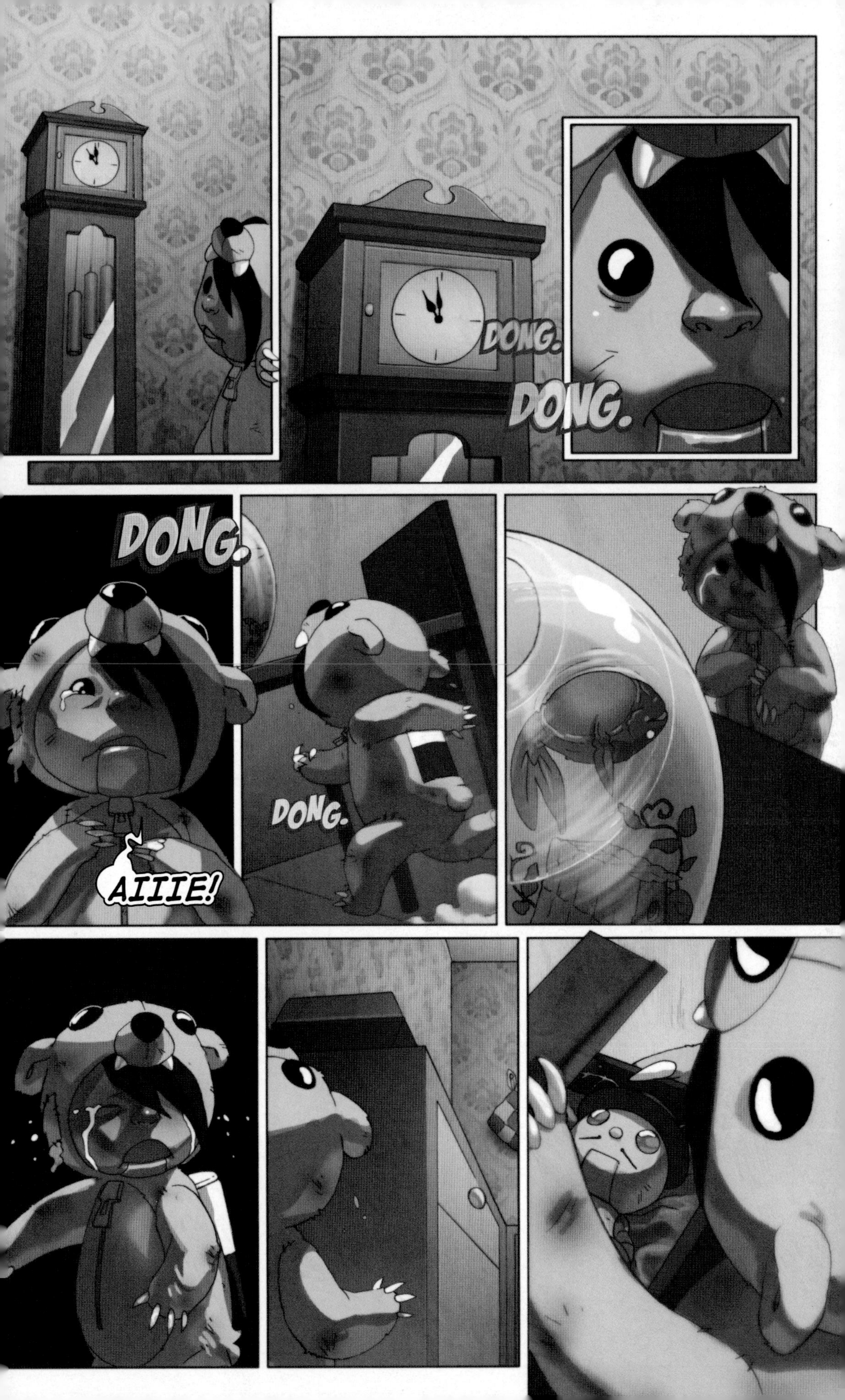
DONG.
DONG.
DONG.
AIIIE!
DONG.

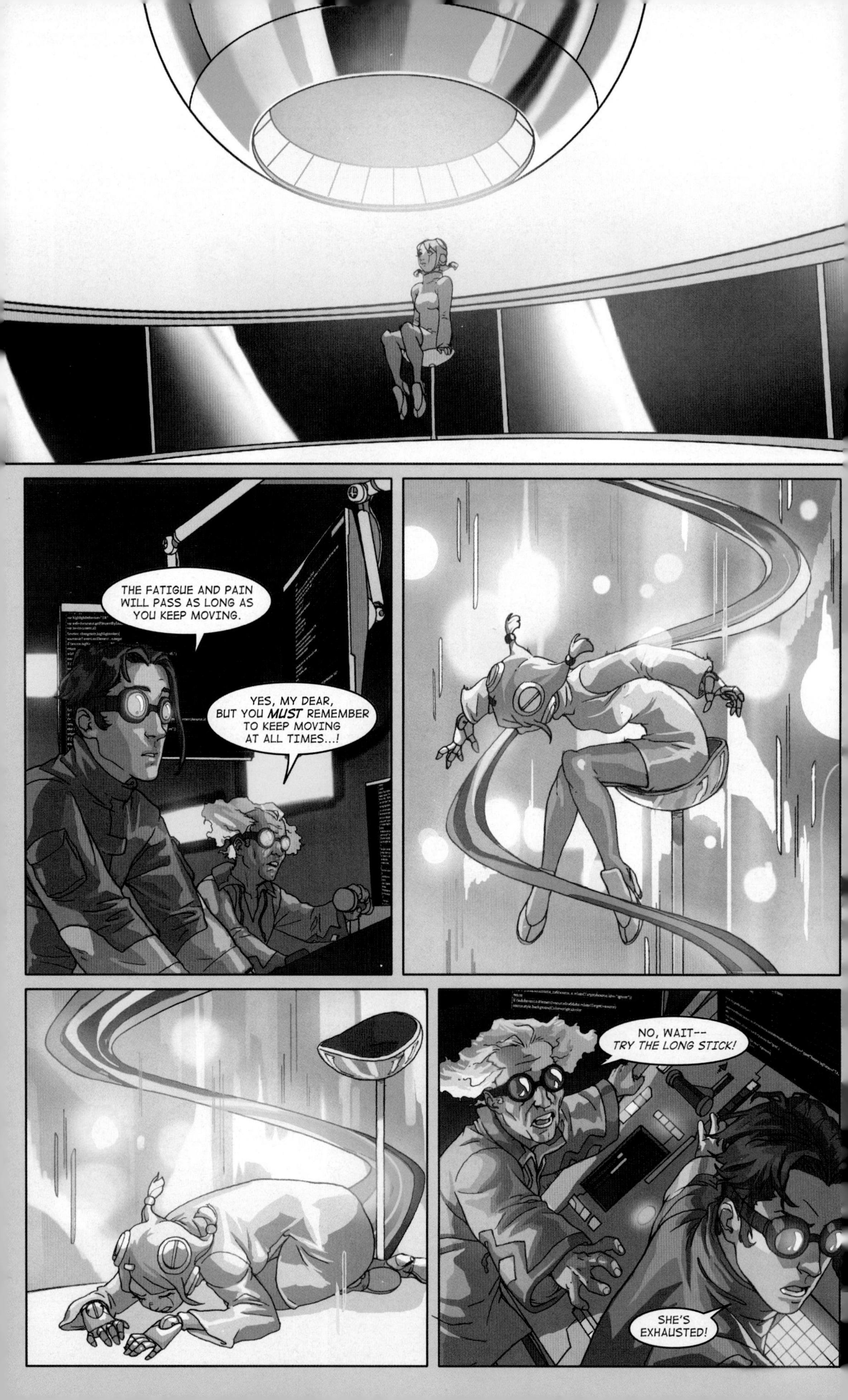
THE FATIGUE AND PAIN WILL PASS AS LONG AS YOU KEEP MOVING.
YES, MY DEAR, BUT YOU *MUST* REMEMBER TO KEEP MOVING AT ALL TIMES...!
NO, WAIT-- *TRY THE LONG STICK!*
SHE'S EXHAUSTED!

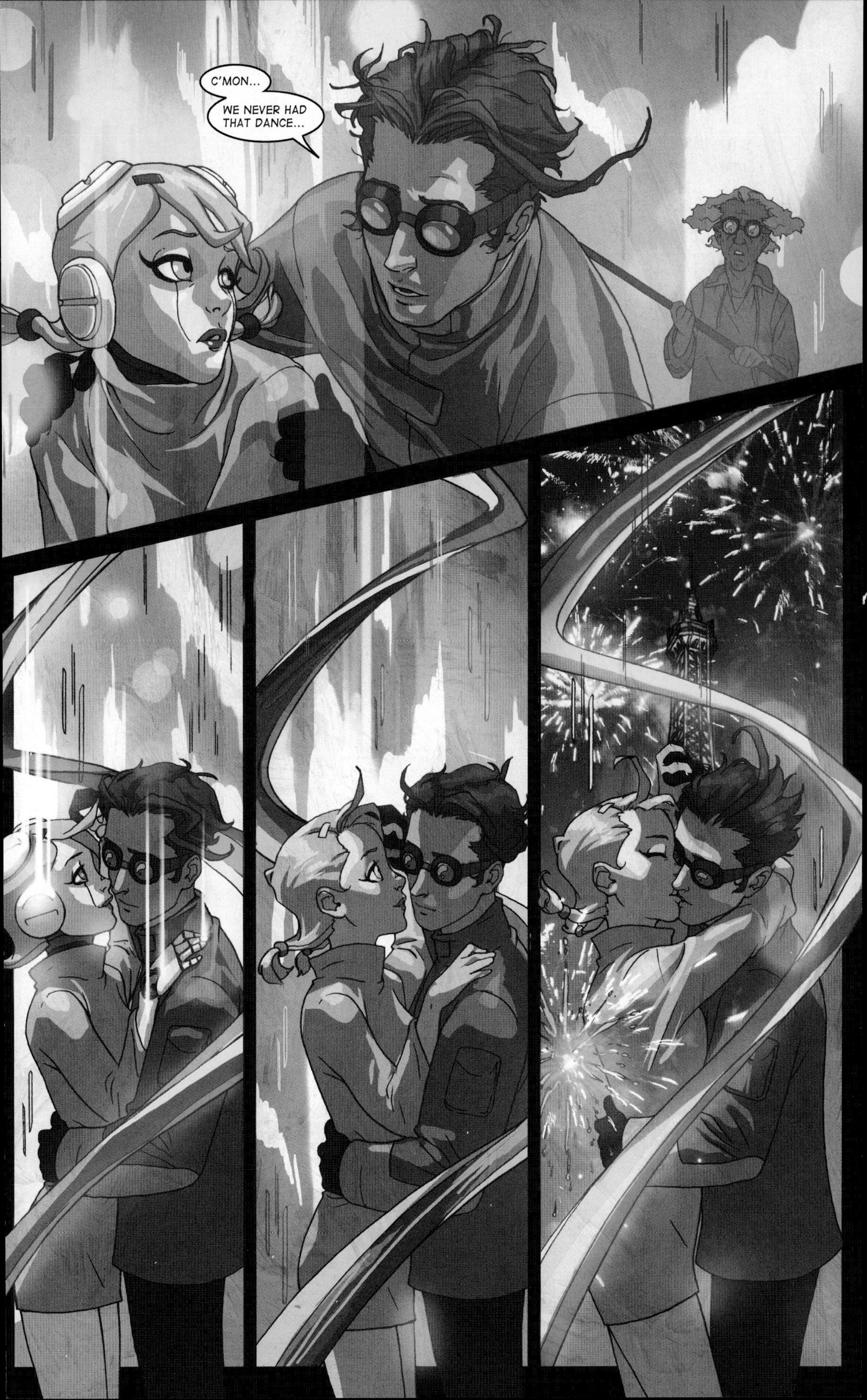
C'MON...
WE NEVER HAD THAT DANCE...

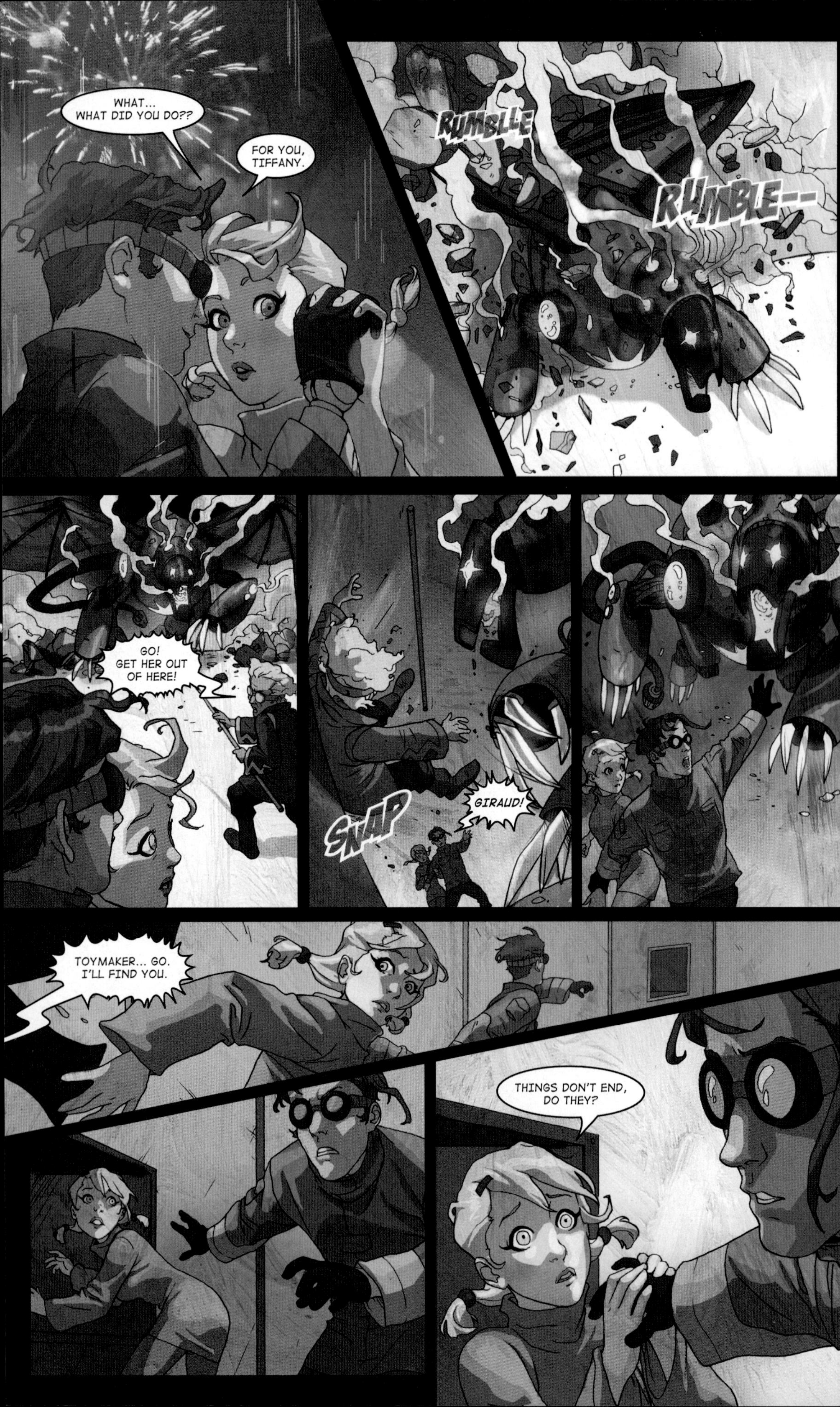

WHAT... WHAT DID YOU DO??
FOR YOU, TIFFANY.
RUMBLLE
RUMBLE--
GO! GET HER OUT OF HERE!
SNAP
GIRAUD!
TOYMAKER... GO. I'LL FIND YOU.
THINGS DON'T END, DO THEY?

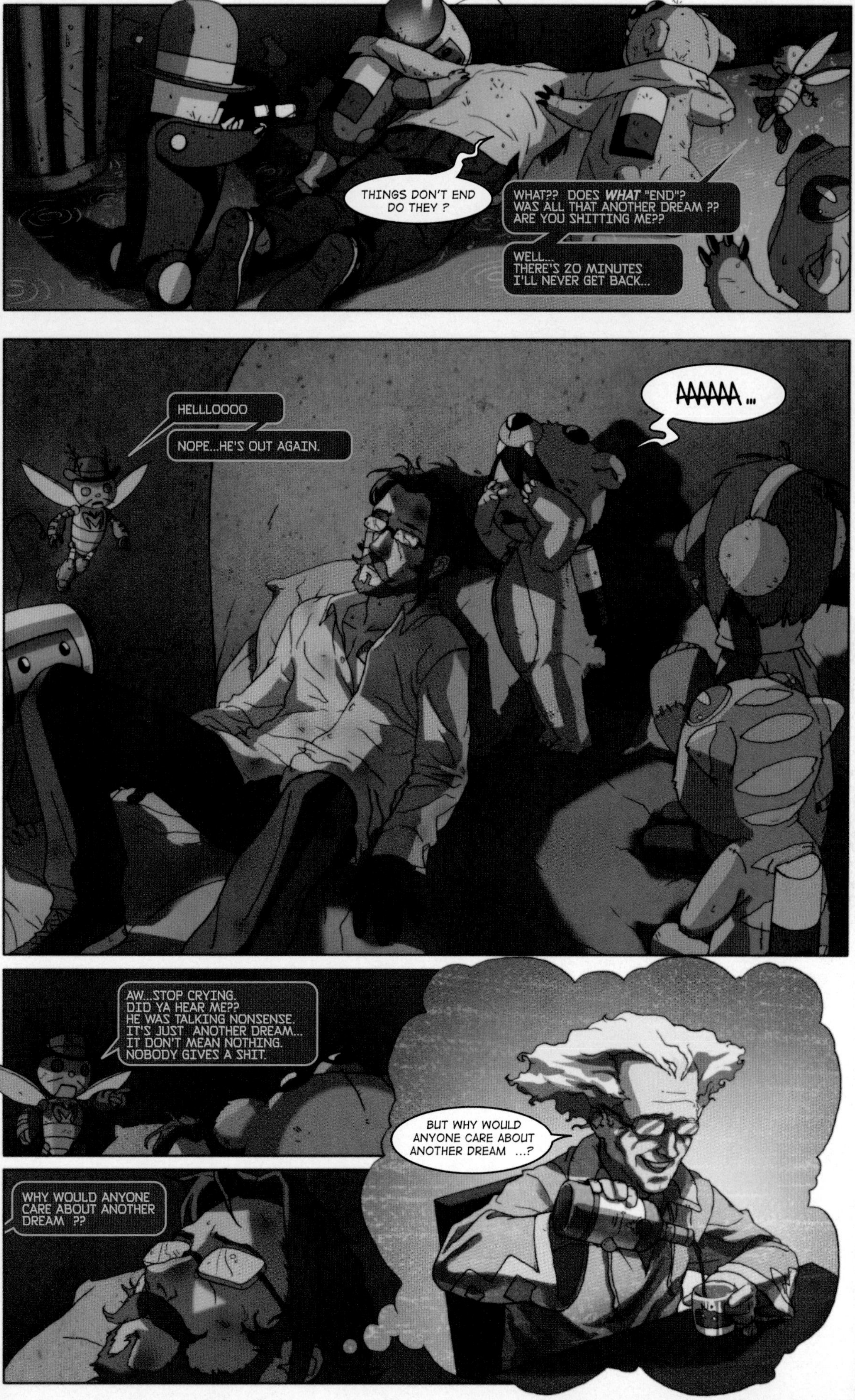
THINGS DON'T END DO THEY ?
WHAT?? DOES *WHAT* "END"? WAS ALL THAT ANOTHER DREAM ?? ARE YOU SHITTING ME??
WELL... THERE'S 20 MINUTES I'LL NEVER GET BACK...
HELLLOOOO
NOPE...HE'S OUT AGAIN.
AAAAAA...
AW...STOP CRYING. DID YA HEAR ME?? HE WAS TALKING NONSENSE. IT'S JUST ANOTHER DREAM... IT DON'T MEAN NOTHING. NOBODY GIVES A SHIT.
BUT WHY WOULD ANYONE CARE ABOUT ANOTHER DREAM ...?
WHY WOULD ANYONE CARE ABOUT ANOTHER DREAM ??

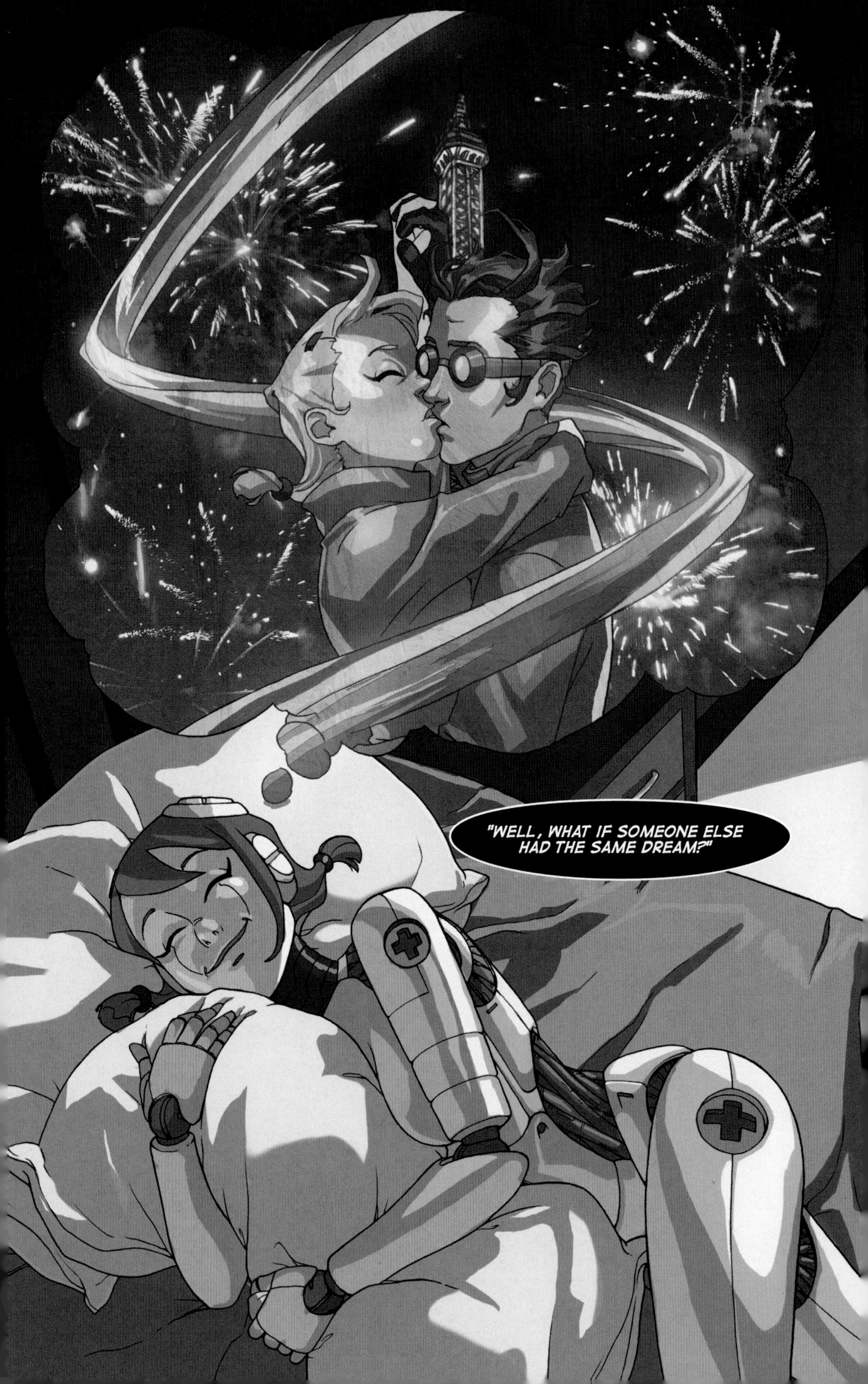
"WELL, WHAT IF SOMEONE ELSE HAD THE SAME DREAM?"

CHAPTER FOUR

"WHY WOULD ANYONE CARE ABOUT ANOTHER DREAM?"

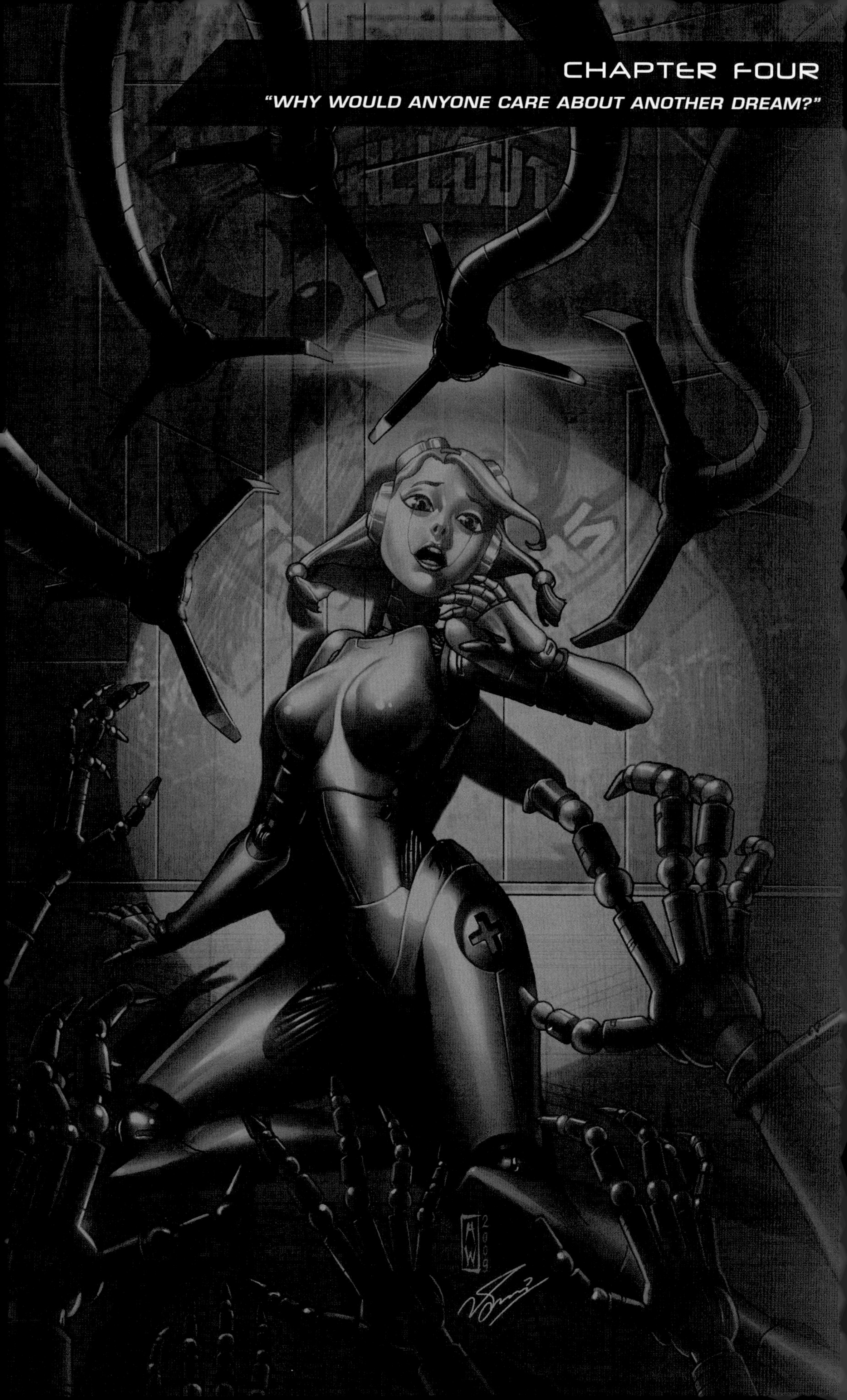

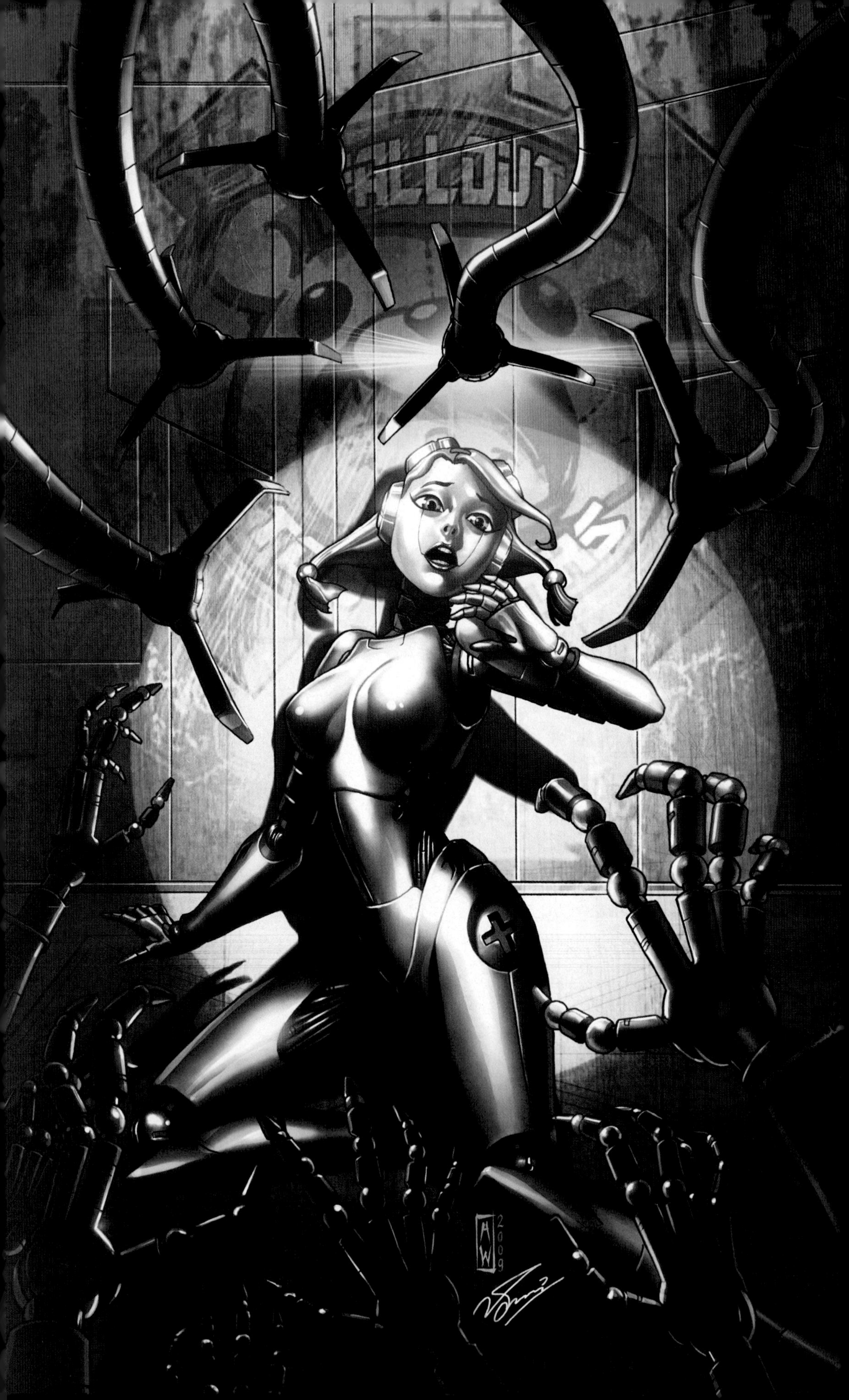

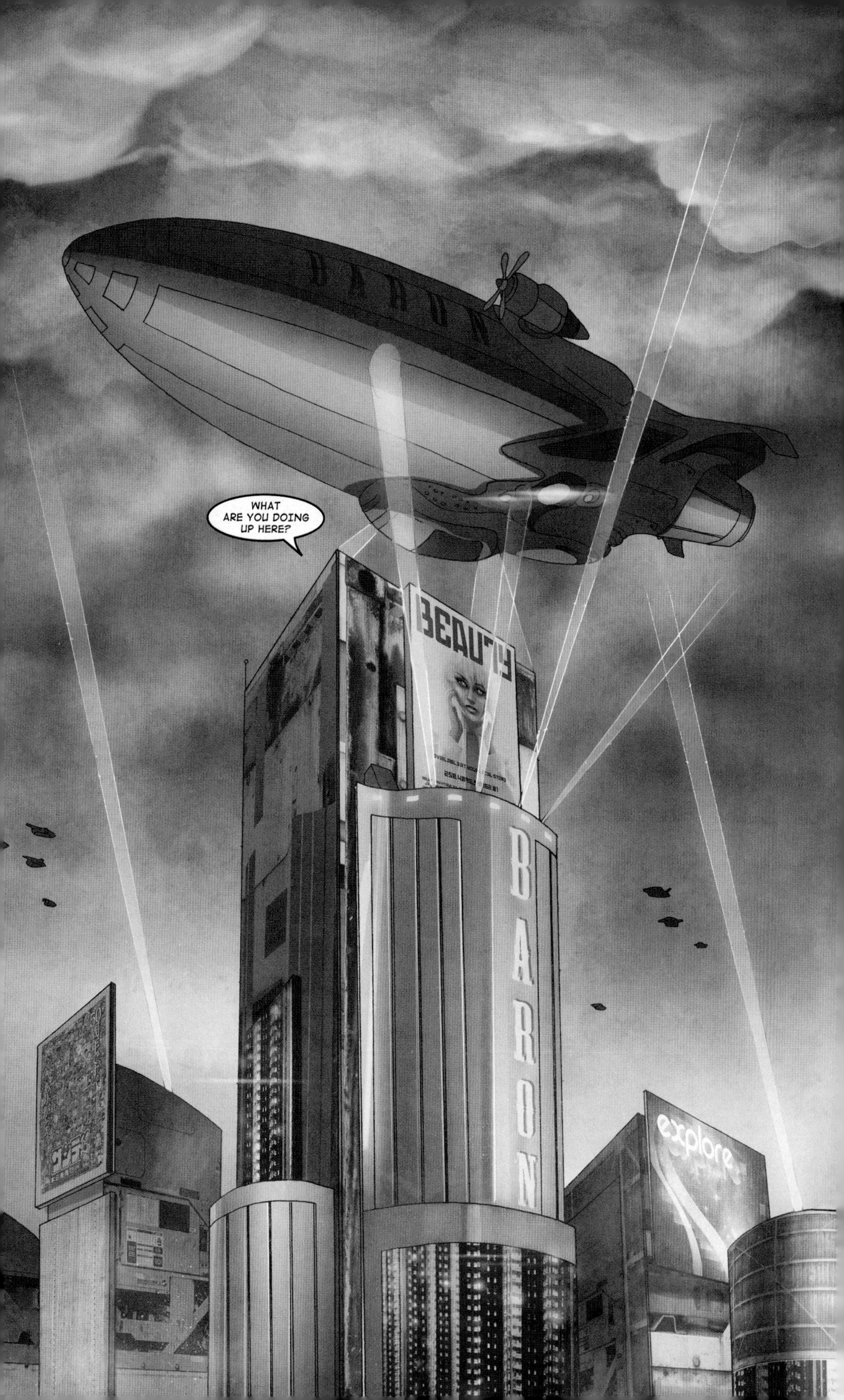

WHAT ARE YOU DOING UP HERE?
BEAUTY
BARON
explore

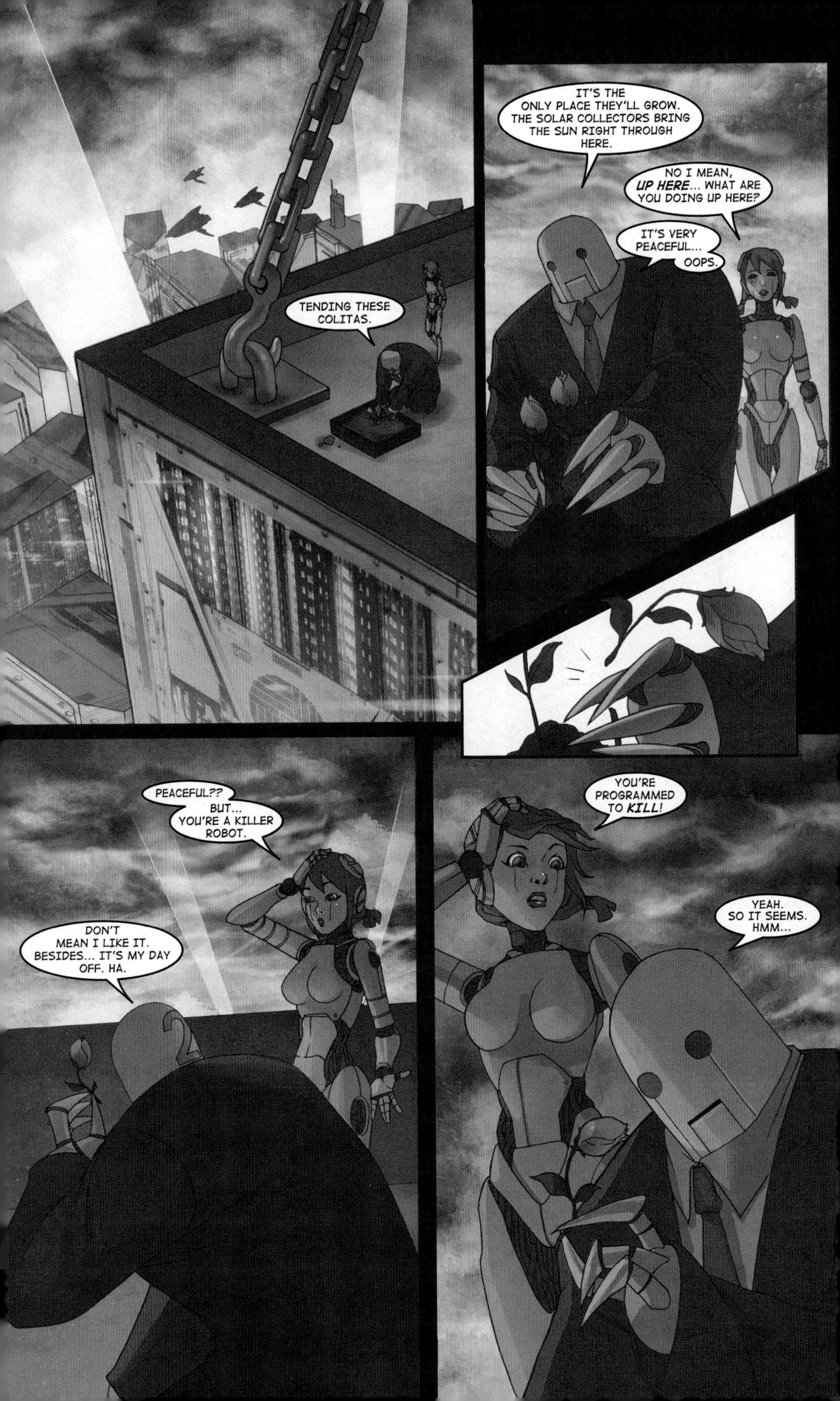
TENDING THESE COLITAS.
IT'S THE ONLY PLACE THEY'LL GROW. THE SOLAR COLLECTORS BRING THE SUN RIGHT THROUGH HERE.
NO I MEAN, *UP HERE*... WHAT ARE YOU DOING UP HERE?
IT'S VERY PEACEFUL...
OOPS.
PEACEFUL?? BUT... YOU'RE A KILLER ROBOT.
DON'T MEAN I LIKE IT. BESIDES... IT'S MY DAY OFF. HA.
YOU'RE PROGRAMMED TO *KILL*!
YEAH. SO IT SEEMS. HMM...

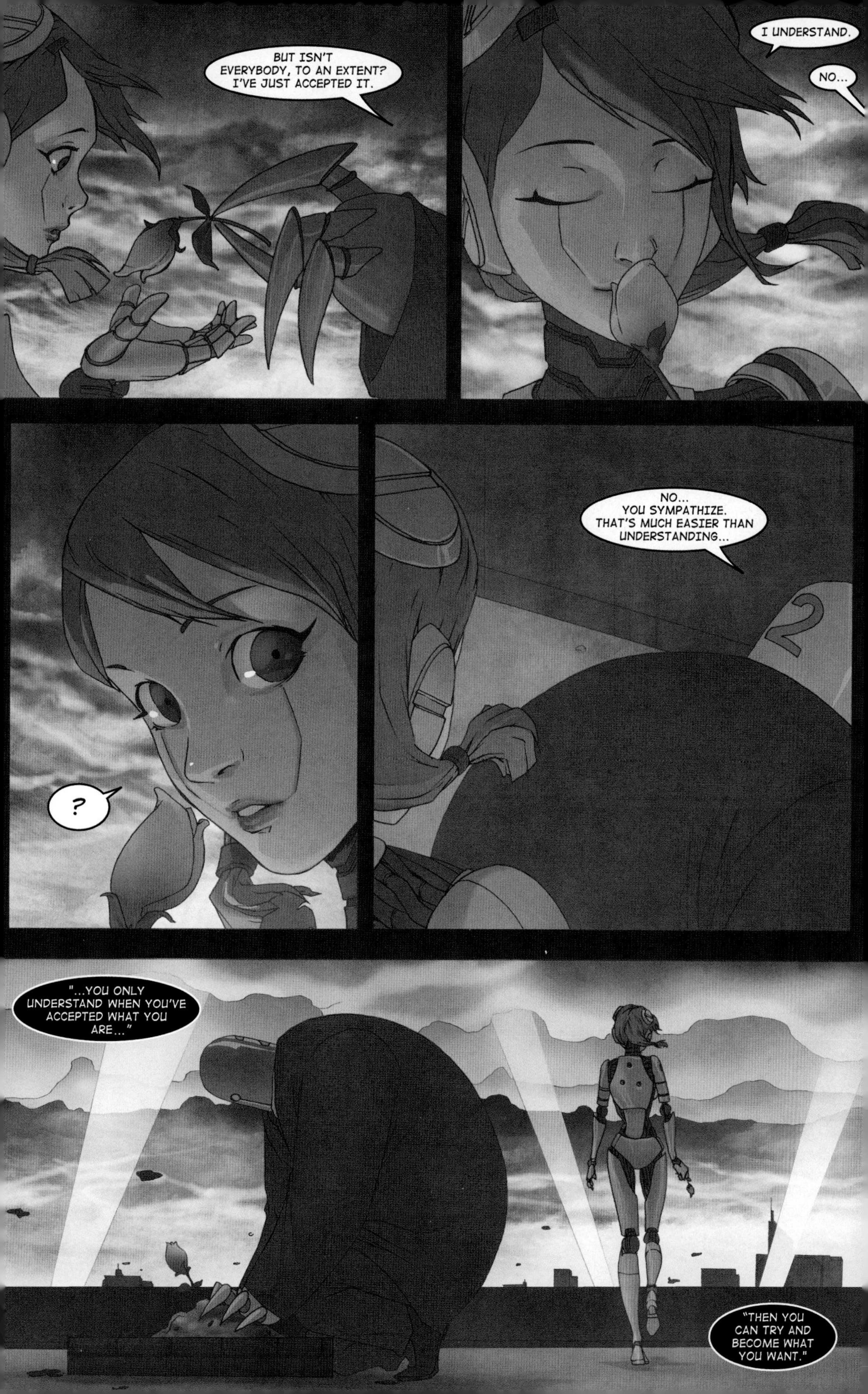
BUT ISN'T EVERYBODY, TO AN EXTENT? I'VE JUST ACCEPTED IT.
I UNDERSTAND.
NO...
?
NO... YOU SYMPATHIZE. THAT'S MUCH EASIER THAN UNDERSTANDING...
"...YOU ONLY UNDERSTAND WHEN YOU'VE ACCEPTED WHAT YOU ARE..."
"THEN YOU CAN TRY AND BECOME WHAT YOU WANT."

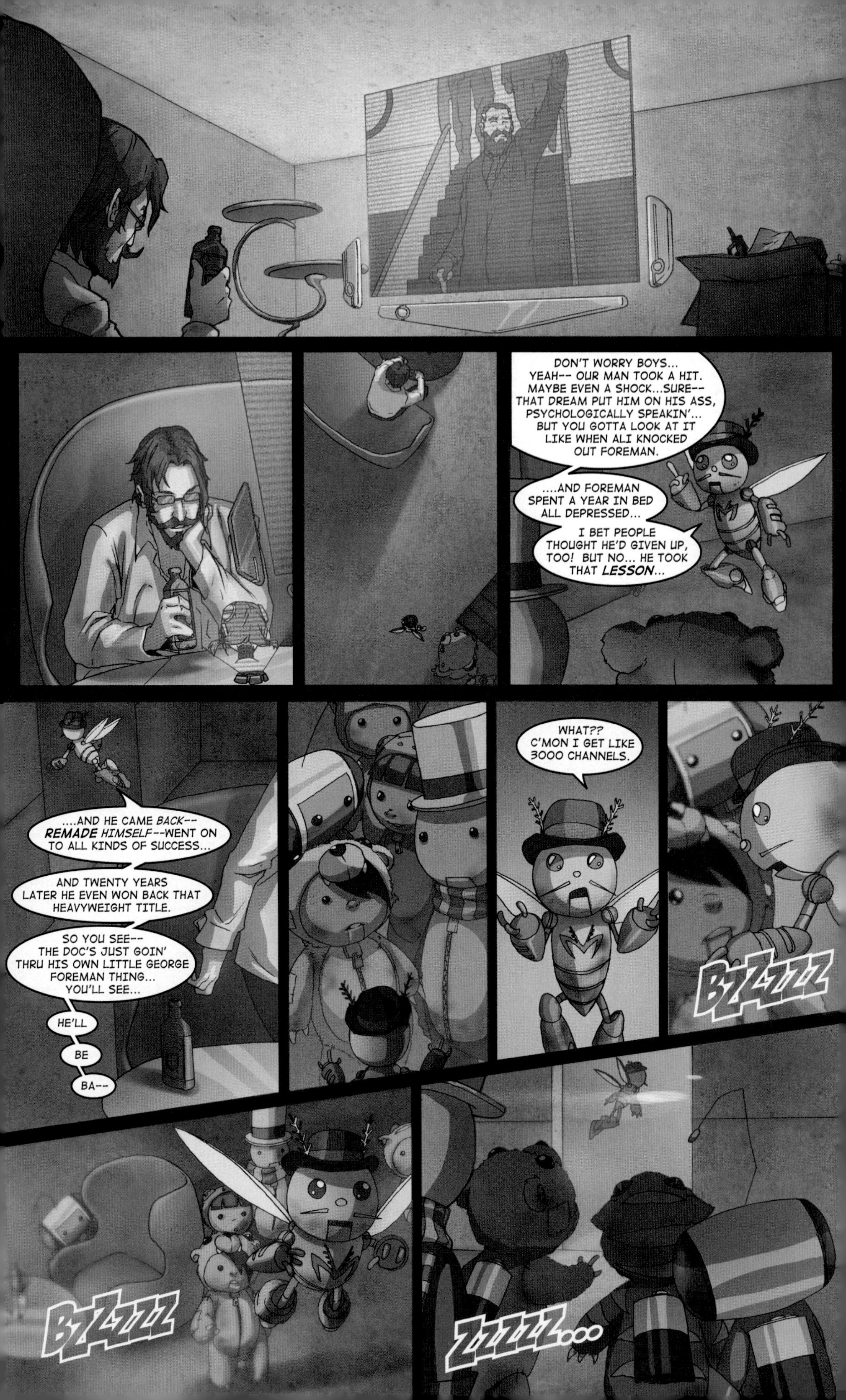
DON'T WORRY BOYS... YEAH-- OUR MAN TOOK A HIT. MAYBE EVEN A SHOCK...SURE-- THAT DREAM PUT HIM ON HIS ASS, PSYCHOLOGICALLY SPEAKIN'... BUT YOU GOTTA LOOK AT IT LIKE WHEN ALI KNOCKED OUT FOREMAN.
....AND FOREMAN SPENT A YEAR IN BED ALL DEPRESSED...
I BET PEOPLE THOUGHT HE'D GIVEN UP, TOO! BUT NO... HE TOOK THAT LESSON...
....AND HE CAME BACK-- REMADE HIMSELF--WENT ON TO ALL KINDS OF SUCCESS...
AND TWENTY YEARS LATER HE EVEN WON BACK THAT HEAVYWEIGHT TITLE.
SO YOU SEE-- THE DOC'S JUST GOIN' THRU HIS OWN LITTLE GEORGE FOREMAN THING... YOU'LL SEE...
HE'LL
BE
BA--
WHAT?? C'MON I GET LIKE 3000 CHANNELS.
BZZZZZ
BZZZZZ
ZZZZZ...

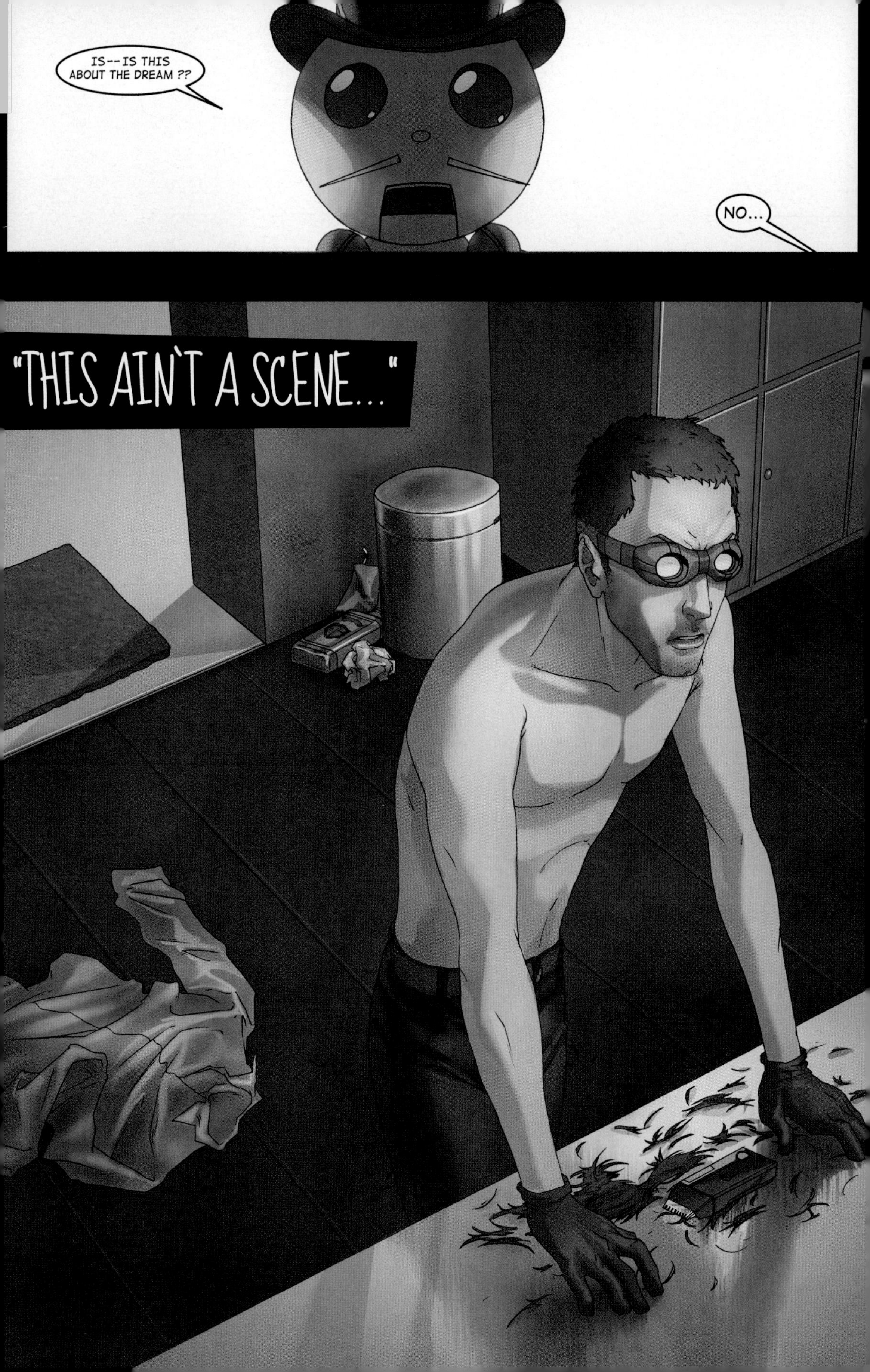
IS--IS THIS ABOUT THE DREAM ??
NO...
"THIS AIN'T A SCENE..."

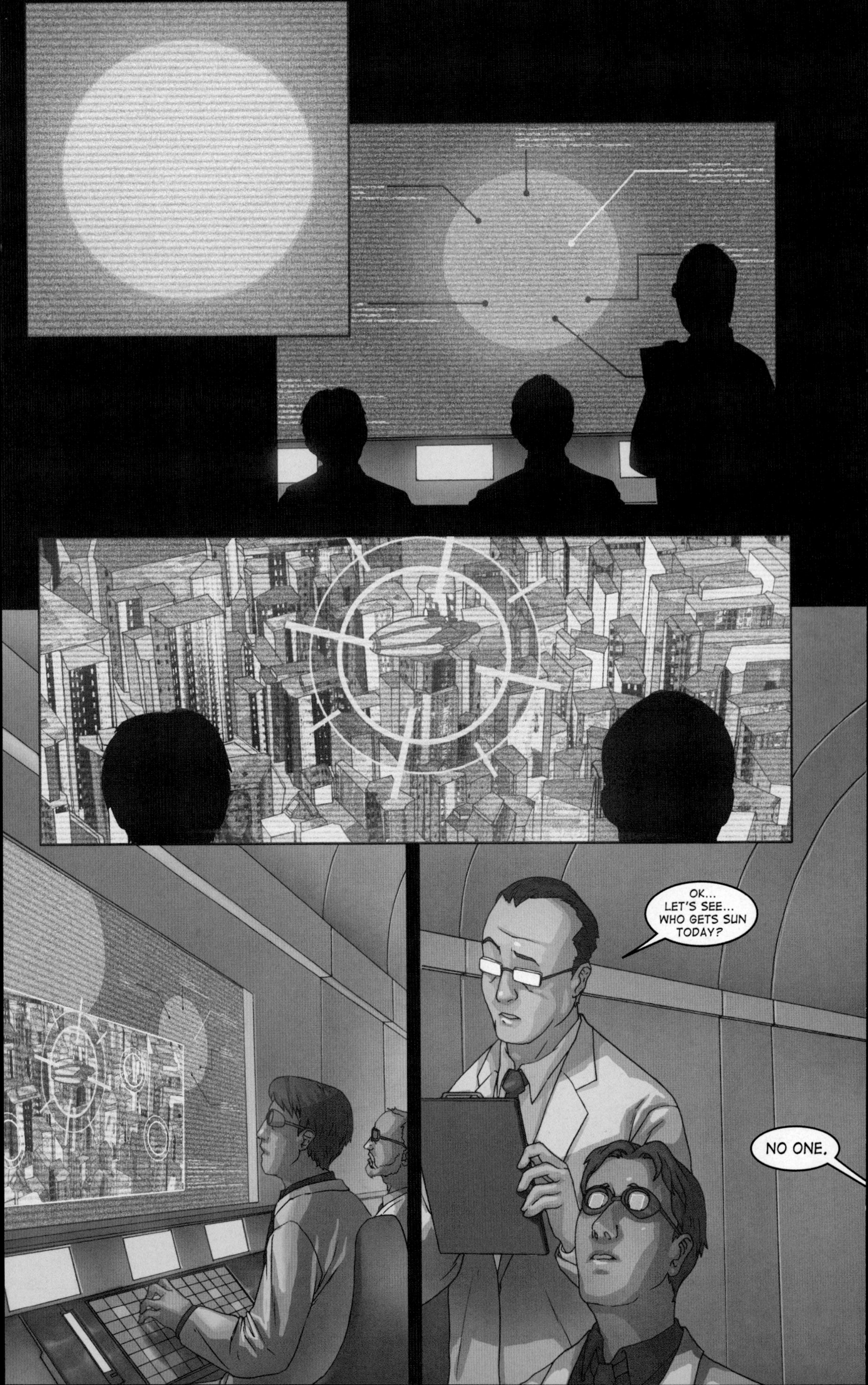
OK... LET'S SEE... WHO GETS SUN TODAY?
NO ONE.

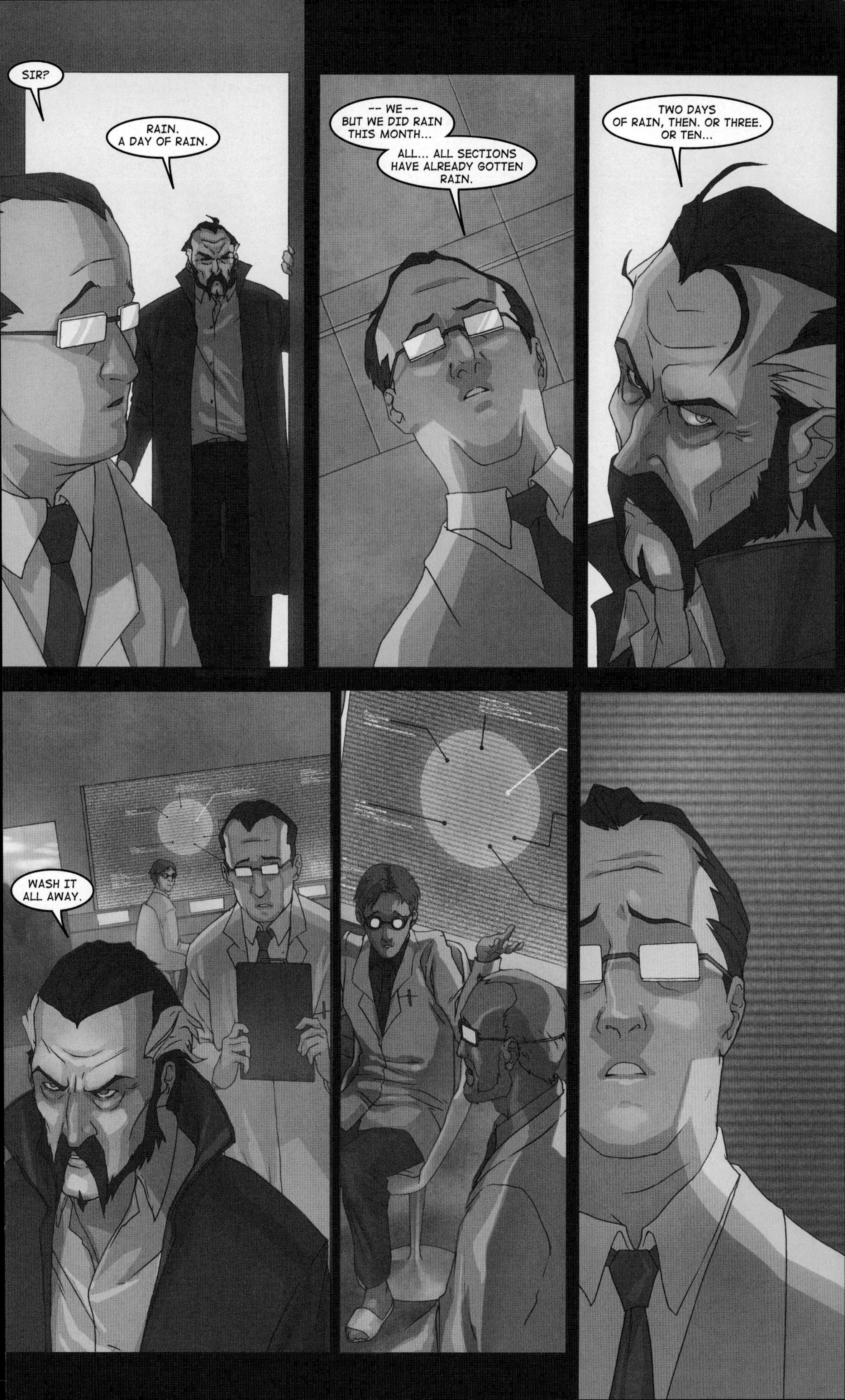
SIR?
RAIN. A DAY OF RAIN.
-- WE -- BUT WE DID RAIN THIS MONTH...
ALL... ALL SECTIONS HAVE ALREADY GOTTEN RAIN.
TWO DAYS OF RAIN, THEN. OR THREE. OR TEN...
WASH IT ALL AWAY.

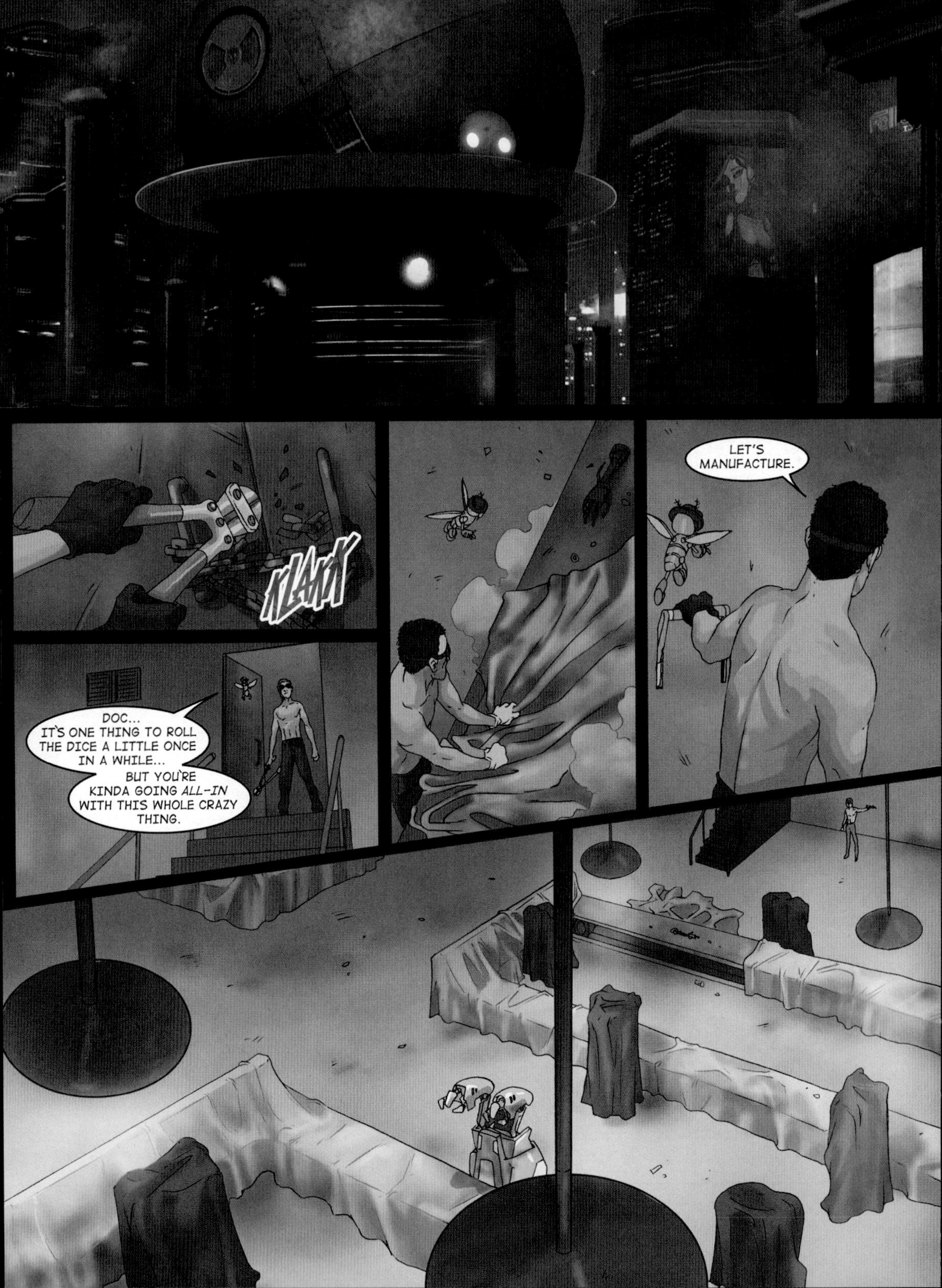
KLANK
LET'S MANUFACTURE.
DOC... IT'S ONE THING TO ROLL THE DICE A LITTLE ONCE IN A WHILE...
BUT YOU'RE KINDA GOING *ALL-IN* WITH THIS WHOLE CRAZY THING.

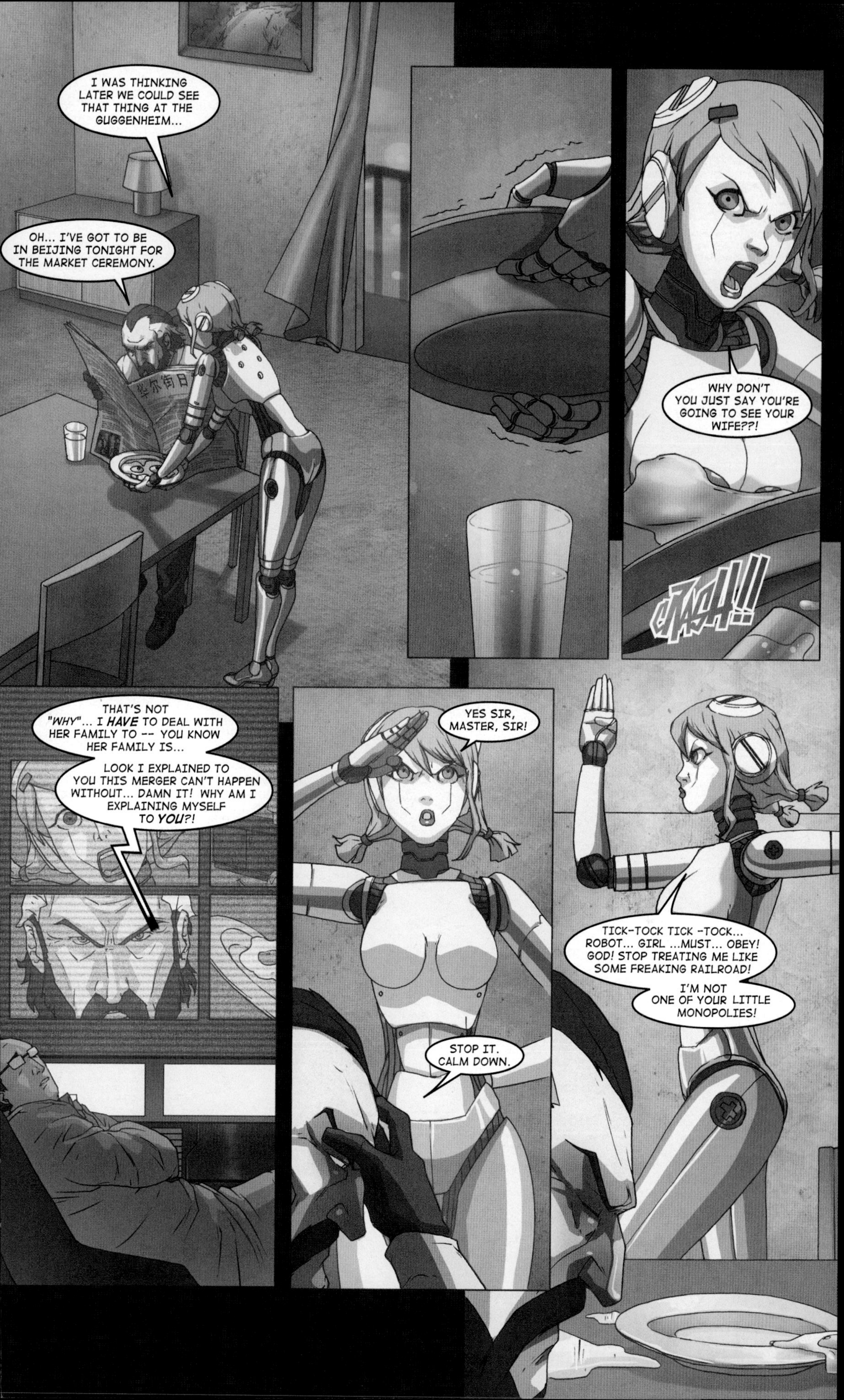
I WAS THINKING LATER WE COULD SEE THAT THING AT THE GUGGENHEIM...
OH... I'VE GOT TO BE IN BEIJING TONIGHT FOR THE MARKET CEREMONY.
华尔街日
WHY DON'T YOU JUST SAY YOU'RE GOING TO SEE YOUR WIFE??!
CRASH!!!
THAT'S NOT "*WHY*"... I ***HAVE*** TO DEAL WITH HER FAMILY TO -- YOU KNOW HER FAMILY IS...
LOOK I EXPLAINED TO YOU THIS MERGER CAN'T HAPPEN WITHOUT... DAMN IT! WHY AM I EXPLAINING MYSELF TO ***YOU***?!
YES SIR, MASTER, SIR!
STOP IT. CALM DOWN.
TICK-TOCK TICK -TOCK... ROBOT... GIRL ...MUST... OBEY! GOD! STOP TREATING ME LIKE SOME FREAKING RAILROAD!
I'M NOT ONE OF YOUR LITTLE MONOPOLIES!

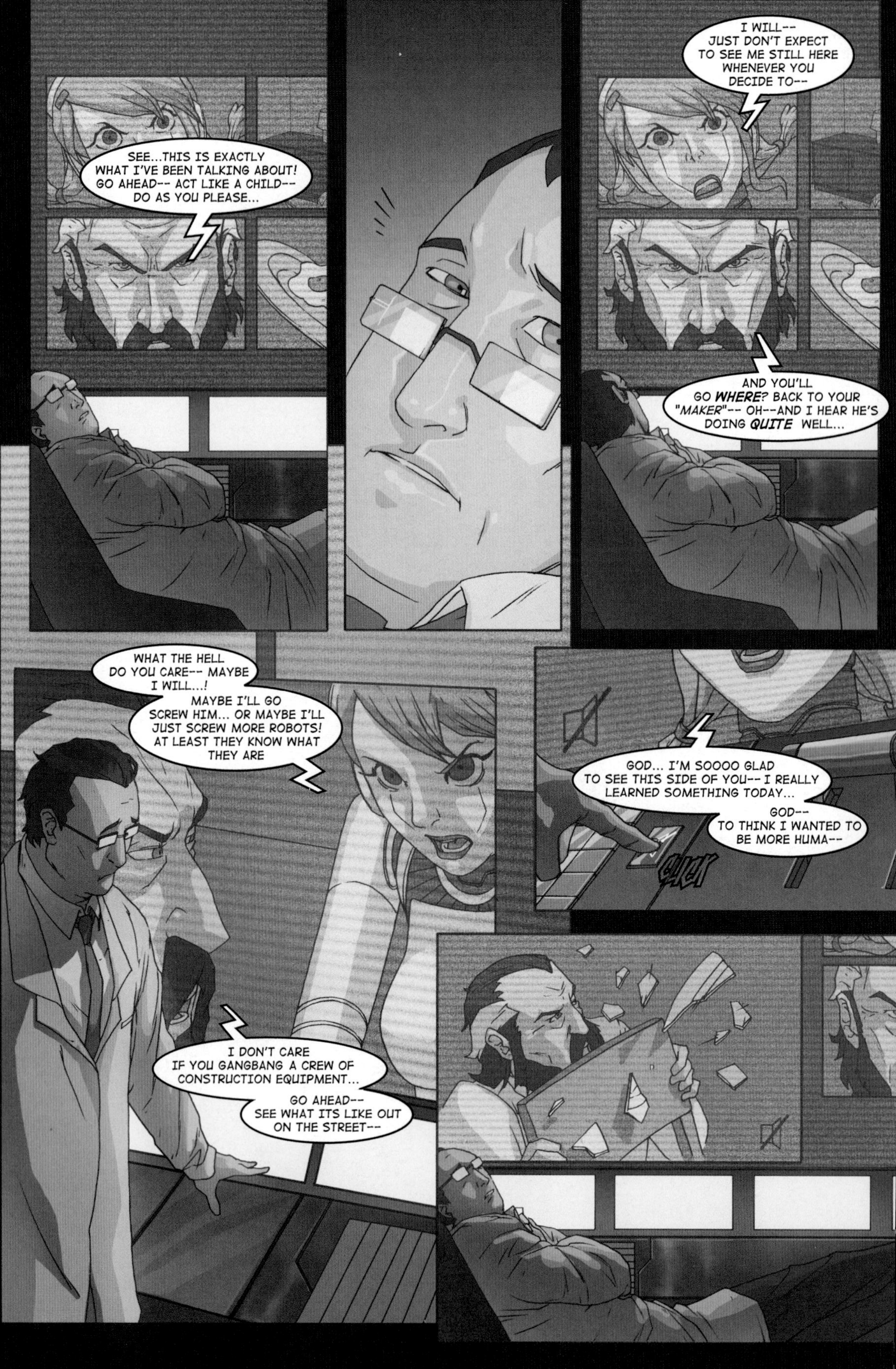
SEE...THIS IS EXACTLY WHAT I'VE BEEN TALKING ABOUT! GO AHEAD-- ACT LIKE A CHILD-- DO AS YOU PLEASE...
I WILL-- JUST DON'T EXPECT TO SEE ME STILL HERE WHENEVER YOU DECIDE TO--
AND YOU'LL GO WHERE? BACK TO YOUR "MAKER"-- OH--AND I HEAR HE'S DOING QUITE WELL...
WHAT THE HELL DO YOU CARE-- MAYBE I WILL...!
MAYBE I'LL GO SCREW HIM... OR MAYBE I'LL JUST SCREW MORE ROBOTS! AT LEAST THEY KNOW WHAT THEY ARE
I DON'T CARE IF YOU GANGBANG A CREW OF CONSTRUCTION EQUIPMENT...
GO AHEAD-- SEE WHAT ITS LIKE OUT ON THE STREET--
GOD... I'M SOOOO GLAD TO SEE THIS SIDE OF YOU-- I REALLY LEARNED SOMETHING TODAY...
GOD-- TO THINK I WANTED TO BE MORE HUMA--
CLICK

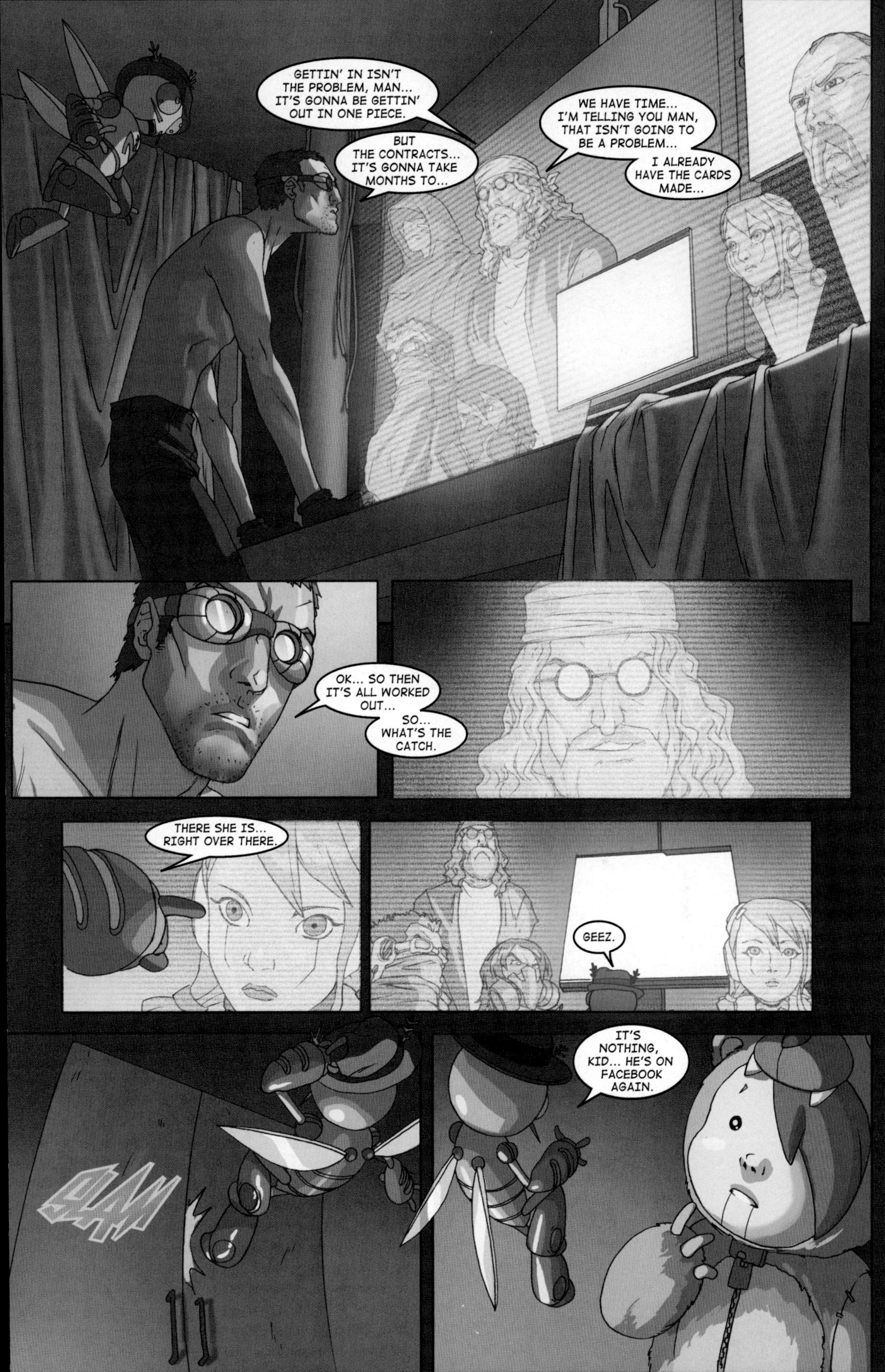
GETTIN' IN ISN'T THE PROBLEM, MAN... IT'S GONNA BE GETTIN' OUT IN ONE PIECE.
BUT THE CONTRACTS... IT'S GONNA TAKE MONTHS TO...
WE HAVE TIME... I'M TELLING YOU MAN, THAT ISN'T GOING TO BE A PROBLEM...
I ALREADY HAVE THE CARDS MADE...
OK... SO THEN IT'S ALL WORKED OUT...
SO... WHAT'S THE CATCH.
THERE SHE IS... RIGHT OVER THERE.
GEEZ.
SLAM
IT'S NOTHING, KID... HE'S ON FACEBOOK AGAIN.

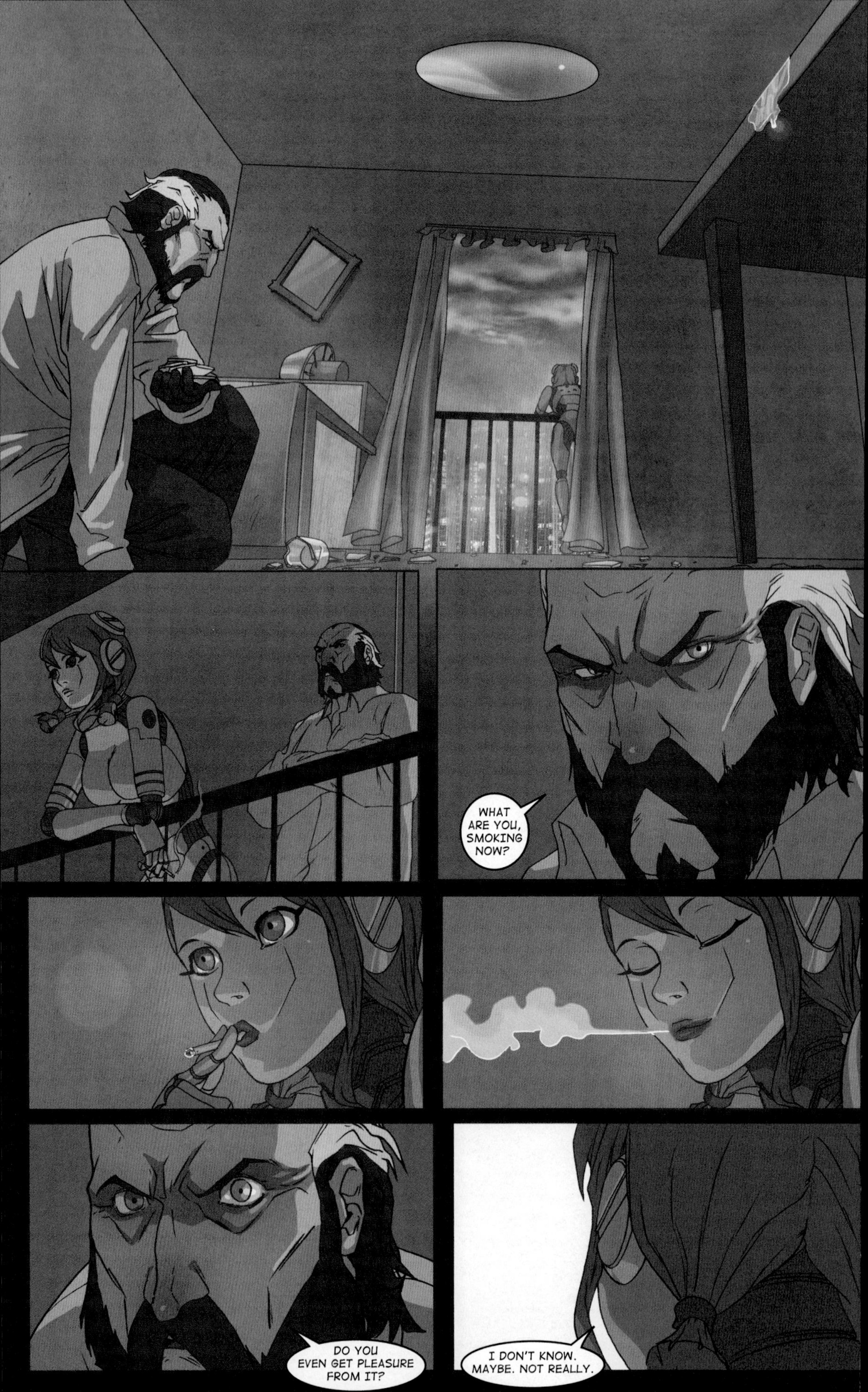
WHAT ARE YOU, SMOKING NOW?
DO YOU EVEN GET PLEASURE FROM IT?
I DON'T KNOW. MAYBE. NOT REALLY.

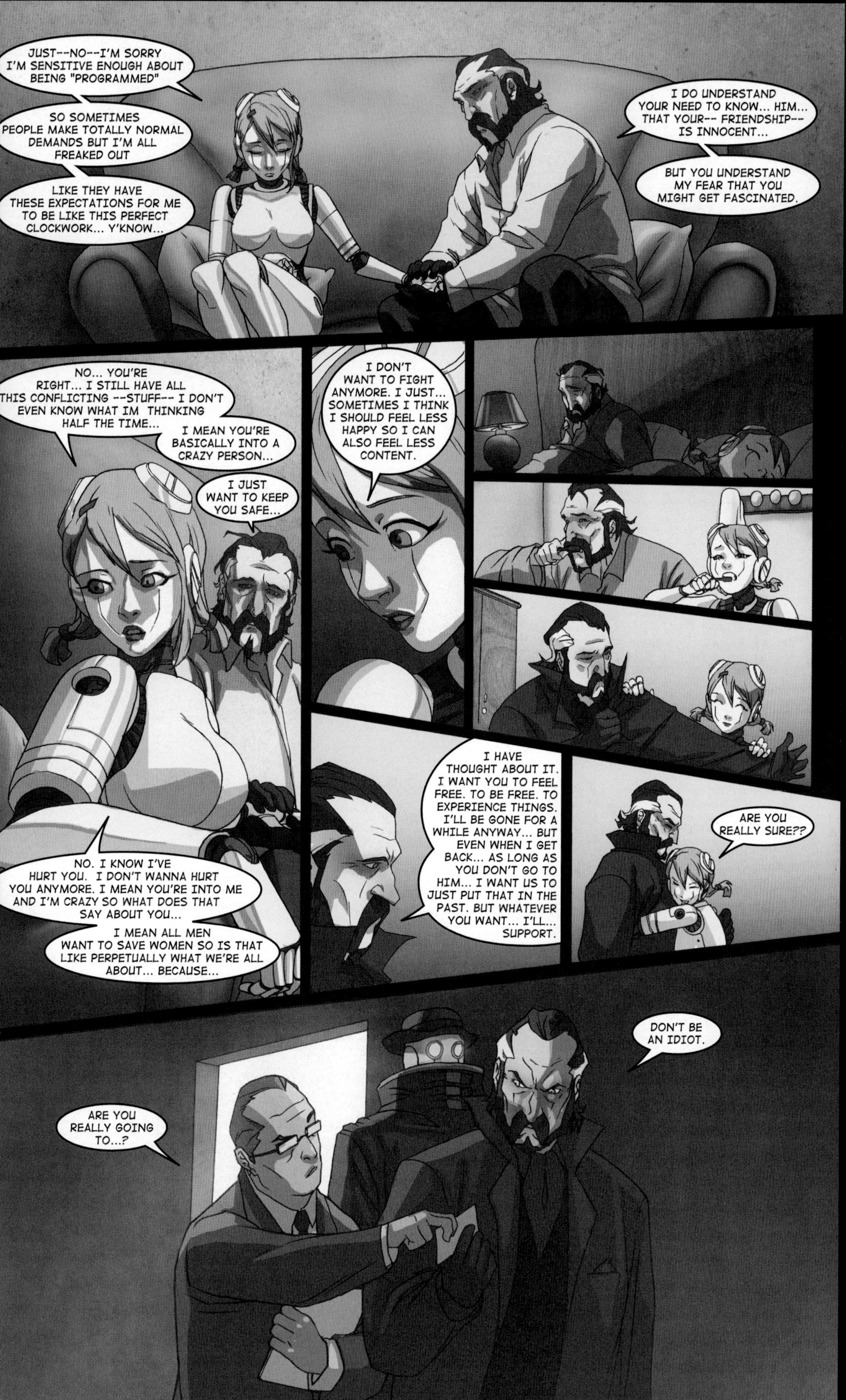
JUST--NO--I'M SORRY I'M SENSITIVE ENOUGH ABOUT BEING "PROGRAMMED"
SO SOMETIMES PEOPLE MAKE TOTALLY NORMAL DEMANDS BUT I'M ALL FREAKED OUT
LIKE THEY HAVE THESE EXPECTATIONS FOR ME TO BE LIKE THIS PERFECT CLOCKWORK... Y'KNOW...
I DO UNDERSTAND YOUR NEED TO KNOW... HIM... THAT YOUR-- FRIENDSHIP-- IS INNOCENT...
BUT YOU UNDERSTAND MY FEAR THAT YOU MIGHT GET FASCINATED.
NO... YOU'RE RIGHT... I STILL HAVE ALL THIS CONFLICTING --STUFF-- I DON'T EVEN KNOW WHAT IM THINKING HALF THE TIME...
I MEAN YOU'RE BASICALLY INTO A CRAZY PERSON...
I JUST WANT TO KEEP YOU SAFE...
NO. I KNOW I'VE HURT YOU. I DON'T WANNA HURT YOU ANYMORE. I MEAN YOU'RE INTO ME AND I'M CRAZY SO WHAT DOES THAT SAY ABOUT YOU...
I MEAN ALL MEN WANT TO SAVE WOMEN SO IS THAT LIKE PERPETUALLY WHAT WE'RE ALL ABOUT... BECAUSE...
I DON'T WANT TO FIGHT ANYMORE. I JUST... SOMETIMES I THINK I SHOULD FEEL LESS HAPPY SO I CAN ALSO FEEL LESS CONTENT.
I HAVE THOUGHT ABOUT IT. I WANT YOU TO FEEL FREE. TO BE FREE. TO EXPERIENCE THINGS. I'LL BE GONE FOR A WHILE ANYWAY... BUT EVEN WHEN I GET BACK... AS LONG AS YOU DON'T GO TO HIM... I WANT US TO JUST PUT THAT IN THE PAST. BUT WHATEVER YOU WANT... I'LL... SUPPORT.
ARE YOU REALLY SURE??
ARE YOU REALLY GOING TO...?
DON'T BE AN IDIOT.

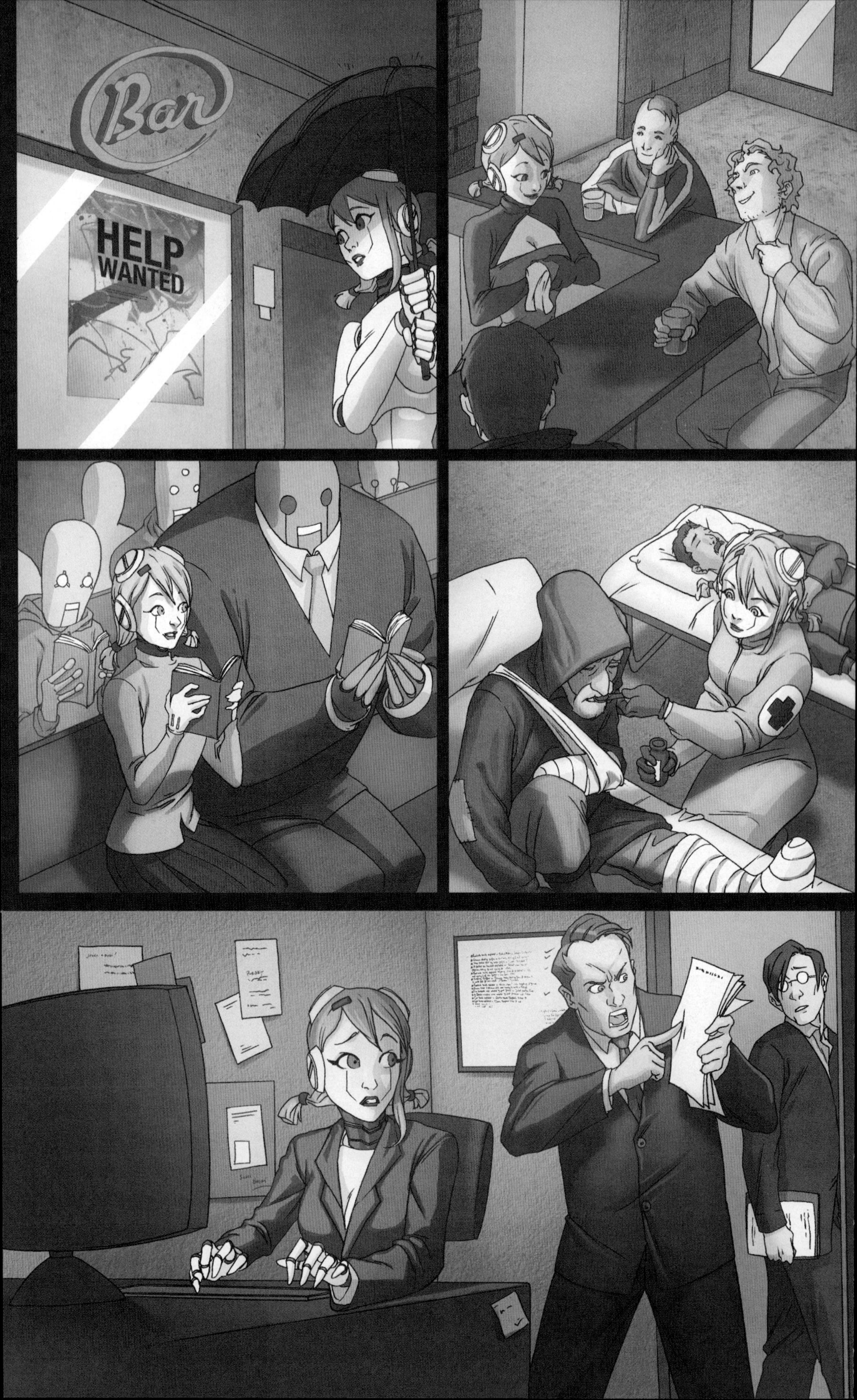
Bar
HELP WANTED

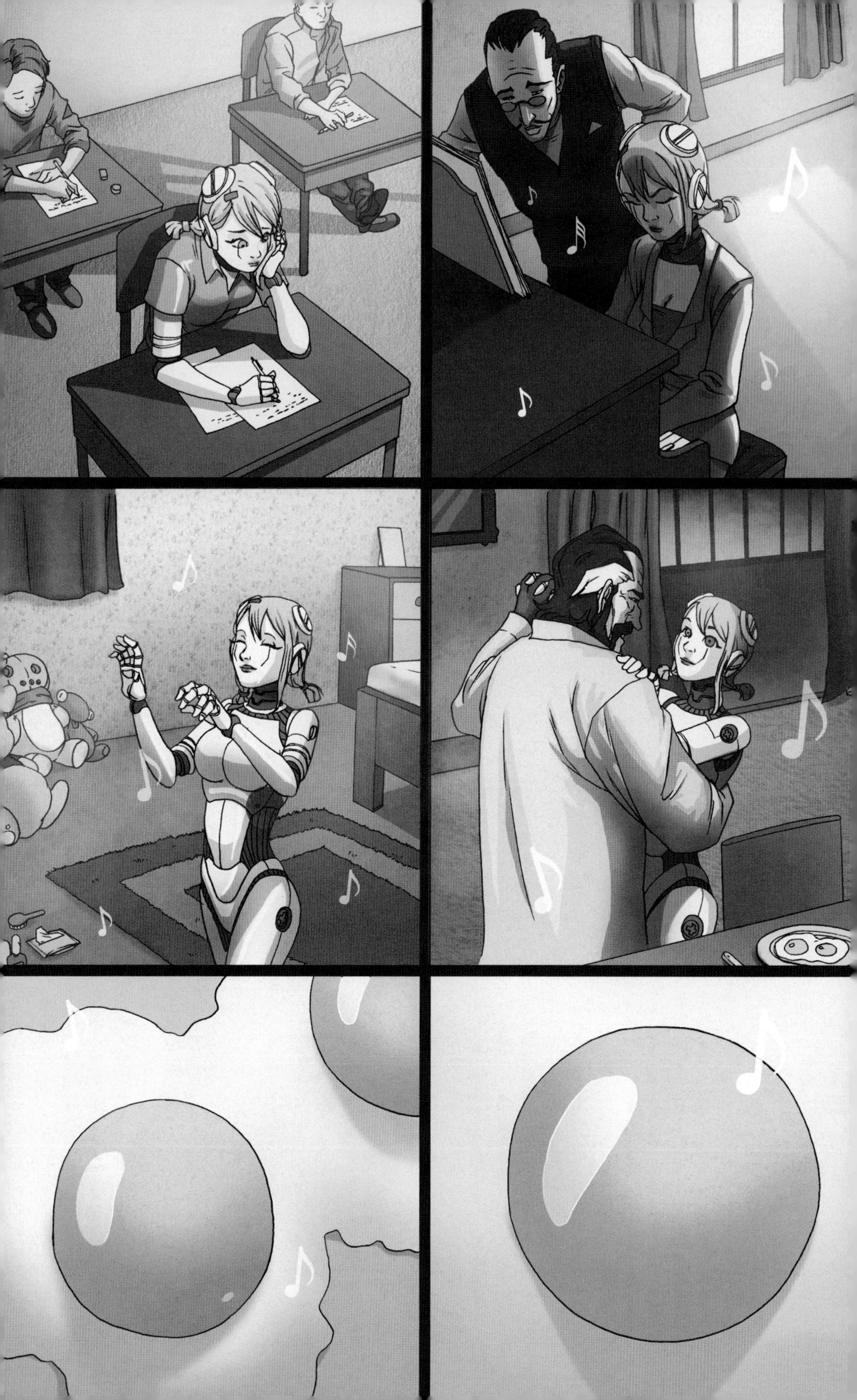

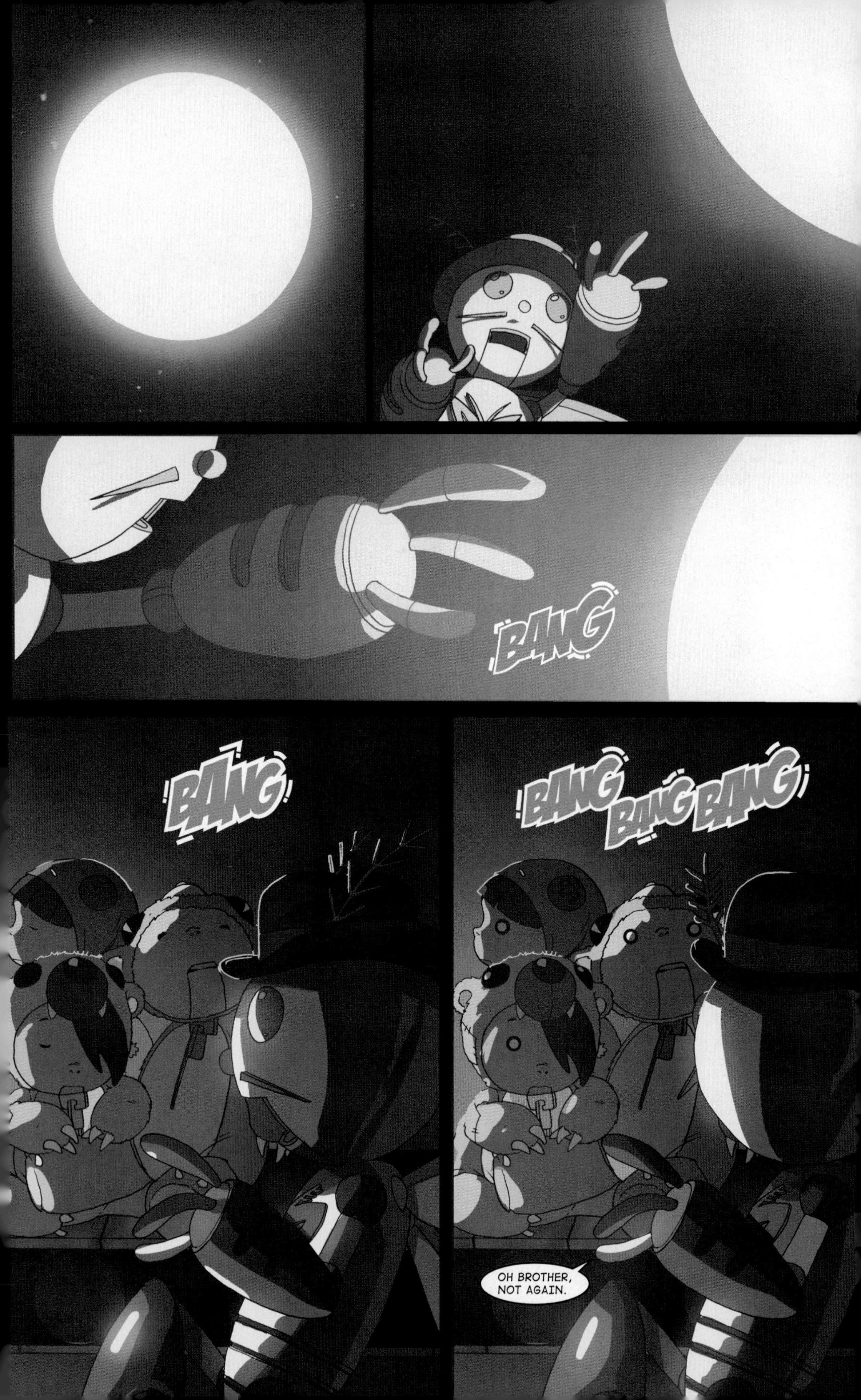
BANG
BANG
BANG
BANG
BANG
OH BROTHER, NOT AGAIN.

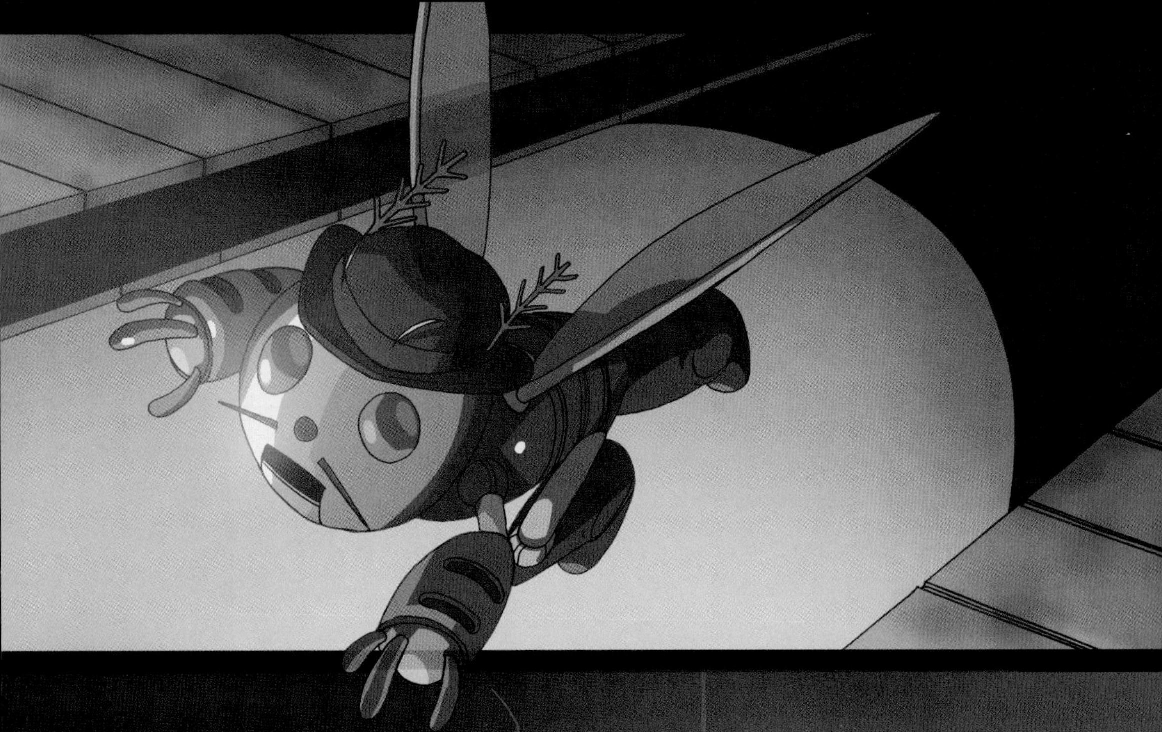

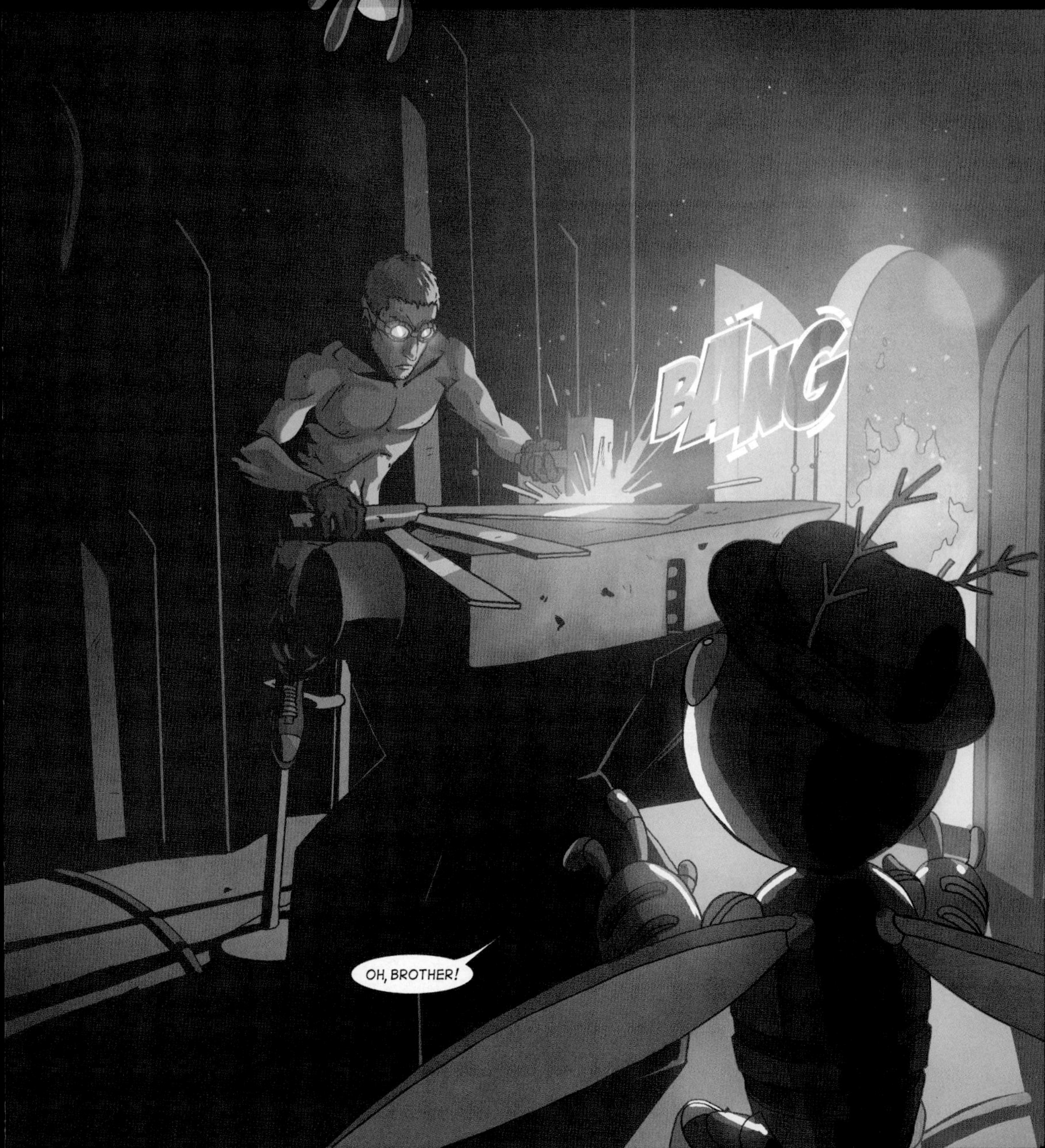
BANG
OH, BROTHER!

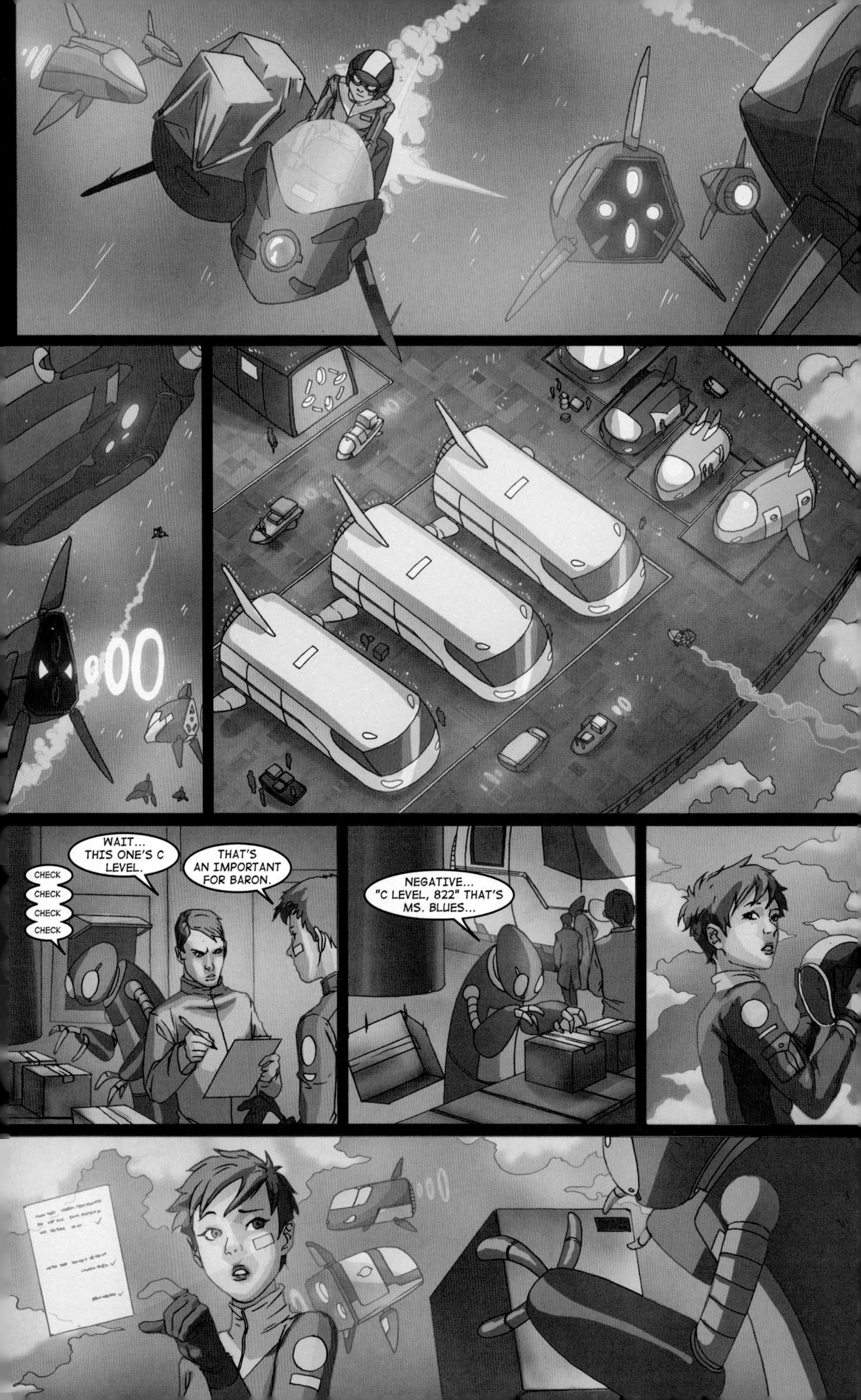
CHECK
CHECK
CHECK
CHECK
WAIT... THIS ONE'S C LEVEL.
THAT'S AN IMPORTANT FOR BARON.
NEGATIVE... "C LEVEL, 822" THAT'S MS. BLUES...

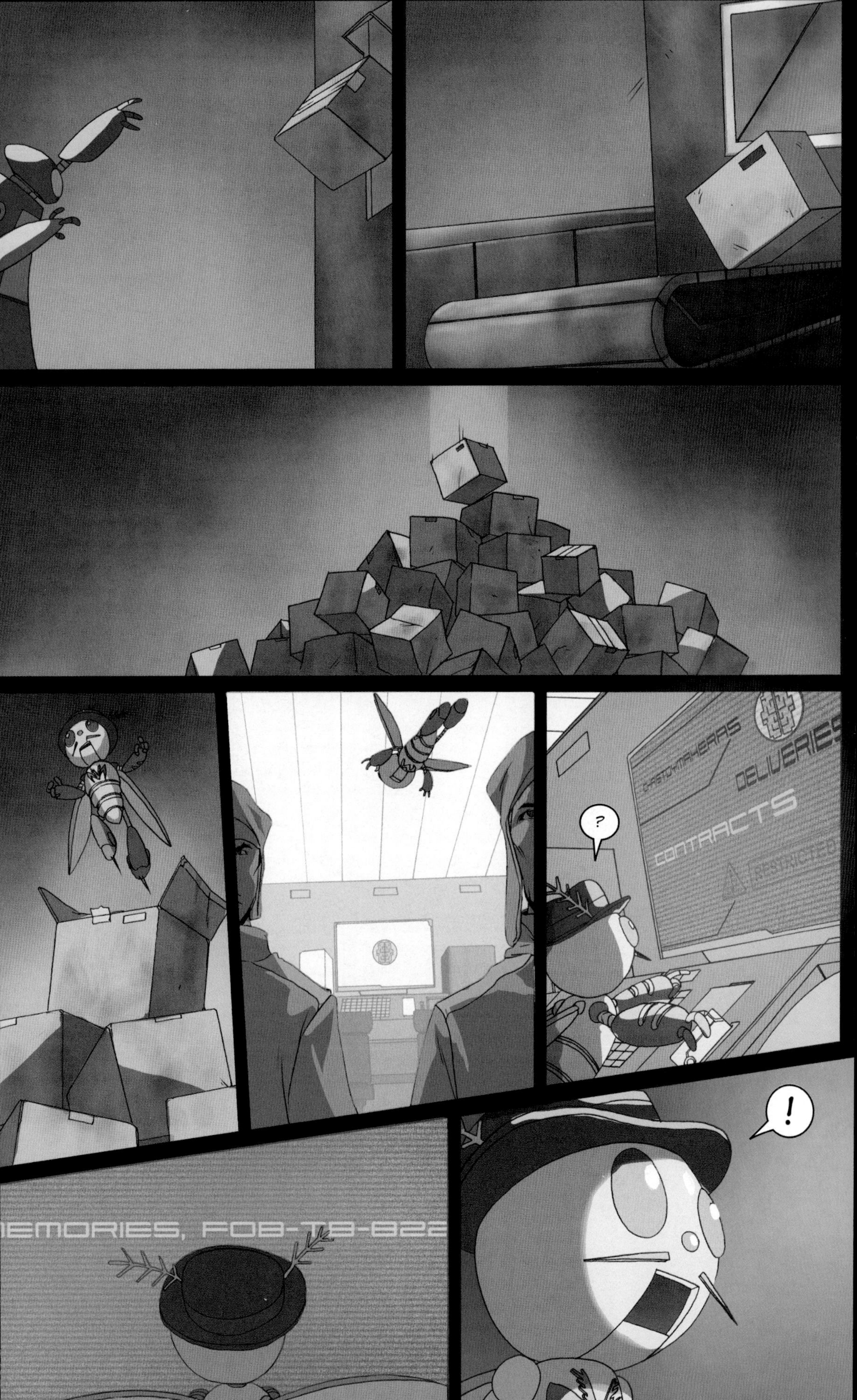
DELIVERIES
CONTRACTS
?
!

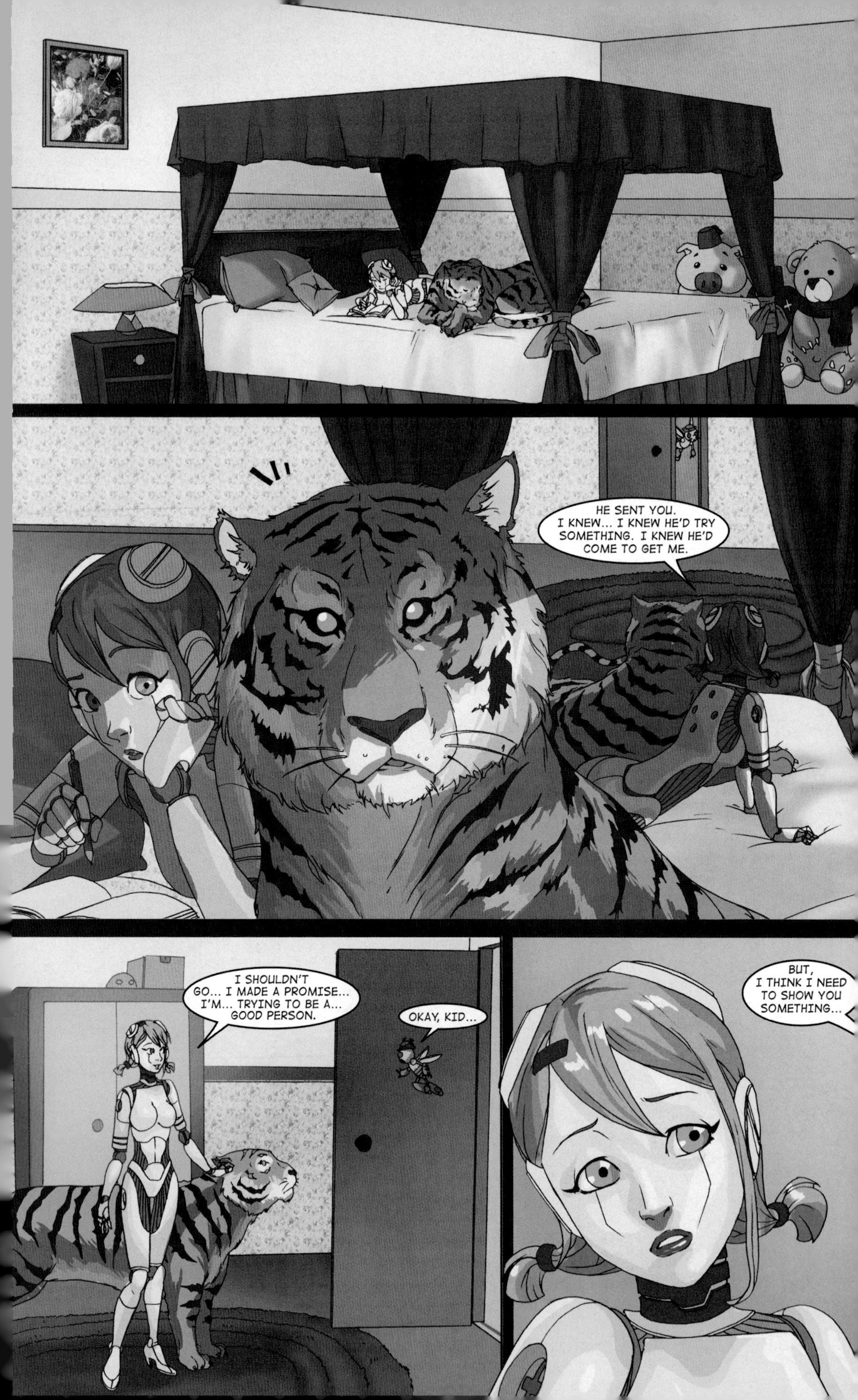
HE SENT YOU. I KNEW... I KNEW HE'D TRY SOMETHING. I KNEW HE'D COME TO GET ME.
I SHOULDN'T GO... I MADE A PROMISE... I'M... TRYING TO BE A... GOOD PERSON.
OKAY, KID...
BUT, I THINK I NEED TO SHOW YOU SOMETHING...

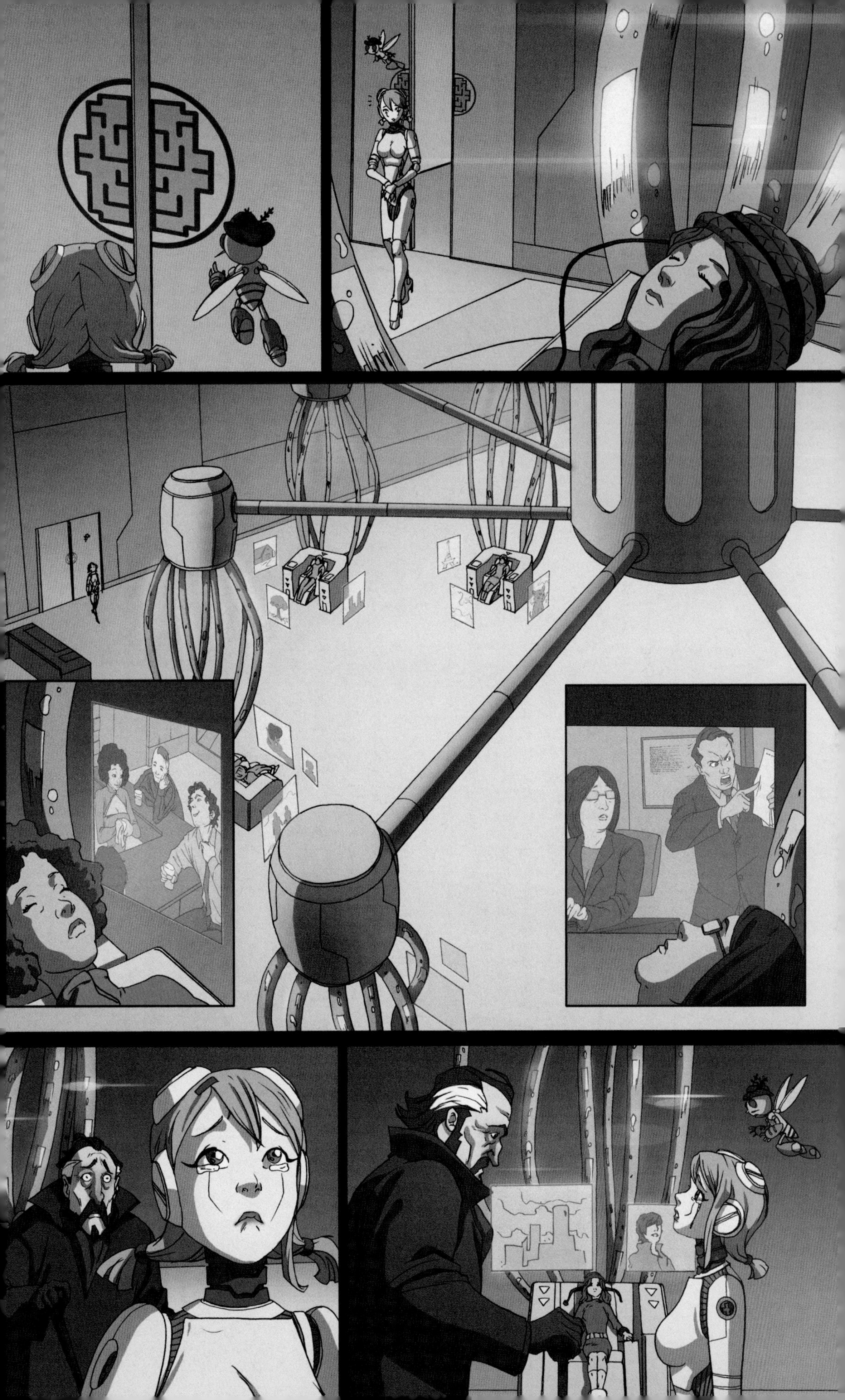

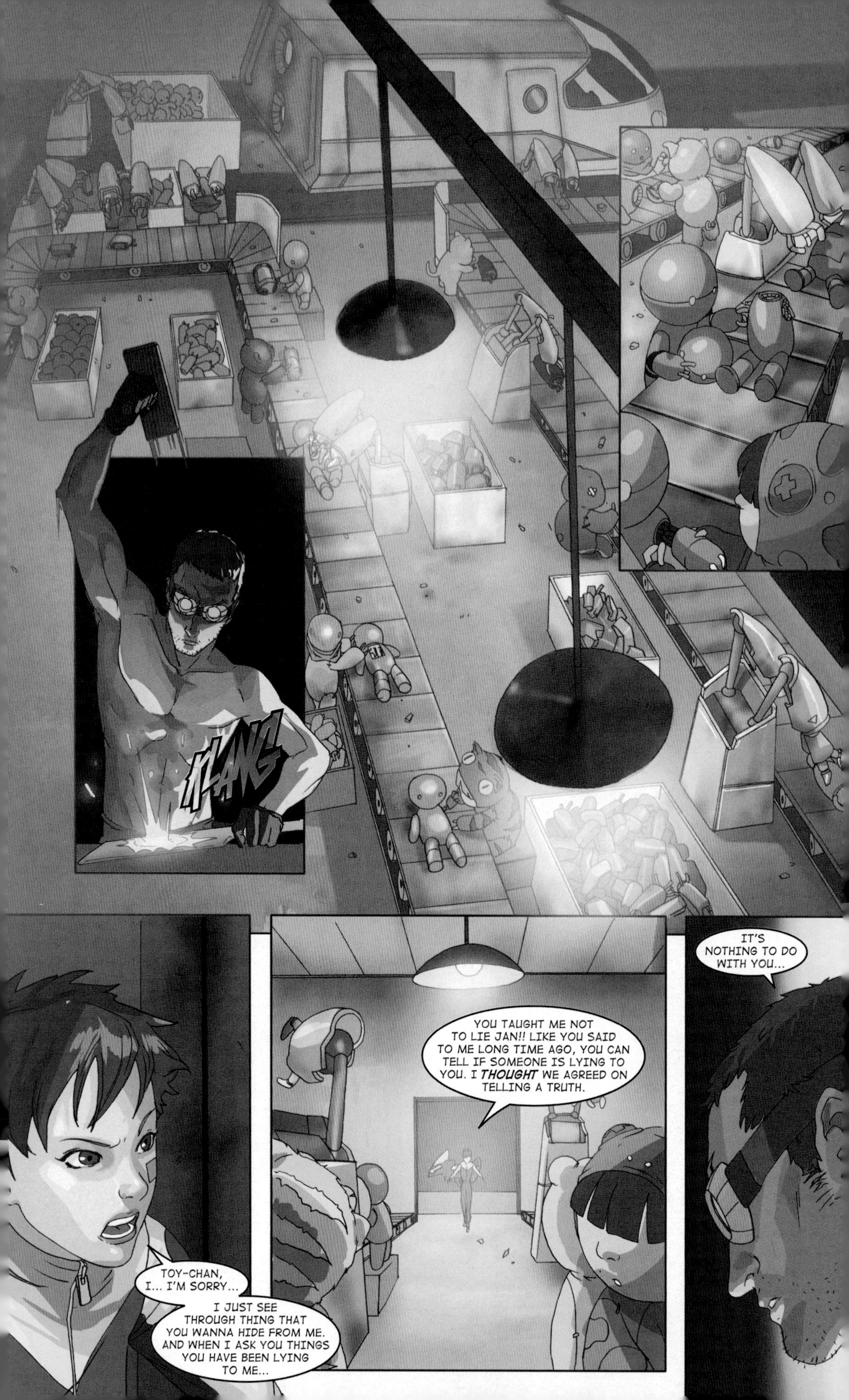
KLANG
TOY-CHAN, I... I'M SORRY...
I JUST SEE THROUGH THING THAT YOU WANNA HIDE FROM ME. AND WHEN I ASK YOU THINGS YOU HAVE BEEN LYING TO ME...
YOU TAUGHT ME NOT TO LIE JAN!! LIKE YOU SAID TO ME LONG TIME AGO, YOU CAN TELL IF SOMEONE IS LYING TO YOU. I *THOUGHT* WE AGREED ON TELLING A TRUTH.
IT'S NOTHING TO DO WITH YOU...

JUST CAN'T BELIEVE YOU ANYMORE OR RESPECT. AFTER ALL THOSE LYING. ENOUGH!!

YOU SAID *I* GO CRAZY CUZ *I* DON'T SEE THE FACT!! *GET IT?* I REALLY DIDN'T WANT TO FIND THIS LIKE THIS, BUT... I'M GLAD I DID TO MYSELF.

I'M SOOOOO DISAPPOINTED YOU. I THOUGHT YOU WERE DIFFERENT.... WAS WRONG... SAME DOUCHES AROUND.

I LOVE HER. I'M GOING TO GO GET HER BACK.

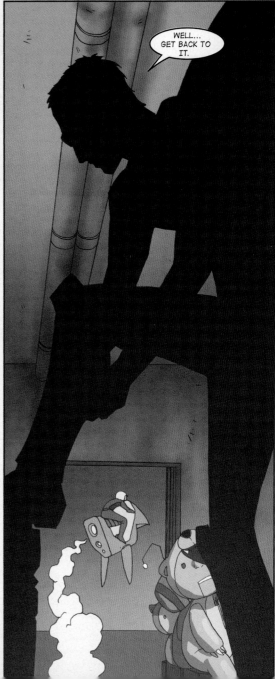

WELL... GET BACK TO IT.

WHY DON'T YOU GO JUST PUT YOUR CHINKO IN THE TOASTER! SAME THING, DAI-YO! SAD-CHARACTER!

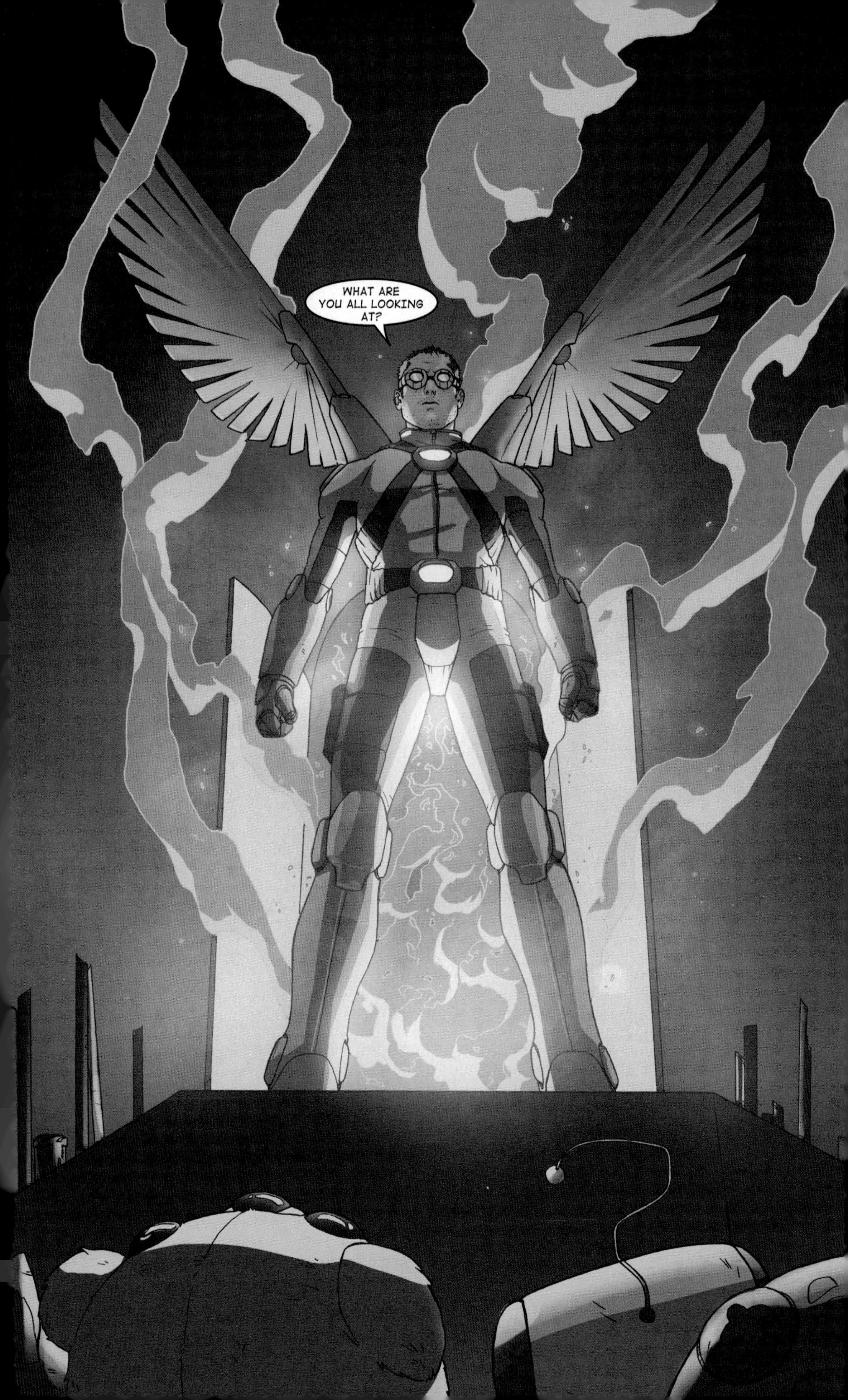
WHAT ARE YOU ALL LOOKING AT?

CHAPTER FIVE

"DROP A HEART, BREAK A NAME"

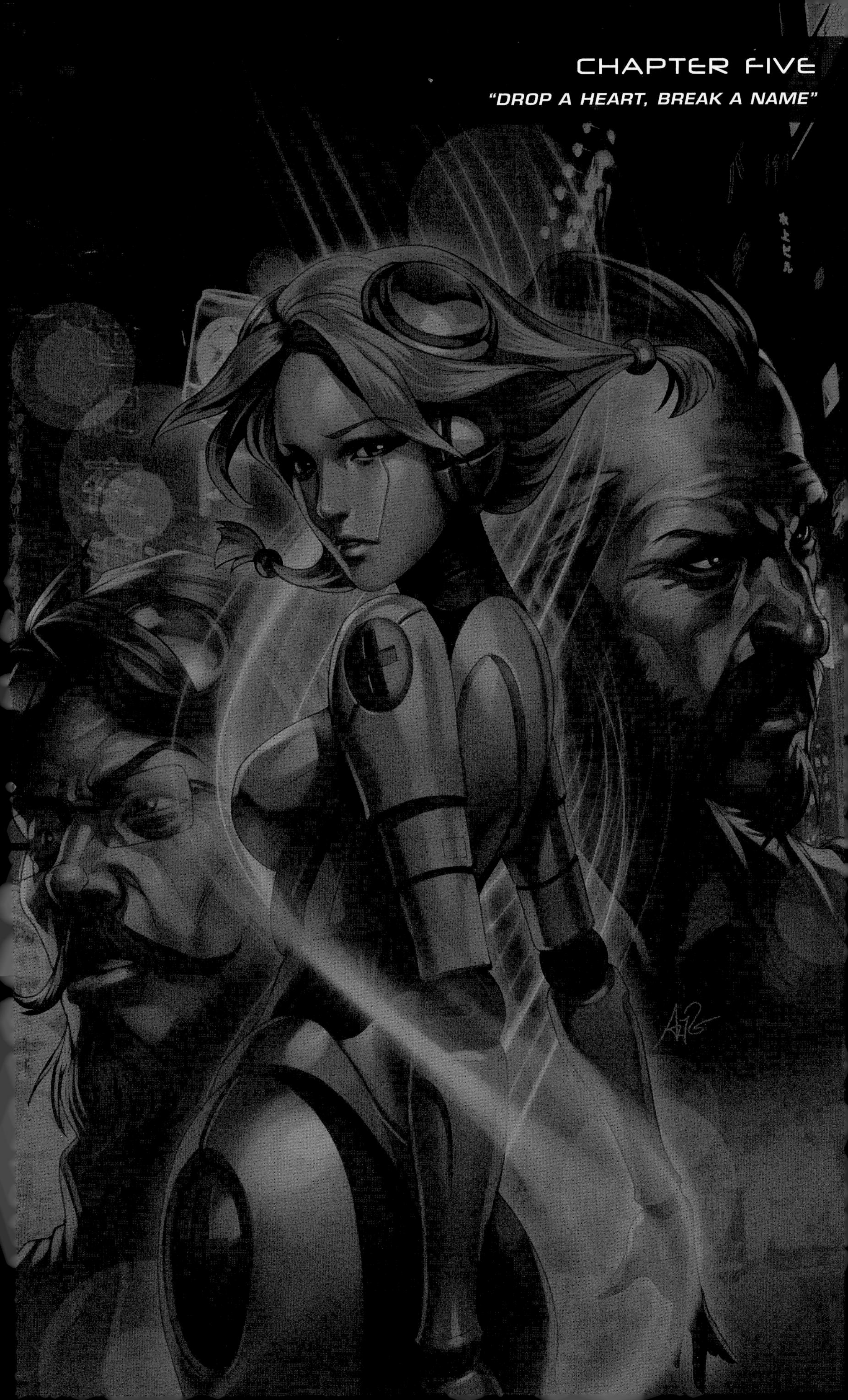

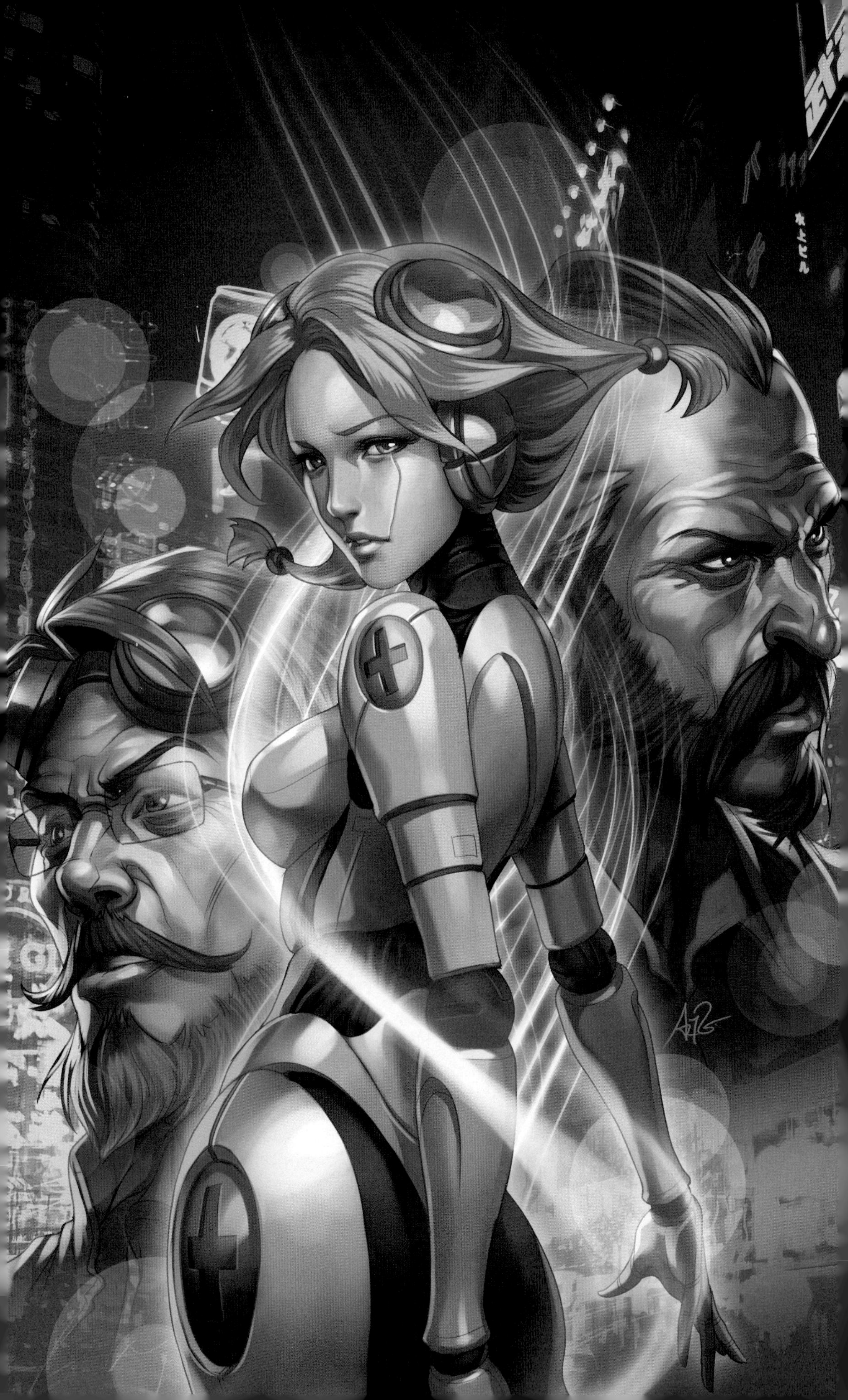

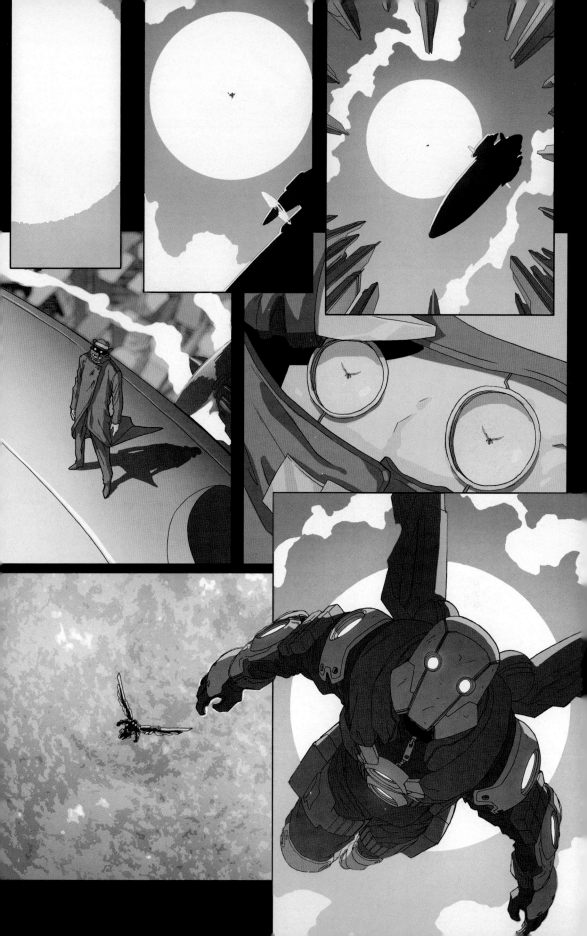

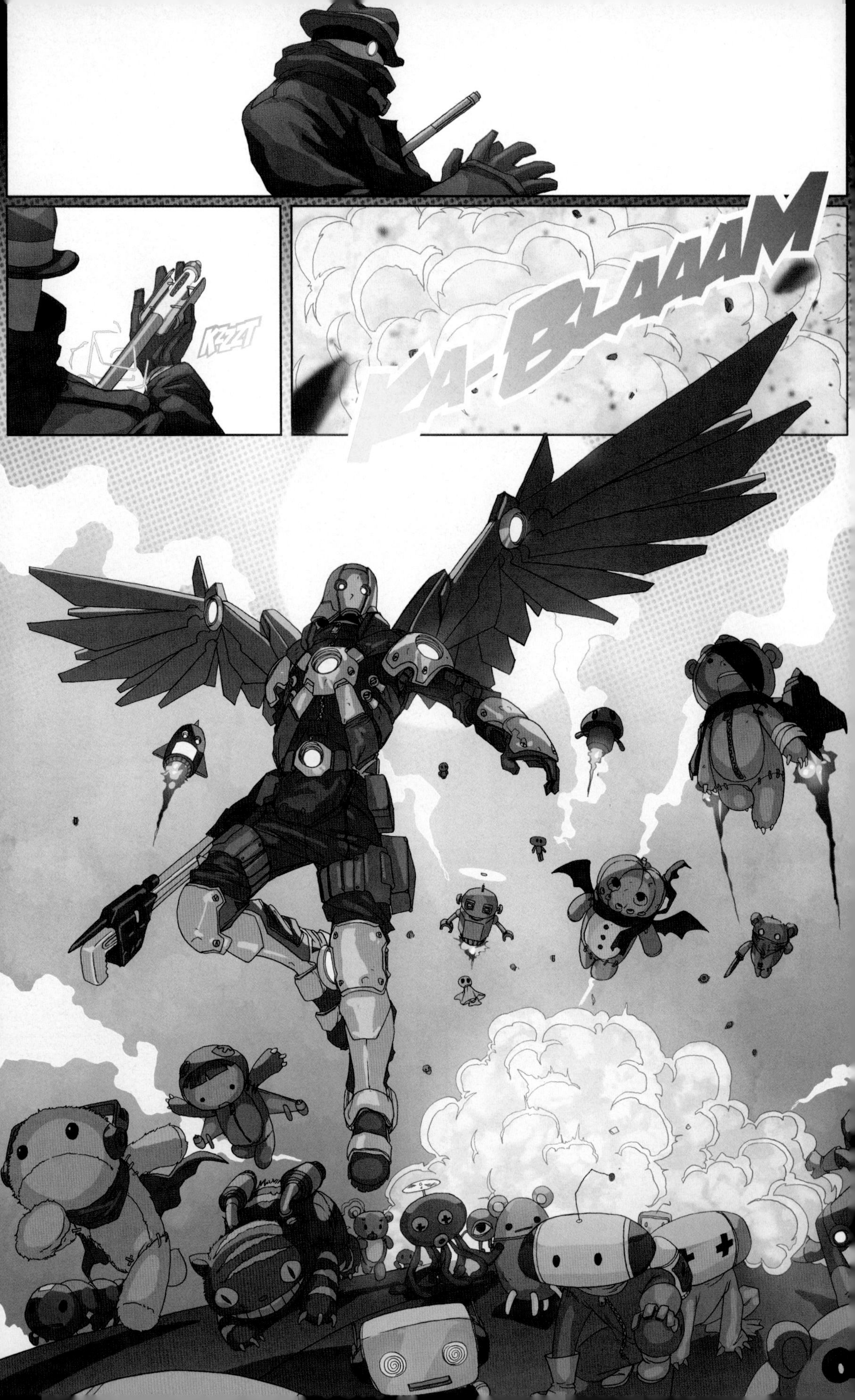
KZZT
KA-BLAAAM

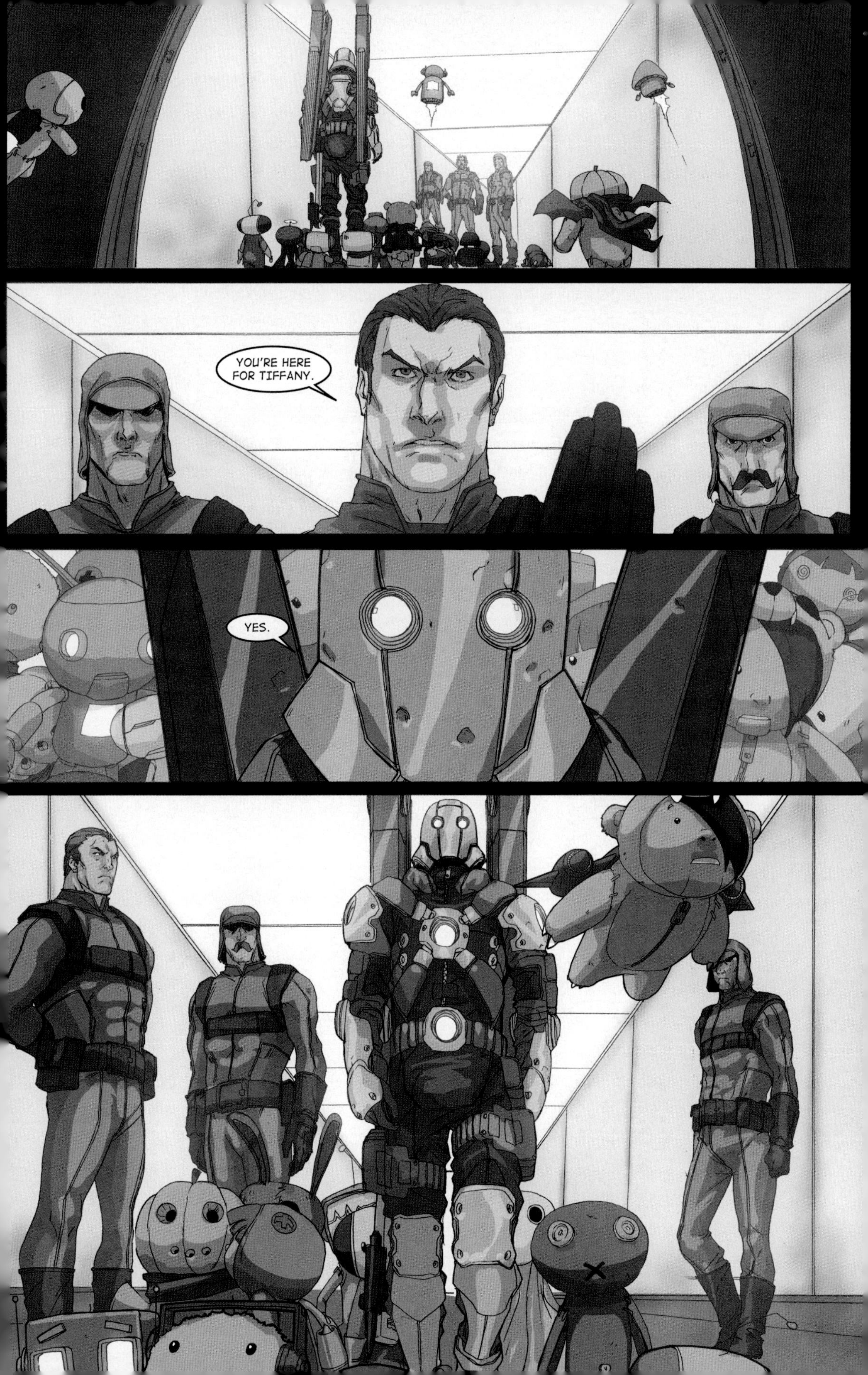
YOU'RE HERE FOR TIFFANY.
YES.

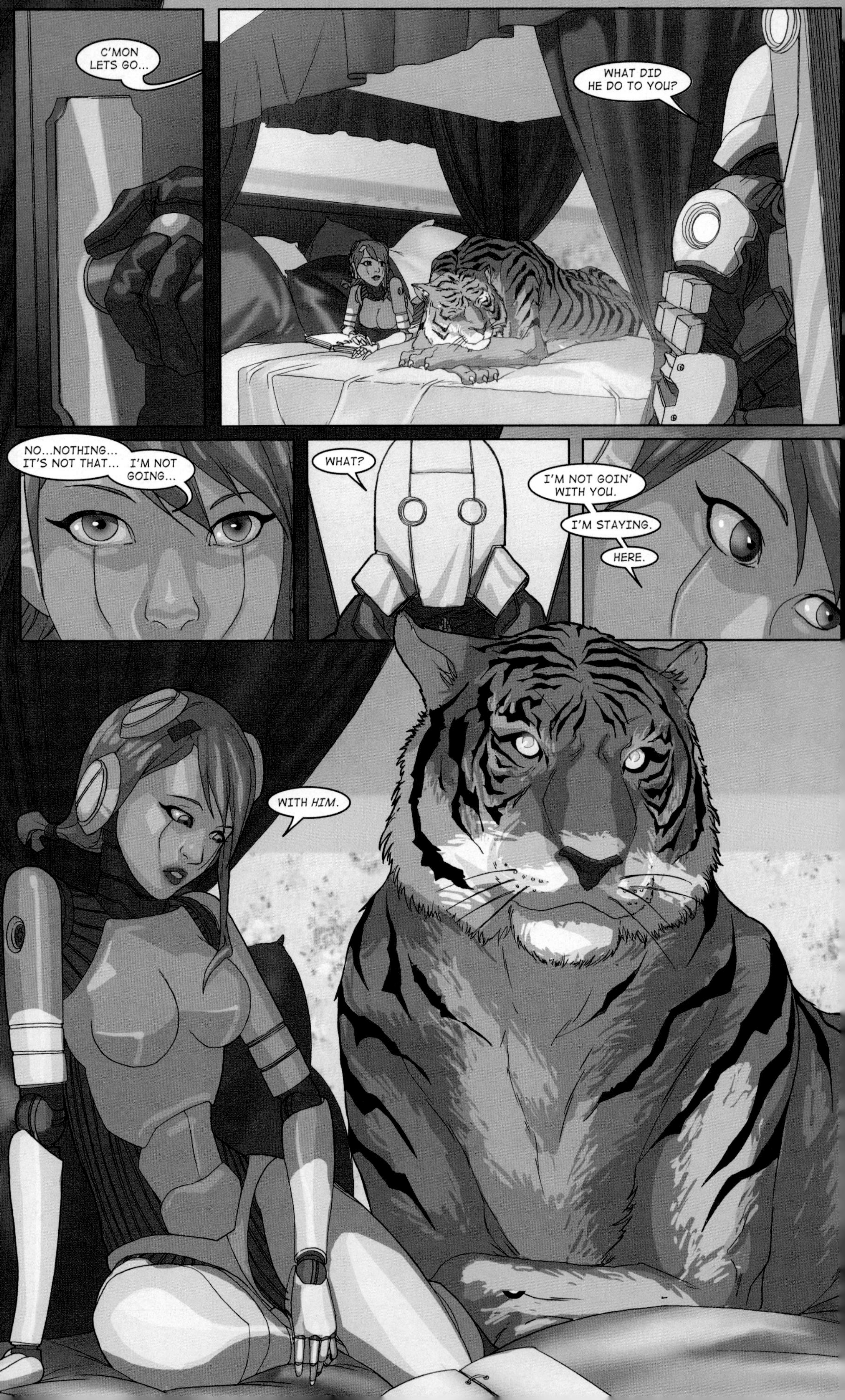
C'MON LETS GO...
WHAT DID HE DO TO YOU?
NO...NOTHING... IT'S NOT THAT... I'M NOT GOING...
WHAT?
I'M NOT GOIN' WITH YOU.
I'M STAYING.
HERE.
WITH *HIM*.

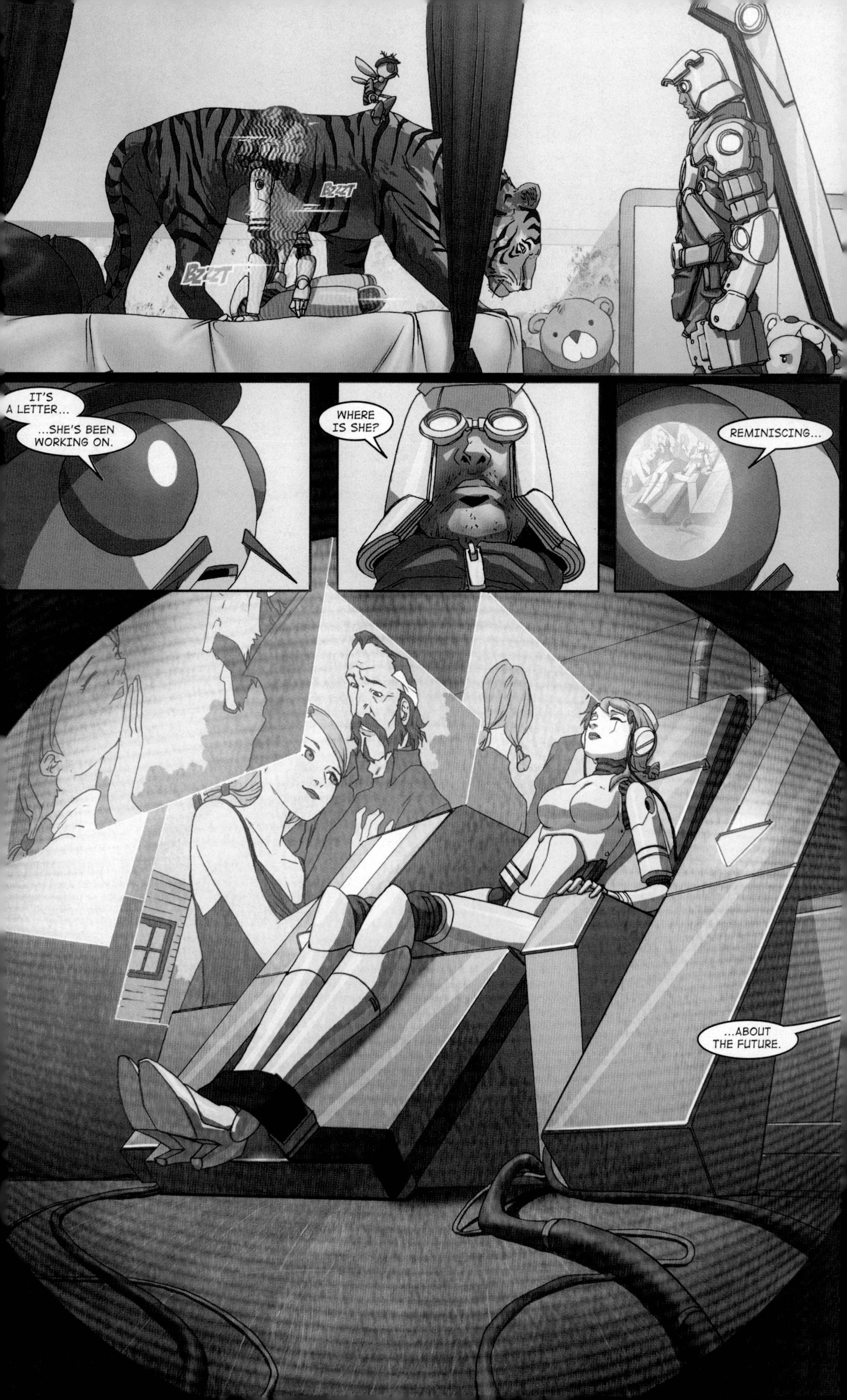
BZZZT
BZZZT
IT'S A LETTER...
...SHE'S BEEN WORKING ON.
WHERE IS SHE?
REMINISCING...
...ABOUT THE FUTURE.

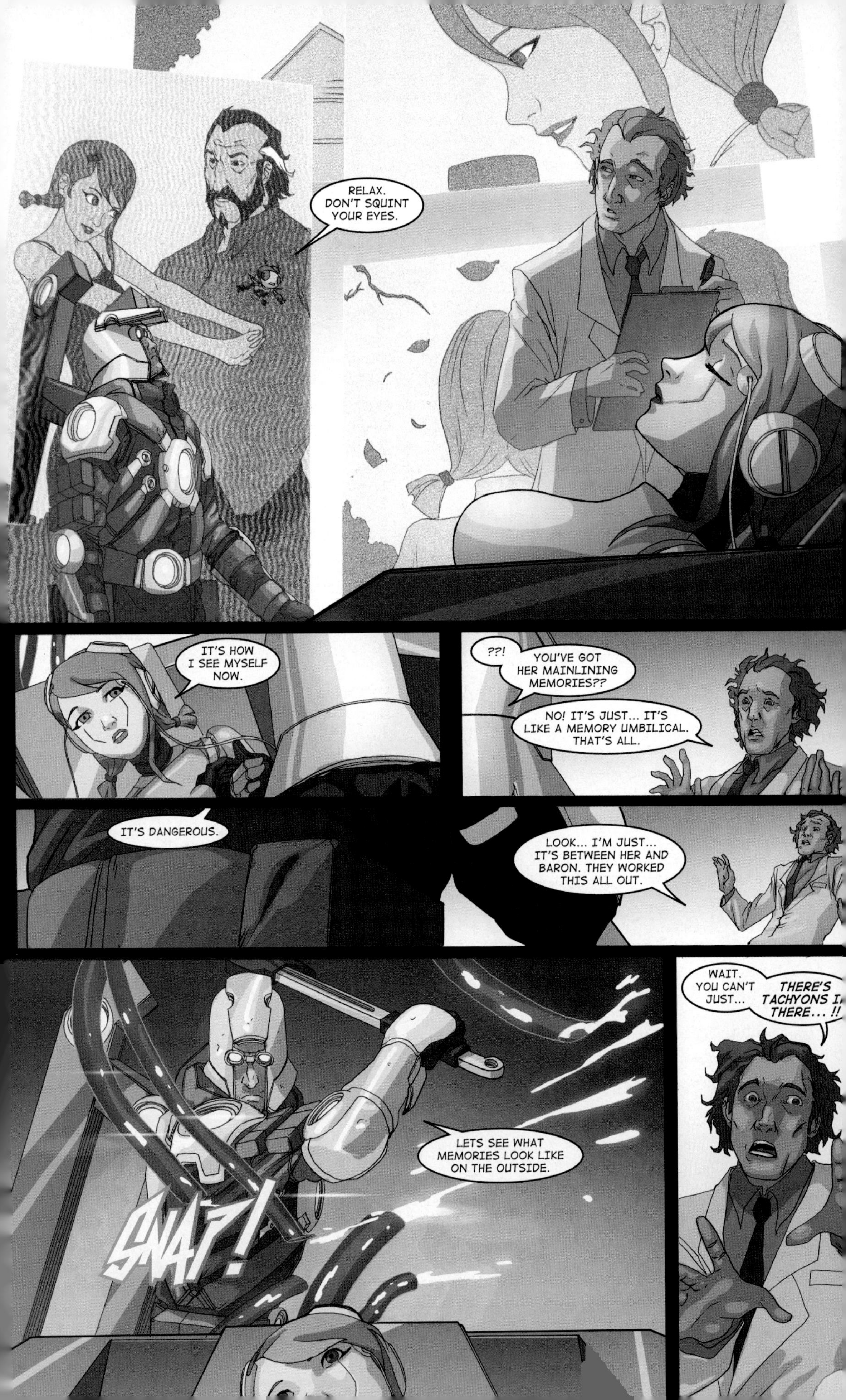

RELAX. DON'T SQUINT YOUR EYES.
IT'S HOW I SEE MYSELF NOW.
??!
YOU'VE GOT HER MAINLINING MEMORIES??
NO! IT'S JUST... IT'S LIKE A MEMORY UMBILICAL. THAT'S ALL.
IT'S DANGEROUS.
LOOK... I'M JUST... IT'S BETWEEN HER AND BARON. THEY WORKED THIS ALL OUT.
LETS SEE WHAT MEMORIES LOOK LIKE ON THE OUTSIDE.
SNAP!
WAIT. YOU CAN'T JUST...
THERE'S TACHYONS IN THERE... !!

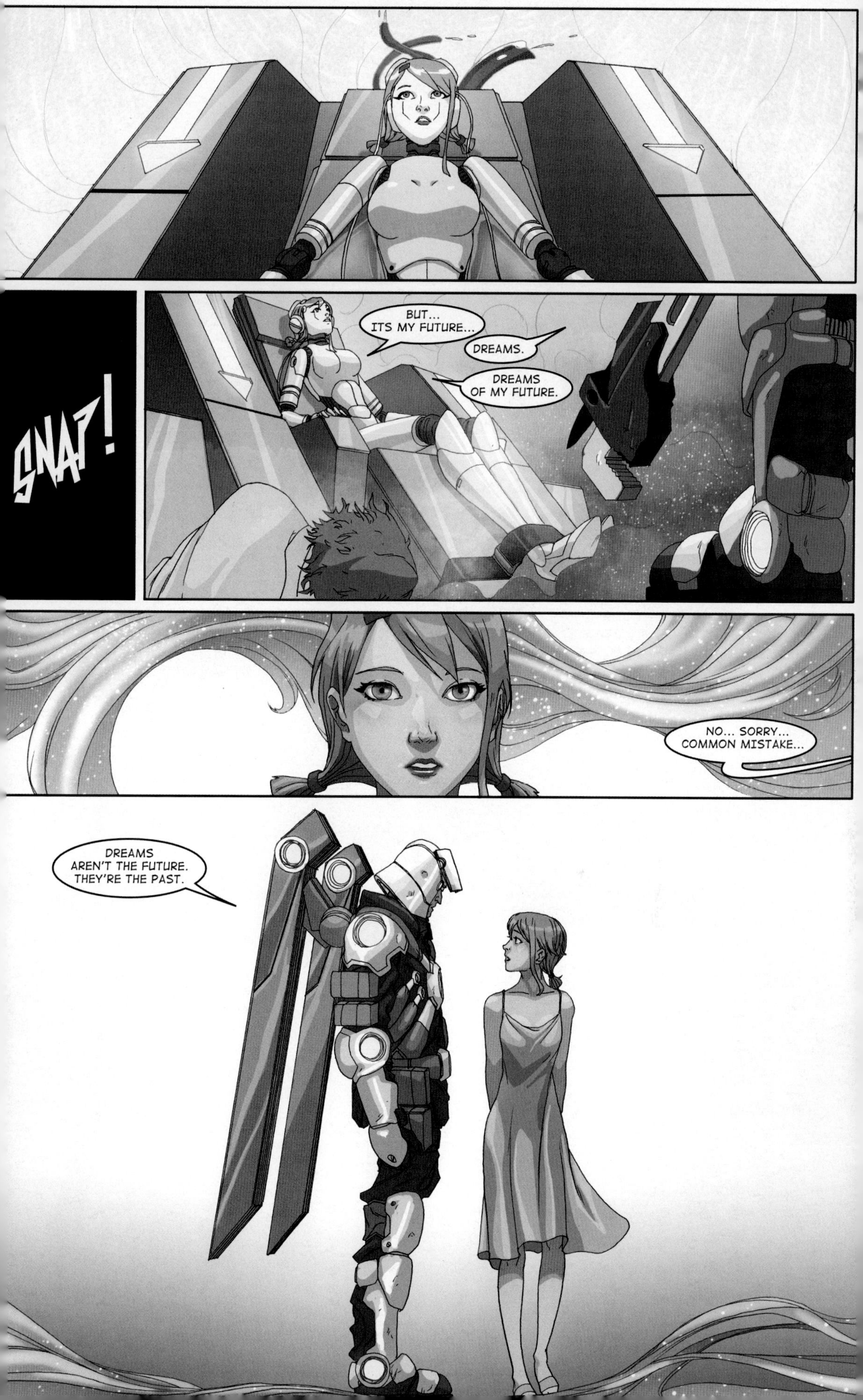
SNAP!
BUT... ITS MY FUTURE...
DREAMS.
DREAMS OF MY FUTURE.
NO... SORRY... COMMON MISTAKE...
DREAMS AREN'T THE FUTURE. THEY'RE THE PAST.

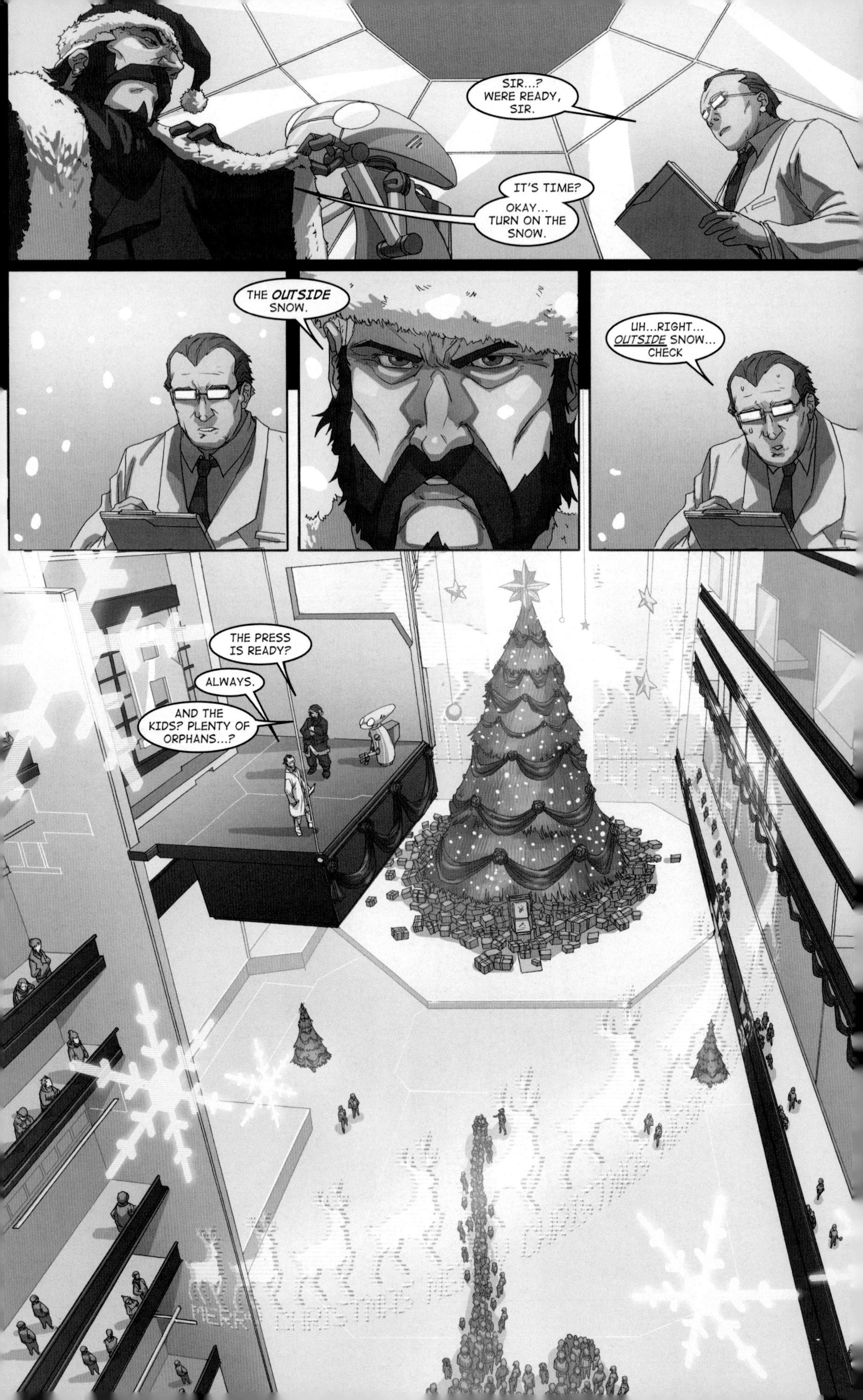
SIR...? WERE READY, SIR.
IT'S TIME?
OKAY... TURN ON THE SNOW.
THE *OUTSIDE* SNOW.
UH...RIGHT... OUTSIDE SNOW... CHECK
THE PRESS IS READY?
ALWAYS.
AND THE KIDS? PLENTY OF ORPHANS...?

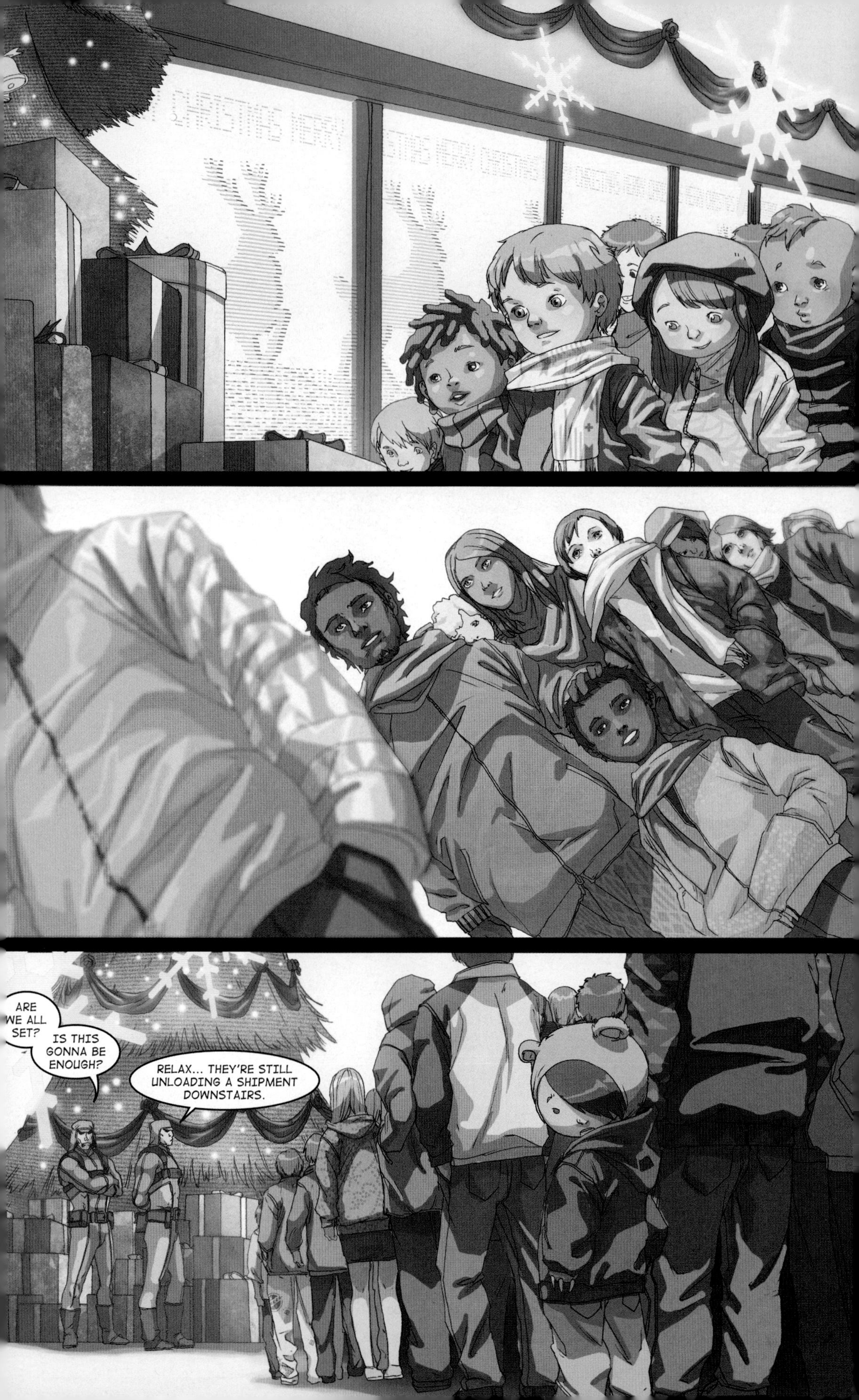

ARE WE ALL SET?
IS THIS GONNA BE ENOUGH?
RELAX... THEY'RE STILL UNLOADING A SHIPMENT DOWNSTAIRS.

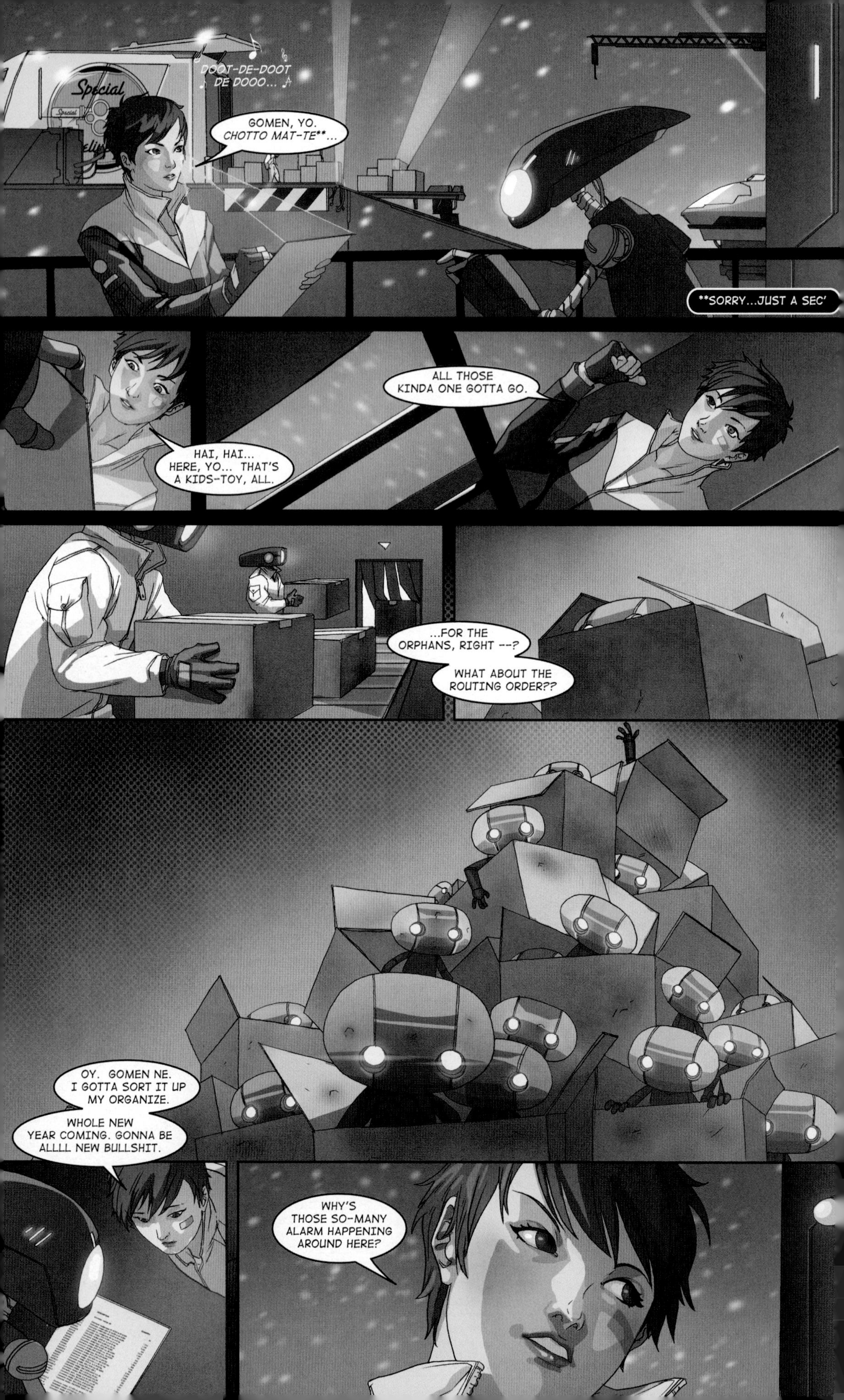
DOOT-DE-DOOT DE DOOO...
GOMEN, YO. CHOTTO MAT-TE**...
**SORRY...JUST A SEC'
ALL THOSE KINDA ONE GOTTA GO.
HAI, HAI... HERE, YO... THAT'S A KIDS-TOY, ALL.
...FOR THE ORPHANS, RIGHT --?
WHAT ABOUT THE ROUTING ORDER??
OY. GOMEN NE. I GOTTA SORT IT UP MY ORGANIZE.
WHOLE NEW YEAR COMING. GONNA BE ALLLL NEW BULLSHIT.
WHY'S THOSE SO-MANY ALARM HAPPENING AROUND HERE?

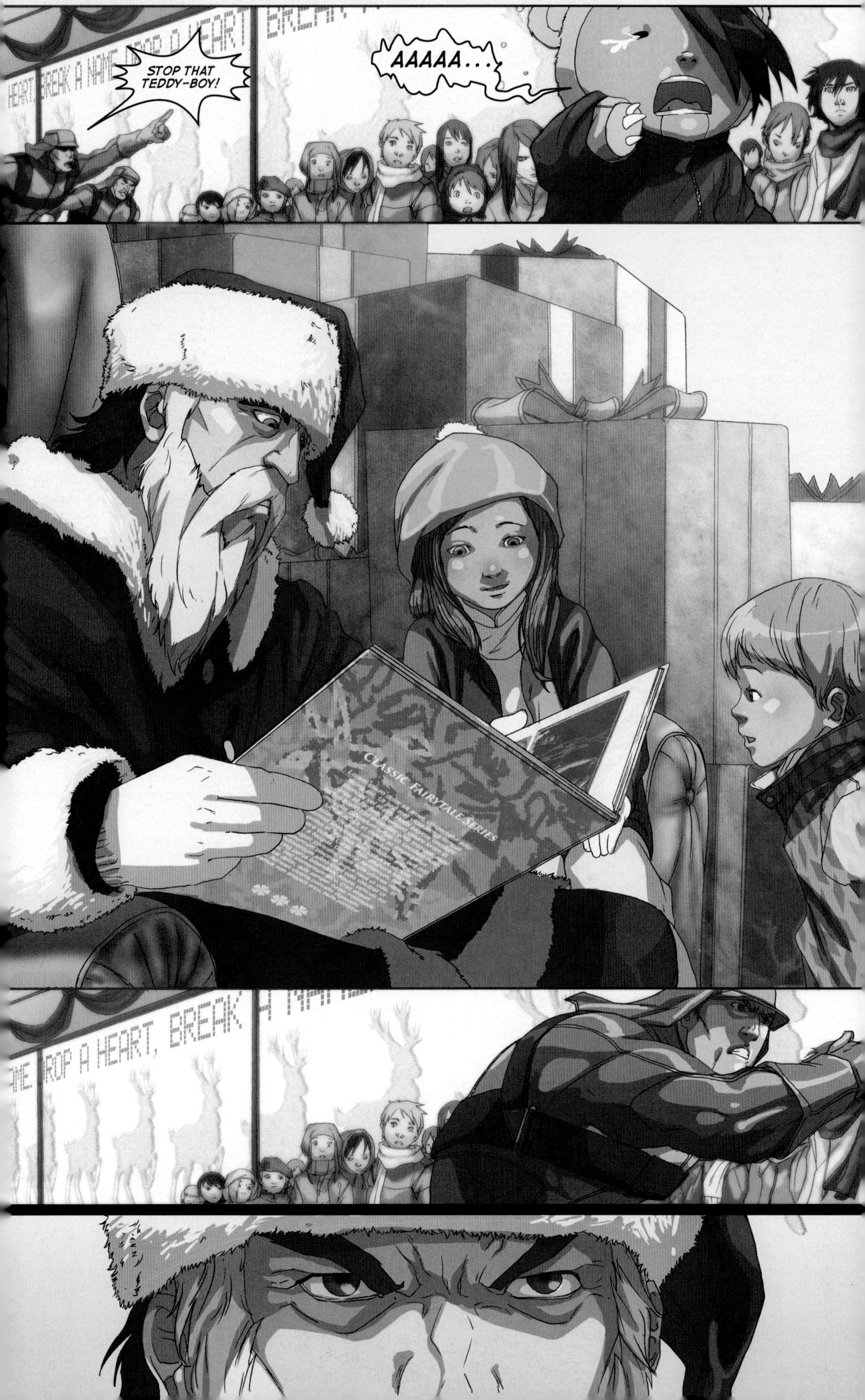
STOP THAT TEDDY-BOY!
AAAAA...
CLASSIC FAIRYTALE SERIES

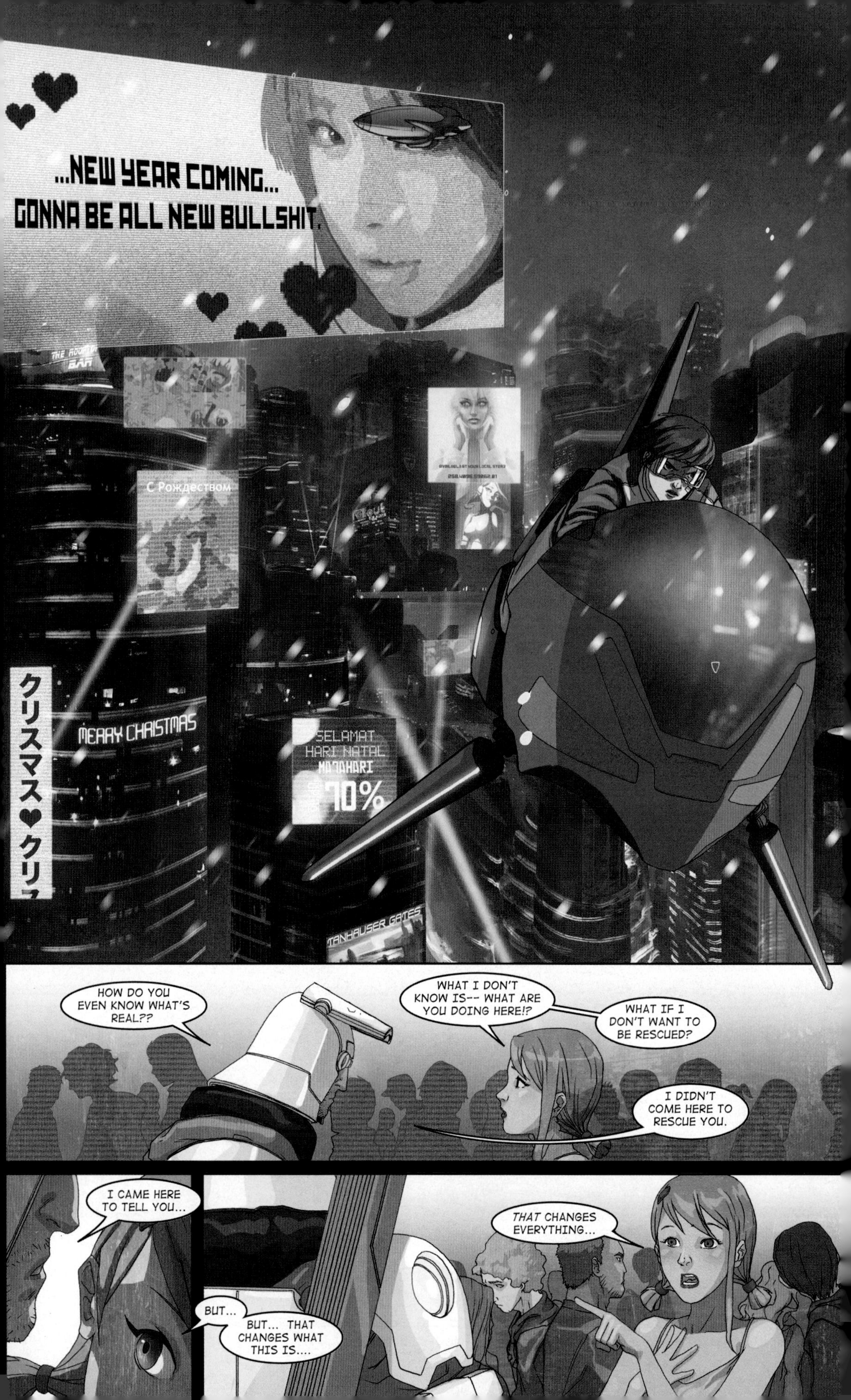

...NEW YEAR COMING...
GONNA BE ALL NEW BULLSHIT.
С Рождеством
MERRY CHRISTMAS
クリスマス
SELAMAT HARI NATAL
MATAHARI
70%
TANHAUSER GATES
HOW DO YOU EVEN KNOW WHAT'S REAL??
WHAT I DON'T KNOW IS-- WHAT ARE YOU DOING HERE!?
WHAT IF I DON'T WANT TO BE RESCUED?
I DIDN'T COME HERE TO RESCUE YOU.
I CAME HERE TO TELL YOU...
THAT CHANGES EVERYTHING...
BUT...
BUT... THAT CHANGES WHAT THIS IS....

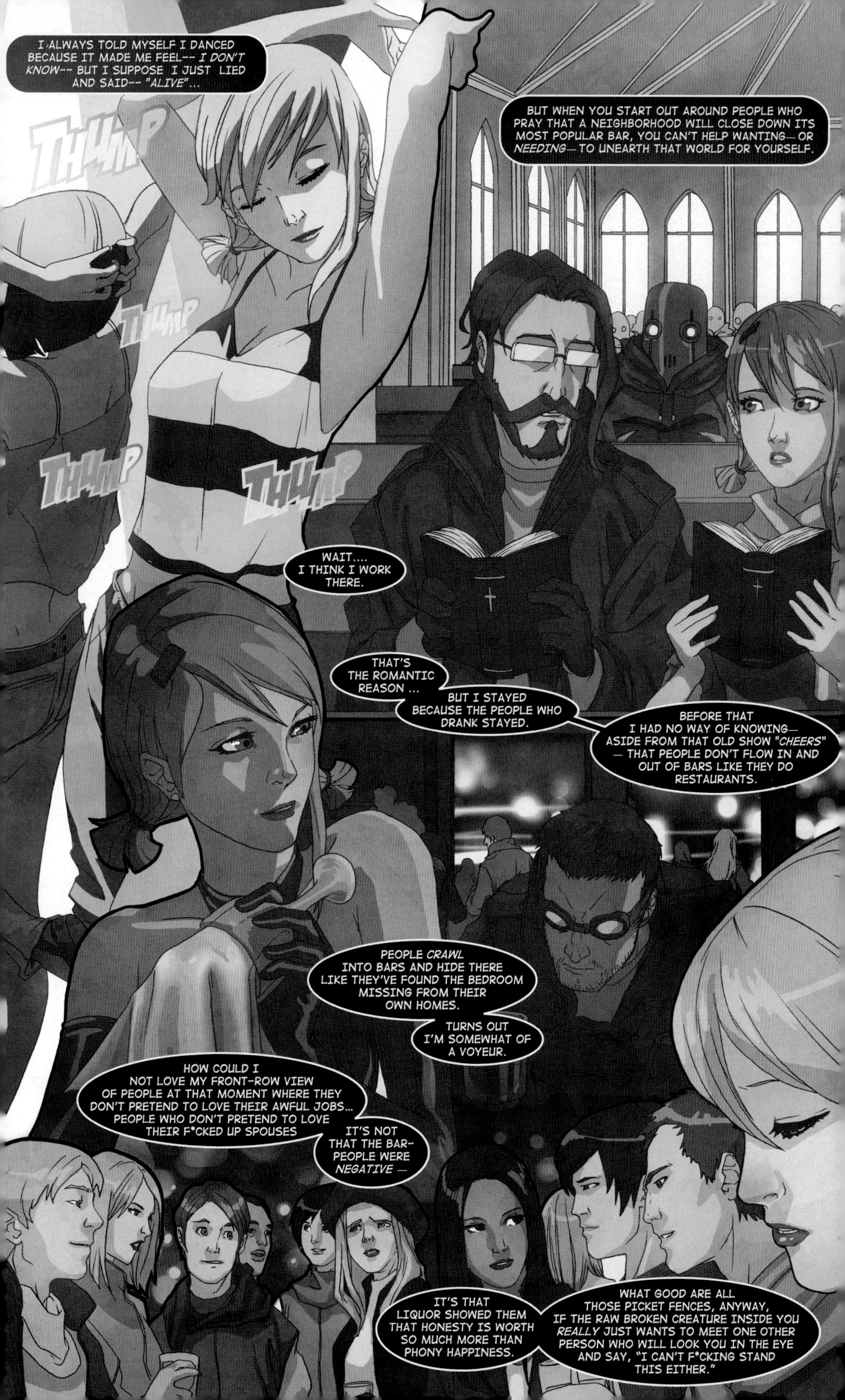
I ALWAYS TOLD MYSELF I DANCED BECAUSE IT MADE ME FEEL-- *I DON'T KNOW*-- BUT I SUPPOSE I JUST LIED AND SAID-- "*ALIVE*"...
THUMP
BUT WHEN YOU START OUT AROUND PEOPLE WHO PRAY THAT A NEIGHBORHOOD WILL CLOSE DOWN ITS MOST POPULAR BAR, YOU CAN'T HELP WANTING— OR *NEEDING*— TO UNEARTH THAT WORLD FOR YOURSELF.
THUMP
THUMP
THUMP
WAIT.... I THINK I WORK THERE.
THAT'S THE ROMANTIC REASON ...
BUT I STAYED BECAUSE THE PEOPLE WHO DRANK STAYED.
BEFORE THAT I HAD NO WAY OF KNOWING— ASIDE FROM THAT OLD SHOW "*CHEERS*" — THAT PEOPLE DON'T FLOW IN AND OUT OF BARS LIKE THEY DO RESTAURANTS.
PEOPLE *CRAWL* INTO BARS AND HIDE THERE LIKE THEY'VE FOUND THE BEDROOM MISSING FROM THEIR OWN HOMES.
TURNS OUT I'M SOMEWHAT OF A VOYEUR.
HOW COULD I NOT LOVE MY FRONT-ROW VIEW OF PEOPLE AT THAT MOMENT WHERE THEY DON'T PRETEND TO LOVE THEIR AWFUL JOBS... PEOPLE WHO DON'T PRETEND TO LOVE THEIR F*CKED UP SPOUSES
IT'S NOT THAT THE BAR-PEOPLE WERE *NEGATIVE* —
IT'S THAT LIQUOR SHOWED THEM THAT HONESTY IS WORTH SO MUCH MORE THAN PHONY HAPPINESS.
WHAT GOOD ARE ALL THOSE PICKET FENCES, ANYWAY, IF THE RAW BROKEN CREATURE INSIDE YOU *REALLY* JUST WANTS TO MEET ONE OTHER PERSON WHO WILL LOOK YOU IN THE EYE AND SAY, "I CAN'T F*CKING STAND THIS EITHER."

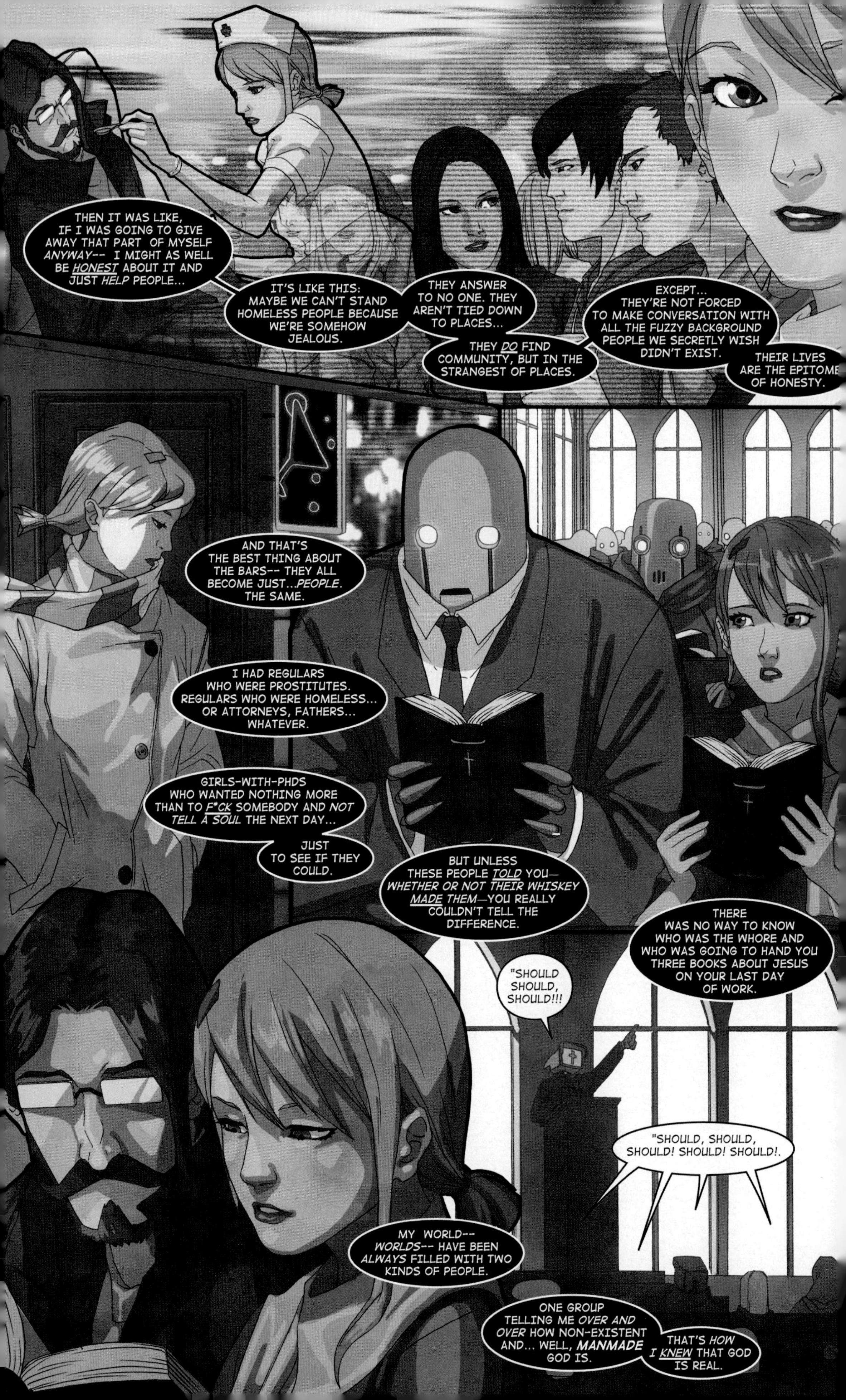
THEN IT WAS LIKE, IF I WAS GOING TO GIVE AWAY THAT PART OF MYSELF *ANYWAY*-- I MIGHT AS WELL BE *HONEST* ABOUT IT AND JUST *HELP* PEOPLE...
IT'S LIKE THIS: MAYBE WE CAN'T STAND HOMELESS PEOPLE BECAUSE WE'RE SOMEHOW JEALOUS.
THEY ANSWER TO NO ONE. THEY AREN'T TIED DOWN TO PLACES...
THEY *DO* FIND COMMUNITY, BUT IN THE STRANGEST OF PLACES.
EXCEPT... THEY'RE NOT FORCED TO MAKE CONVERSATION WITH ALL THE FUZZY BACKGROUND PEOPLE WE SECRETLY WISH DIDN'T EXIST.
THEIR LIVES ARE THE EPITOME OF HONESTY.
AND THAT'S THE BEST THING ABOUT THE BARS-- THEY ALL BECOME JUST...*PEOPLE*. THE SAME.
I HAD REGULARS WHO WERE PROSTITUTES. REGULARS WHO WERE HOMELESS... OR ATTORNEYS, FATHERS... WHATEVER.
GIRLS-WITH-PHDS WHO WANTED NOTHING MORE THAN TO *F*CK* SOMEBODY AND *NOT TELL A SOUL* THE NEXT DAY...
JUST TO SEE IF THEY COULD.
BUT UNLESS THESE PEOPLE *TOLD* YOU—*WHETHER OR NOT THEIR WHISKEY MADE THEM*—YOU REALLY COULDN'T TELL THE DIFFERENCE.
THERE WAS NO WAY TO KNOW WHO WAS THE WHORE AND WHO WAS GOING TO HAND YOU THREE BOOKS ABOUT JESUS ON YOUR LAST DAY OF WORK.
"SHOULD SHOULD, SHOULD!!!
"SHOULD, SHOULD, SHOULD! SHOULD! SHOULD!.
MY WORLD-- *WORLDS*-- HAVE BEEN *ALWAYS* FILLED WITH TWO KINDS OF PEOPLE.
ONE GROUP TELLING ME *OVER AND OVER* HOW NON-EXISTENT AND... WELL, ***MANMADE*** GOD IS.
THAT'S *HOW I KNEW* THAT GOD IS REAL.

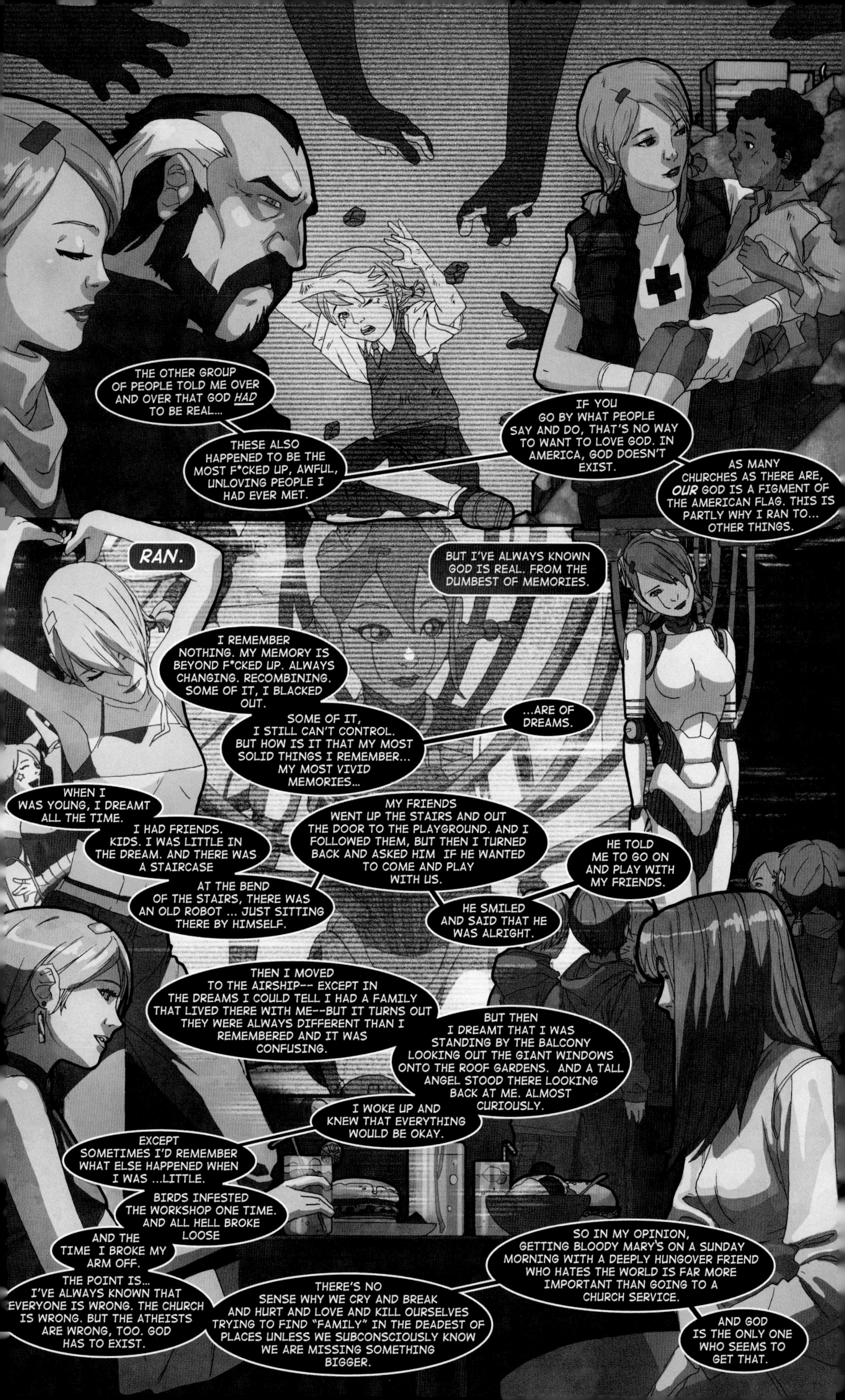
THE OTHER GROUP OF PEOPLE TOLD ME OVER AND OVER THAT GOD HAD TO BE REAL...
THESE ALSO HAPPENED TO BE THE MOST F*CKED UP, AWFUL, UNLOVING PEOPLE I HAD EVER MET.
IF YOU GO BY WHAT PEOPLE SAY AND DO, THAT'S NO WAY TO WANT TO LOVE GOD. IN AMERICA, GOD DOESN'T EXIST.
AS MANY CHURCHES AS THERE ARE, OUR GOD IS A FIGMENT OF THE AMERICAN FLAG. THIS IS PARTLY WHY I RAN TO... OTHER THINGS.
RAN.
BUT I'VE ALWAYS KNOWN GOD IS REAL. FROM THE DUMBEST OF MEMORIES.
I REMEMBER NOTHING. MY MEMORY IS BEYOND F*CKED UP. ALWAYS CHANGING. RECOMBINING. SOME OF IT, I BLACKED OUT.
SOME OF IT, I STILL CAN'T CONTROL. BUT HOW IS IT THAT MY MOST SOLID THINGS I REMEMBER... MY MOST VIVID MEMORIES...
...ARE OF DREAMS.
WHEN I WAS YOUNG, I DREAMT ALL THE TIME.
I HAD FRIENDS. KIDS. I WAS LITTLE IN THE DREAM. AND THERE WAS A STAIRCASE
AT THE BEND OF THE STAIRS, THERE WAS AN OLD ROBOT ... JUST SITTING THERE BY HIMSELF.
MY FRIENDS WENT UP THE STAIRS AND OUT THE DOOR TO THE PLAYGROUND. AND I FOLLOWED THEM, BUT THEN I TURNED BACK AND ASKED HIM IF HE WANTED TO COME AND PLAY WITH US.
HE SMILED AND SAID THAT HE WAS ALRIGHT.
HE TOLD ME TO GO ON AND PLAY WITH MY FRIENDS.
THEN I MOVED TO THE AIRSHIP-- EXCEPT IN THE DREAMS I COULD TELL I HAD A FAMILY THAT LIVED THERE WITH ME--BUT IT TURNS OUT THEY WERE ALWAYS DIFFERENT THAN I REMEMBERED AND IT WAS CONFUSING.
BUT THEN I DREAMT THAT I WAS STANDING BY THE BALCONY LOOKING OUT THE GIANT WINDOWS ONTO THE ROOF GARDENS. AND A TALL ANGEL STOOD THERE LOOKING BACK AT ME. ALMOST CURIOUSLY.
I WOKE UP AND KNEW THAT EVERYTHING WOULD BE OKAY.
EXCEPT SOMETIMES I'D REMEMBER WHAT ELSE HAPPENED WHEN I WAS ...LITTLE.
BIRDS INFESTED THE WORKSHOP ONE TIME. AND ALL HELL BROKE LOOSE
AND THE TIME I BROKE MY ARM OFF.
THE POINT IS... I'VE ALWAYS KNOWN THAT EVERYONE IS WRONG. THE CHURCH IS WRONG. BUT THE ATHEISTS ARE WRONG, TOO. GOD HAS TO EXIST.
THERE'S NO SENSE WHY WE CRY AND BREAK AND HURT AND LOVE AND KILL OURSELVES TRYING TO FIND "FAMILY" IN THE DEADEST OF PLACES UNLESS WE SUBCONSCIOUSLY KNOW WE ARE MISSING SOMETHING BIGGER.
SO IN MY OPINION, GETTING BLOODY MARY'S ON A SUNDAY MORNING WITH A DEEPLY HUNGOVER FRIEND WHO HATES THE WORLD IS FAR MORE IMPORTANT THAN GOING TO A CHURCH SERVICE.
AND GOD IS THE ONLY ONE WHO SEEMS TO GET THAT.

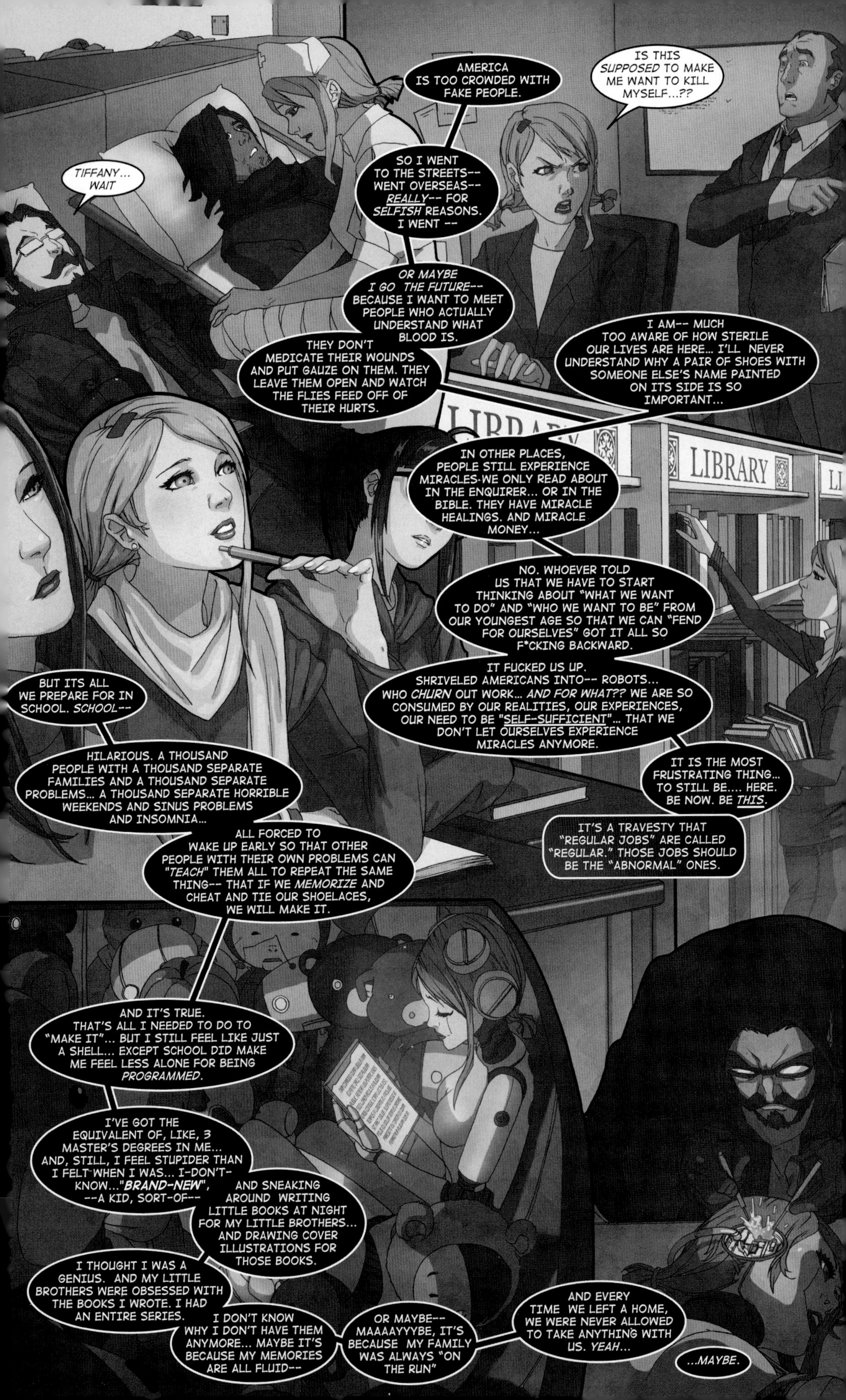

TIFFANY... WAIT
AMERICA IS TOO CROWDED WITH FAKE PEOPLE.
SO I WENT TO THE STREETS-- WENT OVERSEAS-- REALLY-- FOR SELFISH REASONS. I WENT --
OR MAYBE I GO THE FUTURE-- BECAUSE I WANT TO MEET PEOPLE WHO ACTUALLY UNDERSTAND WHAT BLOOD IS.
THEY DON'T MEDICATE THEIR WOUNDS AND PUT GAUZE ON THEM. THEY LEAVE THEM OPEN AND WATCH THE FLIES FEED OFF OF THEIR HURTS.
IS THIS SUPPOSED TO MAKE ME WANT TO KILL MYSELF...??
I AM-- MUCH TOO AWARE OF HOW STERILE OUR LIVES ARE HERE... I'LL NEVER UNDERSTAND WHY A PAIR OF SHOES WITH SOMEONE ELSE'S NAME PAINTED ON ITS SIDE IS SO IMPORTANT...
LIBRARY
IN OTHER PLACES, PEOPLE STILL EXPERIENCE MIRACLES-WE ONLY READ ABOUT IN THE ENQUIRER... OR IN THE BIBLE. THEY HAVE MIRACLE HEALINGS. AND MIRACLE MONEY...
NO. WHOEVER TOLD US THAT WE HAVE TO START THINKING ABOUT "WHAT WE WANT TO DO" AND "WHO WE WANT TO BE" FROM OUR YOUNGEST AGE SO THAT WE CAN "FEND FOR OURSELVES" GOT IT ALL SO F*CKING BACKWARD.
IT FUCKED US UP. SHRIVELED AMERICANS INTO-- ROBOTS... WHO CHURN OUT WORK... AND FOR WHAT?? WE ARE SO CONSUMED BY OUR REALITIES, OUR EXPERIENCES, OUR NEED TO BE "SELF-SUFFICIENT"... THAT WE DON'T LET OURSELVES EXPERIENCE MIRACLES ANYMORE.
IT IS THE MOST FRUSTRATING THING... TO STILL BE.... HERE. BE NOW. BE THIS.
IT'S A TRAVESTY THAT "REGULAR JOBS" ARE CALLED "REGULAR." THOSE JOBS SHOULD BE THE "ABNORMAL" ONES.
BUT ITS ALL WE PREPARE FOR IN SCHOOL. SCHOOL--
HILARIOUS. A THOUSAND PEOPLE WITH A THOUSAND SEPARATE FAMILIES AND A THOUSAND SEPARATE PROBLEMS... A THOUSAND SEPARATE HORRIBLE WEEKENDS AND SINUS PROBLEMS AND INSOMNIA...
ALL FORCED TO WAKE UP EARLY SO THAT OTHER PEOPLE WITH THEIR OWN PROBLEMS CAN "TEACH" THEM ALL TO REPEAT THE SAME THING-- THAT IF WE MEMORIZE AND CHEAT AND TIE OUR SHOELACES, WE WILL MAKE IT.
AND IT'S TRUE. THAT'S ALL I NEEDED TO DO TO "MAKE IT"... BUT I STILL FEEL LIKE JUST A SHELL... EXCEPT SCHOOL DID MAKE ME FEEL LESS ALONE FOR BEING PROGRAMMED.
I'VE GOT THE EQUIVALENT OF, LIKE, 3 MASTER'S DEGREES IN ME... AND, STILL, I FEEL STUPIDER THAN I FELT WHEN I WAS... I-DON'T-KNOW..."BRAND-NEW", --A KID, SORT-OF--
AND SNEAKING AROUND WRITING LITTLE BOOKS AT NIGHT FOR MY LITTLE BROTHERS... AND DRAWING COVER ILLUSTRATIONS FOR THOSE BOOKS.
I THOUGHT I WAS A GENIUS. AND MY LITTLE BROTHERS WERE OBSESSED WITH THE BOOKS I WROTE. I HAD AN ENTIRE SERIES.
I DON'T KNOW WHY I DON'T HAVE THEM ANYMORE... MAYBE IT'S BECAUSE MY MEMORIES ARE ALL FLUID--
OR MAYBE-- MAAAAYYYBE, IT'S BECAUSE MY FAMILY WAS ALWAYS "ON THE RUN"
AND EVERY TIME WE LEFT A HOME, WE WERE NEVER ALLOWED TO TAKE ANYTHING WITH US. YEAH...
...MAYBE.

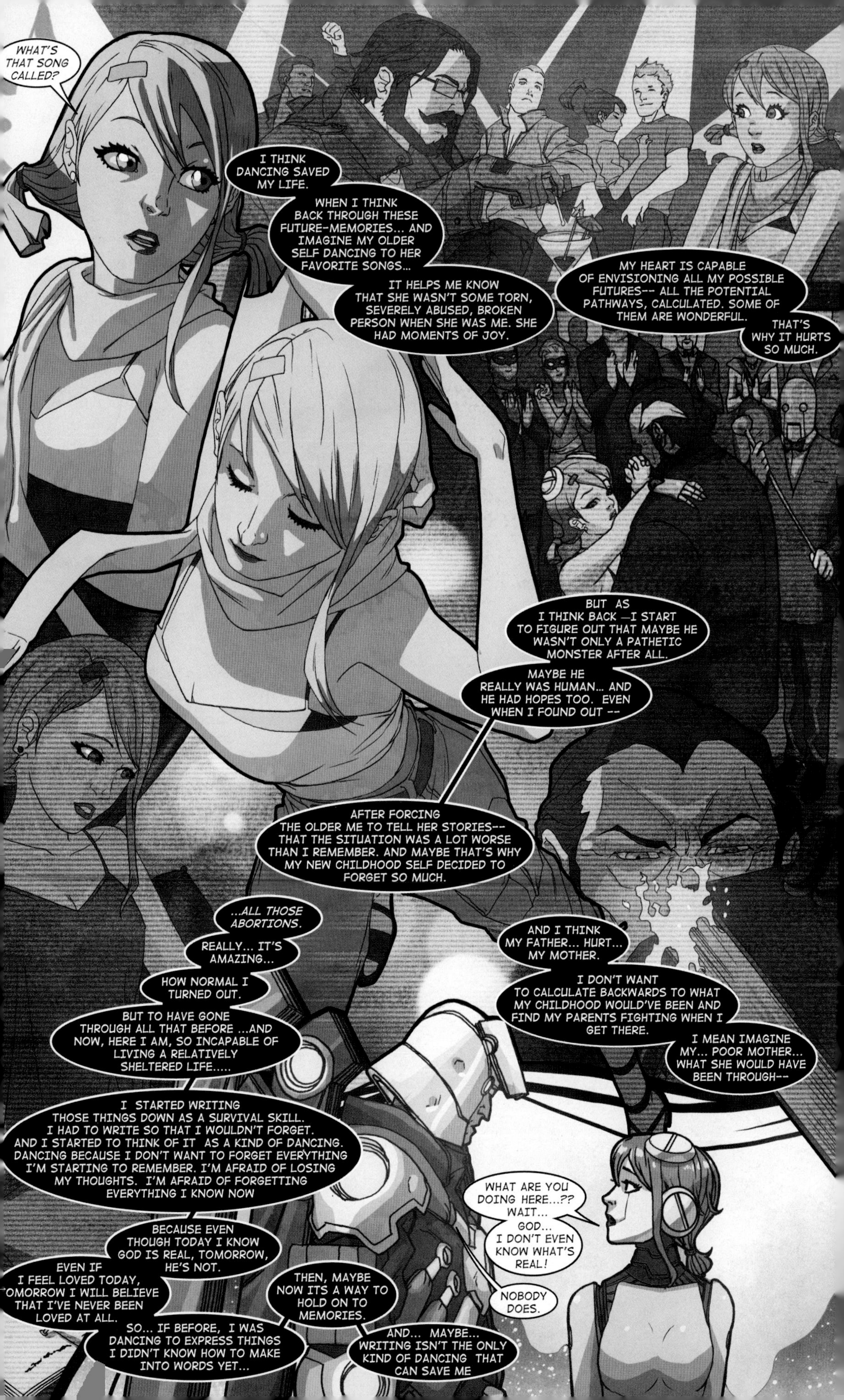
WHAT'S THAT SONG CALLED?
I THINK DANCING SAVED MY LIFE.
WHEN I THINK BACK THROUGH THESE FUTURE-MEMORIES... AND IMAGINE MY OLDER SELF DANCING TO HER FAVORITE SONGS...
IT HELPS ME KNOW THAT SHE WASN'T SOME TORN, SEVERELY ABUSED, BROKEN PERSON WHEN SHE WAS ME. SHE HAD MOMENTS OF JOY.
MY HEART IS CAPABLE OF ENVISIONING ALL MY POSSIBLE FUTURES-- ALL THE POTENTIAL PATHWAYS, CALCULATED. SOME OF THEM ARE WONDERFUL.
THAT'S WHY IT HURTS SO MUCH.
BUT AS I THINK BACK —I START TO FIGURE OUT THAT MAYBE HE WASN'T ONLY A PATHETIC MONSTER AFTER ALL.
MAYBE HE REALLY WAS HUMAN... AND HE HAD HOPES TOO. EVEN WHEN I FOUND OUT --
AFTER FORCING THE OLDER ME TO TELL HER STORIES-- THAT THE SITUATION WAS A LOT WORSE THAN I REMEMBER. AND MAYBE THAT'S WHY MY NEW CHILDHOOD SELF DECIDED TO FORGET SO MUCH.
...ALL THOSE ABORTIONS.
REALLY... IT'S AMAZING...
HOW NORMAL I TURNED OUT.
BUT TO HAVE GONE THROUGH ALL THAT BEFORE ...AND NOW, HERE I AM, SO INCAPABLE OF LIVING A RELATIVELY SHELTERED LIFE.....
AND I THINK MY FATHER... HURT... MY MOTHER.
I DON'T WANT TO CALCULATE BACKWARDS TO WHAT MY CHILDHOOD WOULD'VE BEEN AND FIND MY PARENTS FIGHTING WHEN I GET THERE.
I MEAN IMAGINE MY... POOR MOTHER... WHAT SHE WOULD HAVE BEEN THROUGH--
I STARTED WRITING THOSE THINGS DOWN AS A SURVIVAL SKILL. I HAD TO WRITE SO THAT I WOULDN'T FORGET. AND I STARTED TO THINK OF IT AS A KIND OF DANCING. DANCING BECAUSE I DON'T WANT TO FORGET EVERYTHING I'M STARTING TO REMEMBER. I'M AFRAID OF LOSING MY THOUGHTS. I'M AFRAID OF FORGETTING EVERYTHING I KNOW NOW
WHAT ARE YOU DOING HERE...?? WAIT... GOD... I DON'T EVEN KNOW WHAT'S REAL!
NOBODY DOES.
BECAUSE EVEN THOUGH TODAY I KNOW GOD IS REAL, TOMORROW, HE'S NOT.
EVEN IF I FEEL LOVED TODAY, TOMORROW I WILL BELIEVE THAT I'VE NEVER BEEN LOVED AT ALL.
SO... IF BEFORE, I WAS DANCING TO EXPRESS THINGS I DIDN'T KNOW HOW TO MAKE INTO WORDS YET...
THEN, MAYBE NOW ITS A WAY TO HOLD ON TO MEMORIES.
AND... MAYBE... WRITING ISN'T THE ONLY KIND OF DANCING THAT CAN SAVE ME

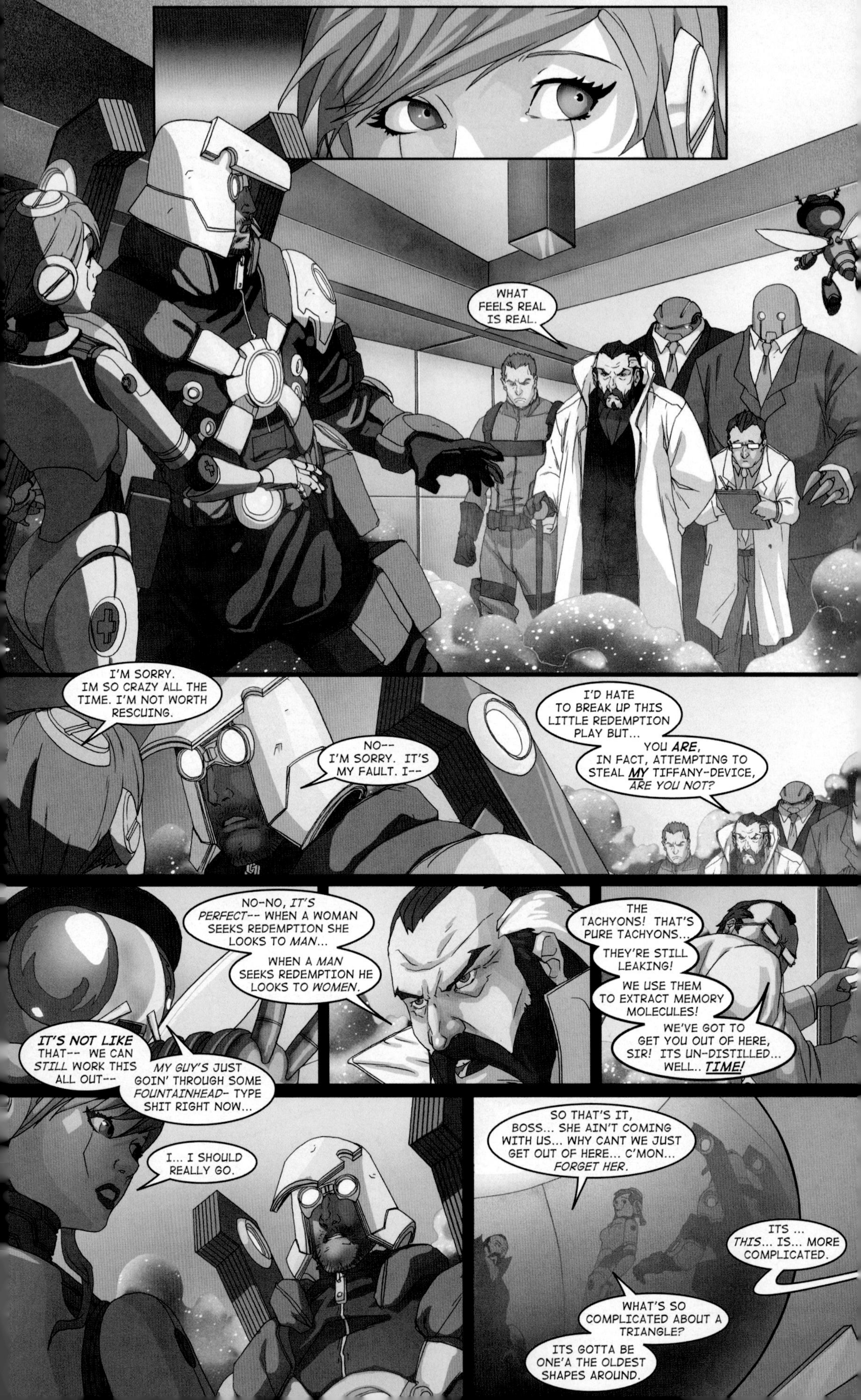
WHAT FEELS REAL IS REAL.
I'M SORRY. IM SO CRAZY ALL THE TIME. I'M NOT WORTH RESCUING.
NO-- I'M SORRY. IT'S MY FAULT. I--
I'D HATE TO BREAK UP THIS LITTLE REDEMPTION PLAY BUT...
YOU *ARE*, IN FACT, ATTEMPTING TO STEAL *MY* TIFFANY-DEVICE, *ARE YOU NOT?*
NO-NO, *IT'S PERFECT*-- WHEN A WOMAN SEEKS REDEMPTION SHE LOOKS TO *MAN*...
WHEN A *MAN* SEEKS REDEMPTION HE LOOKS TO *WOMEN*.
IT'S NOT LIKE THAT-- WE CAN *STILL* WORK THIS ALL OUT--
MY GUY'S JUST GOIN' THROUGH SOME *FOUNTAINHEAD*- TYPE SHIT RIGHT NOW...
THE TACHYONS! THAT'S PURE TACHYONS...
THEY'RE STILL LEAKING!
WE USE THEM TO EXTRACT MEMORY MOLECULES!
WE'VE GOT TO GET YOU OUT OF HERE, SIR! ITS UN-DISTILLED... WELL.. ***TIME!***
I... I SHOULD REALLY GO.
SO THAT'S IT, BOSS... SHE AIN'T COMING WITH US... WHY CANT WE JUST GET OUT OF HERE... C'MON... *FORGET HER*.
ITS ... *THIS*... IS... MORE COMPLICATED.
WHAT'S SO COMPLICATED ABOUT A TRIANGLE?
ITS GOTTA BE ONE'A THE OLDEST SHAPES AROUND.

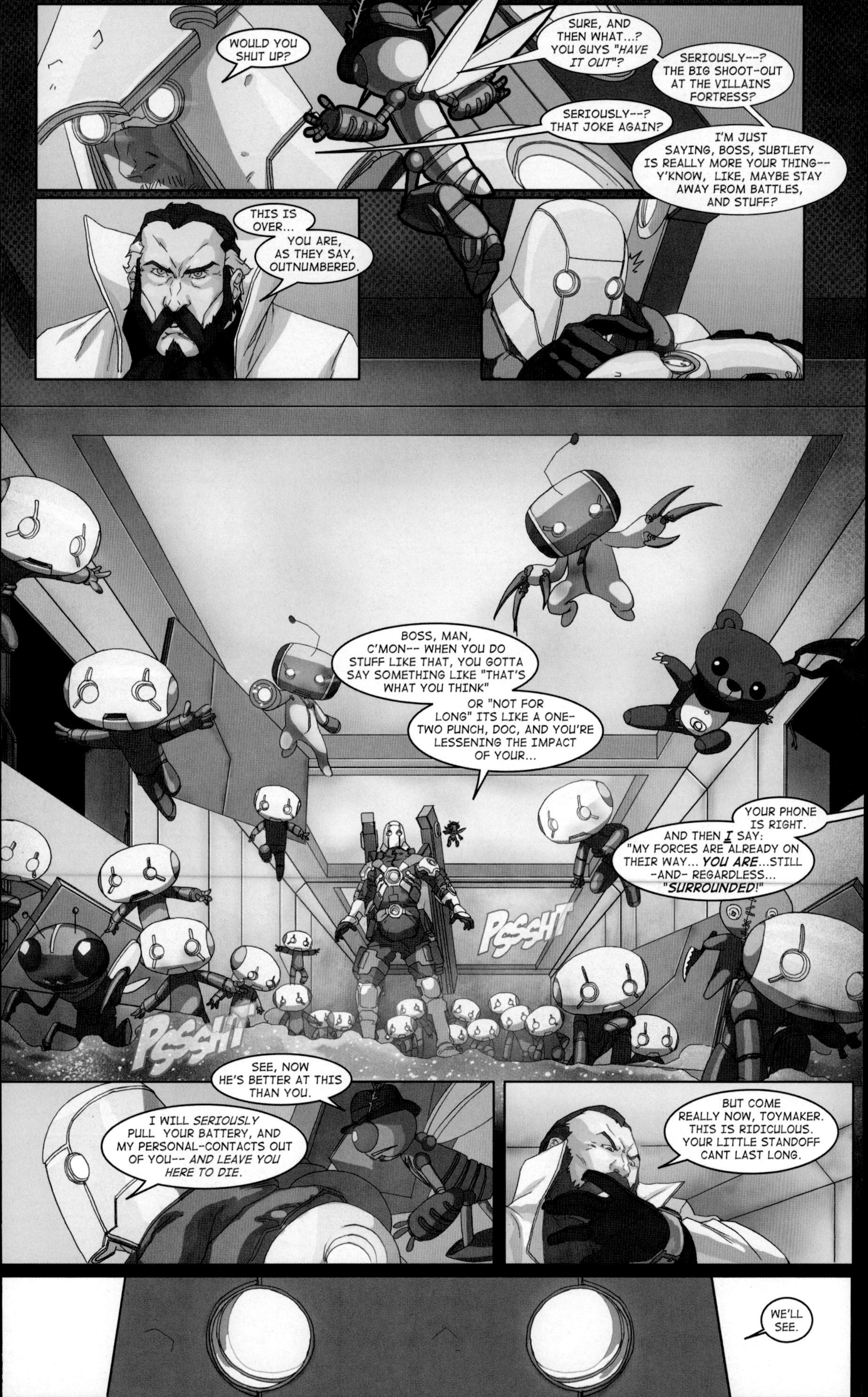
WOULD YOU SHUT UP?
SURE, AND THEN WHAT...? YOU GUYS "HAVE IT OUT"?
SERIOUSLY--? THE BIG SHOOT-OUT AT THE VILLAINS FORTRESS?
SERIOUSLY--? THAT JOKE AGAIN?
I'M JUST SAYING, BOSS, SUBTLETY IS REALLY MORE YOUR THING-- Y'KNOW, LIKE, MAYBE STAY AWAY FROM BATTLES, AND STUFF?
THIS IS OVER...
YOU ARE, AS THEY SAY, OUTNUMBERED.
BOSS, MAN, C'MON-- WHEN YOU DO STUFF LIKE THAT, YOU GOTTA SAY SOMETHING LIKE "THAT'S WHAT YOU THINK"
OR "NOT FOR LONG" ITS LIKE A ONE-TWO PUNCH, DOC, AND YOU'RE LESSENING THE IMPACT OF YOUR...
YOUR PHONE IS RIGHT.
AND THEN I SAY: "MY FORCES ARE ALREADY ON THEIR WAY... YOU ARE...STILL -AND- REGARDLESS... "SURROUNDED!"
PSSSHT
PSSSHT
SEE, NOW HE'S BETTER AT THIS THAN YOU.
I WILL SERIOUSLY PULL YOUR BATTERY, AND MY PERSONAL-CONTACTS OUT OF YOU-- AND LEAVE YOU HERE TO DIE.
BUT COME REALLY NOW, TOYMAKER. THIS IS RIDICULOUS. YOUR LITTLE STANDOFF CANT LAST LONG.
WE'LL SEE.

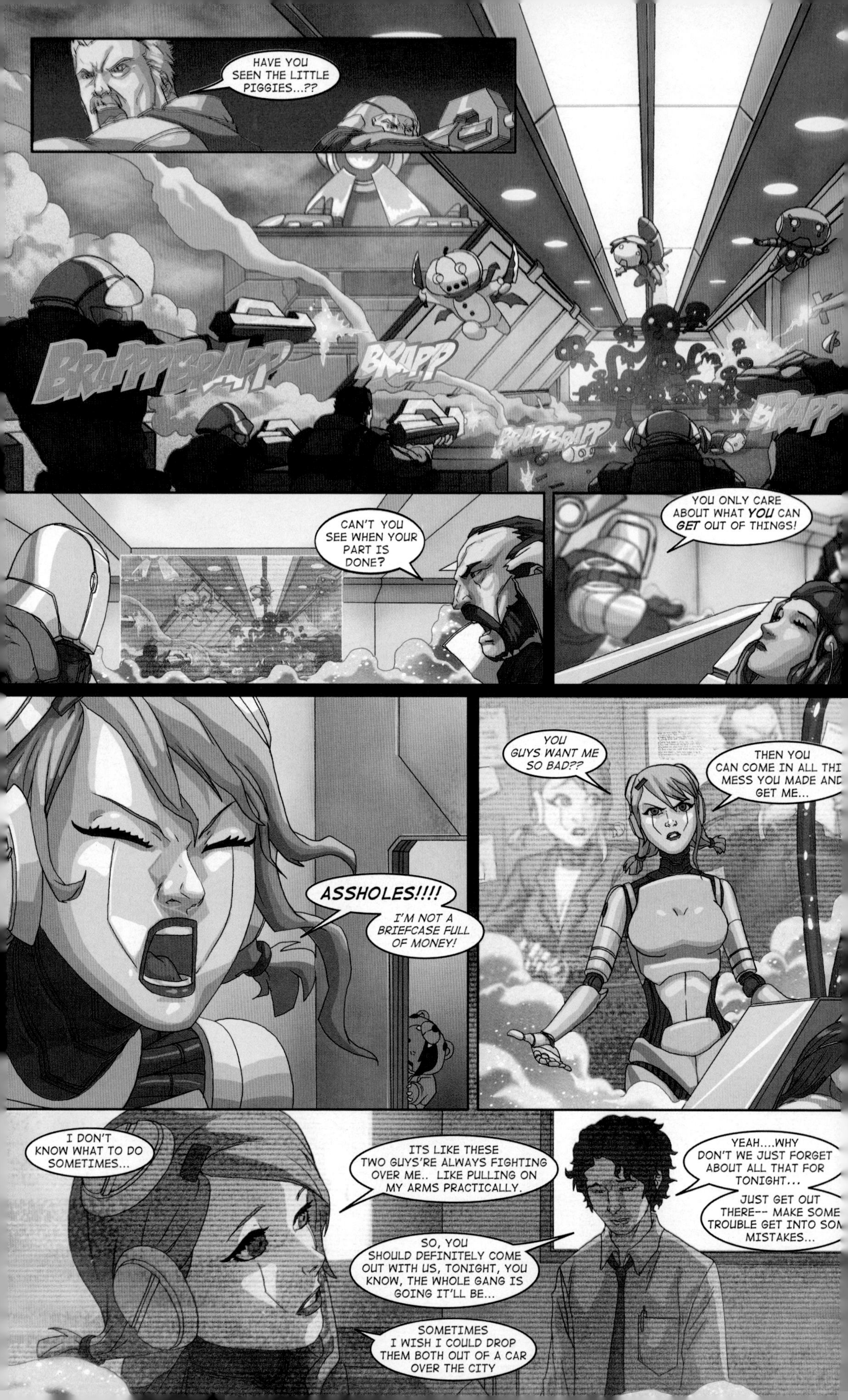
HAVE YOU SEEN THE LITTLE PIGGIES...??
BRAPPBRAPP
BRAPP
BRAPPBRAPP
BRAPP
CAN'T YOU SEE WHEN YOUR PART IS DONE?
YOU ONLY CARE ABOUT WHAT YOU CAN GET OUT OF THINGS!
ASSHOLES!!!!
I'M NOT A BRIEFCASE FULL OF MONEY!
YOU GUYS WANT ME SO BAD??
THEN YOU CAN COME IN ALL THI MESS YOU MADE AND GET ME...
I DON'T KNOW WHAT TO DO SOMETIMES...
ITS LIKE THESE TWO GUYS'RE ALWAYS FIGHTING OVER ME.. LIKE PULLING ON MY ARMS PRACTICALLY.
YEAH....WHY DON'T WE JUST FORGET ABOUT ALL THAT FOR TONIGHT...
JUST GET OUT THERE-- MAKE SOME TROUBLE GET INTO SON MISTAKES...
SO, YOU SHOULD DEFINITELY COME OUT WITH US, TONIGHT, YOU KNOW, THE WHOLE GANG IS GOING IT'LL BE...
SOMETIMES I WISH I COULD DROP THEM BOTH OUT OF A CAR OVER THE CITY

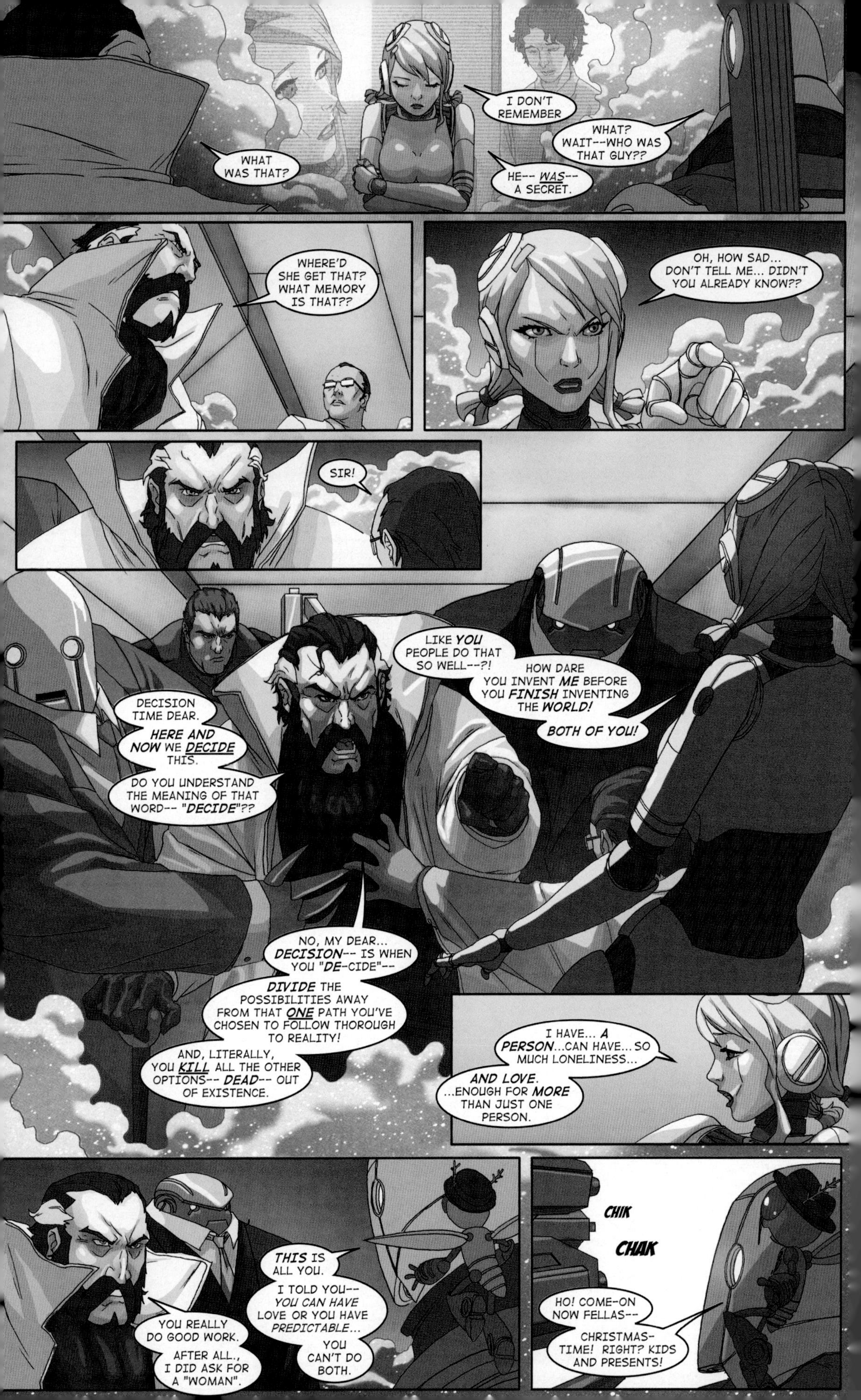
WHAT WAS THAT?
I DON'T REMEMBER
WHAT? WAIT--WHO WAS THAT GUY??
HE-- WAS-- A SECRET.
WHERE'D SHE GET THAT? WHAT MEMORY IS THAT??
OH, HOW SAD... DON'T TELL ME... DIDN'T YOU ALREADY KNOW??
SIR!
LIKE YOU PEOPLE DO THAT SO WELL--?!
HOW DARE YOU INVENT ME BEFORE YOU FINISH INVENTING THE WORLD!
BOTH OF YOU!
DECISION TIME DEAR. HERE AND NOW WE DECIDE THIS.
DO YOU UNDERSTAND THE MEANING OF THAT WORD-- "DECIDE"??
NO, MY DEAR... DECISION-- IS WHEN YOU "DE-CIDE"--
DIVIDE THE POSSIBILITIES AWAY FROM THAT ONE PATH YOU'VE CHOSEN TO FOLLOW THOROUGH TO REALITY!
AND, LITERALLY, YOU KILL ALL THE OTHER OPTIONS-- DEAD-- OUT OF EXISTENCE.
I HAVE... A PERSON...CAN HAVE... SO MUCH LONELINESS...
AND LOVE. ...ENOUGH FOR MORE THAN JUST ONE PERSON.
YOU REALLY DO GOOD WORK.
AFTER ALL., I DID ASK FOR A "WOMAN".
THIS IS ALL YOU.
I TOLD YOU-- YOU CAN HAVE LOVE OR YOU HAVE PREDICTABLE...
YOU CAN'T DO BOTH.
CHIK
CHAK
HO! COME-ON NOW FELLAS--
CHRISTMAS-TIME! RIGHT? KIDS AND PRESENTS!

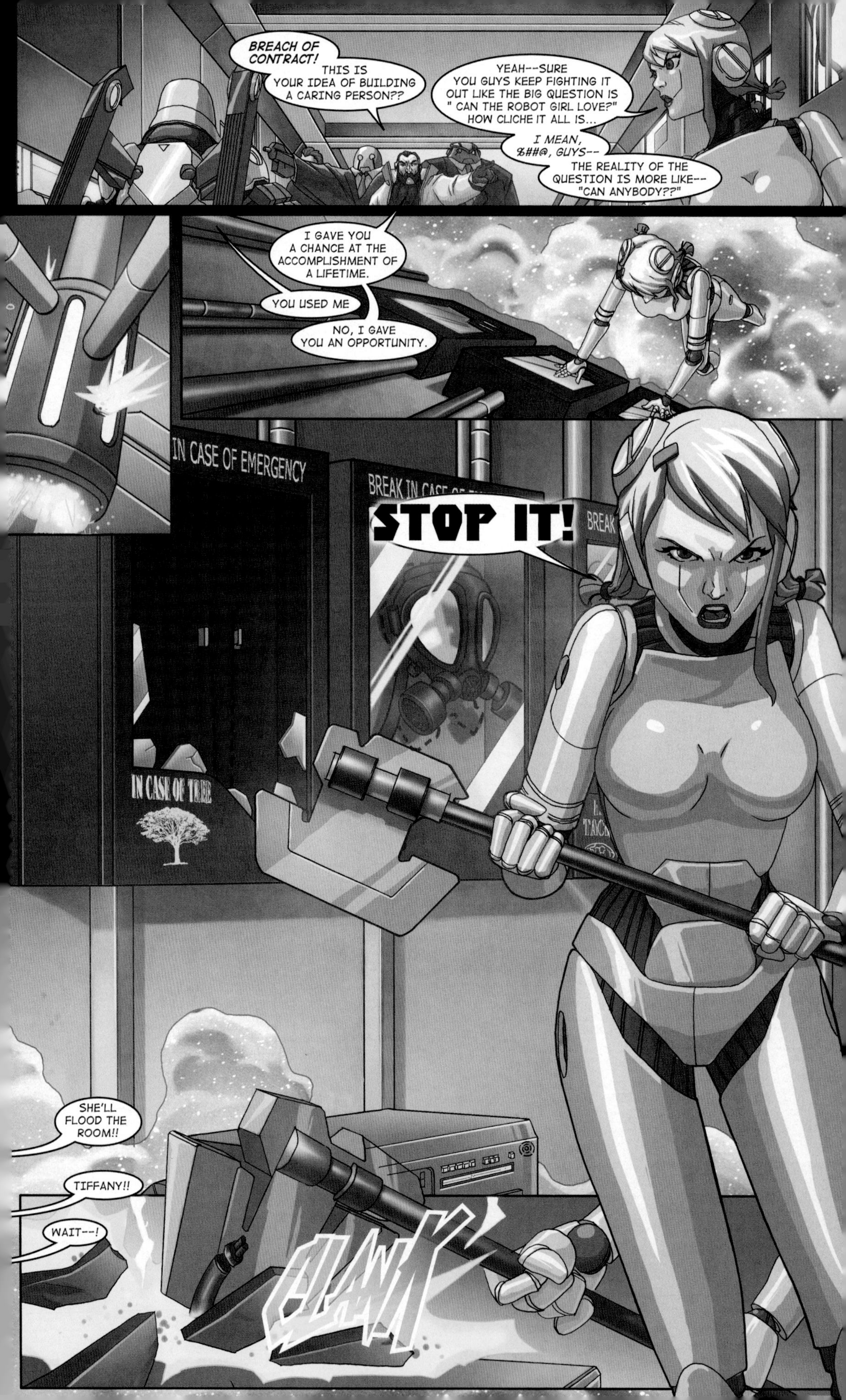
BREACH OF CONTRACT! THIS IS YOUR IDEA OF BUILDING A CARING PERSON??
YEAH--SURE YOU GUYS KEEP FIGHTING IT OUT LIKE THE BIG QUESTION IS " CAN THE ROBOT GIRL LOVE?" HOW CLICHE IT ALL IS...
I MEAN, %##@, GUYS--
THE REALITY OF THE QUESTION IS MORE LIKE-- "CAN ANYBODY??"
I GAVE YOU A CHANCE AT THE ACCOMPLISHMENT OF A LIFETIME.
YOU USED ME
NO, I GAVE YOU AN OPPORTUNITY.
IN CASE OF EMERGENCY
BREAK IN CASE OF
STOP IT!
BREAK
IN CASE OF TREE
SHE'LL FLOOD THE ROOM!!
TIFFANY!!
WAIT--!
CLANK

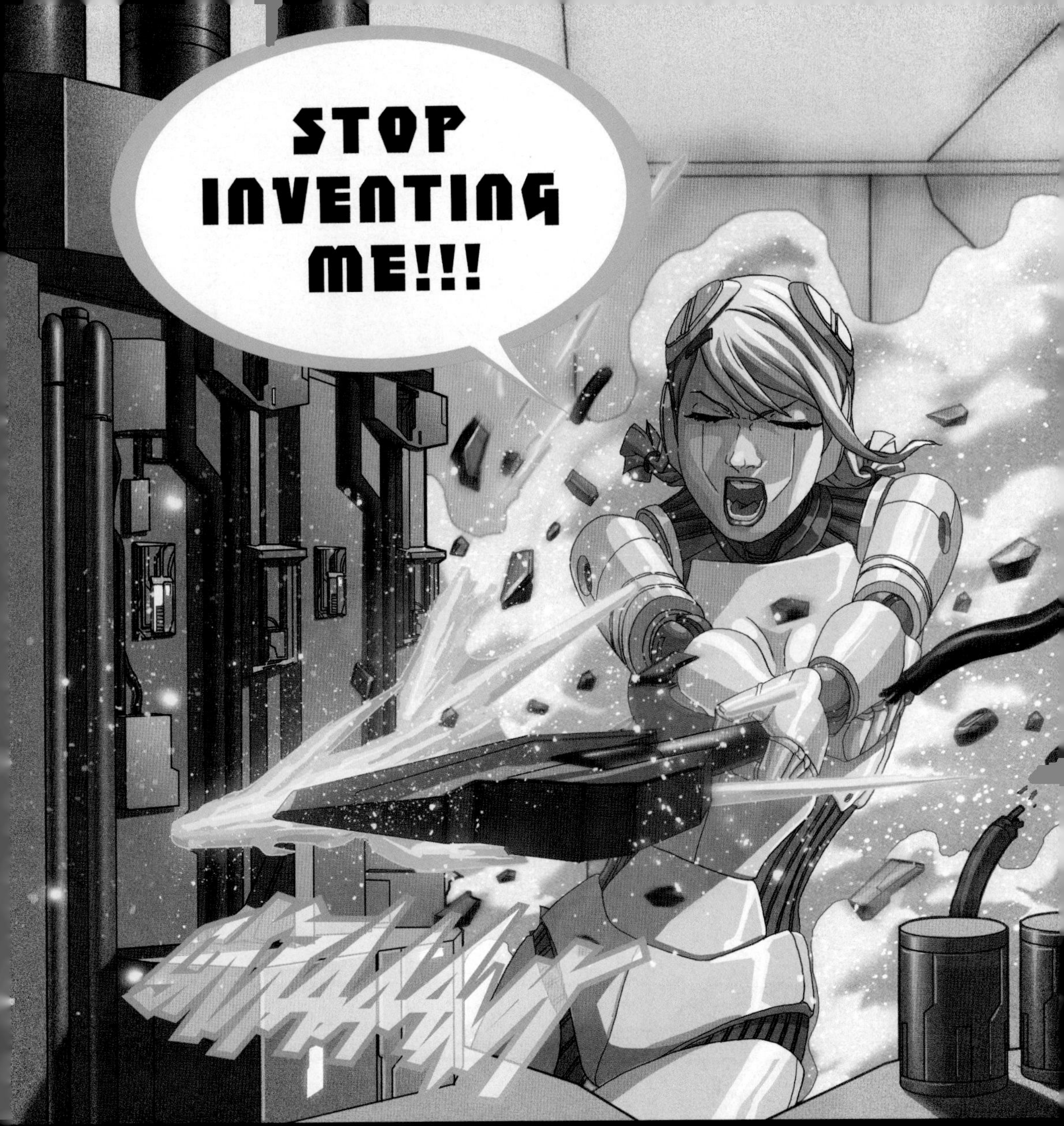
STOP INVENTING ME!!!

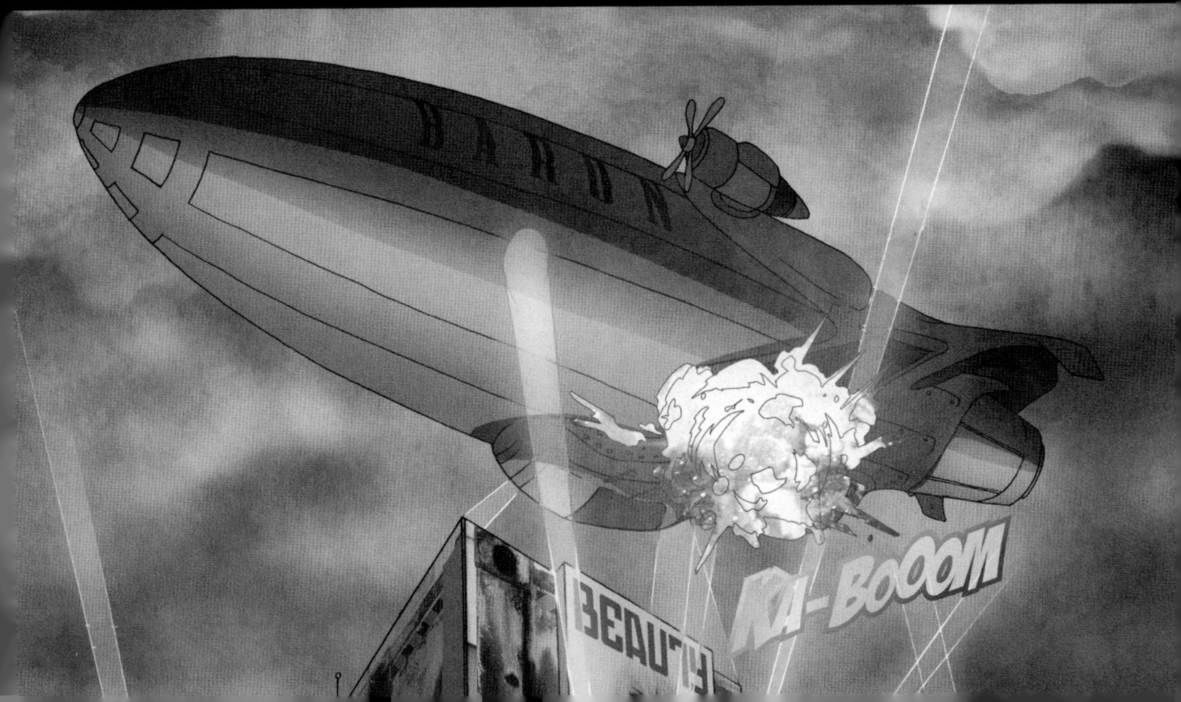
KA-BOOOM

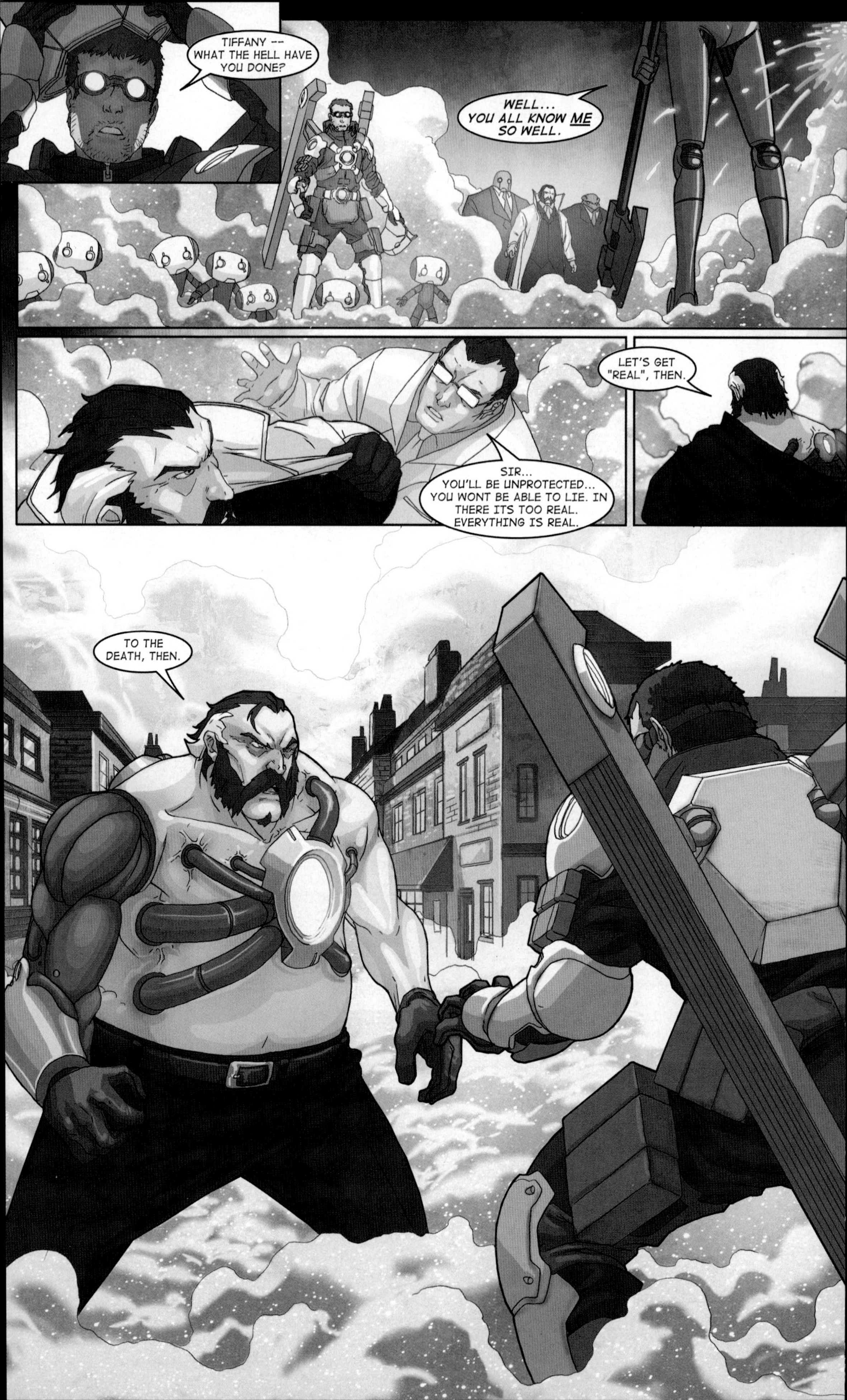
TIFFANY -- WHAT THE HELL HAVE YOU DONE?
WELL... YOU ALL KNOW ME SO WELL.
SIR... YOU'LL BE UNPROTECTED... YOU WONT BE ABLE TO LIE. IN THERE ITS TOO REAL. EVERYTHING IS REAL.
LET'S GET "REAL", THEN.
TO THE DEATH, THEN.

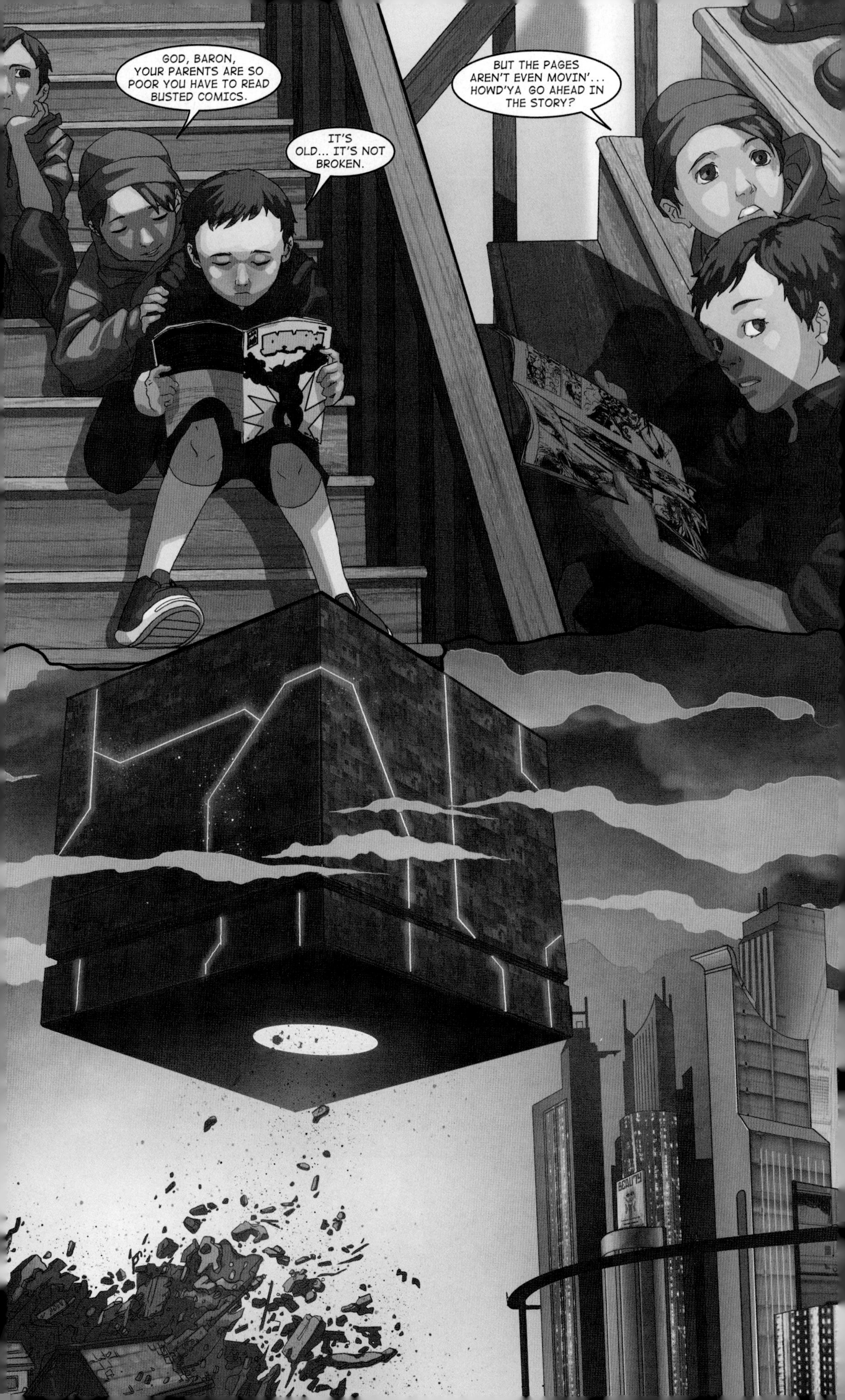
GOD, BARON, YOUR PARENTS ARE SO POOR YOU HAVE TO READ BUSTED COMICS.
IT'S OLD... IT'S NOT BROKEN.
BUT THE PAGES AREN'T EVEN MOVIN'... HOWD'YA GO AHEAD IN THE STORY?
BEAUTY

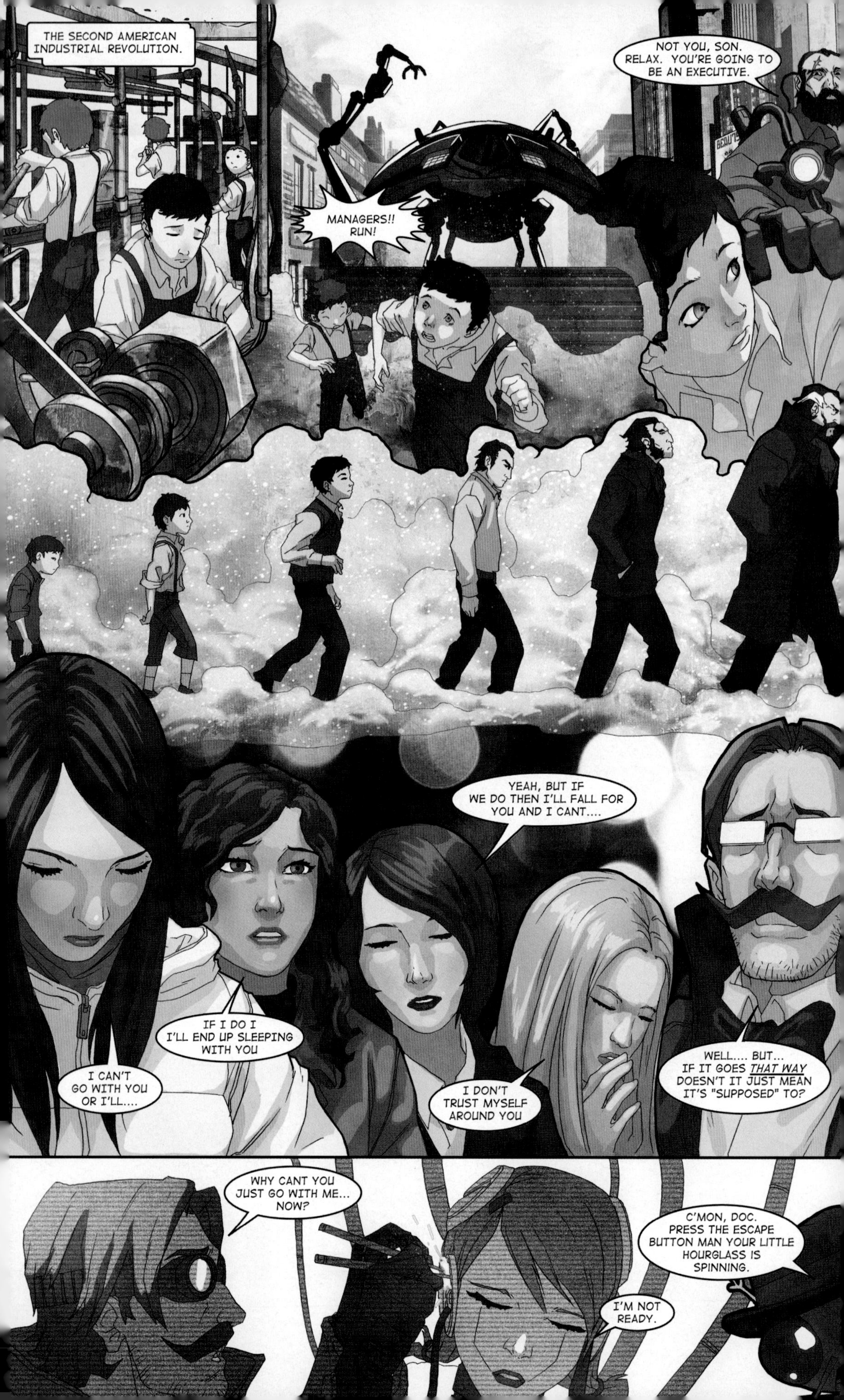
THE SECOND AMERICAN INDUSTRIAL REVOLUTION.
MANAGERS!! RUN!
NOT YOU, SON. RELAX. YOU'RE GOING TO BE AN EXECUTIVE.
YEAH, BUT IF WE DO THEN I'LL FALL FOR YOU AND I CANT....
I CAN'T GO WITH YOU OR I'LL....
IF I DO I I'LL END UP SLEEPING WITH YOU
I DON'T TRUST MYSELF AROUND YOU
WELL.... BUT... IF IT GOES *THAT WAY* DOESN'T IT JUST MEAN IT'S "SUPPOSED" TO?
WHY CANT YOU JUST GO WITH ME... NOW?
C'MON, DOC. PRESS THE ESCAPE BUTTON MAN YOUR LITTLE HOURGLASS IS SPINNING.
I'M NOT READY.

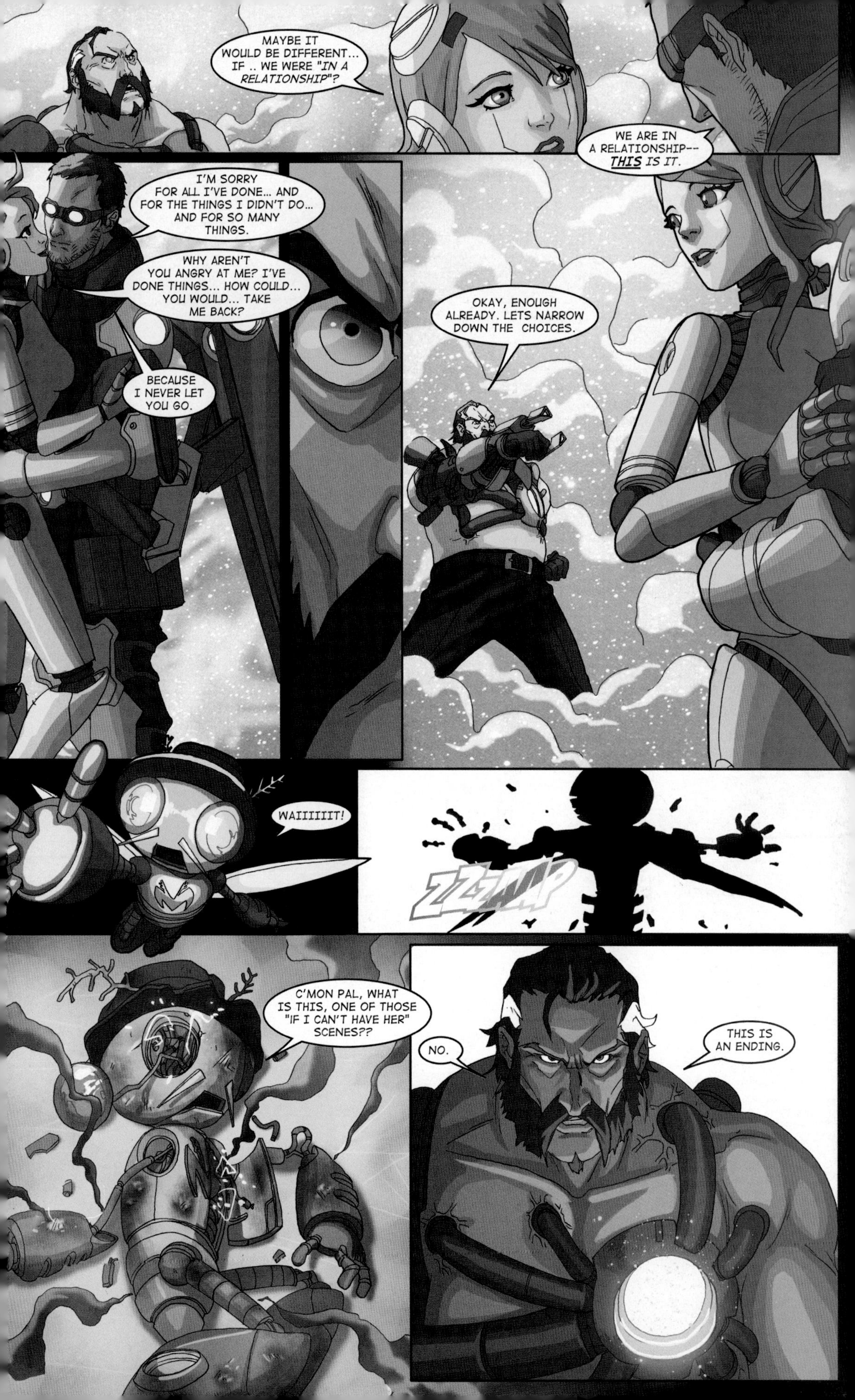
MAYBE IT WOULD BE DIFFERENT... IF .. WE WERE "IN A RELATIONSHIP"?
WE ARE IN A RELATIONSHIP-- THIS IS IT.
I'M SORRY FOR ALL I'VE DONE... AND FOR THE THINGS I DIDN'T DO... AND FOR SO MANY THINGS.
WHY AREN'T YOU ANGRY AT ME? I'VE DONE THINGS... HOW COULD... YOU WOULD... TAKE ME BACK?
BECAUSE I NEVER LET YOU GO.
OKAY, ENOUGH ALREADY. LETS NARROW DOWN THE CHOICES.
WAIIIIIIT!
ZZZAAP
C'MON PAL, WHAT IS THIS, ONE OF THOSE "IF I CAN'T HAVE HER" SCENES??
NO.
THIS IS AN ENDING.

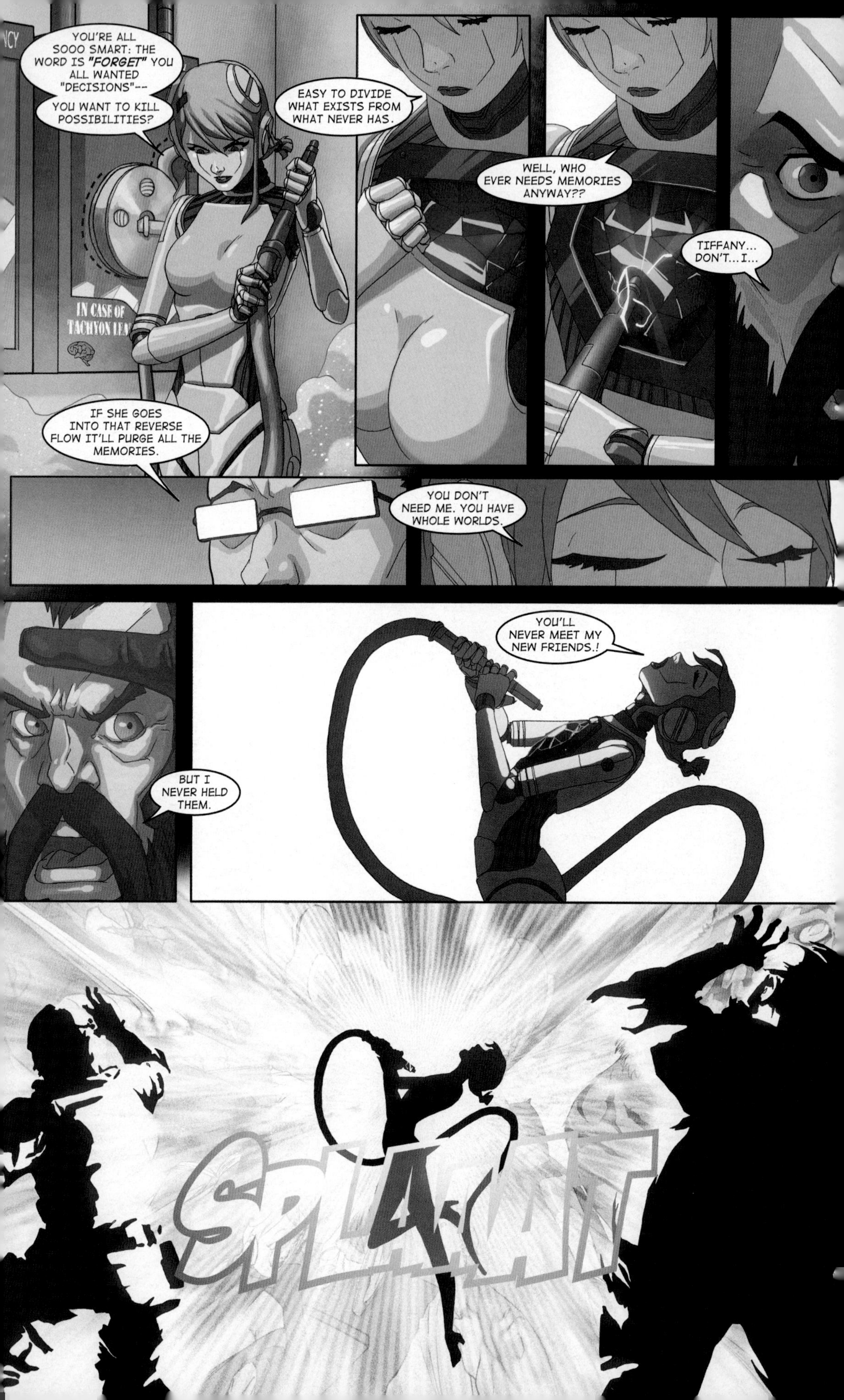
YOU'RE ALL SOOO SMART: THE WORD IS "FORGET" YOU ALL WANTED "DECISIONS"--
YOU WANT TO KILL POSSIBILITIES?
IN CASE OF TACHYON LEA
EASY TO DIVIDE WHAT EXISTS FROM WHAT NEVER HAS.
WELL, WHO EVER NEEDS MEMORIES ANYWAY??
TIFFANY... DON'T...I...
IF SHE GOES INTO THAT REVERSE FLOW IT'LL PURGE ALL THE MEMORIES.
YOU DON'T NEED ME. YOU HAVE WHOLE WORLDS.
BUT I NEVER HELD THEM.
YOU'LL NEVER MEET MY NEW FRIENDS.!
SPLAT

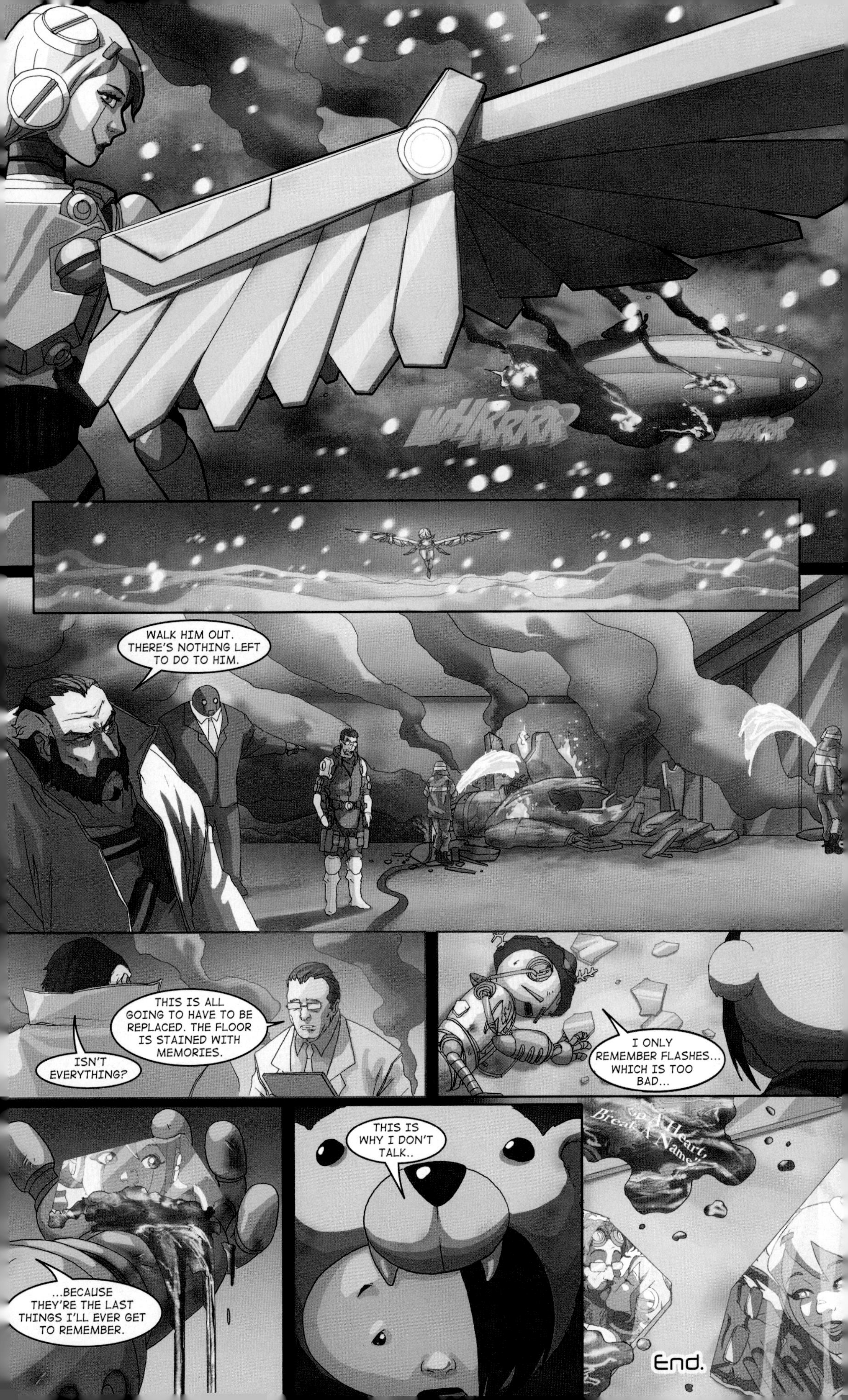
WHRRRR
WHRRR
WALK HIM OUT. THERE'S NOTHING LEFT TO DO TO HIM.
THIS IS ALL GOING TO HAVE TO BE REPLACED. THE FLOOR IS STAINED WITH MEMORIES.
ISN'T EVERYTHING?
I ONLY REMEMBER FLASHES... WHICH IS TOO BAD...
...BECAUSE THEY'RE THE LAST THINGS I'LL EVER GET TO REMEMBER.
THIS IS WHY I DON'T TALK..
A Heart, Break A Name
End.

PETE WENTZ / DARREN ROMANELLI INTERVIEW

by Andrew Steven Harris

*So, you think you're holding a copy of **Fall Out Toy Works** in your hands. But you're not. **Fall Out Toy Works** is actually not something you can simply hold; it's not just a book, it's a concept, and one that crosses over between music, fashion, art, storytelling, the Internet and more. Co-creators Darren "The Doctor" Romanelli, one of the new breaking-edge designers of the fashion world, and Pete Wentz, best known as the frontman/bassist of **Fall Out Boy** and now **Black Cards**, sat down to outline their vision, its origin, and the concept fragment of it that you now hold in your hands.*

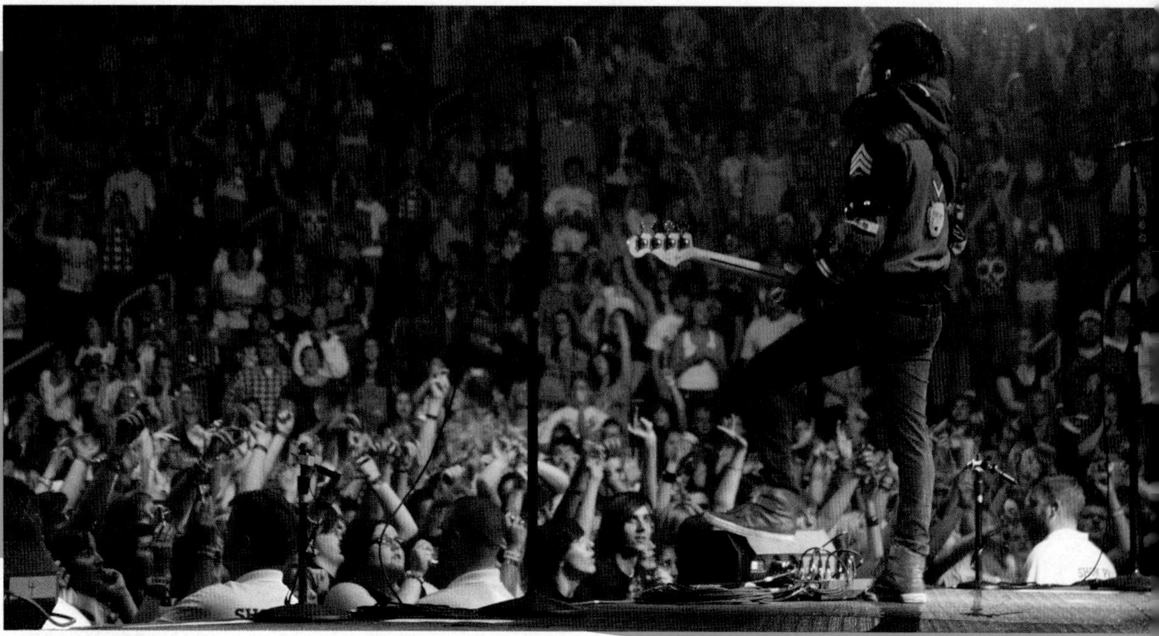

Q: ***So, music and fashion. Obvious partners since the days of the Beatles and Bowie. How'd you two come to hook up?***

DARREN: I met Pete originally because Pete was into my gear. It was totally organic, not a business thing at all. From there we became friends, and one day Pete said to me, "How do you feel about flipping some gear for Fall Out Boy for the next tour?" And that's when we began to collaborate. I made each of them jackets, sort of signature items for them.

PETE: I was into a bunch of stuff that Romanelli was doing, Coca Cola vests and the Dr. Love collection, so I contacted him through his gallery. I wanted to meet him, because the type of stuff he was doing you didn't really see anywhere else and I was totally connecting with it. When we talked, we were totally in synch. I kept going into different corners of ideas -- "What about this?" "What about that?" – and it developed that we both saw a kind of kindred spirit. We both had the same way of viewing art, of viewing the world, and how you make statements with pop art. There are very few people doing it across different media, using different media to relate different aspects of a single statement.

Q: So what we're talking about here is fashion, music, performance, visual art—the way that a song or album becomes a stage show and then a comic book, but it's all part of one single pop art statement. And in a way the combination itself becomes another part of the art.

PETE: Exactly right.

Q: How do you turn that statement into stage gear?

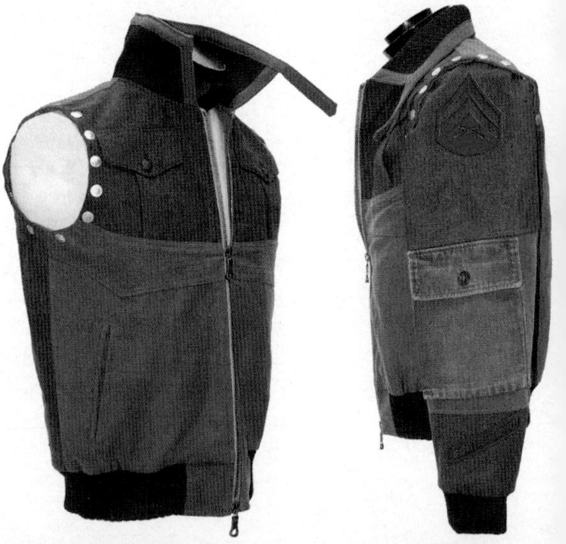

DARREN: We synched on some themes we wanted to come up with, and the garments I used deconstruct vintage military items. I deconstructed military items as if the world was blown apart, very post-apocalyptic, but with the majority of the items from the 1960s. All this has several meanings to me, since people often associate the military with war, but those military garments also helped save people's lives. So there's all that energy in them, and I wanted to bring as much of that energy to the set as I could.

I also had to work very organically, intuitively, since I didn't even know their sizes; I watched videos of them playing and had to go off their style—Andy's a vegan, so didn't want to use leather in his creations and also being that he's the drummer I made his gear with the option to go sleeveless, and so on. I had to come up with pieces that felt right, so I really worked off my flow with Pete.

PETE: It changed how the band played, too. The jackets, for example, have completely amped up what we're doing. We'd come out to this video shoot, and there'd be this crazy collection of riots, security would come out as SWAT police at the edge of the stage; then halfway through the set we would change and come out in Romanelli jackets as part of the post-economic collapse, and re-enter as the new Fall Out Boy.

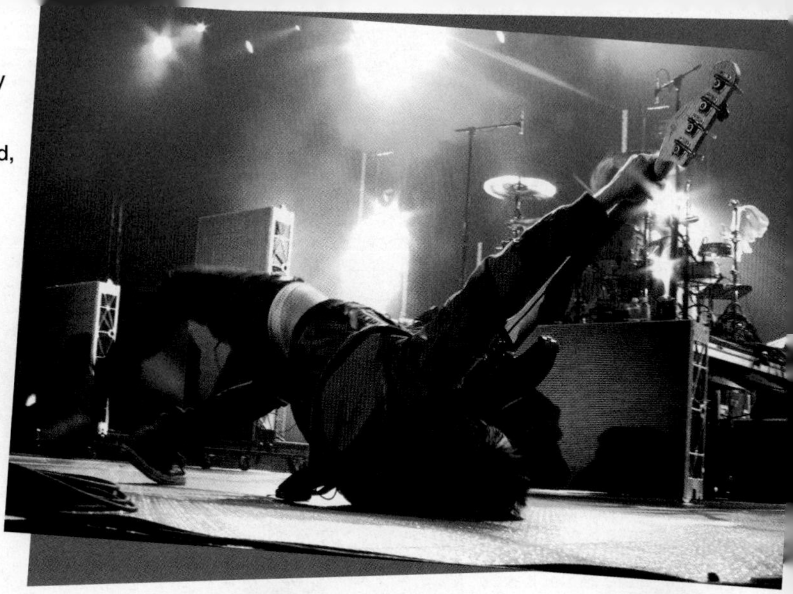

DARREN: And then right after that, we lost touch, and I didn't know how to find Pete. So I tracked him down on JDate.com.

(laughter)

No, seriously, everyone was stoked, and we immediately were like "how do we keep this going", we had a really good flow. So we met at one of our houses and started tossing around ideas, about the world we had started to create. I had always wanted to do a comic book, but I think Pete at the beginning was a bit skeptical. I said "hit me with some ideas", and he said: *Tiffany Blews.*

PETE: There's already a futuristic feeling for the songs on the record, it's the kind of thing that could be playing in the world of Fall Out Toy Works. We've got Lil Wayne on it, and he was like, "Do you want me to rap on it?" And we said, "No, we definitely want you to sing." So it's all these different voices already coming out of *Tiffany Blews* in general. And we thought, "Could we create characters in the expanse of this song?" And the ideas started coming from there.

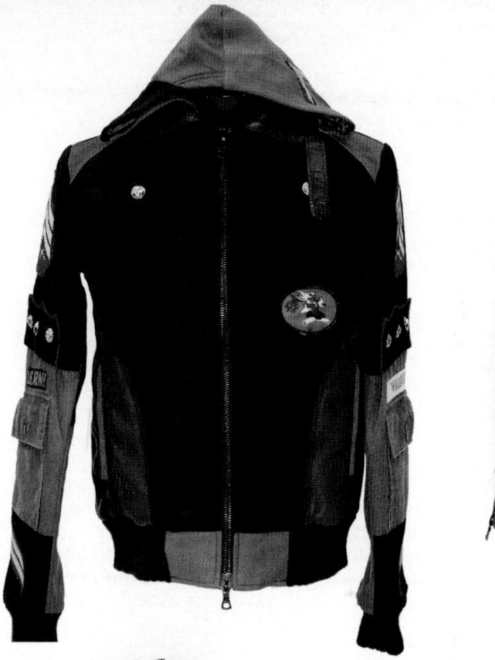

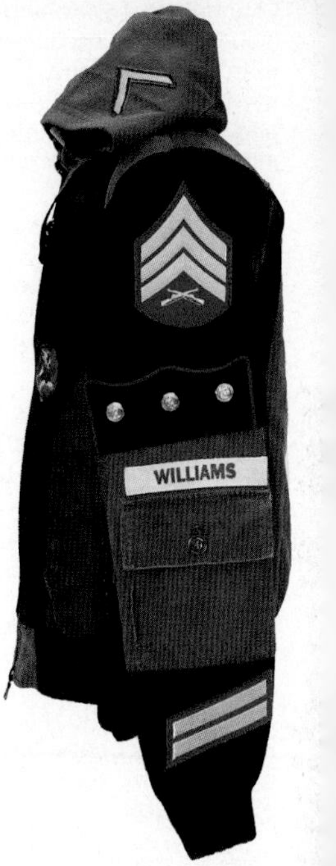
WILLIAMS

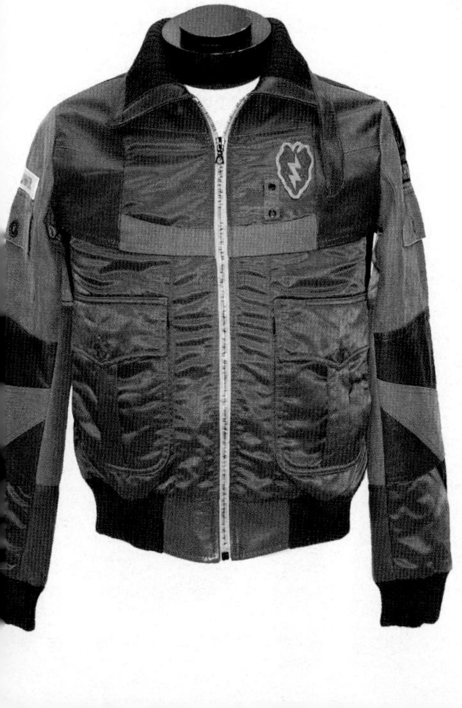

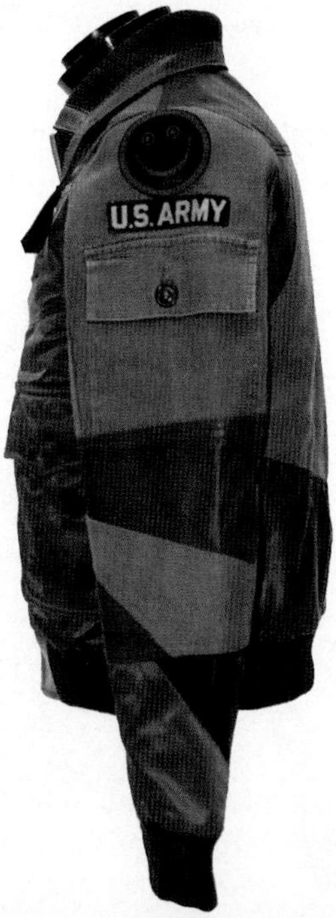
U.S.ARMY

Q: It seems like you drew on all sorts of influences too.

PETE: Oh, definitely. You can find a bit of Pinocchio, Blade Runner, a little of Metropolis—the anime version that came out about 10 years ago—lots of influences. And not just entertainment, either. I'm interested in exploring where society is going in general; Twitter, texting, email…it seems that the more connectivity we have, the less connected we are. A computer does all these things, and eventually if you could create a cyborg human, it raises the question: What are the morals that fit into that? What if your computer could feel something? Can something artificial actually fall in love? And if it was designed to be that way, does that make its feelings any less real? It's definitely that kind of grey area, and it's where technology is leading us. Art and music and storytelling have to start examining those questions.

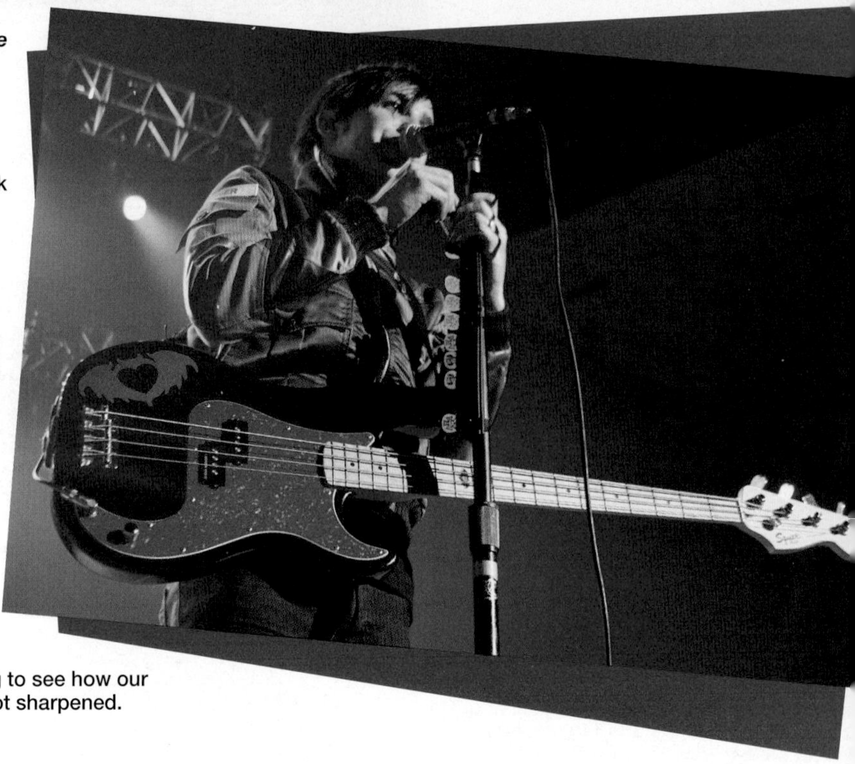

Q: That sounds like a massive challenge. How well do you think you did with it?

DARREN: Well, we're just getting started. The book is incredible, it was a ton of work bringing this thing to life, and everyone collectively is really proud of the end product, which is just the first phase of what's to come. It's nice to be working on the trade paperback now, we really feel like it was both a creative and commercial success.

PETE: Yeah, about that…the truth is, when we started out, we didn't completely realize what a process it was. The intense amount of work that goes into every issue. It was very different watching each issue created, so different than writing a song. It really made us bring our game, and it's been really interesting to see how our initial ideas that were blunt got sharpened.

Q: So what happens now?

DARREN: There's a motion comic in the works right now. Anna Farris is playing Tiffany, and that's definitely exciting. The end game here for us would be a feature film. That's obviously in the stars. And creating toys and collectibles – definitely something that's on the radar down the road.

PETE: The idea that we both agreed on was that it would actually be a series of cohesive ideas, across numerous formats: music, comic books, toys, the stage show, T-shirts, the interactive world, web sites…that's what's so inspiring to me about Darren. I didn't initially have it on such a grandiose level; it's what got me so excited. It's also been really important to find all the right partners for these different aspects. For clothes and toys, Darren has that locked. But Darren and I had never written a comic ourselves, so finding the right partners to help navigate each individual area was essential.

DARREN: I sat down with Nathan Cabrera, tossed around ideas with him for two weeks and really ran with it. When we were done I brought these initial designs to Pete, and he loved them. Jeff introduced us to Brett Lewis, a really tripped-out guy in a nice way, who gave me copies of his series DC Comics trade Winter Men. His work is supercreative; he really nailed it on the story. For art, Sami Basri and the guys at Imaginary Friends Studio totally nailed every character, even the city itself. Dave Elliott wrangled everybody together, he was completely in synch with what we were doing. Dave's got this ability to see exactly what you want before you want it. They all did an excellent job.

Q: Motion comics are still pretty much brand-new, so you're definitely out there on the cutting edge. What do you have planned even further past that?

DARREN: We're working on a couple of ideas, but I really can't announce them yet. There's the cutting edge, and right now we're past the cutting edge. That means you'll have to come all the way up to the edge to see it.

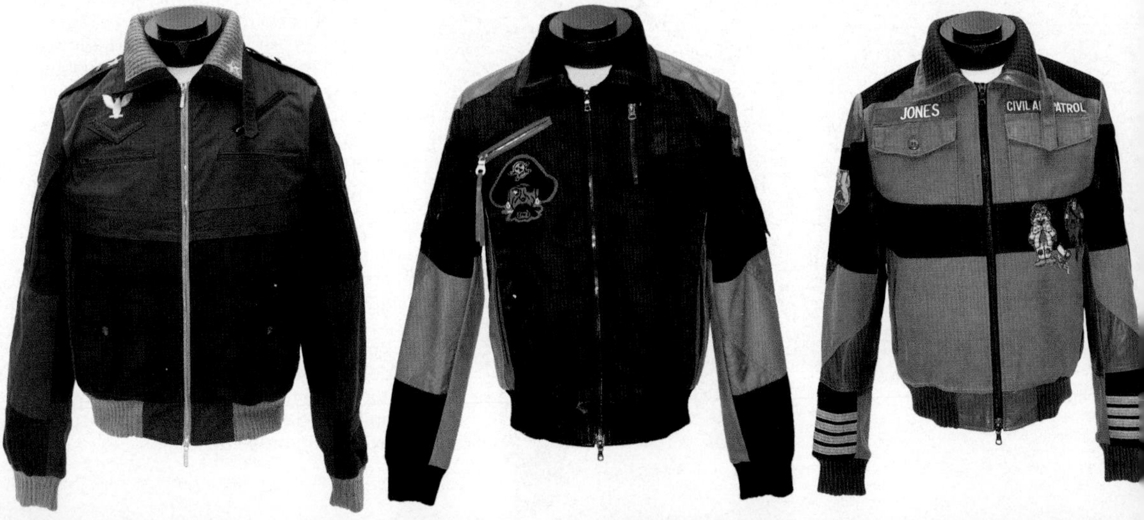
JONES

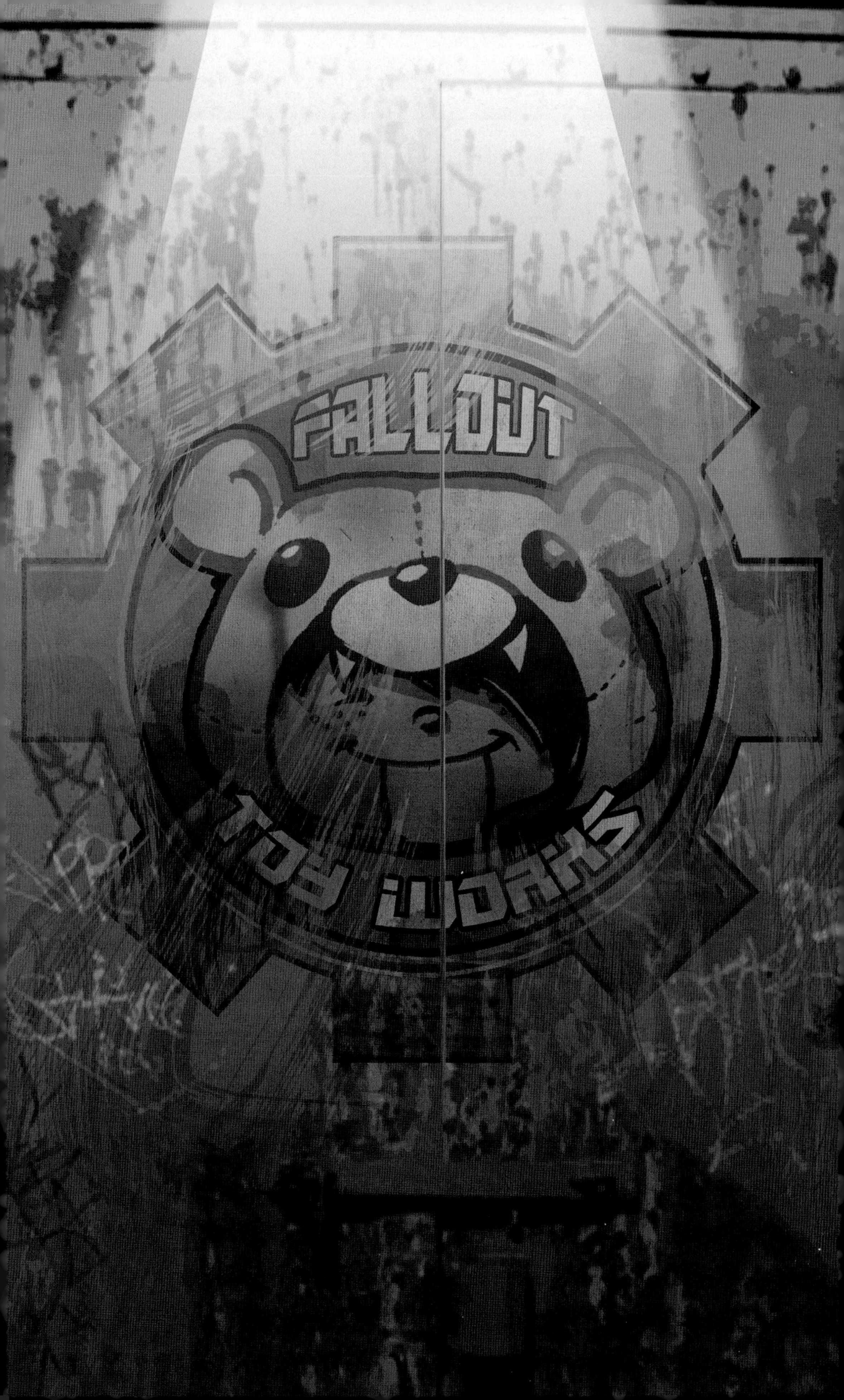
FALLOUT
TOY WORKS

THE TOY MAKER

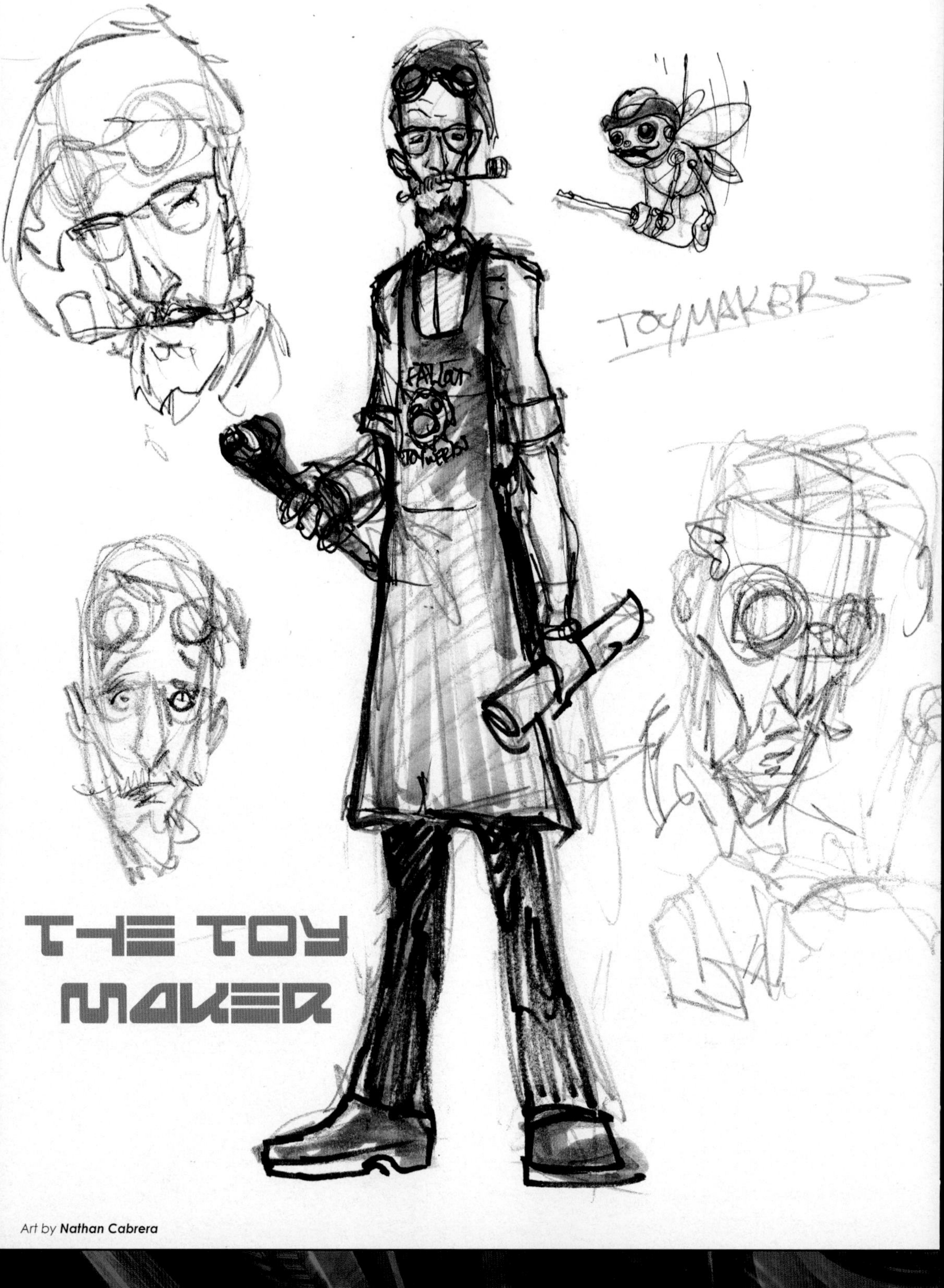
TOYMAKER

Art by ***Nathan Cabrera***

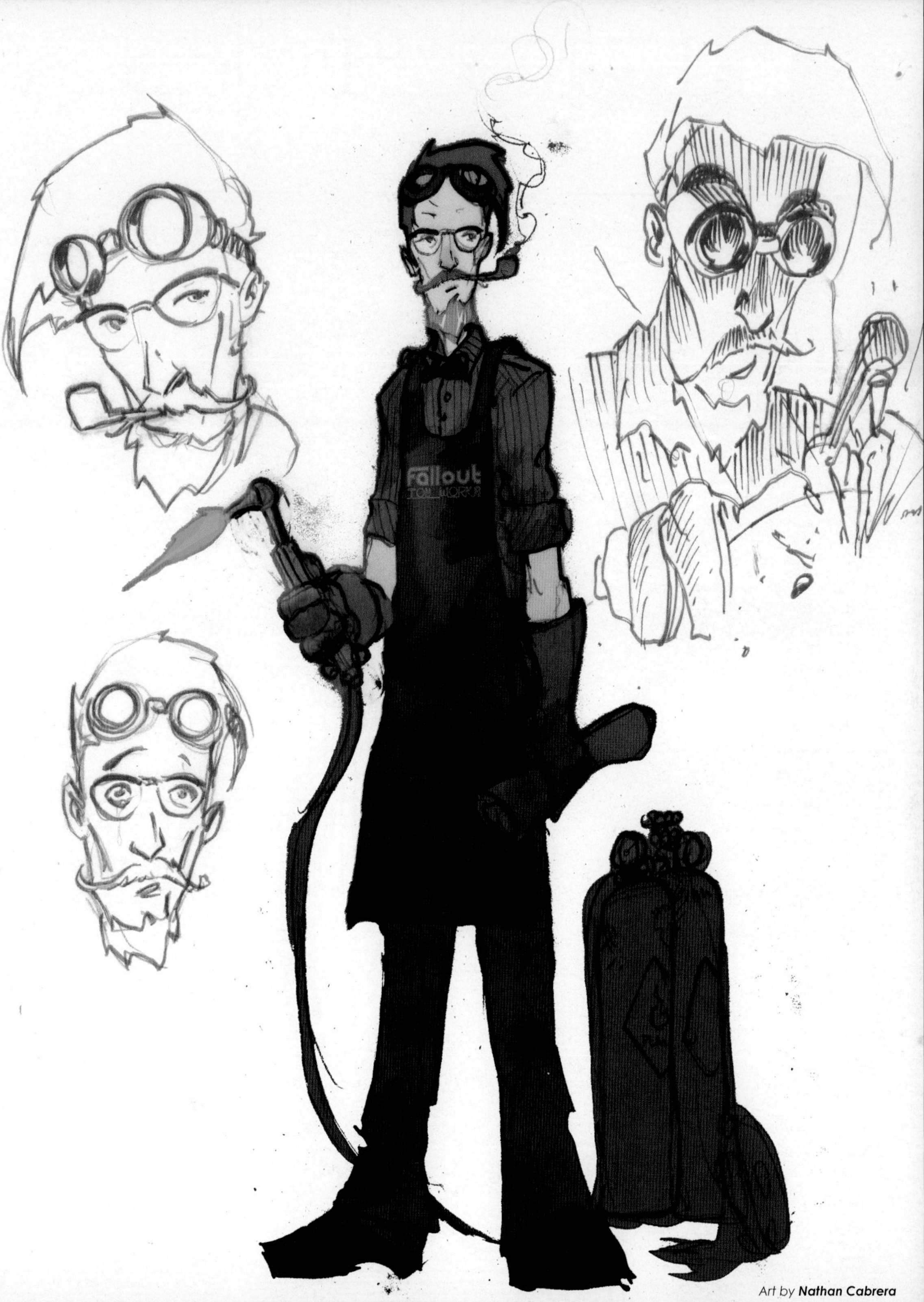
Fallout

Art by **Nathan Cabrera**

TIFFANY

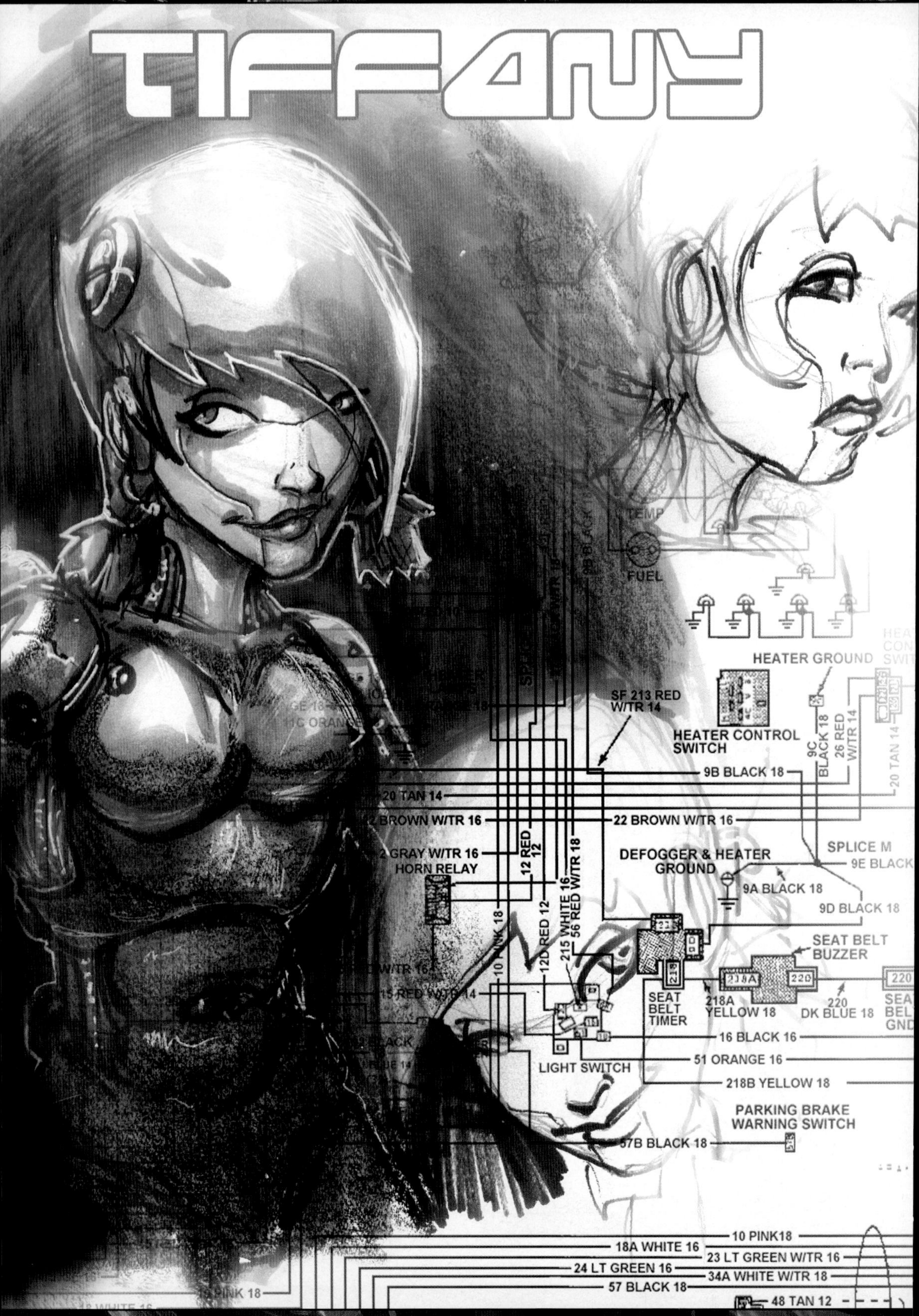

Art by ***Nathan Cabrera***

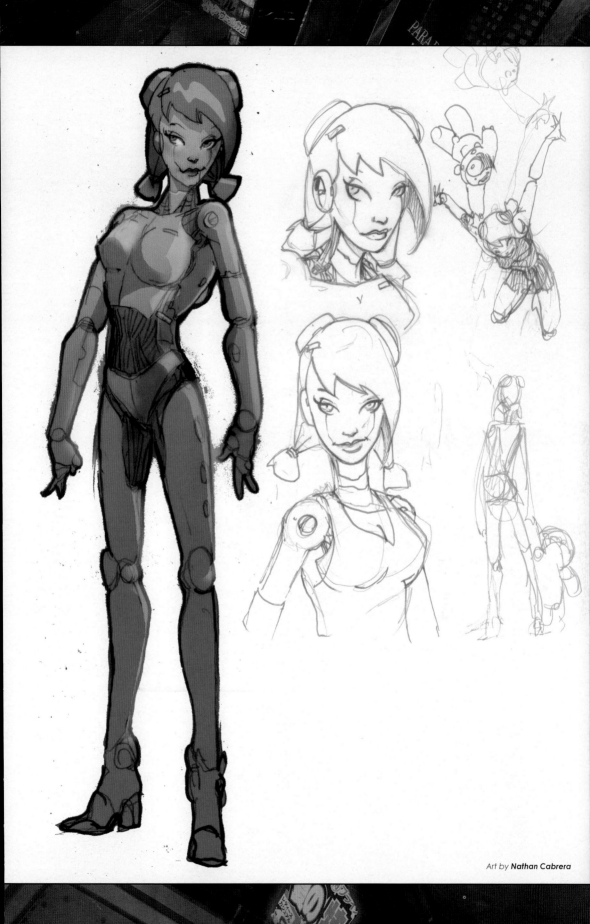

Art by **Nathan Cabrera**

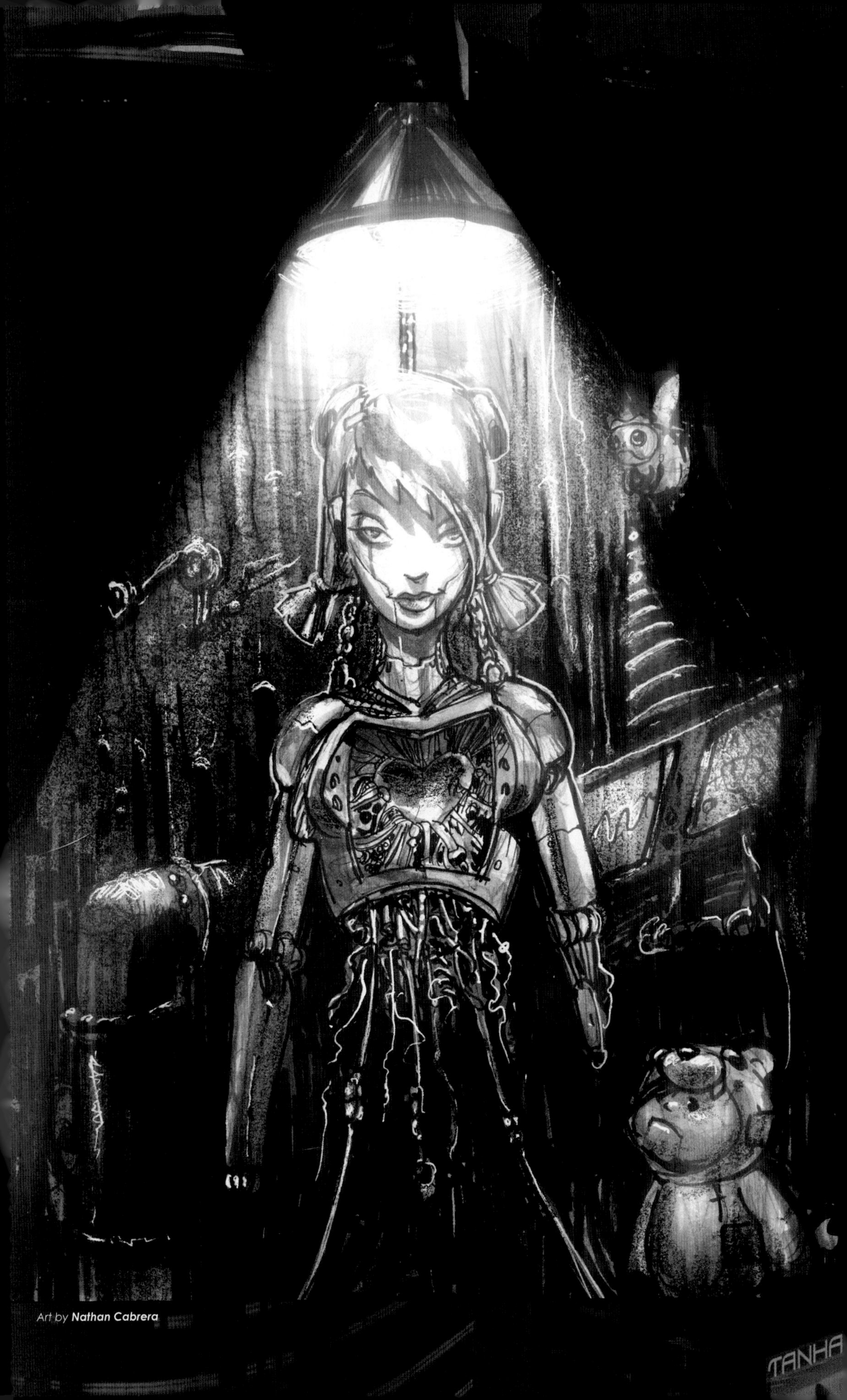

Art by **Nathan Cabrera**

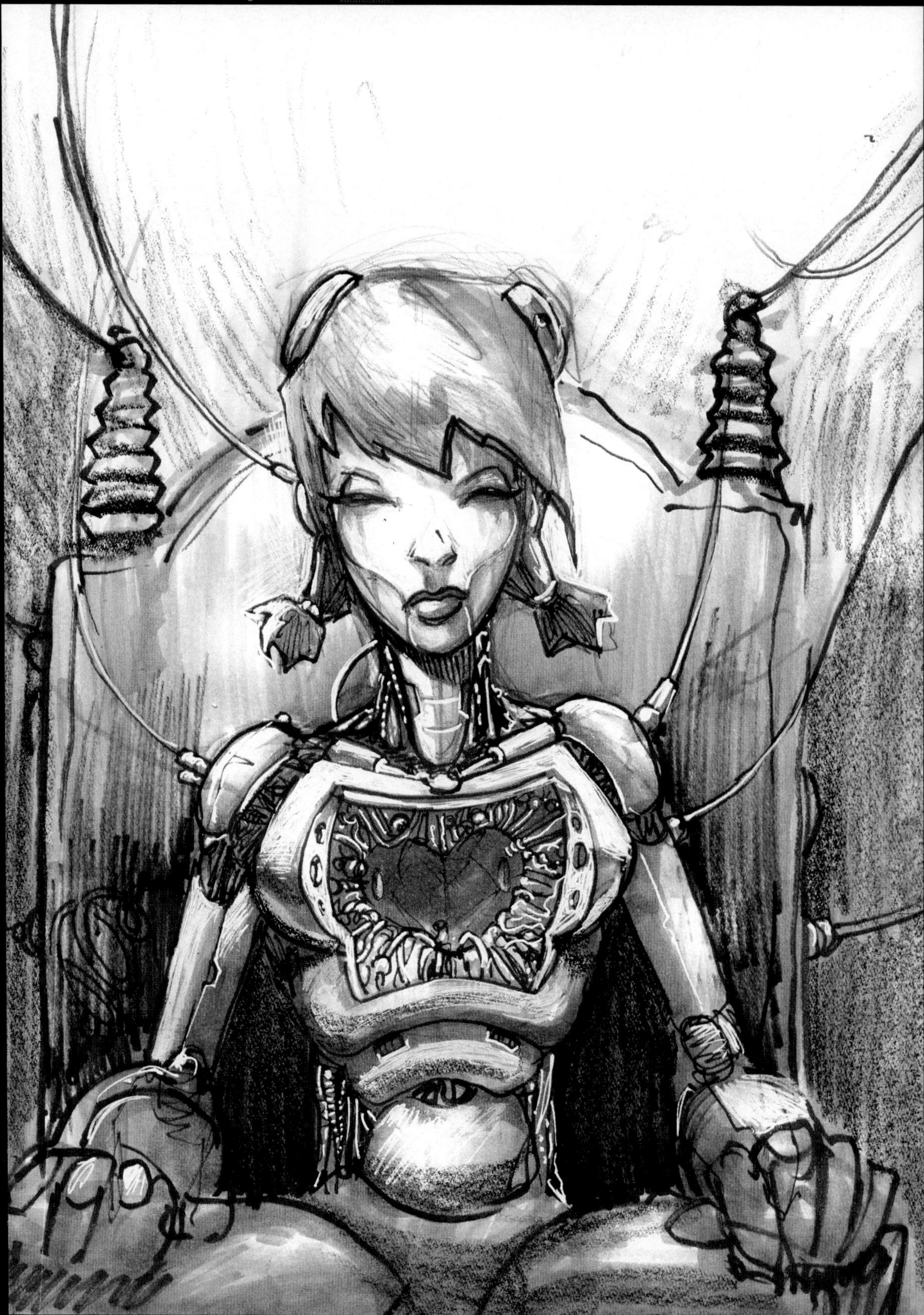

Art by **Nathan Cabrera**

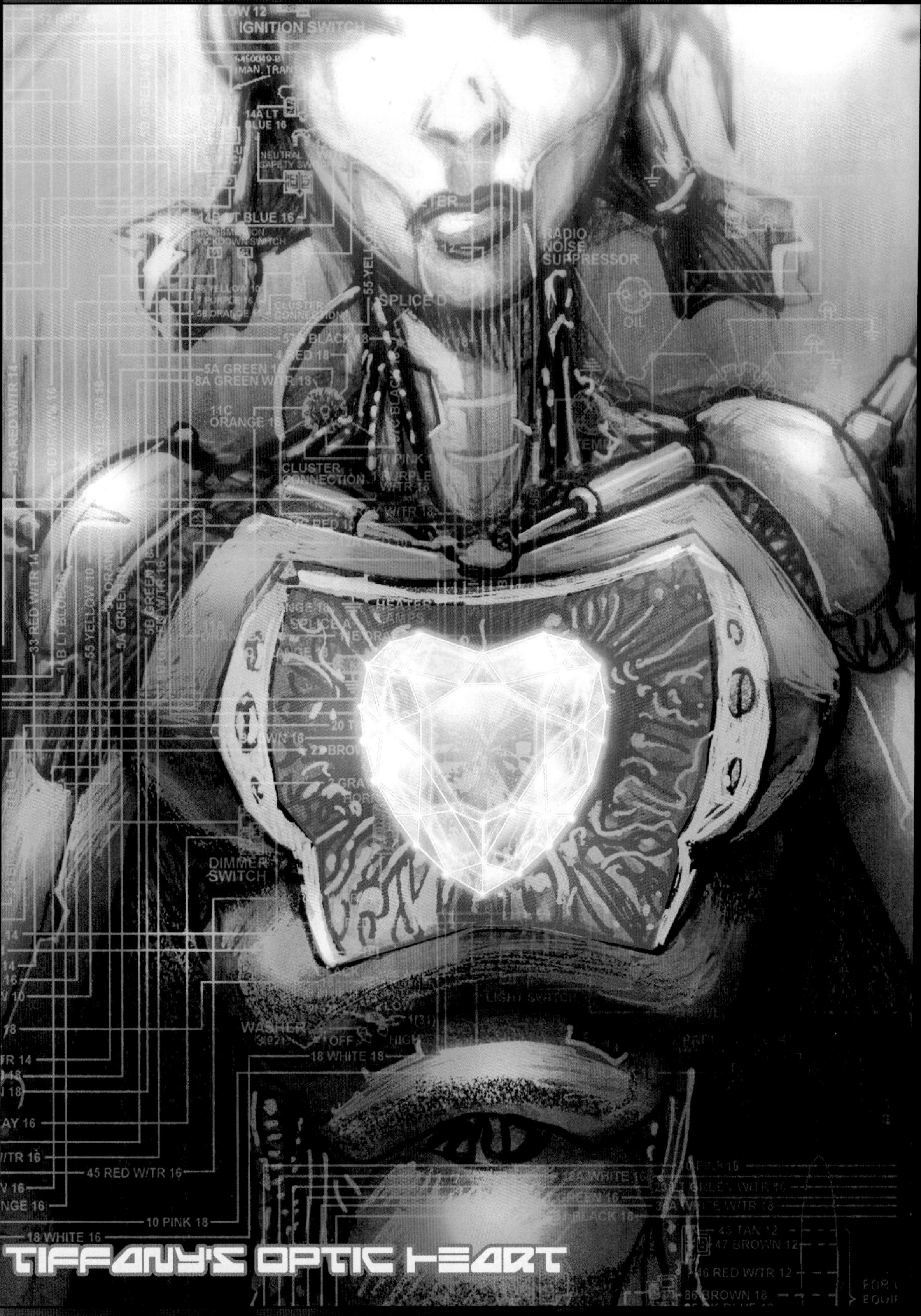
IGNITION SWITCH
14A LT BLUE 16
NEUTRAL SAFETY SWITCH
RADIO NOISE SUPPRESSOR
SPLICE D
OIL
5A GREEN 18
8A GREEN W/TR 18
11C ORANGE 18
CLUSTER CONNECTION
55 YELLOW 10
33 RED W/TR 14
HEATER LAMPS
DIMMER SWITCH
WASHER
18 WHITE 18
45 RED W/TR 16
10 PINK 18
18 WHITE 16
48 TAN 12
47 BROWN 12
46 RED W/TR 12
86 BROWN 18

TIFFANY'S OPTIC HEART

Art by **Nathan Cabrera**

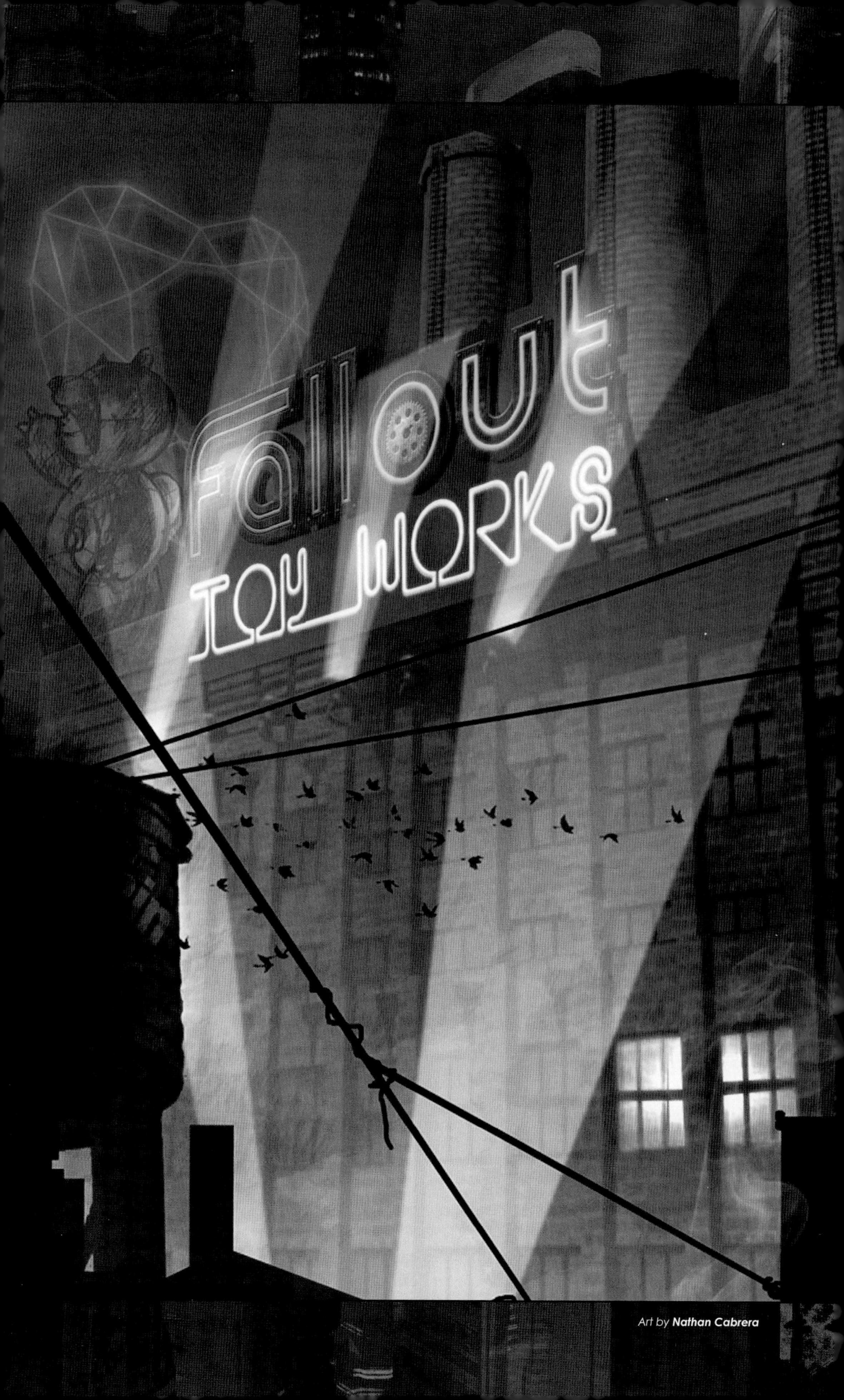
Fallout
TOY WORKS

Art by **Nathan Cabrera**

Art by **Nathan Cabrera**

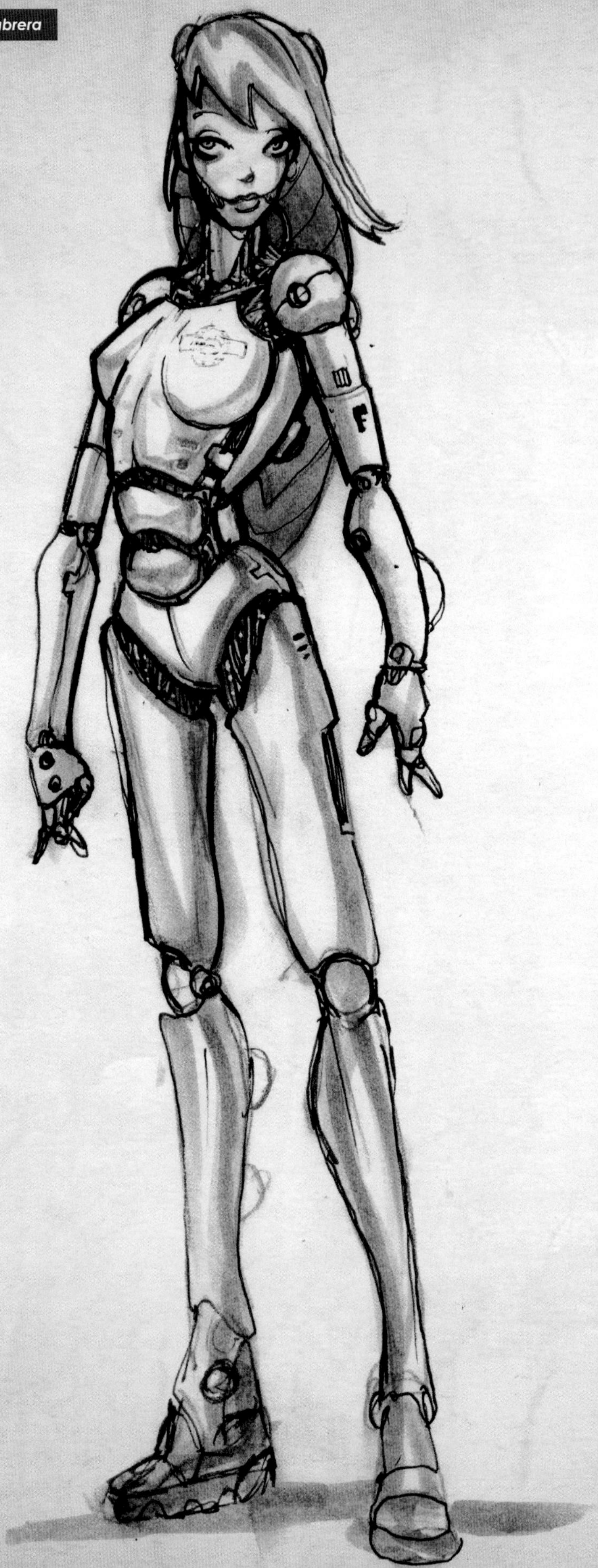

F

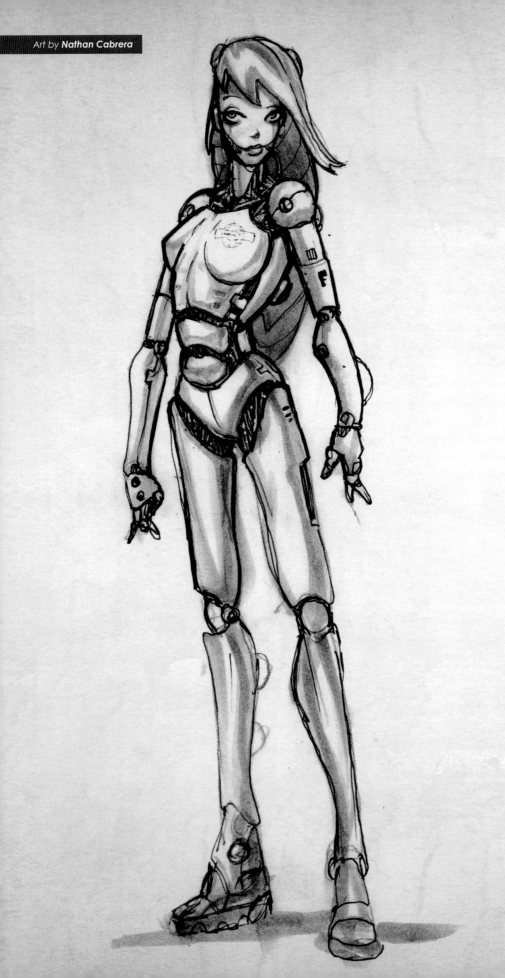

Art by **Hendry Prasetyo**

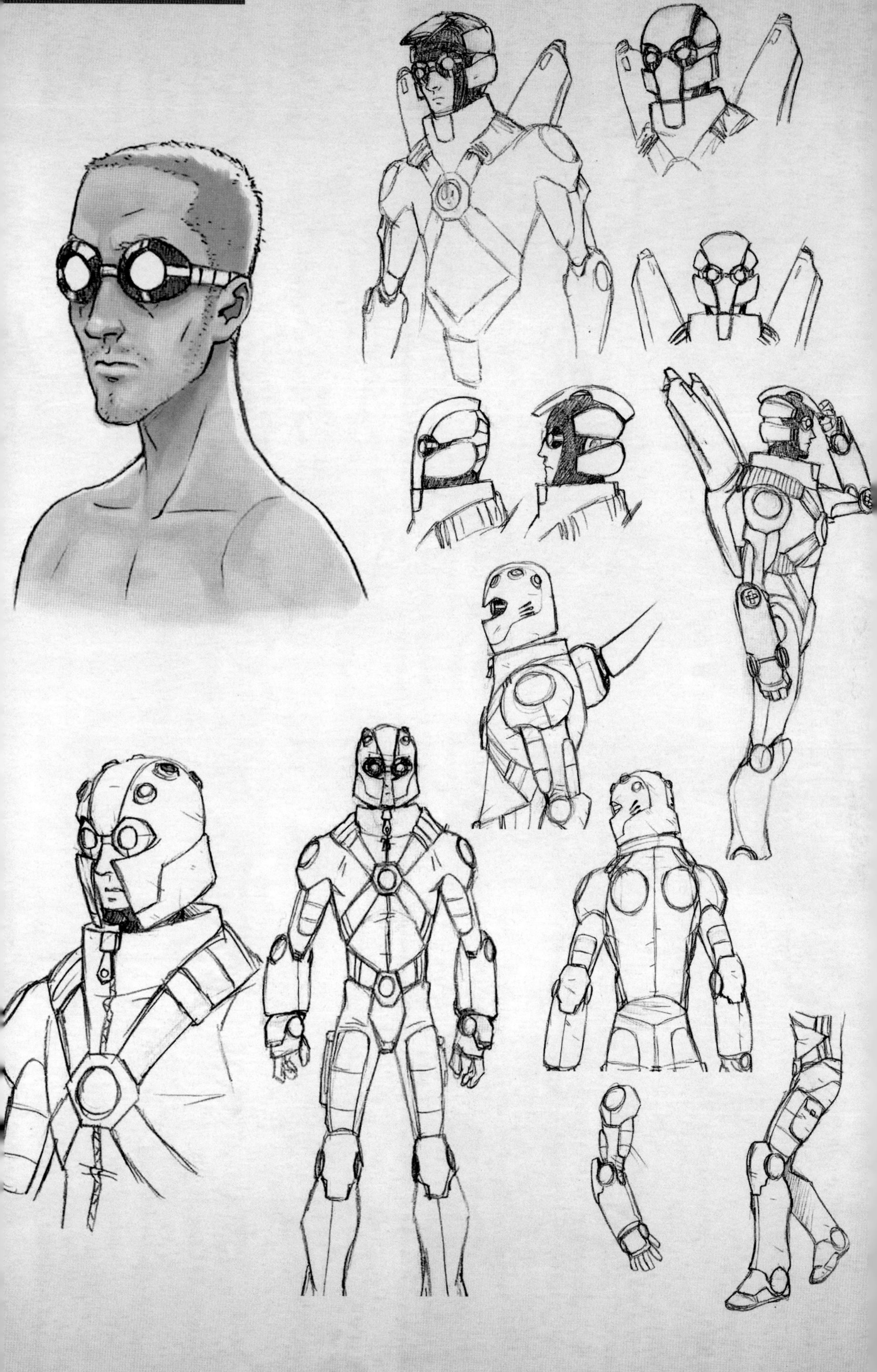

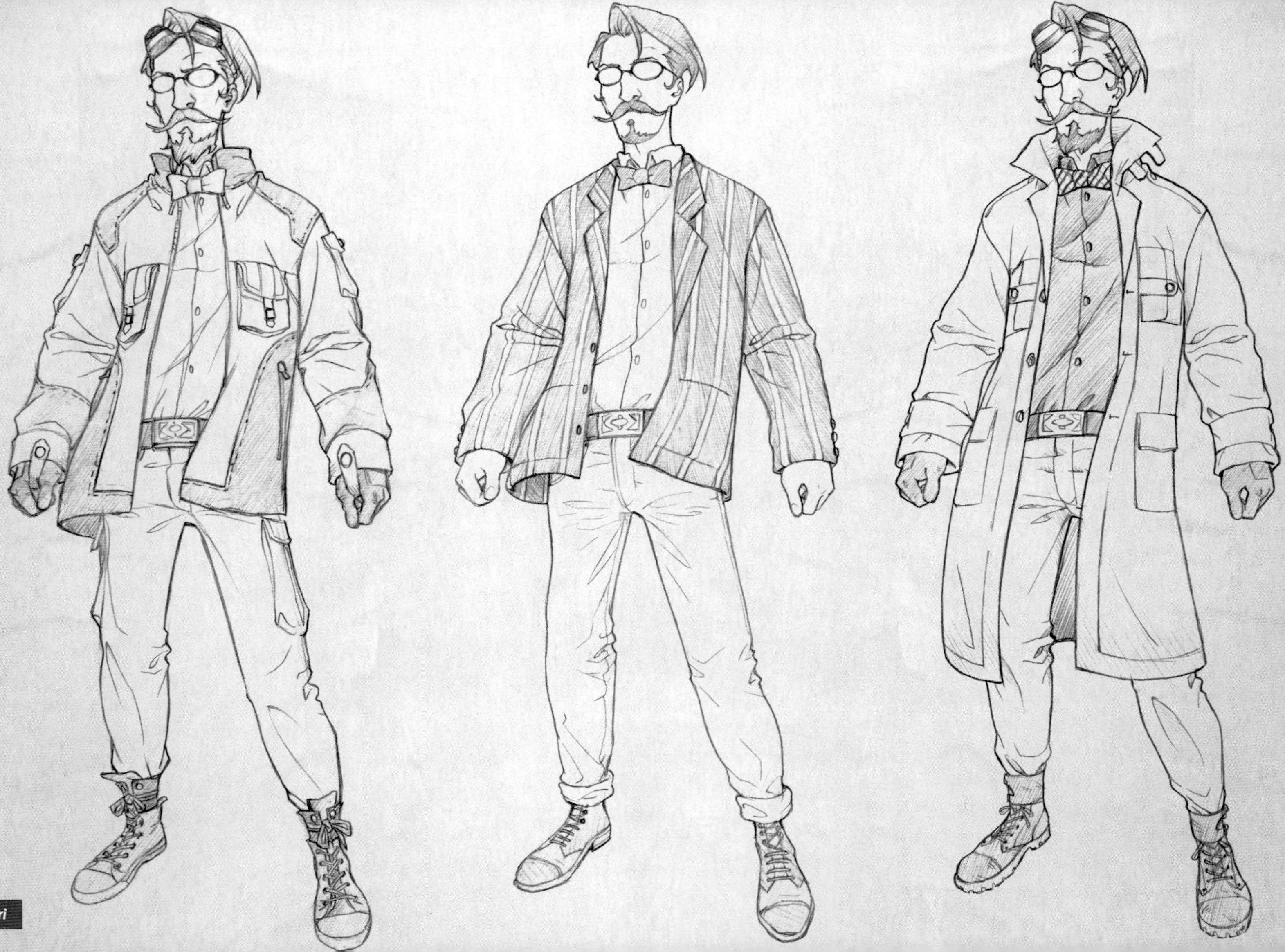

Art by **Sami Basri**

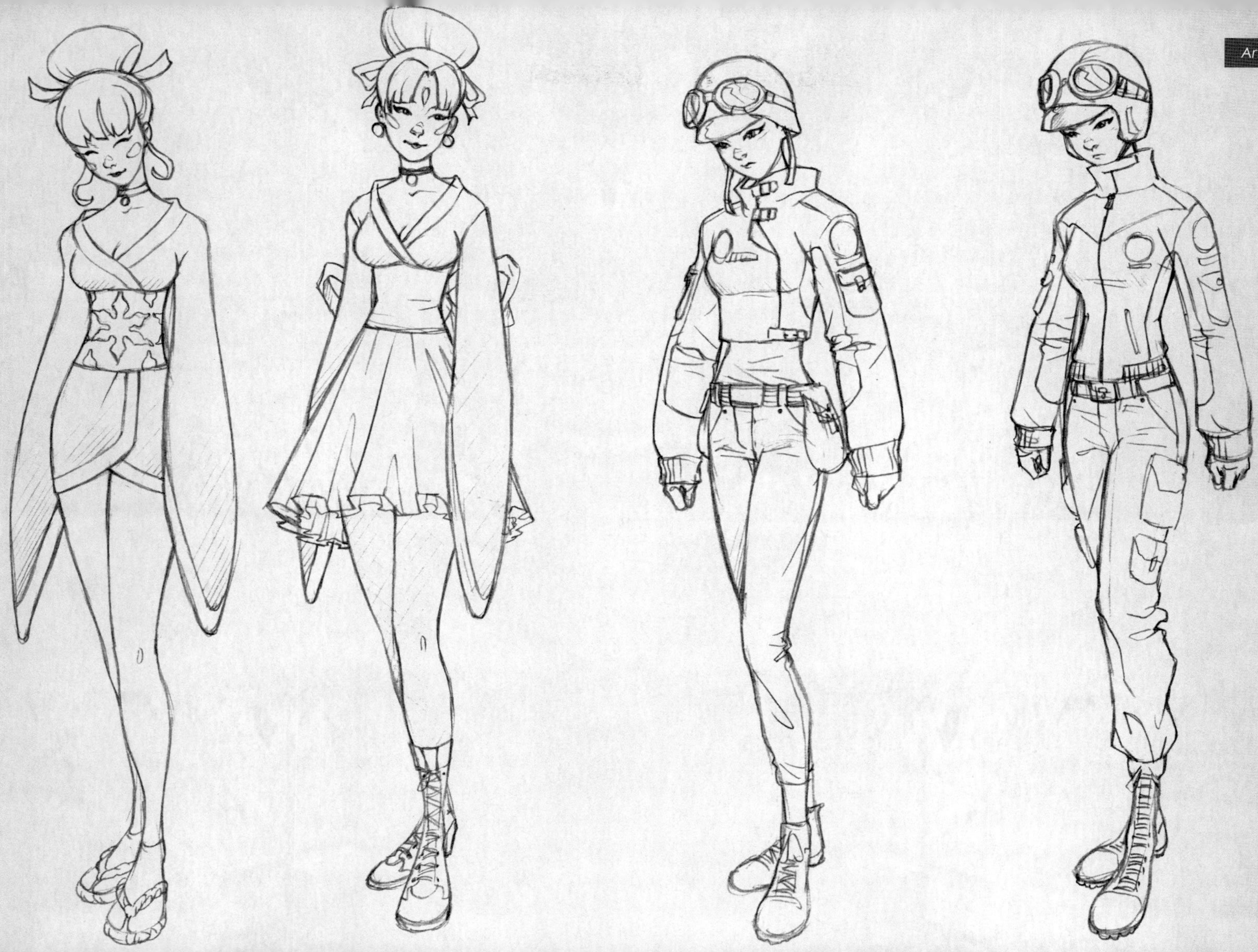

Art by **Sami Basri**

Art by **Sami Basri**

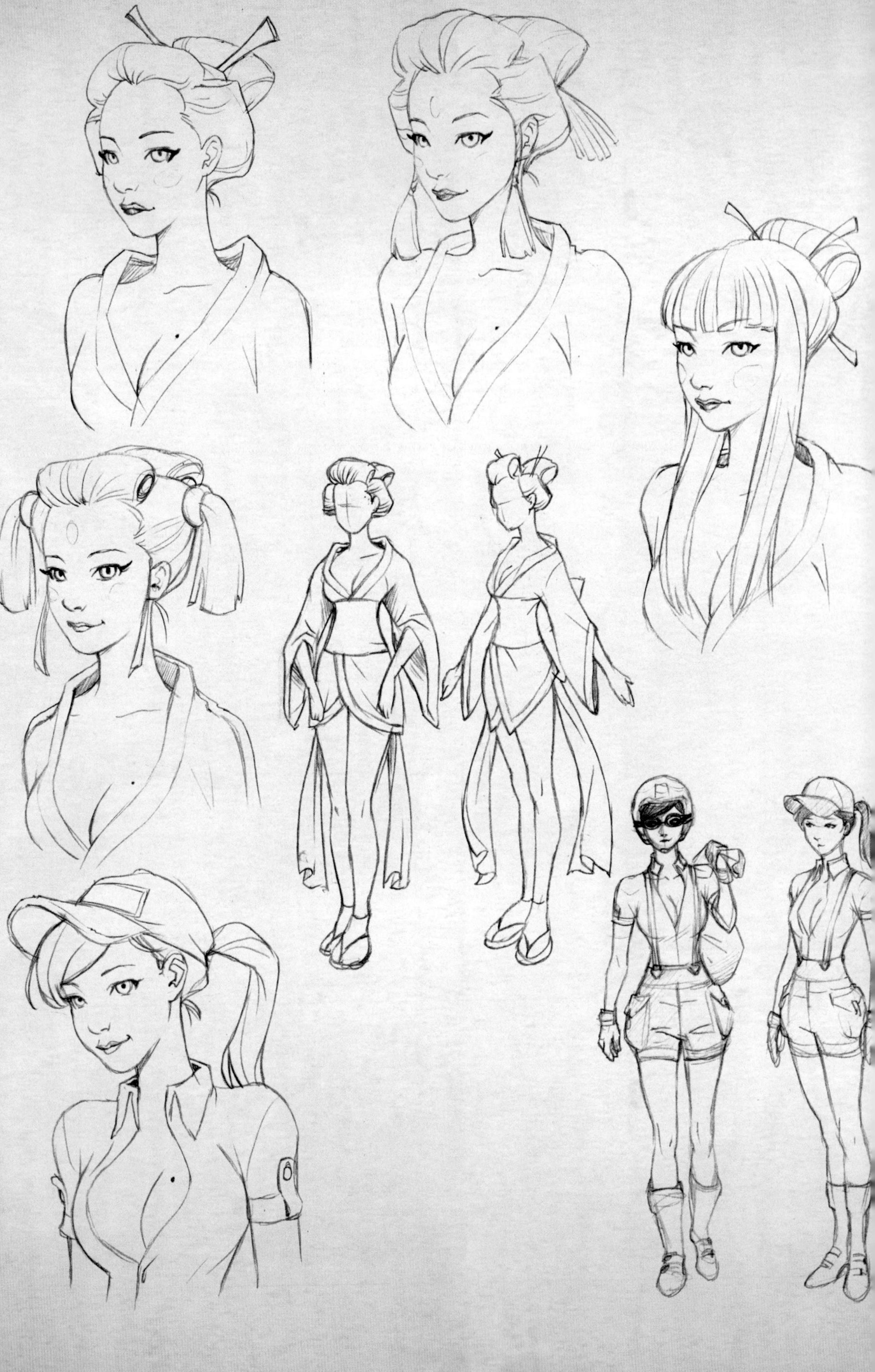

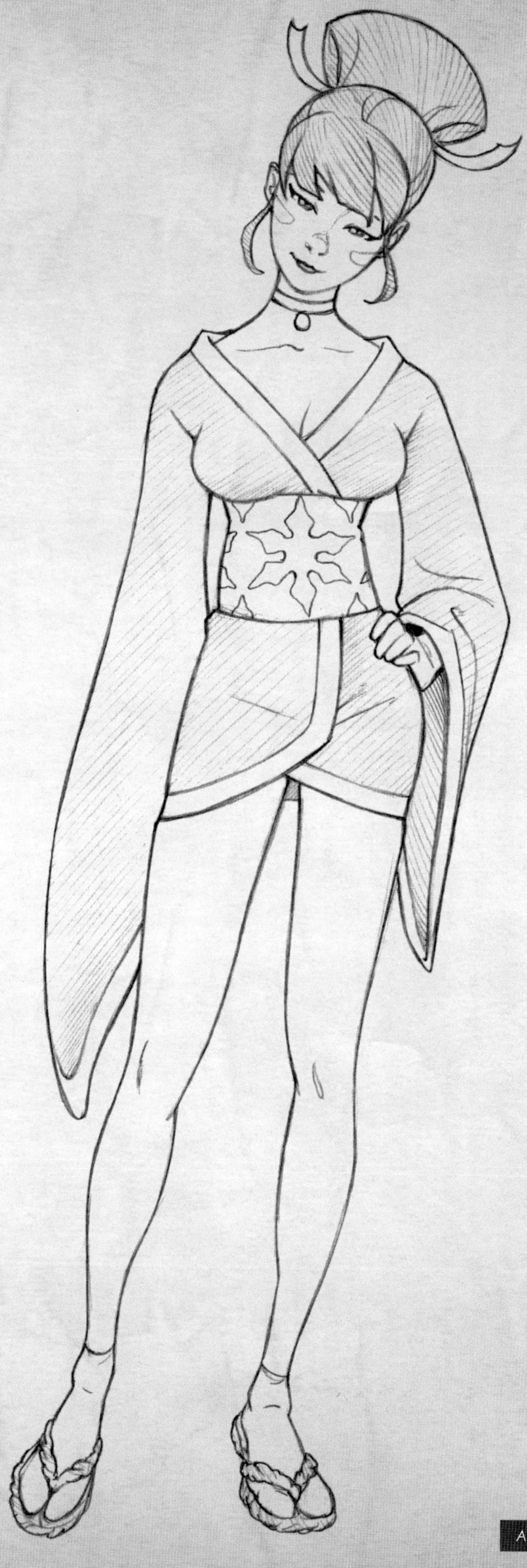

Art by **Sami Basri**

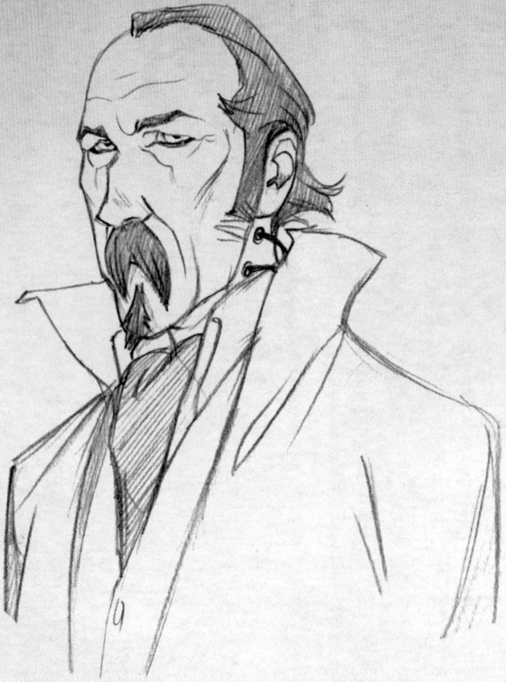
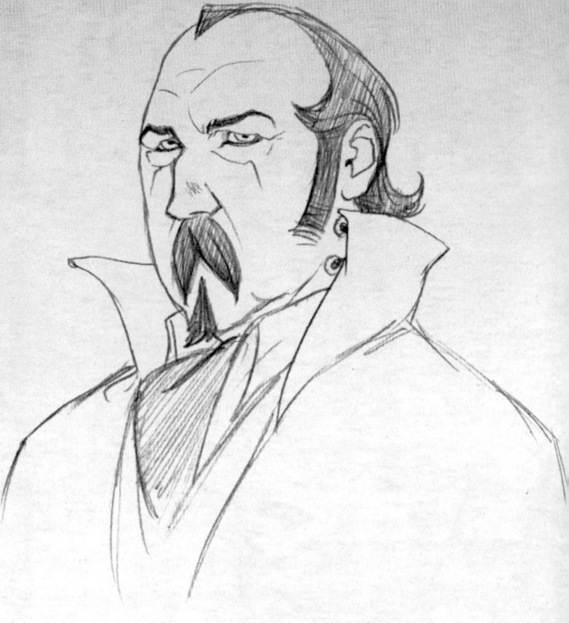
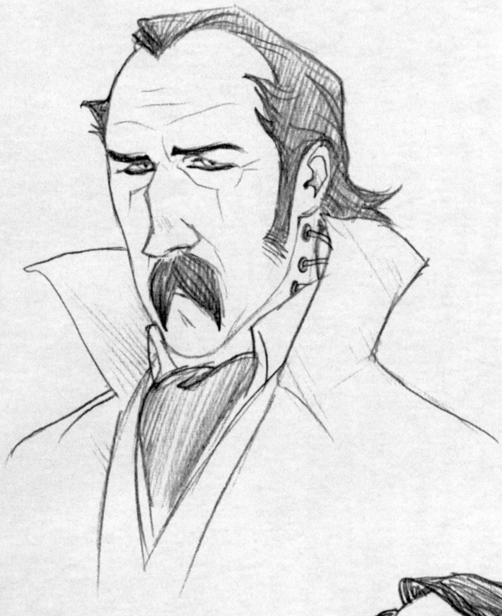
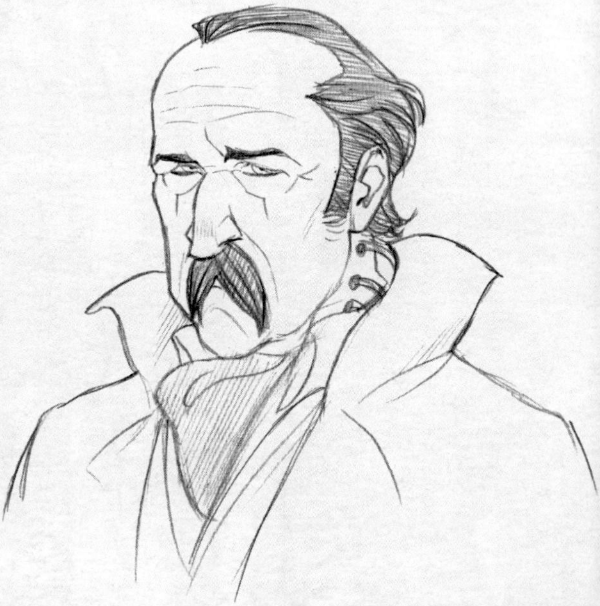
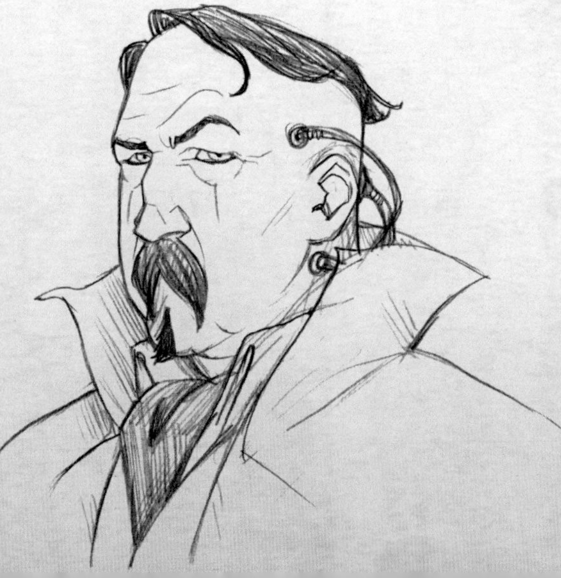

Art by **Sami Basri**

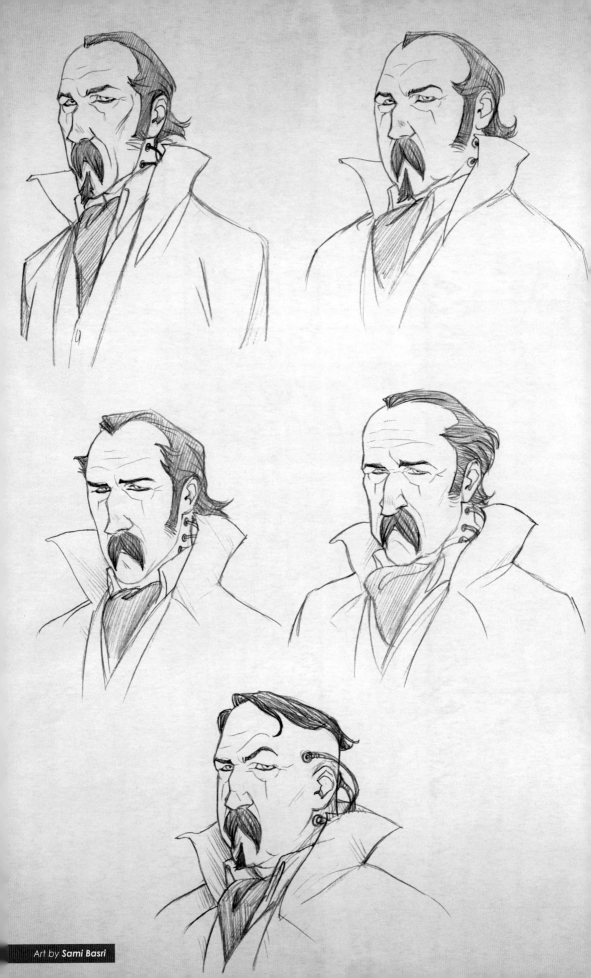

Art by **Sami Basri**

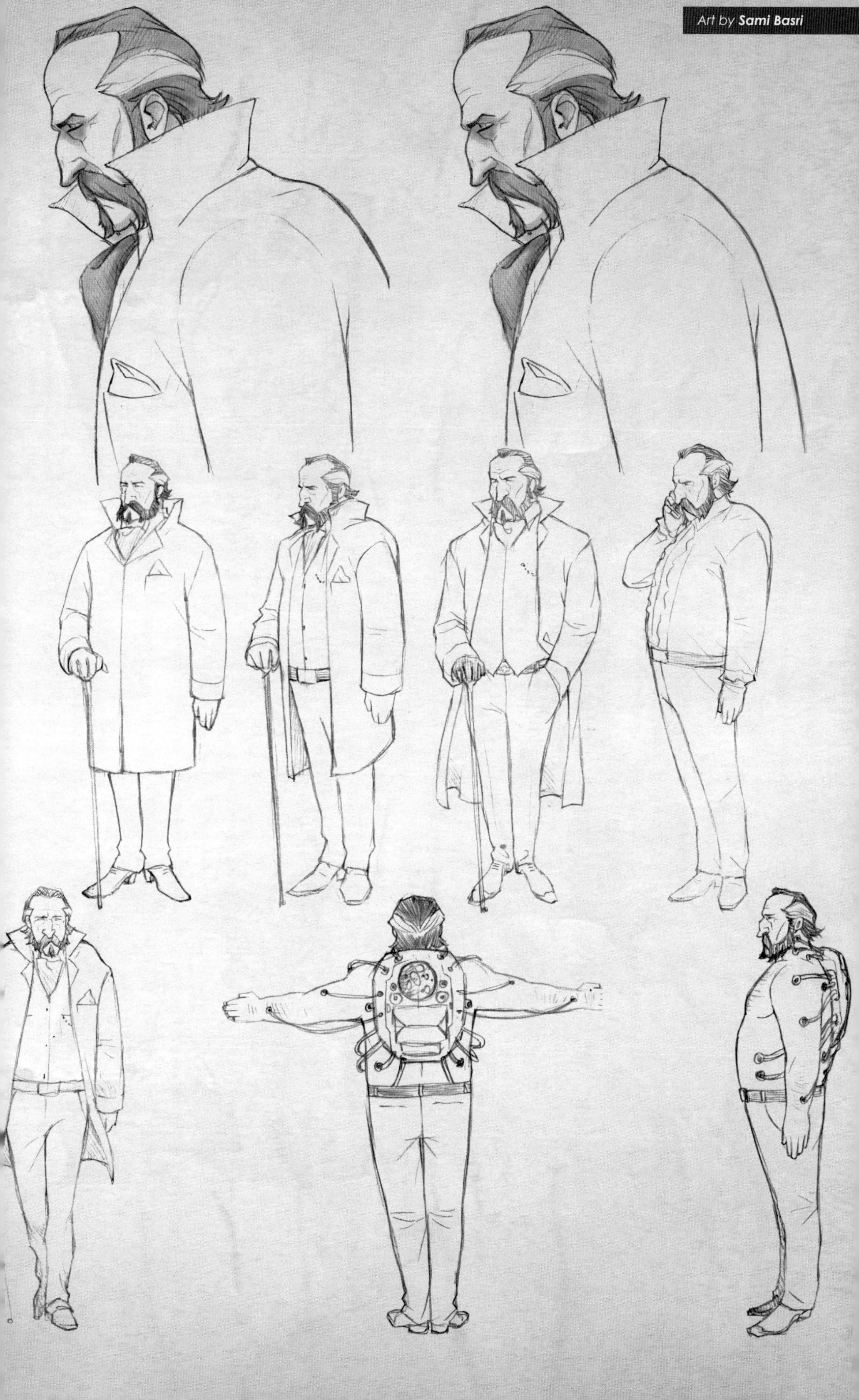

Art by **Sami Basri**

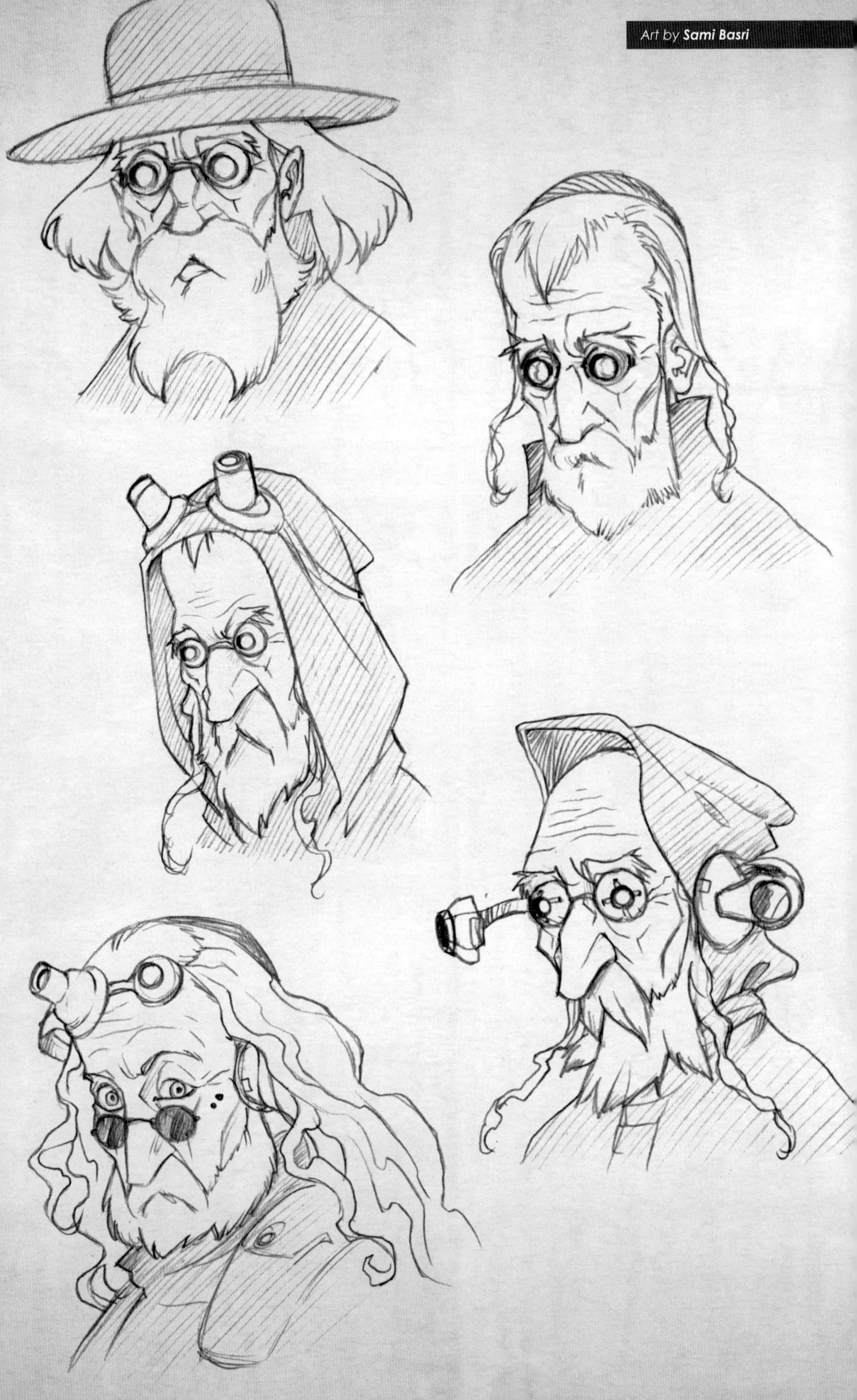

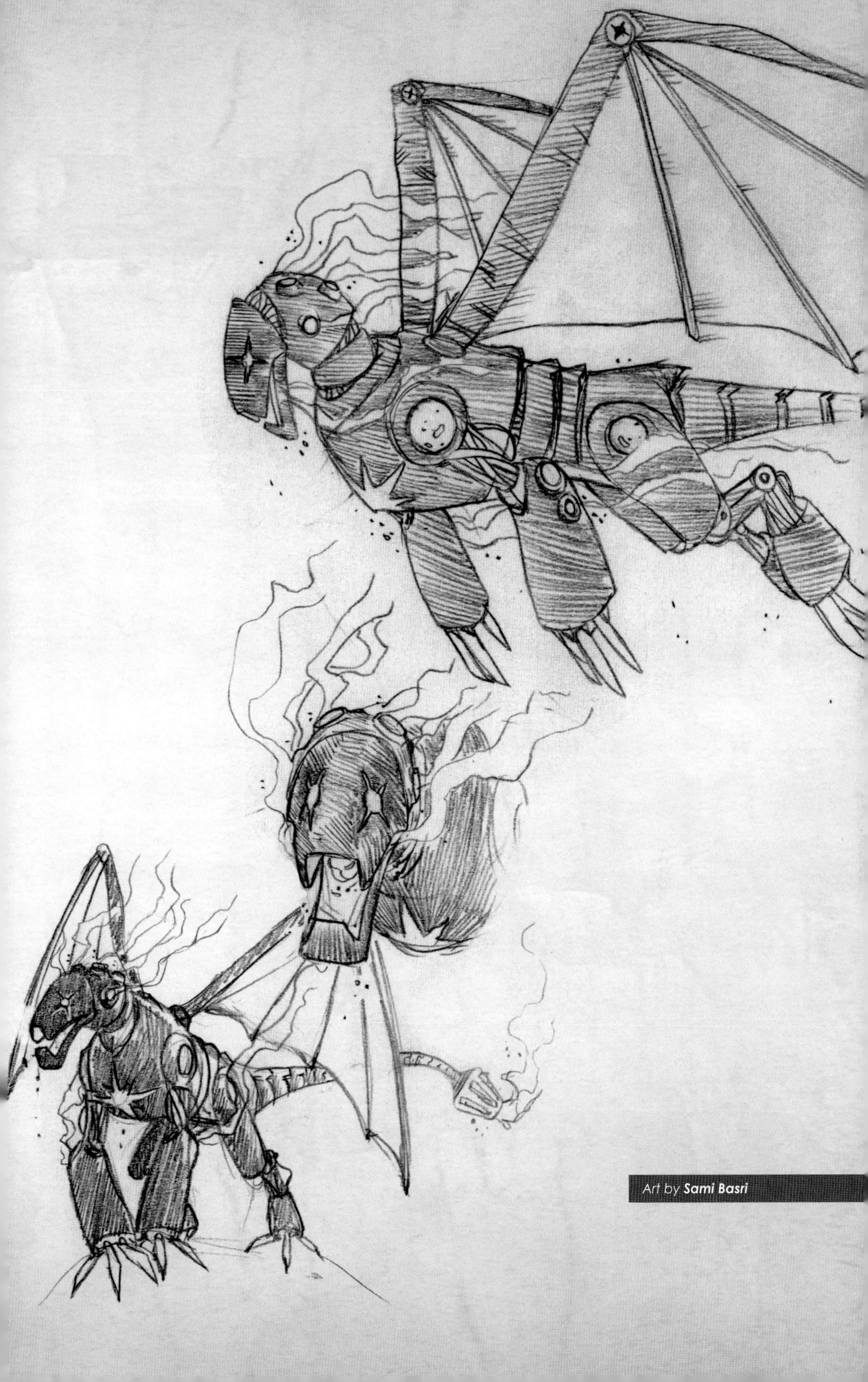

Art by **Sami Basri**

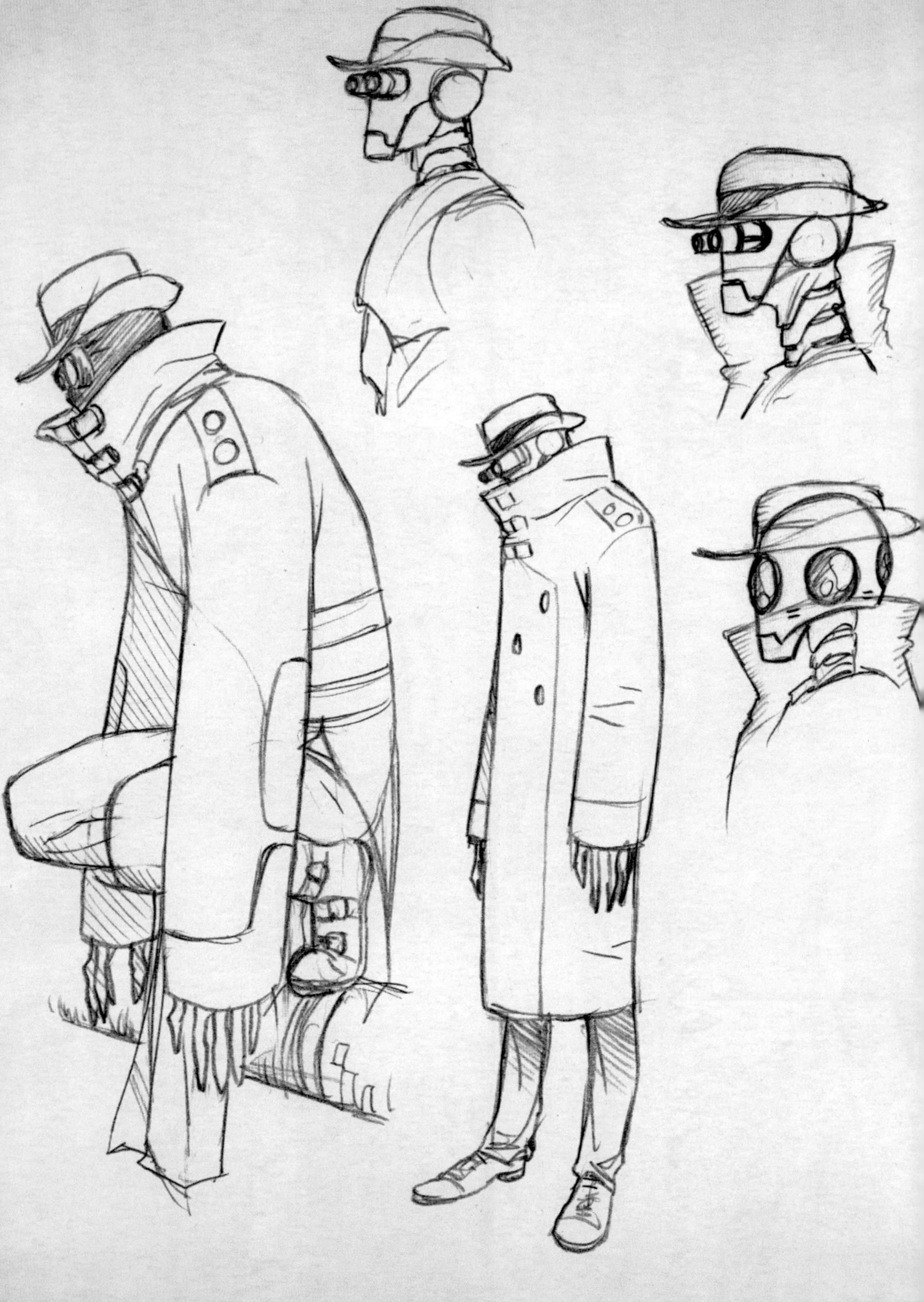

Art by **Sami Basri**

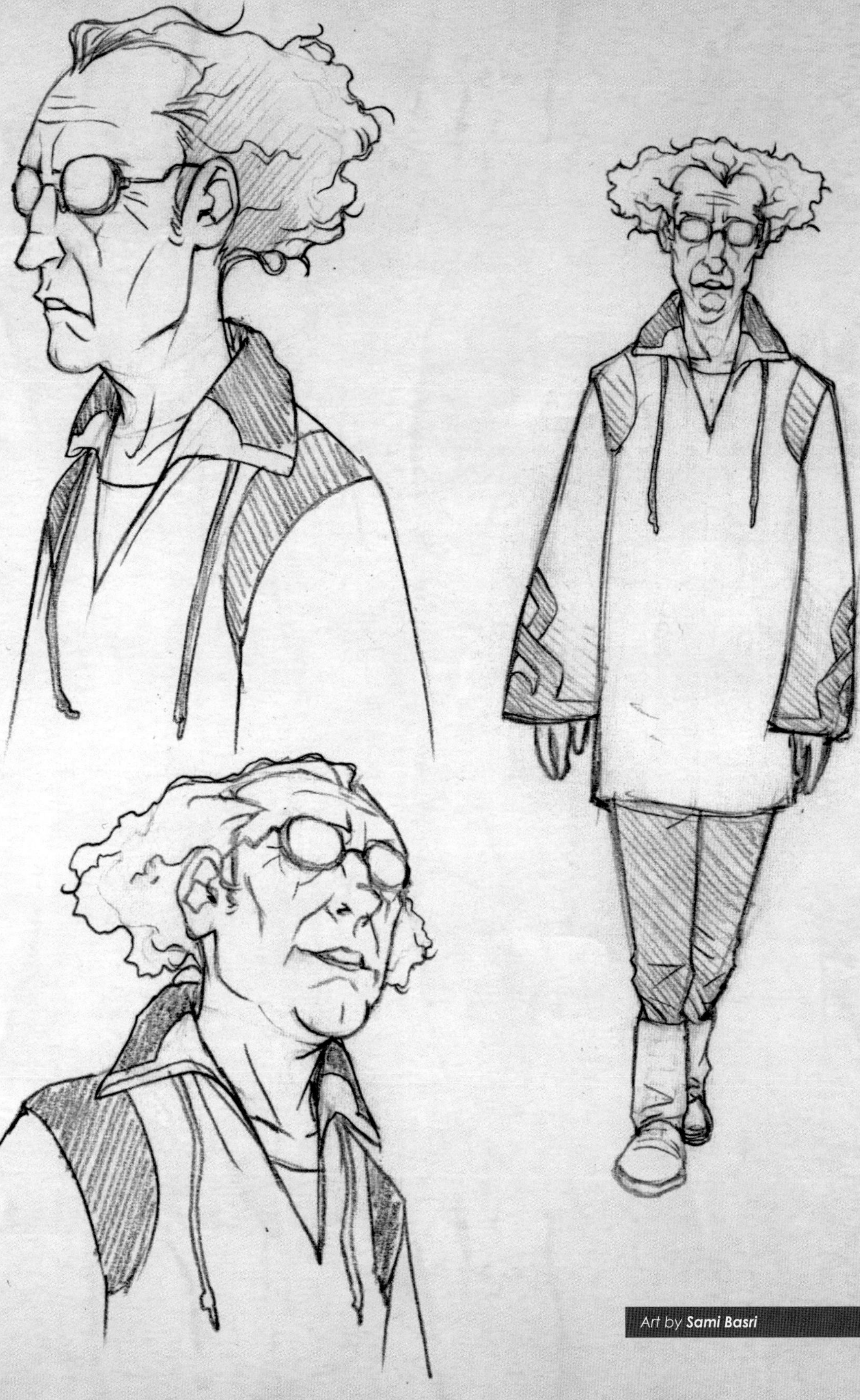

Art by **Sami Basri**

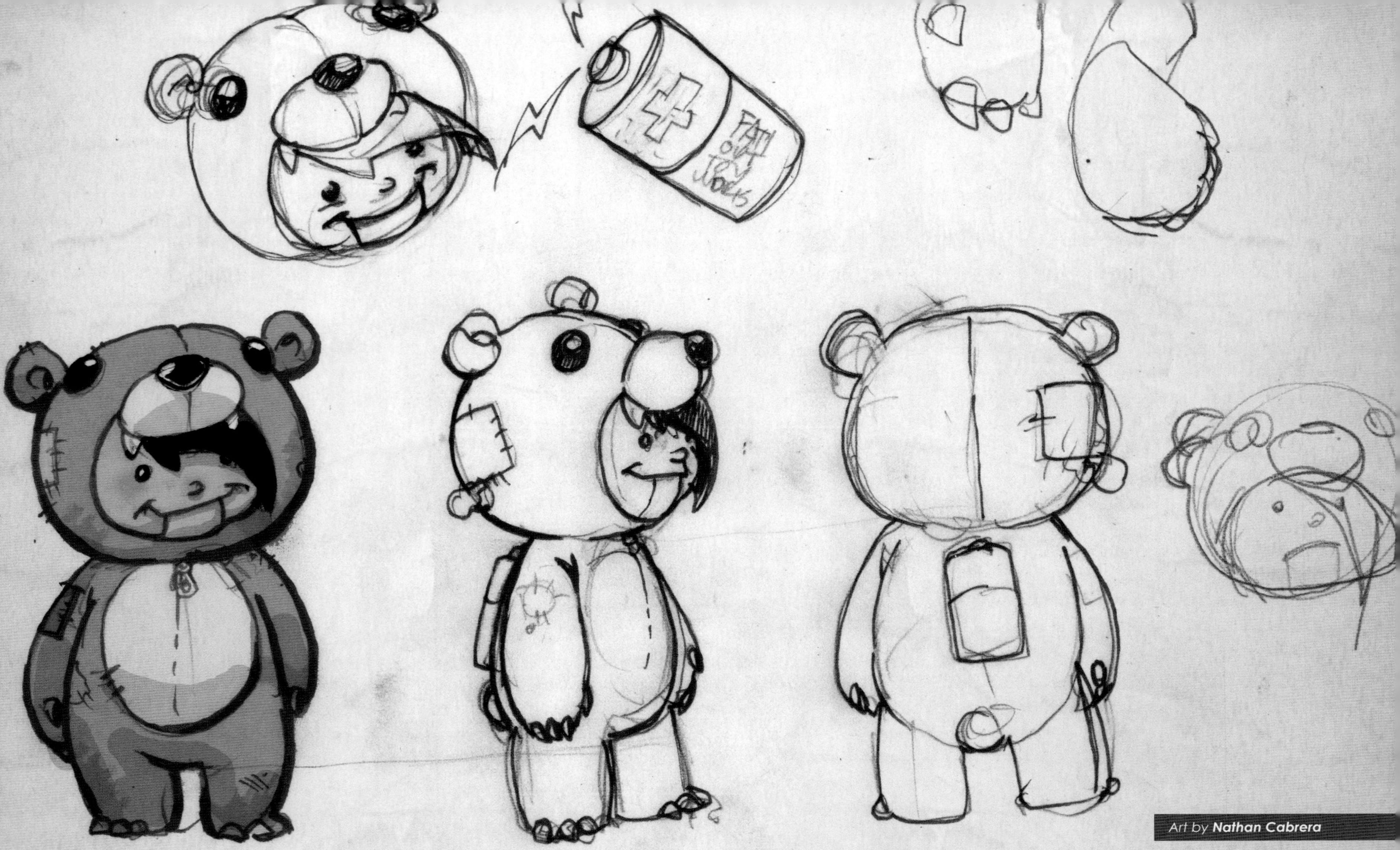

Art by ***Nathan Cabrera***

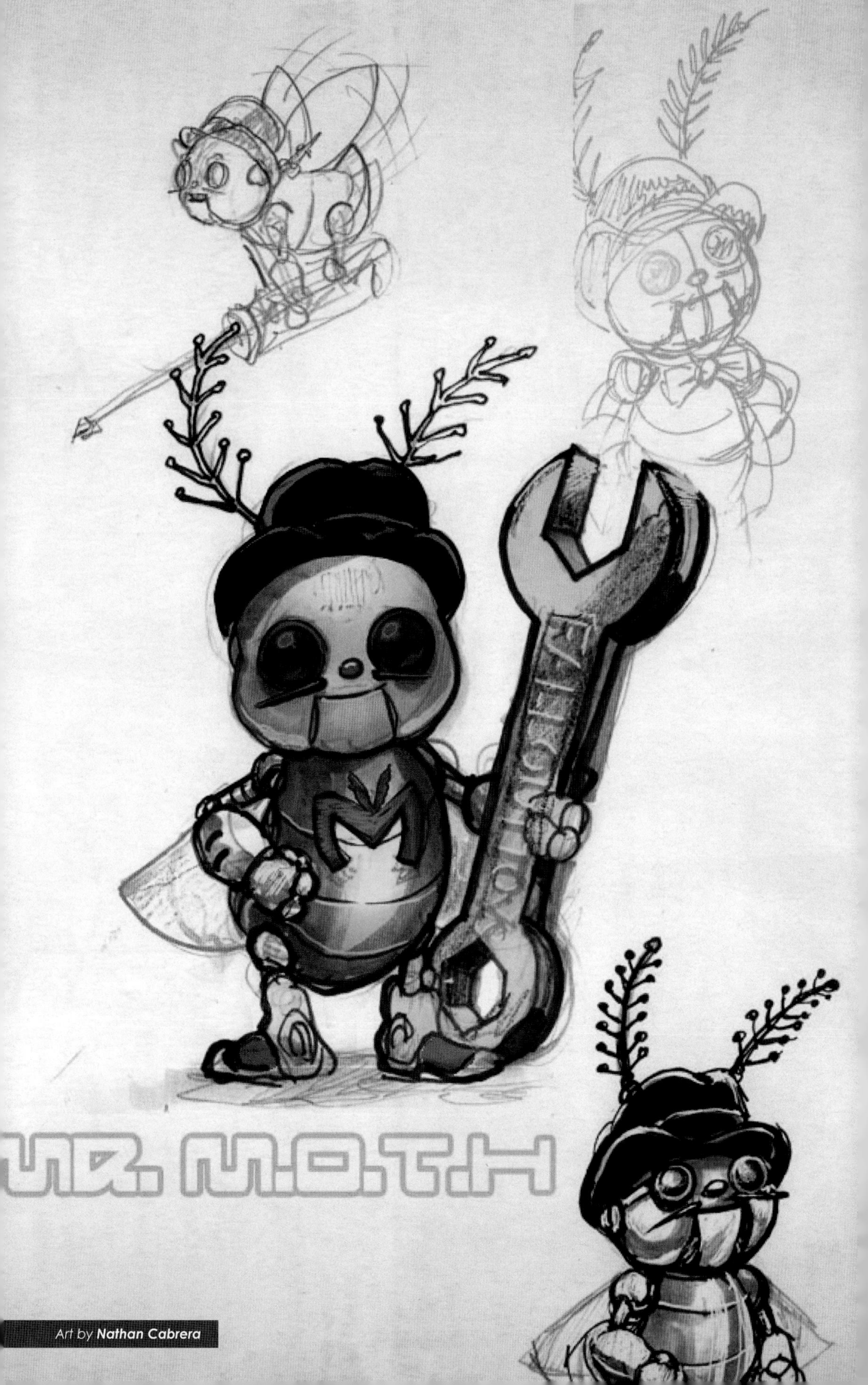
M.O.T.H

Art by **Nathan Cabrera**

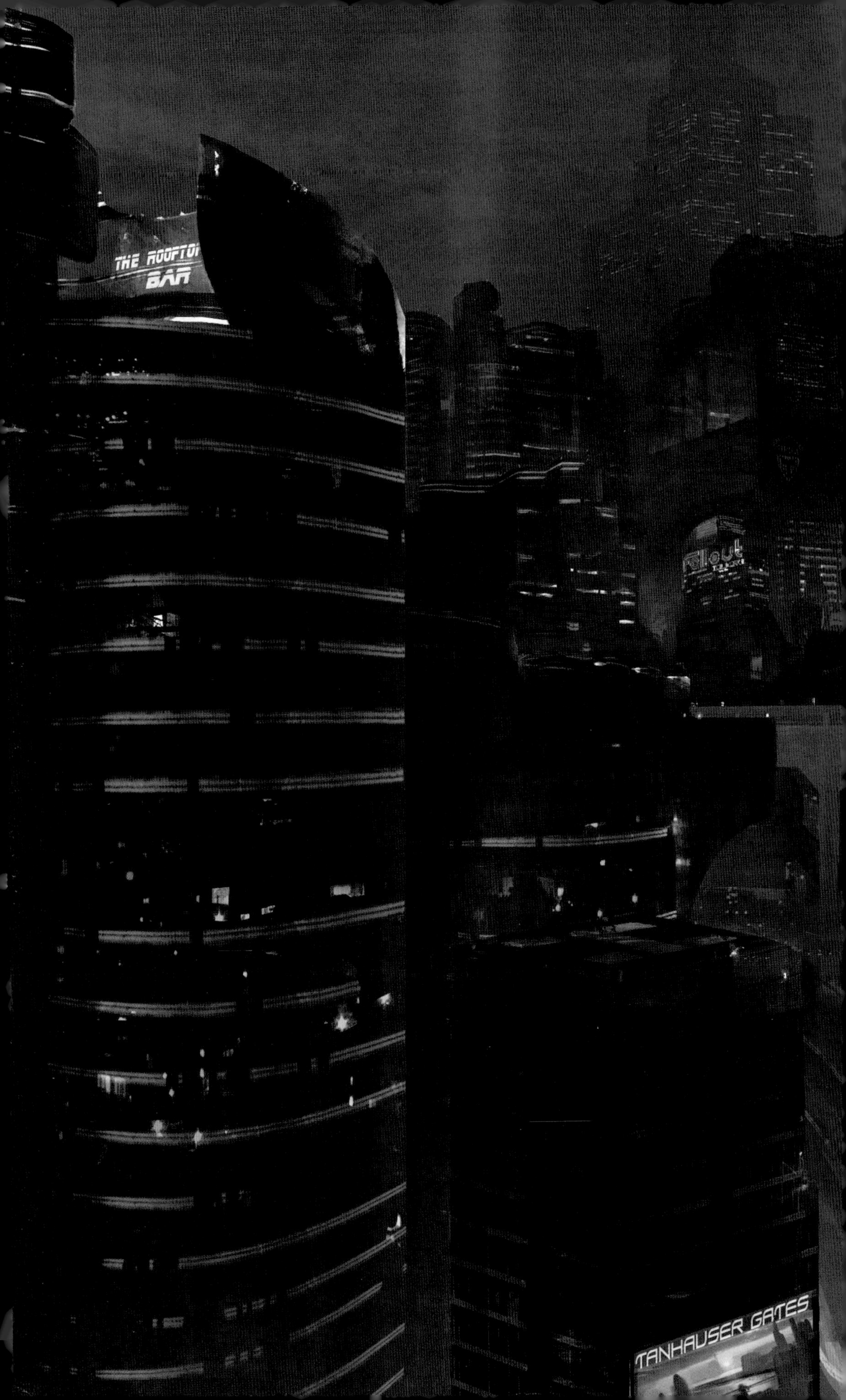
THE ROOFTO
BAR
TANHAUSER GATES